Studies in Neurolinguistics

VOLUME 3

PERSPECTIVES IN
NEUROLINGUISTICS AND PSYCHOLINGUISTICS

Harry A. Whitaker, Series Editor
DEPARTMENT OF PSYCHOLOGY
THE UNIVERSITY OF ROCHESTER
ROCHESTER, NEW YORK

HAIGANOOSH WHITAKER and HARRY A. WHITAKER (Eds.).
  Studies in Neurolinguistics, Volumes 1, 2, and 3.
NORMAN J. LASS (Ed.). Contemporary Issues in Experimental Phonetics
JASON W. BROWN. Mind, Brain, and Consciousness: The Neuropsychology
  of Cognition
S. J. SEGALOWITZ and F. A. GRUBER (Eds.). Language Development and
  Neurological Theory
SUSAN CURTISS. Genie: A Psycholinguistic Study of a Modern-Day "Wild
  Child"

In preparation

I. M. SCHLESINGER and LILA NAMIR (Eds.). Sign Language of the Deaf:
  Psychological, Linguistic, and Sociological Perspectives
JOHN MACNAMARA (Ed.). Language Learning and Thought

Vibrators
  basics of, 274–75
  tips for using, 178–79, 275–76
  types of, 276–81, **277**, **278**,
    279, **280**
Visual stimulation, 10
Vitamins, 205
Vulnerability, 52
Vulva, 176–79, **177**

W

Waermark, 78
Wand style vibrator, 277, **277**
Waterproof vibrators, 278
Watson, Cynthia Mervis,
  262–63
Wave of Bliss technique, steps in
  connecting breath to breath,
    316
  cultivating arousal, 313–14
  infinite cycle, 317–18, **317**
  opening to your inner light,
    316–17
  pelvic rocking, 313
  playful wave, 314–16, **315**
Waxing, pubic hair, 206
Webster, Ben, 79

Whipple, Beverly, 110, 121, 122,
  159
Windham Hill Retrospective, 79
Wine, 77
*Wise Woman's Guide to Erotic
  Videos, The*, 12
Woman superior (woman on top)
  position, 160, 236–38,
    237
Woodhull, Victoria, <u>117</u>
Woody Woodpecker kiss, 85, 86
World Is Your Oyster position,
  192, **192**
Worwood, Valerie Anne, 97
Wrists, 95–96

Y

Yab Yum position, 301–3, **302**
Yeast infections, 201
Y-Knot position, 190–91, **191**

Z

Zilbergeld, Bernie, 25, 36, 144
Zimmerman, Jack, 292
Zone orgasms, 167

Studies in Neurolinguistics

Volume 3

Edited by

HAIGANOOSH WHITAKER

HARRY A. WHITAKER

Department of Psychology
The University of Rochester
Rochester, New York

ACADEMIC PRESS   New York   San Francisco   London   1977

A Subsidiary of Harcourt Brace Jovanovich, Publishers

COPYRIGHT © 1977, BY ACADEMIC PRESS, INC.
ALL RIGHTS RESERVED.
NO PART OF THIS PUBLICATION MAY BE REPRODUCED OR
TRANSMITTED IN ANY FORM OR BY ANY MEANS, ELECTRONIC
OR MECHANICAL, INCLUDING PHOTOCOPY, RECORDING, OR ANY
INFORMATION STORAGE AND RETRIEVAL SYSTEM, WITHOUT
PERMISSION IN WRITING FROM THE PUBLISHER.

ACADEMIC PRESS, INC.
111 Fifth Avenue, New York, New York 10003

United Kingdom Edition published by
ACADEMIC PRESS, INC. (LONDON) LTD.
24/28 Oval Road, London NW1

Library of Congress Cataloging in Publication Data

Main entry under title:

Studies in neurolinguistics.

(Perspectives in neurolinguistics and psycholin-
guistics)
Includes bibliographies and indexes.
1.   Speech, Disorders of.   2.   Languages—
Physiological aspects.   3.   Neuropsychology.
I.   Whitaker, Haiganoosh.   II.   Whitaker, Harry A.
[DNLM: 1.   Language.   2.   Neurophysiology.   WL102
S933]
RC423.S74   616.8'552   75-13100
ISBN 0–12–746303–8 (v. 3)

PRINTED IN THE UNITED STATES OF AMERICA

Contents

4 The Limbic System in Human Communication   157

   John T. Lamendella

5 A Model of Individual Differences in Hemispheric Functioning   223

   Curtis Hardyck

6 Variability and Constraint in Acquired Dyslexia   257

   John C. Marshall and Freda Newcombe

List of Contributors

Numbers in parentheses indicate the pages on which the authors' contributions begin.

François Boller (1), Case Western Reserve University School of Medicine and Cleveland Veterans Administration Hospital, Cleveland, Ohio

Eugene Green (123), Boston University and Boston Veterans Administration Hospital, Boston, Massachusetts

Curtis Hardyck (223), Institute of Human Learning, University of California, Berkeley, California

Davis H. Howes (123), Boston University School of Medicine and Boston Veterans Administration Hospital, Boston, Massachusetts

Youngjai Kim (1), Case Western Reserve University School of Medicine and Cleveland Veterans Administration Hospital, Cleveland, Ohio

John T. Lamendella (157), School of Humanities and the Arts, San Jose State University, San Jose, California

Ronald S. Levy (287), Hennepin County Medical Center, Minneapolis, Minnesota

James L. Mack (1), Case Western Reserve University School of Medicine and Cleveland Veterans Administration Hospital, Cleveland, Ohio

John C. Marshall (257), Interfakultaire Werkgroep Tall-en Spraakgedrag, University of Nijmegen, The Netherlands

Freda Newcombe (257), Department of Neurology, The Churchill Hospital, Headington, Oxford, England

Michel Paradis (65), Department of Linguistics, McGill University, Montreal, Quebec, Canada

Preface

This is the third in a series of volumes of original research papers in neuro-linguistics. We are planning to extend the series to at least five volumes and perhaps more. It is our opinion that subdivisions of the field of neurolinguistics would be contrived at best, and we are not attempting thematic volumes. Therefore we are publishing these papers as they are received rather than holding some back in an attempt to subdivide each volume into more specialized areas. Although the focus on the relationships between language and the nervous system remains predominant, it has become clear to us since the time of the conception of this series that to truly represent the field of neurolinguistics, both subject matter and methodology must be broadly conceived. In this and successive volumes we will publish detailed case histories, multisubject experimental studies, as well as literature reviews; we will also publish research papers that employ a variety of experimental and observational techniques. The criteria for the choice of topics is the same as that for the selection of papers to be published in a journal, with the added luxury of a greater number of pages so that a topic or a problem can be fully examined.

In our opinion, much of the excitement of neurolinguistics is its interdisciplinary character. Ideas originate from many disciplines, and attempts at synthesis must take account of many different kinds of data. As is well known, there are a number of substantial disagreements among researchers in this field. Rather than attempt to present a falsely unified perspective, we have deliberately solicited papers that present viewpoints which will not meet with uniform acceptance from our readership. We have also solicited papers that attempt to pull together commonly known information into new syntheses and hopefully will provide the impetus for further research.

Boller, Kim, and Mack (Chapter 1) have reviewed the challenging problem of "Auditory Comprehension in Aphasia, discussing both historical and current approaches. A number of aphasia tests used to measure auditory comprehension are analyzed and compared. Particular attention is given to the phonological, semantic, syntactic, and paralinguistic aspects of comprehension.

The world's literature on "Bilingualism and Aphasia" is surveyed by Paradis (Chapter 2); the focus of his synthesis is on the modes of restitution of the various languages of the polyglot aphasic. The explanations for the various types of recovery range from linguistic to social to psychological.

One of the puzzling problems in aphasic research has been "The Nature of Conduction Aphasia." It is discussed and reviewed by Green and Howes (Chapter 3). In their chapter they consider the anatomic findings and the clinical features of 52 reported cases and then they examine different models and explanations for the syndrome.

Although we are all implicitly aware of "The Limbic System in Human Communication," Lamendella (Chapter 4) makes it explicit in his synthesis of anatomic, physiologic and behavioral research. Evidence is adduced from comparative studies in other species as well as from studies of patients with brain damage.

Hardyck (Chapter 5) presents "A Model of Individual Differences in Hemispheric Functioning," in which he analyzes and compares a number of the current theories about the left and right hemispheres. He examines data which relate hemispheric functions to handedness and then he presents his own model which takes into account the available data and makes some specific experimental predictions.

Marshall and Newcombe (Chapter 6) consider the psycholinguistic nature of reading errors in their paper "Variability and Constraint in Acquired Dyslexia." They present eight case histories in which some aspect of dyslexic impairment is a prominent feature. These cases are analyzed in terms of their linguistic similarities and differences, to show how different levels of language are revealed.

Levy (Chapter 7) addresses "The Question of Electrophysiological Asymmetries Preceding Speech" in a study of the readiness potentials over the motor and premotor regions in eight subjects. He combines a sophisticated statistical analysis with a detailed phonological analysis of speech and other vocal tract gestures, to develop hypotheses about what is shown in the readiness potential.

Clinicians and research scientists alike will find material of interest in these volumes. For the clinical neurologist or speech pathologist, neurolinguistics adds powerful and interesting theories and methods derived from the behavioral sciences. For the linguist, neurolinguistics represents the addition of a new data base against which to test theories of language, as well as the addition of experimental methods to language research. For the psychologist, neurolinguistics can represent a means for neuropsychology and physiological psychology to focus on the problems of language and brain. Our ultimate goal is a synthesis of the brain sciences, the behavioral sciences, and the clinical sciences, regardless of whether one's primary interest is in language, in the brain, or in the therapy and rehabilitation of the brain-damaged person. These volumes are the first in this field to present a multiauthored, multitopic study of neurolinguistics; we hope they will give the reader a sense of the breadth and the interest of many of the problems in the field.

Contents of Previous Volumes

1

Auditory Comprehension in Aphasia[1]

François Boller
Youngjai Kim
James L. Mack
CASE WESTERN UNIVERSITY
SCHOOL OF MEDICINE
AND CLEVELAND VETERANS
ADMINISTRATION HOSPITAL

INTRODUCTION

This chapter deals with disturbances of auditory comprehension in aphasia. Although the most obvious aspect of an aphasic patient's disturbance is his oral, written, or gestural output, it was recognized quite early in the history of aphasia research that expressive problems were often associated with impairments of comprehension. Nevertheless, the comprehension of aphasics has been studied less often than their expression, perhaps because the analysis of comprehension must be based, of course, on observation of overt responses and thus is confounded by output deficits. While a disorder of spontaneous output can be reasonably interpreted as an expressive disorder, a deficient response to an external stimulus may or may not reflect impairment of comprehension per se.

It is quite difficult to provide a precise definition for the term "comprehension." Most would agree, however, that a disorder of comprehension is an inability to understand linguistic utterances which cannot be attributed to deficient sensory input, generalized cognitive deficits, or defective attention. This chapter consists of an analysis of disorders of auditory comprehension in adult aphasics. Impaired comprehension of written (see Marshall & Newcombe, this volume) or gestural material (see Gainotti & Lemmo, 1976) is not discussed.

[1] Research presented in this chapter was supported in part by The Cleveland Veterans Administration, Project Number 1017-05.

1

A brief outline of the commonly used categories of aphasia is presented in order to indicate the extent to which comprehension deficits have been considered to be associated with each such category. Other, nonaphasic syndromes which result or appear to result in comprehension difficulties are also described. After discussing some early contributions to the study of comprehension deficits in aphasia, we review various techniques that have been developed for the assessment of comprehension, including single tests and large test batteries. Finally, an analysis of experimental studies of auditory comprehension is presented.

COMPREHENSION DISORDERS IN VARIOUS SYNDROMES

The terminology used in this section and in the remainder of this chapter is generally that proposed by Benson and Geschwind (1971) and Goodglass and Kaplan (1972). For each syndrome, however, the terms used by other authors are also indicated. Aphasia is defined as a loss of language ability that is secondary to cerebral damage and that causes a disorder of translation of thoughts into words and words into thoughts. Within this broad definition, aphasic syndromes may be divided initially into two types, those with *nonfluent* and those with *fluent* output (Benson, 1970).

Nonfluent Aphasias

BROCA'S APHASIA

This syndrome corresponds to what Broca (1861) called *aphemia*, later referred to by Wernicke (1874, 1908) and Goldstein (1948) as *motor aphasia.* Other synonyms include *cortical motor aphasia* (Lichtheim, 1885), *verbal aphasia* (Head, 1926), *expressive aphasia* (Weisenburg & McBride, 1935), and *efferent motor aphasia* (Luria, 1966). The diagnosis of this form of aphasia is based principally on the observation of reduced (nonfluent) verbal output in both speech and writing. Comprehension often appears intact or nearly intact on informal examination. In fact, it is rarely perfect, as shown by the poor performance of patients when asked to carry out complex commands requiring a succession of responses. Written questions and commands are particularly likely to elicit defective responses (Isserlin, 1936). In some cases, comprehension is more grossly impaired, so there may be considerable overlap between this form of aphasia and global aphasia. Not infrequently, an initial global aphasia evolves, as the patient's comprehension and output improve, into a typical Broca's aphasia. About 20% of all patients with aphasia have Broca's aphasia (Vignolo, 1973).

GLOBAL APHASIA

Weisenburg and McBride (1935) called this syndrome *expressive–receptive aphasia.* The most deficient of all types, the global aphasic shows severe impairment of all linguistic functions. He says little, understands only a few questions and commands, and repeats only the simplest sounds. It is not unusual to observe this condition initially followed by a residual picture of another type of aphasia (as, for example, Broca's aphasia, as just stated). Global aphasia is the most frequent type of aphasia (20 to 25%; Vignolo, 1973).

TRANSCORTICAL MOTOR APHASIA

Transcortical motor aphasia is Lichtheim's (1885) term; Luria (1966) described a somewhat similar condition he called *dynamic aphasia.* Patients with this syndrome have markedly reduced output with relatively intact comprehension. Naming is also quite good; repetition is practically perfect. Reading is preserved, but writing is nearly always impaired. In the case of those patients whose reduced output is linguistically correct and who can name, understand, repeat, and read quite well, it is doubtful that the disorder is an aphasia, a fact that led Von Stockert (1974) to dub the syndrome *aphasia sine aphasia.*

Fluent Aphasias

WERNICKE'S APHASIA

The disorder we know as *Wernicke's aphasia* was referred to by Wernicke (1874) and Goldstein (1948) as *sensory aphasia,* while Lichtheim (1885) called it *sensory cortical aphasia,* and Head, *syntactic aphasia* (1926; cf., for example, his Case 14, Vol. 2, p. 215). Luria refers to it as *acoustic aphasia* (1966); Weisenburg and McBride (1935) term it *receptive aphasia.* Diagnosis is based principally on the observation of fluent yet meaningless jargon. Alajouanine, Sabouraud, and Ribaucourt (1952) and Alajouanine, Lhermitte, Ledoux, Renaud, and Vignolo (1964) have described two, sometimes coexistent types of this disorder, distinguished by their tendencies to use primarily phonemic or semantic jargon, a distinction discussed in detail later (see pp. 34–36). In a retrospective analysis of his own cases, Hécaen (1969, 1972) has differentiated Wernicke's aphasia into three forms: (*a*) "predominant word-deafness," in which there is impairment in the reception of auditory signals but a relatively preserved ability to read; (*b*) "predominant impairment of verbal comprehension," with inability to decode both oral and written language; and (*c*) "attentional disorganization," with failure to attend consistently to messages.

In Wernicke's aphasia, comprehension, as a rule, is severely impaired, but some patients with severe jargonaphasia can show good performance on tests of auditory comprehension (Alajouanine, Sabouraud, & de Ribaucourt, 1952; Kinsbourne & Warrington, 1963). The typical patient, when questioned or given commands, usually stops talking and appears to listen to what he is told, only to fall back into a jargon that often bears no apparent relationship to the examiner's words. The incidence of Wernicke's aphasia is similar to that of Broca's apahsia, that is, 15 to 20 % (Vignolo, 1973).

CONDUCTION APHASIA

Conduction aphasia was a term introduced by Wernicke (1874). Goldstein calls it *central aphasia* (1948), and Luria's *afferent motor aphasia* (1966) probably corresponds to this form. Wernicke (1874) thought that, in some patients, there could be a lesion of the pathway connecting "the central termination of the acoustic nerve," what we now call "Wernicke's area," and the areas controlling "the representation of movements in the cerebral cortex which are necessary for the production of sounds," or "Broca's area" in modern parlance. Thus Wernicke chose the term *Leitungsaphasie,* which implies "failure to conduct." He noted that these patients could "understand everything" and "express themselves" but that their "ability to choose the correct word is disturbed." As was pointed out later (Lichtheim, 1885), these patients repeat quite poorly. Diagnosis is often based on a discrepancy between relatively preserved comprehension and clearly impaired repetition. Varying data on the incidence of this type of aphasia have been reported, from "rare" (Goldstein, 1948) to 4% (Vignolo, 1973) and 5 to 10% (Benson, Sheramata, Bouchard, Segarra, Price, & Geschwind, 1973).

ANOMIC APHASIA

Synonyms for this type of aphasia include *amnestic aphasia* (Goldstein, 1948) and *nominal aphasia* (Head, 1926). Here the main disturbance consists of difficulties in naming on confrontation and in word-finding in spontaneous speech. The naming and word finding problems occur with a wide variety of word types and must be distinguished from problems in naming specific types of stimuli, such as colors or other visual or tactual stimuli. The latter type of difficulty is seen in nonaphasic agnosic conditions which Geschwind (1967a) considers to reflect lesions which separate specific sensory systems from the speech areas. Nonaphasic misnaming may occur with diffuse or generalized neurological involvement as well. Actual anomic aphasics represent about 8% of the total number of cases of aphasia (Vignolo, 1973).

TRANSCORTICAL SENSORY APHASIA

The name *transcortical sensory aphasia* was proposed by Lichtheim (1885). Von Monakow (1914) calls it *sensory associative aphasia.* In this syndrome repetition is quite good while comprehension is grossly impaired. In extreme cases, repetition is the only remaining language function, a condition leading to echolalia. This more severe form was called by Goldstein (1948) and by Geschwind, Quadfasel, and Segarra (1968) "isolation of the speech area." The name *transcortical sensory aphasia* is thus reserved for the less severe form in which comprehension, though somewhat preserved, is clearly worse than repetition. This syndrome occurs in about 2% of aphasics (Vignolo, 1973).

Other Syndromes

Finally, mention must be made of syndromes in which a single language modality is impaired.

ALEXIA WITHOUT AGRAPHIA

This syndrome was first identified by Dejerine (1914), who called it *pure word blindness.* In the classical form, the patient has no disorder of spoken language. However, particularly in the initial stages, the patient often has some difficulty in naming objects, and impaired ability to name colors has usually been observed in association with the syndrome (Geschwind & Fusillo, 1966; Geschwind, 1967a). Furthermore, some difficulty in comprehending spoken language may occur in the initial phases of the disorder. This syndrome is rare (Vignolo, 1973).

WORD DEAFNESS

Word deafness was first used by Kussmaul (1877), and the syndrome was later termed *subcortical sensory aphasia* by Lichtheim (1885). In its very rare pure form, comprehension of spoken language is severely impaired despite normal hearing ability, but oral expression, writing, reading aloud, and comprehension of written material are allegedly intact. More frequently, spontaneous speech, writing, and comprehension of written material show some abnormality; the diagnosis, however, is based on the observation of far greater relative impairment of auditory comprehension.

APHEMIA

As stated above, the term *aphemia* was used by Broca (1861), but Bastian (1887) is generally credited with giving it its present meaning. Lichtheim (1885) called this syndrome *subcortical motor aphasia,* and Brown (1972) calls it *pure motor aphasia.* Aphemia is a disorder in which only oral expression is impaired. Writing, reading, and comprehension are preserved. This disorder is extremely rare.

Nonaphasic Disturbances of Comprehension

Aphasic disturbances of comprehension must be distinguished from a series of conditions in which there is also failure to respond to questions and commands, which makes the assessment of language quite difficult. These conditions include paralysis of the cranial nerves, due either to a bulbar lesion (as seen in amyotrophic lateral sclerosis or syringobulbia) or to pseudobulbar paralysis (also called pseudobulbar palsy), wherein bilateral lesions affect the suprasegmental motor fibers that innervate the cranial nerve nuclei. In such cases, a neurological examination may be necessary for differential diagnosis, although pseudobulbar palsy often includes a marked loss of emotional control, with unprovoked outbursts of laughing or crying (Brown, 1967; Merritt, 1973, p. 195), making a behavioral diagnosis possible.

Akinetic mutism, or *vigilant coma* (Jennet & Plum, 1972), must also be distinguished from aphasic disturbance of comprehension. In this condition, the patient appears awake, looking about with open eyes, but he responds to neither verbal nor nonverbal stimuli. In extreme cases, he may not even chew food placed in his mouth. These symptoms may be (*a*) iatrogenic, or induced by drugs such as steroids or amphetamines; (*b*) psychiatric, as, for example, in affective psychoses, catatonic schizophrenia, or transient situational disturbances such as "shell-shock"; or (*c*) indicative of a general medical condition such as infection, dehydration, or anemia, when such a condition is unaccompanied by signs of neurological involvement; finally, (*d*) they may be seen in such neurological disorders as trauma or vascular lesions. The term *akinetic mutism* is properly applied only in the last of these situations. In a related condition, the "locked-in syndrome" (Plum & Posner, 1972), the patient is entirely awake, responsive, and sentient, but a general paralysis limits his repertoire of responses to little more than jaw and eye movements and blinking. In some cases, the patient may occasionally be observed to spontaneously produce linguistically correct speech. Furthermore, the nonresponsiveness of the typical patient clearly extends to areas of nonlanguage behavior, a condition distinguishing him from aphasics.

Finally, aphasic comprehension deficits must be clearly differentiated from generalized disorders associated with severe dementia and confusional states. It is often very difficult or impossible to establish verbal or nonverbal communication with demented or confused patients who may fail to pay attention to the examiner and may, for example, continue a monologue even when directly addressed. Some demented patients, however, particularly those with Alzheimer's disease, may exhibit specific aphasic symptoms, such as poor naming ability, impaired repetition, and abnormal performance on tests of auditory comprehension (De Renzi & Vignolo, 1966).

In summarizing our discussion of aphasic syndromes, several comments are in order. First, one should recall Pierre Marie's (1906; translated by Cole & Cole, 1971) strongly expressed view that "there is only one aphasia" and that subdivision of this disorder into different syndromes is totally arbitrary. The system of classification outlined above is followed by most authors, although there have been some notable exceptions (Bay, 1962; Schuell, Jenkins, & Jimenez-Pabón, 1964). Even the strongest proponents of the existence of different aphasic syndromes concede, however, that these syndromes are seldom seen in pure form. Sometimes patients evolve from one form into another or present with a combination of symptoms, making reliable classification impossible. The question of the validity of classifying aphasics into various syndromes will be examined at the end of the chapter.

Regardless of whether or not aphasics may be reliably classified into distinct syndromes, comparisons of the degree of comprehension deficit in various patients implies some consensus as to the nature of comprehension. Although we did not attempt to provide a precise definition of comprehension, it has thus far been discussed as if it were a unitary function which can be scaled. However, as will be seen below, evaluations of the nature and extent of comprehension deficit vary considerably as a function of the methods used to assess comprehension. Further elucidation of the nature of comprehension must thus be deferred until the techniques of assessment have been presented.

Finally, evaluating comprehension in aphasics is complicated by the fact that comprehension tends to improve more rapidly than other language functions, whether or not the patient receives speech therapy (Vignolo, 1965). Thus the problem of an evolving clinical picture may make the analysis of comprehension more difficult than the analysis of other language functions.

EARLY CONTRIBUTIONS TO THE STUDY OF COMPREHENSION DEFICITS IN APHASIA

Although Wernicke (1874) is credited with the first systematic description of comprehension deficits in aphasia, his was not the first reported case (Boller, in press). As pointed out by Benton (1965a,b), Gesner, in his chapter entitled "Speech Amnesia" (1770), described a patient who complained of difficulty in understanding other people's language, perhaps the earliest account of comprehension difficulties. Lordat (1843 [1969]) published a description of his own aphasia, which he termed "alalia." He wrote, "I was no longer able to receive the ideas of others because the amnesia which prevented me from speaking also made me unable to understand the sounds I heard fast enough to catch their meaning. I would have needed time to make the effort of remembering each sound; conversation is too fluent for me to understand enough words." While Bay (1969) has argued that Lordat's description was influenced by his preconceived vitalistic notions of language, Lordat's report certainly corresponds closely to many aphasics' descriptions of comprehension deficits (see Alajouanine, 1968, pp. 301–332; Gardner, 1975, pp. 397–422).

Broca (1861 [1969]) did not specifically deal with problems of auditory comprehension in aphasia, but in his report of his patient, Leborgne ("Tan-Tan"), he commented that at times the patient failed to respond to questions that could have been answered with a simple gesture. Although some of the patient's responses could not be clearly understood, at other times they were intelligible and clearly incorrect: "although he had no children, he responded that he had some." Indeed, Leborgne's comprehension deficits combined with his lack of fluency suggest that he was perhaps globally aphasic.

In 1869, Bastian spoke of defects that might exist "in the auditory perceptive centers or in the different fibers with which they are connected, [as a result of which] the individual could not appreciate the meaning of spoken words; they would be to him mere sounds." Although this paper was apparently not known to Wernicke in 1874, later (1908) he gave credit to Bastian and also to Schmidt, who, in 1871, had described a case of his own (Boller, in press).

It remained for Wernicke to provide the first detailed and systematic description of comprehension impairment along with a model of the relationship between specific aphasic syndromes and focal neuroanatomical lesions. Wernicke (1874 [1968]), on the basis of Meynert's work (see, for example, Meynert, 1866), regarded the brain as divided into two large areas of functionally different significance: the frontal lobes (all the area anterior to the fissure of Rolando), which he considered to contain representations of movement; and the temporo-occipital lobes (regarded as a single unit), which he thought contained memory images of past impressions. He was not certain of the function of the parietal lobes. Wernicke considered that "the first temporal convolution, a sensory area, is the center for sound images—the central termination of the acoustic nerve." He schematically represented both functional and anatomical relationships in a diagram (see Figure 1.1) in which a represents the point at which the acoustic nerve enters the medulla, b is Broca's area, a_1 is the "central termination of the acoustic nerve" (what we now call "Wernicke's area"), and b_1 represents the "place where the sound producing motor nerves leave the brain." By means of this schema, Wernicke was able to analyze the functional nature of comprehension deficits. He reasoned that if the pathway from a to a_1 were interrupted in an adult with normally developed speech, only deafness would result, whereas the same lesion should produce mutism in a preverbal child. Most important for our purposes, Wernicke discussed the effects of the destruction of area a_1, stating that "the sound images of the names of all possible objects will

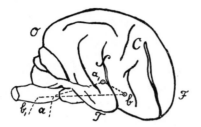

Figure 1.1 Functional anatomy of the brain according to Wernicke. C = Central fissure; S = Sylvian fissure; F = Frontal lobe; O = Occipital lobe; T = Temporal lobe; a = place where acoustic nerve enters medulla; a_1 = central termination of acoustic nerve; b = representations of movements in cerebral cortex necessary for production of sounds; b_1 = place where most sound-producing motor nerves leave the brain. [Wernicke, 1874.]

be lost." Such a patient is "capable neither of repeating spoken words, since this is the characteristic function of the path $a–a_1–b–b_1$, nor of understanding a spoken word. . . . Aside from his deficient comprehension, the patient has aphasic manifestations in speaking because of the absence of the corrective function exercised unconsciously by the sound images." Agraphia in such patients was explained as a consequence of the fact that writing is "always executed under the guidance of sound." Furthermore, these patients would not be able to read aloud or understand written materials unless they were "scholars practiced since childhood to skim over a page and understand its meaning without becoming conscious of individual words." Thus a single lesion and disruption of a specific function could have broad consequences. Wernicke explained the absence of reports of cases of this type not just as a consequence of case infrequency but because of the fact that they well may have been considered confusional states. He went on to apply his model to explain the deficits seen in conduction and nonfluent aphasia as well.

It should be noted that Wernicke's diagram is of the right hemisphere and that in the first three sections of his monograph, Wernicke does not give much emphasis to the question of hemispheric dominance for language. In addition, in the first case of sensory aphasia which he describes in detail, hemispheric localization seems uncertain. In the next nine cases, however, he presents clinical data and, in four cases, post mortem evidence clearly pointing to left hemisphere lesions.

The successful reception of Wernicke's monograph was all the more striking in view of the fact that he was young (only 26 years of age at the time of publication), affiliated with a provincial university (Breslau), and without either academic rank or support from major academic figures. Furthermore, his later interests and achievements were not related to aphasia. Geschwind (1967b) has discussed possible reasons for the monograph's acceptance. Wernicke brought new clinical facts to light. He differentiated sensory aphasia from confusional states and distinguished the syndrome both clinically and anatomically from motor aphasia. As Geschwind (1967b) points out, Wernicke "made the first searching attempt to link the facts of anatomy with facts of behavior in a way that permitted both prediction of syndromes and organized testing of hypotheses." Wernicke also made important points in regard to the nature of language. Stressing the auditory–verbal aspects of language, he excluded the effects of lesions of the optic pathways from the clinical syndromes of aphasia, contrary to the position taken by Bastian. He also clearly distinguished between disturbances of language and more generalized intellectual deficits such as Finkelnburg's (1870) asymbolia. For Wernicke, "there could be nothing worse for the theory of aphasia than to interpret the disturbances of intelligence that accompany it—and that can occasionally be observed in every other localized disorder of the brain—as essential to the clinical picture."

Hughlings Jackson, in spite of the fact that he wrote widely on aphasia, did not clearly identify disturbances of comprehension. Discussing the process of dissolution of language (Jackson, 1874 [1915]), he distinguished three different levels: utterances that are not speech, utterances that are inferior speech (oaths, exclamations), and utterances that express relationships. For Jackson, only the third level represented true speech, and the loss of this level was seen following lesions of the left hemisphere. Thus his entire discussion of aphasic disturbances was carried out without reference to comprehension. In his discussion of the role of the right hemisphere, which he considered the seat of automatic acts, he stated, "The right hemisphere is the half by which we receive propositions" (Jackson, 1874 [1915]). This statement appears to relegate comprehension to the right hemisphere; however, Jackson added, "When we receive a proposition, the process is entirely automatic." Thus it is not at all clear to what extent Jackson considered the reception of propositions—an automatic activity—synonymous with comprehension, a process that is hard to conceive of as entirely automatic.

Following Wernicke many authors recognized the existence of comprehension deficits in aphasia. Charcot in 1888 (see Charcot, 1974, pp. 145–149), for example, described several specific syndromes, or what he called "primitive" or "partial" aphasias: agraphia, motor aphasia, verbal deafness, and verbal blindness. He stressed, however, that "in most cases the aphasic patient we see in our clinical practice is a complete aphasic with, in combination and in different proportions, the different types of primitive aphasias." While Charcot, as well as Wernicke, distinguished aphasia from intellectual deficits, Marie (1906) opposed the notion of specific language deficits. He stressed that aphasia was always accompanied by a comprehension deficit which was not due to "deafness for verbal–auditory images" (probably a reference to Lichtheim's *Wortklangsbilder*), but was a consequence of intellectual deterioration.[2] To illustrate his belief that the deficits in aphasia were of a more generalized intellectual nature, he cited the case of an aphasic who used to be a "good cook," but who, when given the implements for frying an egg, produced a result that was "obviously unpresentable." Marie argued that a comprehension deficit (and thus, by his definition, intellectual deterioration) was also present in Broca's aphasia, which he considered to be simply Wernicke's aphasia accompanied by anarthria.

In contrast to Marie's attempt to bring the complex processes involved in aphasia under a single, generalized picture of deficit, Pick (1909; see Spreen, 1973) provided a detailed analysis of a single function, comprehension. He presented a hierarchical model of comprehension, stating that "language understanding is a synthetic process consisting of a series of individual steps." He emphasized that comprehension of single words is achieved through the evocation of associated words that are conceptually related to the stimulus words and that such associational responses precede understanding at more complex levels.

It is notable that these early writers raised many of the basic issues that concern us today in studying comprehension deficits in aphasia.

ASSESSMENT OF COMPREHENSION

Although early contributors to the analysis of comprehension deficits in aphasics discussed the role and nature of comprehension problems, it is very difficult to compare the findings of one writer with another unless each has specified techniques for measuring comprehension. Perhaps the earliest special test for the evaluation of comprehension was the Proust–Lichtheim Test, in which the patient was asked to raise his fingers (Proust, 1872), to squeeze the examiner's hand (Lichtheim), or to make as many "expiration movements" (Dejerine, 1891) as there were syllables in the name of an object shown to the patient. Such a test was intended to evaluate the quality of the "motor images of the inner speech," presumably intact in anarthria but impaired in Wernicke's aphasia.

Benton (1973) has recently reviewed a number of early contributions to the testing of comprehension in aphasia. As early as 1885, Grashey published a

[2] Cole (1968) has recently reviewed Pierre Marie's contribution to aphasia and has discussed the implications of Marie's statement concerning intellectual deterioration in aphasia. His conclusion is that "it is difficult to be fully certain what Marie meant by this deficit in intellect." Cole adds that in his opinion this "circumscribed" deficit could be equated with the patient's deficit in comprehension. For a recent discussion of the problem of the relationship of intelligence to brain lesions and aphasia, see Basso, De Renzi, Faglioni, Scotti, and Spinnler (1973), and Lebrun and Hoops, 1974.

picture test which was designed to evaluate a patient's ability to integrate sensory information presented over time in order to achieve recognition of a complex stimulus. Rieger (1889) was perhaps the first to propose the use of a large-scale battery to test both intellectual and language functions in brain-damaged patients. Liepmann must also be considered one of the first to use a systematic approach in evaluating patients with disorders of higher cortical functions. A little known paper of his, which he modestly called "Kleine Hilfsmittel" ('small helpful hints') (1905), outlines a procedure designed to assess auditory comprehension. Liepmann's test consists of a series of statements, some meaningful and some absurd, in response to which the patient was instructed to nod in agreement or dissent.

Perhaps the most widely known of the early tests of comprehension ability is the famous Three Papers Test of Pierre Marie (1906). The test consisted simply of giving a patient a complex sequential command: "Here on this table are three pieces of paper of different sizes; give me the largest one, crumple the middle-sized one and throw it on the floor; as for the smallest one, put it in your pocket." As an alternative to the Three Papers Test, Marie (1906) also asked the patient to "Stand up, tap three times on the window with your finger, then return to the front of the table, walk around your chair and sit down." In fact, Marie developed a series of tests which ranged from the very simple to tasks as complex as those just described. His aphasia battery has been described in detail by his student, Moutier (1908). The test battery included simple commands, starting with requests such as "Stick out your tongue," "Put a stamp on a letter." When the patient failed to perform an act, he was asked to imitate the examiner's performance of the act. The patient was given a series of commands containing the same critical words, for example, "Give me your hand," and "Spread the fingers of your hand." Of course, it might be quite difficult to assess the quality of the patient's performance in response to many of these commands. Yet, even though these early techniques were not always capable of precisely quantifying or scoring the patient's response, they did afford some controlled means of comparing the performance of one patient with another.

In his book, *Aphasia and Kindred Disorders of Speech,* Head (1926) described a series of tests used in his examination of aphasics. They included naming and recognition of objects (pointing to an object on command); naming and recognition of colors; The Man, Cat, and Dog Test (an easy reading and writing test); and the Clock Test, involving setting the hands of the clock and telling the time. More relevant to auditory comprehension are his last two tests: the Coin in Bowl Test, and the Hand, Eye, and Ear Test. In the first test, four bowls or saucers are set upon a table and a penny is placed in front of each. The patient is then asked to place the pennies in the bowls according to a series of commands. In the second test, the patient is requested to touch an eye or an ear with one or the other hand. In both of these tests, the patient was required first to imitate the examiner, next to imitate a pictured human figure carrying out the command, then to follow oral or written commands, and finally to write a description of the movement performed by the examiner. Head's goals in the construction of these tests were to quantify (*1*) the variability in each patient's performance by having him repeat required behavior several times and (*2*) the severity of the patient's deficits by presenting the required taks in order of increasing difficulty and noting the point at which the patient failed.

Goldstein (1948) stressed the importance of a further dimension in the examination of the aphasic's comprehension by noting the context in which difficulties occurred. He advised the potential examiner to notice whether the patient understood everyday questions "under all conditions or only if they belonged to a situation concerning his own personality, his own interest, etc." In other words, Goldstein evaluated comprehension in terms of the degree to which the patient's understanding of specific, concrete situations could be generalized, or made abstract, an issue with which Goldstein was greatly concerned throughout his work. He also presented a test battery which included a series of commands ranging in complexity from "Close your eyes" to "Put the key in the door, shut the door, and bring the key back." His final command was Marie's Three Papers Test.

A series of tests described by Weisenburg and McBride (1935) is the first of the modern aphasia batteries. In an introduction entitled, "Psychological examination for aphasic patients; a discussion of the essential requirements," they outline some of the principles used in the construction of this battery. They point out that a battery for aphasia should cover all the performances which may be disturbed. As many as possible of the tests selected for a preliminary examination should be standardized, so that the results obtained by one investigator can be compared with those obtained by another. At the same time, the standard tests must be capable of being altered to throw more light on unusual difficulties. Thus, although Weisenburg and McBride realized the importance of standardization, they emphasized that the fundamental purpose of a language test was to provide a thorough analysis of the individual patient's language behavior, including his method of work, the factors which appear to cause his failures, and the nature of the responses he finally achieves. They felt that the least complicated type of tests were most likely to provide such specific information. Weisenburg and McBride also point out the need for adequate testing of comprehension of oral and written material in a comparable manner. Finally, because of the great variability in the performance of aphasics, tasks must be of a sufficient range of difficulty to apply to all patients. The battery developed by these writers consisted of tests designed to evaluate many different aspects of language and nonlanguage abilities, including speaking, naming, repeating, understanding spoken language, reading, writing, arithmetic, language intelligence, reproduction of verbal material, and other general tests of language and nonlanguage abilities.

Comprehension was examined by the following tests:

1. *Response to everyday questions and comments.* Weisenburg and McBride remark, as did Goldstein, that patients tend to understand questions arising from natural situations better than test questions, even though no gestural cues are given.

2. *Comprehension of words and sentences.* This was tested by an oral adaptation of Gates' Reading Test (1927) for words, phrases, and sentences. Items were repeated as many times as the patient asked, in order to make the procedure comparable to a written presentation, where a patient could go over the material repeatedly.

3. *Following directions.* Tasks consisted of commands, ranging from "Close your eyes" and "Put the back of your hand on the top of your head" to a test of three commissions (complicated commands with threefold directions) and Marie's Three Papers Test.

4. *Comprehension of spatial terms and relationships.* This test included Head's Hand, Eye, and Ear Test (1926) and Abelson's Figures (1911). The latter test includes commands such as "Point inside the circle and the triangle but not in the square."

Weisenburg and McBride also used a Language Intelligence Test which consisted of the following:

1. *The Controlled Association Test.*

   a. *Opposites.* "I am going to say a word and I want you to tell me the opposite of it as quickly as you can." Stimuli were taken from a list of words developed by Whipple (1921).

   b. *Part–Whole Test.* "I am going to tell you some words one at a time. Each of them is a part of something. As soon as I say the word, I want you to quickly tell me the word meaning the whole of which the word I said is a part." The stimuli, taken from Healy and Bronner (1927) included such items as "window," "leaf," "beak," and "stamen." The Part–Whole scores obtained with normals were well distributed; the Opposites Test was easily performed by most normals. Because it was so simple, the latter was usually the more valuable test in assessing aphasic patients.

   c. *Van Wagenen's Oral Analogies Test* (1920). "I am going to say three words. I want you to tell me the fourth word that has the same relationship to the third word I say as the second has to the first." Stimuli included such items as "Horn is to blow as bell is to _____?" (ring). The writers comment that this test proved to be an efficient means of detecting slight difficulties in evoking words.

2. *Sentence Completion Test* (Trabue, 1916). This included items ranging from "I see you. Can you see _____?" to "When two persons _____ about _____ which neither _____, they _____ almost _____ to disagree." Not surprisingly, results of this test showed a wide distribution of scores among normals.

3. *Absurdities.* "I am going to read you a paragraph that has something foolish about it, something absurd. When I am finished, I want you to tell me what is foolish about it." This test included such items as, "A showman advertised for a giant and a dwarf. A man of ordinary height presented himself and offered to fill both parts. He claimed to be the smallest giant in the world and the biggest dwarf."

4. *Vocabulary.* In this test, the patient was asked to give an oral definition that would indicate that he recognized the meaning of the words, which were taken from the Stanford–Binet Vocabulary Test.

The foregoing illustrations serve to point out both the contributions and the difficulties introduced by Weisenburg and McBride's approach. The importance of using measures with a wide dispersion of scores so as to permit the comparison of patients with widely varying severities of comprehension deficits cannot be ignored. At the same time, tests with the widest range tended to be heavily weighted on general intellectual factors and therefore difficult to interpret in terms of a patient's specific linguistic abilities. On many of the measures, diagnostic utility appears to have been sacrificed for the sake of obtaining a "satisfactory distribution."

Ombredane (1951) made an important contribution by describing an assessment technique that stressed the role of particular types of words in identifying comprehension problems. In the Cat and Chair Test, six cards were displayed in front of the patient, each showing a cat either on, before, to the right of, below, behind, or to the left of a chair. The patient was asked to point to the card corresponding to a sentence, spoken by the examiner, that described the positional relationship of the cat to the chair by means of a critical preposition. In the Pencils Test, the patient was presented with two groups of pencils, one to his left and one to his right, each group containing a long red pencil, a short red pencil, a long blue pencil, and a short blue pencil. He was then instructed to select from the eight pencils the one described aloud by the examiner, e.g., "the long red pencil on your right." Thus, the patient's ability to comprehend and utilize descriptive attributes and positional relationships was evaluated in a context that did not appear to require a significant amount of general intellectual ability, although, of course, attentional deficits might well influence the patient's performance. These two tests are somewhat reminiscent of Head's Coin in Bowl Test and seem clearly to be precursors of De Renzi and Vignolo's Token Test.

In the introduction to their paper on the Token Test, De Renzi and Vignolo (1962b) discuss the guidelines they followed in designing this new test. The test was developed to examine patients who present very mild receptive disorders that might not be detected by routine clinical examination. It does not require a special apparatus or printed material and can be administered in a short time. The commands are brief and easy to follow from an intellectual standpoint but demanding on a linguistic level. The authors point out that most tests previously suggested for the purpose of testing comprehension were too confusing (e.g., Head's Hand, Eye, and Ear Test), too demanding on the patient's span of attention because of their length (e.g., Marie's Three Papers Test), or too difficult from an intellectual point of view (e.g., many of the tests of Weisenburg & McBride). The authors thought a high degree of linguistic difficulty could be attained, not by using unusual words and syntactic forms but by eliminating the redundancy present in normal speech. Thus they explicitly avoided giving cues provided by the nature of objects used or by the situational or verbal context of a command (De Renzi & Vignolo, 1962a).

The material used for the Token Test consists of twenty plastic chips similar in size to those used in card games and varying in size (large or small), color (red, blue, green, yellow, or white), and shape (circles and rectangles). The tokens are displayed in front of the patient in four rows of five tokens each: large circles, small circles, large rectangles, and small rectangles, with every color represented in each row. The tokens are so arranged that no color is represented twice in one column. When all twenty tokens are present, it takes at least three words designating size, shape, and color to identify a given token. The test consists of five progressively more difficult parts. Before starting, the examiner makes sure that the patient understands the words, "circle," "rectangle" and the five colors which are to be used. The test consists of 61 commands.

One can clearly discern two levels of difficulty within the test. Through Part IV, the task is essentially the same, to "take" a token, the verb serving only to enable the examiner to determine whether or not the patient has correctly identified the described stimulus. From one part of the test to the next, the token or tokens are identified with increasingly greater specificity. In Part V, however, one must not only identify the designated token but respond to commands that call for varied responses and that require an understanding of the positional relationship of the various tokens as conveyed through the use of prepositions; that is, the patient is required to grasp "the semantic complications introduced by the 'small instruments of language.' "

De Renzi and Vignolo (1962b) gave the Token Test to 19 aphasics, none of whom had shown comprehension difficulty either during normal conversation or in a detailed aphasia battery. All 19 made an increasing number of errors as the test progressed, with mistakes becoming very frequent in Parts IV and V.

In the final part of the paper, De Renzi and Vignolo (1962b) considered the theoretical question of whether or not a more specifically linguistic approach would offer increased insight into aphasia but concluded that the Token Test "must be considered above all as a functional clinical tool . . . of great sensitivity, contaminated as little as possible by intellectual difficulties."

TESTS OF COMPREHENSION IN CURRENT APHASIA BATTERIES

The process of evaluating comprehension entails presenting stimulus materials to a subject and, on the basis of his or her response, making an inference as to the extent of the subject's ability to comprehend. The nature of the stimulus materials and the manner in which they are presented are independent variables which can be more or less systematically manipulated in order to determine the critical parameters affecting a subject's response. The examiner is limited, however, to those materials that the constructor of a given battery considered important and relevant in evaluating comprehension ability. Tests of comprehension thus generally consist of carefully worked out administrative procedures and stimulus materials designed to elicit relatively simple responses. In making such simple responses, a wide variety of aphasics, including those with severe expressive difficulties, can convey their degree of comprehension in a manner minimally confounded by the presence of deficits unrelated to comprehension.

The complexity of stimulus materials presented can also be systematically varied across test batteries. The amount of information presented is a simple and quantifiable aspect of stimulus complexity, although its quantification is complicated, of course, by the redundancy of the message. The number of items to be processed (such as phonemes, morphemes, phrases, and sentences) can be systematically increased in order to determine the level at which performance is disrupted by information overload. This critical level can be compared to the subject's performance with relatively nonverbal information to evaluate his or her limitations in attention per se, independent of the linguistic aspects of the task.

Another, more qualitative aspect of complexity can be defined as the level of difficulty of the semantic content of the stimulus material. Obviously, defining the difficulty of the semantic context of the stimulus may be somewhat subjective and thus variable. The semantic difficulty of stimulus materials used to test a subject's comprehension may range from that posed by a simple request to point to an object named by the examiner to that of performing difficult tasks that require the discrimination of logical relationships based on subtle, differential uses of prepositions.

A final aspect of complexity is related to the syntactic structure of the stimulus. Although relatively little research has been done on the response of persons with impaired comprehension to changes in syntax, several tests include items in which sentence structure is modified (as from declarative to interrogative), apparently in order to evaluate the subject's ability to comprehend the essential message across various transformations.

A significant question in any evaluation of comprehension is whether performance of the task breaks down at a peripheral, or prelinguistic, level or at a more central, linguistic level. This distinction is analogous to Eisenson's (1954) distinction between subsymbolic and symbolic processes. In examining comprehension, it is extremely important to determine to what degree an impaired response reflects either deficits in perception or peripheral response or an inability to integrate and comprehend material that has been adequately perceived.

Although most test material is verbal in nature, nonverbal tasks are often used to establish a subject's ability to perceive the materials and to carry out the movements necessary to complete the tests of comprehension. Thus most batteries include some measures of sensory processing, motor skills, and praxis as a preliminary aspect of the evaluation of comprehension. It is important to note, however, that many tasks that appear to be nonverbal may require some rudimentary level of language comprehension, making difficult the formal assessment of sensory processing and motor skills. Often, determining the accuracy of a subject's perceptions and the level of his motor skills requires careful observation of his spontaneous behavior.

In many of the tests of comprehension in standard aphasia batteries, identical or similar tasks are employed. Most of these tasks are variations of the following: matching spoken or written words with their significates, either in the form of objects or pictures, selected from an array; matching spoken phonemes, letters, words, or phrases with their written equivalents; answering spoken or written questions with yes—no or more extended responses; following spoken or written directions by carrying out a single action or a series of actions; and completing written or spoken sentences from which one or more words have been omitted.

To familiarize the reader with the kinds of tasks used for tests of comprehension, the following section describes in detail the comprehension tests from four aphasia batteries (Boston Diagnostic Aphasia Examination, Examining for Aphasia, Minnesota Test for Differential Diagnosis of Aphasia, and Neurosensory Center Comprehensive Examination for Aphasia).

Boston Diagnostic Aphasia Examination

Two subsections of Goodglass and Kaplan's (1972) test are relevant to our discussion.

Auditory Comprehension Test:
1. *Word Discrimination.* Subjects are presented with cards depicting several stimuli (objects, geometric forms, letters, actions, numbers, and colors) and asked to point to the correct stimulus when the examiner names it by saying, "Show me ____."
2. *Body Part Identification.* Subjects are asked to point to their body parts when the examiner says, "Show me your ____."
3. *Commands.* Subjects are asked to carry out simple to complex commands, such as "make a fist" and "tap each shoulder twice with two fingers keeping your eyes shut."
4. *Complex Ideational Material.* Subjects are asked to respond with a single yes or no to materials, read by the examiner, that range from simple and short to complex and long.

Understanding Written Language:
1. *Symbol and Word Discrimination.* This is a visual recognition task in which subjects are asked to match cursive or printed (and either upper or lower case) versions of the same letters and words.
2. *Phonetic Association.* This test consists of two sections, both of which examine the subject's ability to associate sounds with letters.
   Word Recognition. Subjects are required to select from among five written words the one that the examiner has spoken.
   Comprehension of Oral Spelling. The examiner spells a word aloud, and then asks the subject to say the word.
3. *Word–Picture Matching.* Written words are presented to the subject one by one, and he is then asked to select a picture that depicts the word shown, such as a chair, smoking, etc.
4. *Reading Sentences and Paragraphs.* Subjects are asked to complete a sentence or a paragraph by choosing the most appropriate word from among a group of four.

Examining for Aphasia

Eisenson (1954) categorizes deficits of comprehension somewhat differently than do the authors of other test batteries. He considers comprehension, or reception, to be a symbolic activity and distinguishes it from two *subsymbolic* activities: *gnosis,* or recognition of objects, a function he considers to be a preliminary to comprehension, and *praxis,* or utilizing objects, a function he considers to follow comprehension. Eisenson includes several tests to evaluate gnosis and praxis within each sensory modality, as described below.

1. *Visual Agnosia.* In this series of tests, various sets of stimuli are presented, such as common objects, pictures, colors, forms, reduced size pictures, numbers, letters, printed words, and printed sentences, and the subject is asked to do one of the following: name the stimulus, point to the stimulus when it is named by the examiner, demonstrate the use of the stimulus, match the stimulus with another visual presentation of it on the facing page, or select the name from among several given orally by the examiner.

2. *Auditory Agnosia.* With eyes closed, the subject is asked to identify or imitate an activity performed by the examiner such as coughing or whistling. The subject is also asked to point to body parts named by the examiner.

3. *Tactile Agnosia.* With eyes shut, the subject is required to identify objects placed in either hand.

The following are Eisenson's receptive aphasia tests, designed to evaluate symbolic comprehension.

1. *Auditory Verbal Comprehension.*

a. *Oral Sentences.* The subject is required to answer questions read by the examiner. If he or she fails, the examiner presents four choices from which the correct answer is to be selected.

b. *Oral Paragraphs.* Paragraphs are read aloud, followed by questions. If the subject fails, choices are given from which he or she may select the correct answer.

2. *Silent Reading Comprehension.* Subjects are asked to read sentences and paragraphs silently and to select the correct answer from one of four alternatives.

Minnesota Test for Differential Diagnosis of Aphasia

In Schuell's (1965) battery, comprehension tests are organized according to the modality of presentation. With tests of *auditory disturbances* the items are presented in spoken form by the examiner.

1. *Recognizing Common Words.* The subject is presented with pictures and asked to point to the one named by the examiner.

2. *Discriminating between Paired Words.* The subject is presented with pairs of pictures whose names are phonemically similar and asked to point to the picture which the examiner names.

3. *Recognizing Letters.* The subject is required to point to one of an array of letters that corresponds to one the examiner names.

4. *Identifying Items Serially Named.*   The subject is presented with a picture in which several objects and people are depicted and then asked to point to the items in the sequence in which they are named by the examiner.

5. *Understanding Sentences.* Simple questions of common factual information requiring yes–no answers are presented.

6. *Following Directions.* The subject is presented with a number of objects and asked to perform tasks with the objects as directed by the examiner.

7. *Understanding a Paragraph.* A long paragraph is read to the subject. The examiner then asks a series of factual questions about the paragraph, to which the subject must answer yes or no.

The section of tests for auditory disturbances includes two tests of repetition for digits and sentences that although they involve auditory presentation, are not expressly related to comprehension.

The second major section of tests deals with *visual and reading disturbances.*

1. *Matching Forms.*   A card with one of a number of geometric forms is placed in front of the subject, who is then asked to point to the corresponding form on another card with an array of forms.

2. *Matching Letters.* This is the same task as matching forms, with letters as the stimuli.

3. *Matching Printed Words to Pictures.* A series of cards, each with a picture and two words written under it, are presented, and the subject is asked to point to the word which matches the picture.

4. *Matching Printed to Spoken Words.* A series of cards, each with a pair of written words, are presented, and the subject is asked to point to the word which the examiner speaks. On both the third and fourth tasks, the incorrect alternatives are selected so as to be phonetically, semantically, or randomly related to the picture.

5. *Reading Comprehension of Sentences.* A series of simple sentences of factual information are presented and the subject is asked to check "yes" or "no" in response.

6. *Reading Comprehension of Paragraph.* A long paragraph followed by written questions is given to the subject to read silently. He then checks off a "yes" or "no" answer to each question.

Neurosensory Center Comprehension Examination for Aphasia

In Spreen and Benton's (1969) battery, simple and complex comprehension skills are evaluated, by means of both auditory and visual presentation, in four basic tests.

1. *Identification by Name.* A tray of objects is presented, and the subject is asked to point to each of the objects which the examiner names aloud, one at a time.

2. *Identification by Sentence (Token Test).* The subject is shown, in an ordered array, 20 plastic chips which vary in color (white, yellow, red, blue, or green), size (large or small), and form (circle or square) and is asked to perform various tasks which the examiner describes aloud. The commands range from simple ("Show me a circle") to complex ("Put the red circle on the green square").

3. *Reading Sentences for Meaning.* This task is analogous to the Token Test but less lengthy. Subjects are told to read aloud the commands, which are printed individually on cards, and then to carry them out.

4. *Reading Names for Meaning.* This task is analogous to the Identification by Name Test, except that names are presented on individual cards, and the subject is asked, "Show me this object."

If a subject makes errors on the tests described above, several "control tests," included in the battery, may be administered in order to rule out the possibility that perceptual deficits have contributed to the subject's errors.

1. *Tactile–Visual Matching.* A tray of objects is shown, and the subject is asked to reach into a stereognosis blind and palpate an object. He is then asked to point to the same object in the tray. The test is carried out with each hand.

2. *Visual–Visual Matching.* Two identical trays of objects are placed in front of the subject and the examiner respectively. The examiner points to an object in his tray, and the subject is asked to point to the corresponding object in his own tray.

3. *Form Perception.* The subject is given a card which has on it a series of letters. The examiner then shows the subject a series of cards, each with a single letter on it, and in each case the subject is asked to point to the corresponding letter on his card.

Other Aphasia Batteries

The tasks used in Porch's (1967) Index of Communicative Ability (PICA) are similar to those of other batteries and will not be described in detail. The battery is divided into three types of subtests: gestural, verbal, and graphic. Stimuli are presented through either auditory or gestural modalities by the examiner, and the subject is required to respond aloud, gesturally, or in writing. An important contribution of the PICA lies in the comprehensiveness of its scoring system. Each response is scored on a 16-point scale, ranging from 1 for no response to 16 for a correct complex response, taking into consideration the "accuracy," "responsiveness," "completeness," "promptness," and "efficiency" of the response. The response scores are summarized in graphs which are categorized into five basic profile types: aphasia without complications, aphasia with verbal formulation or expressive problems, aphasia complicated by illiteracy, bilateral brain damage, and "aberrant patterns." The response analysis over time also provides an "Aphasia Recovery Curve" which allows the examiner to predict the recovery potential of each subject.

On a less formal level, Luria (1966) examines many of the same functions in his tests of comprehension. He begins with an examination of phonemic ability in which the subject's auditory acuity as well as his ability to discriminate simple and complex phonemic configurations is evaluated. He then examines the subject's word comprehension ability by methods similar to those used in other aphasia batteries, for example, by asking him to point to the word, picture, or body part named by the examiner. Tests of ability to understand simple sentences and logical-grammatical structures follow. In the former, subjects are required to indicate their comprehension of simple spoken or written sentences by pointing to appropriate pictures or by following simple instructions given aloud. In the tests of understanding logical-grammatical structures, tasks similar to those of the Token Test are given, requiring subjects to place an object in a particular spatial relation to another object as instructed by the examiner.

In contrast to the above described tests of aphasia in which standard questions and materials are used, Sarno's (1969) *Functional Communication Profile* is an attempt to evaluate the subject's ability to communicate within a test environment which simulates real life situations. To evaluate comprehension of spoken language, the subject's response in a variety of situations is observed in regard to: awareness of gross environmental sounds, emotional voice tone, and speech; recognition of one's own given name, one's family name, and the names of familiar objects; and understanding of action verbs, directions (both gestural and spoken), simple conversation with one person, television, movies, conversation with more than two people, and rapid complex conversation. To evaluate comprehension of written language, the subject's ability to read single words, rehabilitation program cards, street signs, correspondence, newspaper headlines, articles, magazines, and books is observed.

The evolution of aphasia test batteries corresponds closely to the progress made in aphasia research in general. In view of the recent trend in aphasia studies toward the incorporation of findings from contemporary research in psycholinguistics, it is expected that tests in which syntactic and semantic variables are rigorously controlled and refined will become available in the future.

RESEARCH ON COMPREHENSION

The present review is directed toward analyzing studies of auditory comprehension in order to evaluate the current state of knowledge about the critical aspects of spoken language that influence the aphasic patient's comprehension. Prior to the last decade, relatively few studies of comprehension were carried out. Most early work in this area appears to have been devoted to establishing the efficacy of various techniques and tests in identifying aphasic patients and to evaluating the extent to which nonverbal deficits such as short term memory impairments or reduced general ability might influence performance on tests of language comprehension.

Early Tests

It was clear from the time of their earliest application that many tests of comprehension might be too difficult to be of use in identifying specific language impairments. Moutier (1908) criticized Proust–Lichtheim's test (cf. p. 11 above) which required the subject to designate the number of syllables in the name of an object shown by the examiner. Among the patients at Bicêtre, Moutier found only a handful who knew what a syllable was. Furthermore, he felt the significance of the information provided by the test was quite unclear: "We do not understand the nature of the information which can be obtained from the Proust–Lichtheim Test. . . . This test has never been of the slightest use to us" (1908, p. 181).

Of the tests proposed by Pierre Marie, the Three Papers Test is the only one which has remained in current use. It was included as part of the battery of Weisenburg and McBride (1935), but these authors have not summarized or discussed the results of its use with either aphasics or normals. Boller and Vignolo (1966) used the Three Papers Test with four groups of subjects: normal controls, right brain damaged (RBD) patients, left brain damaged (LBD) patients without evidence of aphasia, and LBD patients with mild receptive deficits. If a subject failed to perform correctly after the first presentation of Marie's test, the command was repeated. A score of one was given for correct performance on each of the three steps. Table 1.1 shows the scores obtained by the four groups with repeated directions. As can be seen, the test is very easy for normals (only one failed) and for the RBD and the LBD nonaphasic subjects (only two failed in each group). Of the LBD aphasic group, 29 out of 34 (85%) also showed no impairment. Without repetition of commands, only 65% of the aphasic subjects performed without error, but the performance of the other three groups also fell. There was no significant difference between normal and aphasic performance either with or without repeated commands, and the test discriminated poorly between groups.

It may be worth repeating, however, that the aphasic group had been selected by Boller and Vignolo (1966) for the presence of only minimal or mild comprehension disturbance. Data on the results of giving the Three Papers Test to an unselected sample of aphasics are not available. Boller and Vignolo do report a tendency of RBD patients to perform more poorly than nonaphasic

TABLE 1.1 Scores of Four Experimental Groups on Marie's Three Papers Test[a]

			Brain-damaged patient					
	Control patients		Right		Left			
Scores					Nonaphasic		Aphasic	
	(N=31)		(N=30)		(N=26)		(N=34)	
	E	S	E	S	E	S	E	S
3	15	15	18	10	13	11	13	15
. . . .								
2			1		1	1	2	1
1	1		1				2	
0							1	

[a]E= patients with elementary education (less than 6 years); S= patients with secondary or superior education (more than 6 years); dotted line (. . .) represents normal cut-off score.

LBD patients. This finding, in the authors' opinion, suggests that response to the test's rather long verbal command may be influenced by cognitive deficits unrelated to language.

The tests proposed by Head (1926) for testing oral comprehension, particularly the Hand, Eye, and Ear Test, have been used by several examiners (Pearson, Alpers, & Weisenburg, 1928; Quadfasel, 1931; Goldstein, 1948; Orgass & Poeck, 1969). Most authors suggest that failure to perform the task in the Hand, Eye, and Ear Test correctly may be due not only to aphasia but also to impairments of visual–spatial ability and to limited intelligence. Even normal adults of superior intelligence may fail on this and other tests in Head's battery (Pearson *et al.,* 1928). On the other hand, Orgass and Poeck (1969), using a series of verbal tests in an effort to identify those with the most specific diagnostic value for aphasia, found that the four tests best able to discriminate between aphasics and nonaphasic brain damaged subjects included Head's Hand, Eye, and Ear Test. The other three tests were a Verbal IQ, an Arithmetic Calculation Test, and the Token Test. It must be noted, however, that Orgass and Poeck (1969) used their own version of Head's test. Therefore, it is possible that the discrepancy between their findings and those of other writers is due to methodological differences. Overall, it seems difficult to determine what aspect of Head's test accounts for the aphasic's impaired response to it and, consequently, to judge the extent to which the Hand, Eye, and Ear Test may be considered a measure of comprehension.

The Token Test

Since its introduction in 1962, De Renzi and Vignolo's Token Test has been studied extensively. Research on the test has been carried out in Italy (Boller & Vignolo, 1966; Boller, 1968), Germany (Orgass & Poeck, 1966a, b; Poeck, Kerschensteiner, & Hartje, 1972; Orgass, Poeck, Hartje, & Kerschensteiner, 1973; Poeck, Hartje, Kerschensteiner, & Orgass, 1973; Hartje, Kerschensteiner, Poeck, & Orgass, 1973; Poeck, Orgass, Kerschensteiner, & Hartje, 1974), North America (Benton, 1967; Peck-Swisher & Taylor-Sarno, 1969; Spellacy & Spreen, 1969; Whitaker & Noll, 1972), Rumania (Kreindler, Gheorghita, & Voinescu, 1971), Holland (Van Dongen & Van Harskamp, 1972), France (Albert, 1972), and England (Lesser, 1974). The original method of De Renzi and Vignolo (1962b) has generally been followed, although Boller and Vignolo (1966) used 22 instead of 21 commands in Part V and, in the first four parts, asked the patients to "touch" rather than "take" the tokens. Others have substituted squares for rectangles (Spreen & Benton, 1969). Shorter versions of the test have also been proposed (Benton, 1967; Spellacy & Spreen, 1969; Spreen & Benton, 1969; Orgass *et al.*, 1973).

Studies have generally found the Token Test to be an accurate and sensitive indicator of the presence of aphasia. Hartje *et al.* (1973), for example, reported a poor Token Test performance in 91% of aphasic patients, while Boller and Vignolo (1966) found that LBD patients who did not appear aphasic on a standard aphasia battery performed significantly more poorly than did RBD patients or normal controls. Generally performance on the Token Test has been found to correlate with clinical assessments of the severity of aphasia (Orgass & Poeck, 1966a) as well as with performance on various standard aphasia batteries (Peck-Swisher & Taylor-Sarno, 1969; Lesser, 1974).

Poeck and his associates have made important contributions to our knowledge of the relationship between the Token Test, type of language disturbance, and noncognitive variables. Type of aphasia apparently does not influence overall Token Test scores of aphasics categorized either into groups with motor, sensory, or anomic aphasia (Orgass & Poeck, 1966a; Poeck *et al.*, 1973) or along the dimension of fluency–nonfluency (Poeck *et al.*, 1972). On the other hand, Kreindler *et al.* (1971) found that severity of receptive disorder was inversely related to Token Test performance, although severity of expressive disorders was not. Furthermore, after the age of 15, age does not seem to influence Token Test performance (Orgass & Poeck, 1966a; Hartje *et al.*, 1973), but subjects with more education tend to have higher scores (Orgass & Poeck, 1966a; Boller & Vignolo, 1966).

An important concern is whether the test can be considered a relatively pure measure of verbal comprehension. If it can be so considered, patients with RBD, and presumably no aphasia, who do poorly on the test will be regarded as "false positive," in that their poor performance will incorrectly suggest comprehension deficits. Peck-Swisher and Taylor-Sarno (1969) found that RBD patients showed an increasing number of errors as the test progressed, from 15% on Part I to 22, 52, 71, and 92% on Parts II through V, respectively. For Parts IV and V, the performance of the RBD patients was significantly worse than that of normal controls. However, the authors point out that they displayed the tokens in an arrangement somewhat different from the array used in the standardized administrative procedure. Consequently, the subjects of Peck-Swisher and Taylor-Sarno (1969) may have been required to use visual scanning and visual–spatial abilities to a greater extent than that normally required by the Token Test; this would increase the difficulty of the task for patients with RBD (De Renzi, Faglioni, & Scotti, 1970). The number of false positives reported in studies using a more standard administrative procedure has been considerably lower, for example, 15% (Van Dongen & Van Harskamp, 1972). Boller and Vignolo (1966) reported only a 5% false positive rate, and Lesser (1974) found no Token Test performance differences between RBDs and normal controls.

In a broader sense, the problem of false positives on the Token Test relates to the questions of what specific factors influence Token Test performance and of the extent to which Token Test performance correlates with nonlanguage abilities. Interestingly, Token Test scores have been reported to be correlated with Performance IQ (Hartje *et al.*, 1973, who used the German version of the Wechsler–Bellevue Intelligence Scale) and scores on the Raven Progressive Matrices (Van Dongen & Van Harskamp, 1972). On the other hand, Boller and Vignolo (1966) and Lesser (1974) found no significant correlation between Token Test performance and Raven Matrices scores.

Kreindler *et al.,* (1971) attempted to analyze specific aspects of Token Test performance separately: the effects of the shapes, colors, and sizes of the tokens, the effect of word position in the commands, and the concrete or abstract aspects of the tokens. In order to equate the set size of each of the properties of the tokens, they reduced the number of colors in the test to two. They further modified the test by placing the tokens in a constant random arrangement, and they reduced the task to simply pointing to the tokens which they named either in standard word order, for example, "large yellow circle," or in atypical order, for example, "yellow large circle." Finally, they introduced two further tokens which could be varied in color and size to make the tokens less abstract; these were in the shapes of a flower and a house.

The authors found that aphasics experienced the greatest difficulty in comprehending (i.e., correctly identifying) the shape of the token and the least difficulty in comprehending size. The abstract (circle, square) tokens were more difficult for aphasics than the concrete (flower, house) tokens only in terms of identifying shape. Finally, the order of the commands significantly influenced performance, in that the last item named was identified most easily. Although this latter finding raises the possibility that short-term memory (STM) deficits may account for some Token Test problems, the authors tested STM independently in all of the patients and found that none were unable to remember a span of three items. Furthermore, they noted that clinically some aphasics were observed to repeat "mechanically" the three words of the command while simultaneously pointing to an incorrect choice. (However, Lesser, 1976, argues that the Token Test does overtax the reduced auditory—verbal sequencing span of aphasics.)

In sum, the findings of Kreindler *et al.* (1971) suggest that it may be possible to isolate some critical aspects of Token Test performance that will provide a basis for evaluating the nature of a patient's performance with more specificity than by simply noting his total score. A logical extension of these findings would be to examine the performance of nonaphasic brain damaged patients in a similar manner.

Another approach to breaking down Token Test performance into some of its critical elements was taken by Whitaker and Noll (1972). Although these authors' study deals mainly with normal children, aged five to twelve, their conclusions are relevant to the present discussion. They applied the method of Boller and Vignolo (1966), including the substitution of the word "touch" for "take" in the commands of Parts I through IV, but their analysis focused on interpreting the errors that subjects made on Part V, the most difficult part of the test. The authors found that 8 of the 22 items in Part V contributed most of the total errors of their subjects. All but one of these 8 critical commands use the word "touch" but only one of the remaining 14 commands in Part V uses this word. The authors point out that an implicit instrumental instruction is associated with the verb "touch." "Touch the red square" implies "Touch with a part of your body," usually your finger. This implicit meaning is attached to the word "touch" in Parts I through IV of the test. But "touch," the authors explain, may also carry an explicit, or overt, instrumental meaning which replaces or supplements the understood one. For example, one may say "touch the blue circle with the red square." Whitaker and Noll (1972) suggest that the high error scores obtained by their subjects on the eight items in Part V reflect the subjects' difficulty in shifting from the implicit to the overt instrumental case, and they cite unpublished studies showing that aphasic adults and disadvantaged children show this same type of difficulty.

Poeck *et al.* (1974) examined the performance of aphasics and nonaphasic adults in the light of the analysis suggested by Whitaker and Noll (1972). The authors found that the eight critical items that had been identified by Whitaker and Noll were not critical in determining the total scores of nonaphasic adults. For aphasics, although these items were clearly more difficult than others, they accounted for only one-third of total errors. This led Poeck *et al.* (1974) to conclude that the explanation proposed by Whitaker and Noll does not fully account for the performance of either normal adults or aphasics in Part V of the Token Test. In comparing these two studies, we must of course keep in mind the possible differences between English and German. However, it is interesting to note that both studies reported similar findings with respect to two items that carry the explicit instrumental instruction. Item 43, "Touch the blue circle with the red rectangle," was the most difficult item for both the aphasic and nonaphasic adults tested by Poeck *et al.* and the children tested by Whitaker and Noll. At the same time, item 44, which gives a similar command but in an unusual word order ("Touch, with the blue circle, the red rectangle"), was of an intermediate level of difficulty for both adult groups and was only the second most difficult item for the children. It may be that although the unusual word order of item 44 serves to alert adult subjects to the changed explicit meaning of "touch," it makes the item more difficult for children. Thus the explanation of Whitaker and Noll may have some bearing on adult performance on the test even though it fails to account completely for the difficulties subjects experience on Part V.

In conclusion, it appears that although the Token Test has now been used by many laboratories throughout the world for well over a decade, the reasons aphasics tend to perform poorly in comparison with groups of other patients and with control groups are not clear. Although quite different types of aphasic patients obtain similar total test scores, it is by no means certain that failure of a single basic process can account for this similarity. Different aphasics may perform poorly for entirely different reasons. It would appear that future research should focus on a qualitative analysis of each subject's performance. Such an analysis could be facilitated by changing the scoring system from an item by item pass–fail type of score (as originally proposed by De Renzi and Vignolo, 1962b) into scoring each aspect of each command separately (as proposed by Benton, 1967, and by Spreen and Benton, 1969). It is important to remember that Token Test performance may also be influenced by motor or visual–motor coordination deficits. This possibility could be investigated by comparing the performance of subjects' under the standard method of administration to their performance under conditions in which they would not be required to perform any act but would simply have to say whether or not a performance demonstrated by an examiner corresponded to the command they had heard.

Current Research

Apart from studies validating, or evaluating the meaning of, tests of comprehension, a number of recent investigations have explored specific aspects of auditory comprehension. For purposes of our discussion, we have classified these studies according to whether they deal primarily with the phonological, the semantic and syntactic, or the "paralinguistic" aspects of comprehension. There is, however, considerable overlap among these categories.

PHONOLOGICAL ASPECTS OF COMPREHENSION

Luria (1947, 1970) has stated that "patients with sensory aphasia usually hear well enough, but they are unable to pick out the phonemically important cues from a steady flow of speech . . . the few features which are significant in discriminating the meaning of words are perceived by these patients as no more distinct than the numerous insignificant features. Thus, the words lose their phonemic constancy and meaning" (1970, p. 401). According to Luria, the comprehension deficit exhibited by Wernicke's aphasics was due principally to disturbance of phonemic perception.

While it is generally agreed that phonemic discrimination tends to be impaired in lesions of the left hemisphere (Goldblum & Albert, 1972; Assal, 1974), Luria's interpretation of his subjects' phonemic abilities has been challenged by several authors. In all of his phonemic discrimination tasks, Luria required subjects to indicate their perceptions either by repeating aloud or writing an utterance of the examiner or by making a gestural response to one phoneme but not another, a task which required the subject to keep in mind a conceptual model of two phonemes. Luria's tasks thus require some linguistic processing, or at least they are more complex than a simple perceptual discrimination task.

Studies of the phonemic discrimination of aphasic patients who exhibit comprehension deficits have generally failed to support Luria's position, except when the discrimination task involved some linguistic elements. The typical paradigm for investigating phonemic discrimination while minimizing linguistic processing involves the sequential presentation of two stimuli which may or may not be phonemically contrasted; the subject is asked to judge whether the stimuli are similar or different. A second paradigm, which appears to increase the linguistic aspects of the task, requires a subject to match a single word, presented aloud, to a single picture that he must select from an array of pictures, all of whose names are phonemically similar. In both of these designs, the phonemic contrasts may involve two principal variables: type of phonological feature, for example, voice, place, manner, nasality; and number of features contrasted, that is, one or more than one (presumably the use of more than one feature heightens the contrast). Analyses of studies of phonemic discrimination of aphasics with comprehension impairment have usually involved either correlating phonemic discrimination scores with scores on a test of comprehension or comparing phonemic discrimination scores of various aphasic subgroups, categorized according to their degree of comprehension impairment.

Performance on tests of phonemic discrimination has been found to be not significantly correlated with comprehension abilitiy as measured by the Boston

Diagnostic Aphasia Examination (Blumstein, Baker, & Goodglass, in press) or the Token Test (Naeser, 1974 and 1976). Blumstein *et al.* actually found a significant correlation in their study, but it was the result of the fact that patients with Broca's aphasia were least impaired on both tasks; when this group was omitted, the correlation dropped to an insignificant level. Furthermore, the group with the poorest comprehension, Wernicke's aphasics, were not the worst group on the phonemic discrimination task. Naeser (1974) obtained a correlation of only .12 between her phonemic discrimination test and the Token Test. It should be noted that both of these studies dealt with relatively small groups of subjects. Neither study, however, supports Luria's hypothesis.

An extensive study of the phonemic discrimination ability of aphasics was carried out by Blumstein *et al.* (1977), who presented subjects with two stimuli which the subjects had to identify as similar or different by pressing the appropriate button. The actual stimuli consisted of two series, one of real and one of nonsense words. The words in each series were contrasted on the basis of voice or place or both of these two phonological features. The authors included two additional sets of stimuli in the test. In one, items were contrasted in terms of the order of their component phonemes. In the other, items were differentiated in terms of syllables; the unstressed syllables in two-syllable words were contrasted. Results indicated that all aphasic groups—Broca's, "mixed anteriors" (nonfluent aphasics with comprehension impairments), Wernicke's, and "residual posteriors" (patients with anomic, conduction, or transcortical sensory aphasia)— performed more poorly with nonsense words than with real words. The authors point out that if the group with the poorest comprehension (the Wernicke's aphasics) had a deficit based on phonemic discrimination difficulty, they should have exhibited the least difference in performance between real and nonsense words, since the phonemic aspects of the two tasks were the same. Actually, the Broca's aphasics showed the smallest difference. The authors suggest that the superior performance of all groups on the real words may reflect the tendency of subjects to encode the words and then compare them at a linguistic level. In this sense, the performance of the Wernicke's was as much a function of meaning as was that of the other groups.

The results on the three types of tasks showed essentially the same pattern. Whether they were discriminating words contrasted on the basis of changes in phonemes, phoneme order, or syllables, the Broca's did best and the mixed anterior group performed most poorly. All groups performed better on the phonemic discrimination task when the contrast involved two phonological features than when it involved only one. On the other hand, the groups performed differently as a function of the specific feature contrasted. There was no difference in the response of the two anterior groups to contrasts of voice and place, but for the two posterior groups, place contrasts were more difficult. Pointing out that place cues are context dependent (place varies as a function of the following vowel), the authors suggest that the posterior groups may have difficulties in using phonological attributes in a linguistically meaningful way.

In contrast to their performance in simple phonemic discrimination studies, when they are asked to match a single spoken word with one picture in an array of pictures, aphasics with comprehension deficits tend to perform more poorly than other aphasics when the other pictures in an array are of objects with names phonemically similar to the target item (Schuell, Jenkins, & Jimenez-Pabón, 1964; Goldblum & Albert, 1972). Naeser (1974) compared the performance of various aphasics on a phonemic discrimination task with their performance on a phoneme picture perception task in which she used the same target words, one at a time, and asked the subject to match each with one of two pictures, the second of which represented the phonemically similar word from the phoneme discrimination task. Her phonemic discrimination task results essentially replicated the findings of Blumstein *et al.* (1977). However, Naeser found that place contrasts were more difficult than voice or manner for all groups. Most important, she found that not only were the Wernicke's poorest on the picture perception task, but they experienced as much difficulty when two phonological features were contrasted as when only one was contrasted, whereas the other groups showed an improved performance when the task was made easier by increasing the number of features contrasted. Naeser interpreted this finding as indicating that the comprehension deficit in Wernicke's aphasia is due to impaired phonemic—semantic association ability. Furthermore, since her anterior aphasics with comprehension deficits failed to show this effect, she argues that their comprehension deficit is qualitatively different from that of the Wernicke's aphasics. She also reported the results for one patient with pure word deafness who performed more poorly than all patients on the phonemic discrimination task but performed relatively better on the picture perception task, which, according to Naeser, suggests that this patient's comprehension deficit may indeed have been based on phonemic deficits. Once the patient had perceived a phoneme correctly, Naeser commented, she had no difficulty in associating it with the correct semantic equivalent in the form of a picture.

Studies such as that of Naeser (1974) suggest that phonemic perception plays either a minimal or no part in the comprehension deficit of Wernicke's aphasics. This conclusion was supported by a study in which the other pictures in the array were not limited to phonemically similar items. Gainotti, Ibba, and Caltagirone (1975) studied LBD patients, both nonaphasic and aphasic, including Broca's, Wernicke's with semantic paraphasia, Wernicke's with phonemic paraphasia, and anomic aphasics, on a task that was similar to Naeser's except that the incorrect choices in the array of pictures included one that was phonemically similar to the target item, one that was semantically similar, and three that were unrelated to the stimulus words. These authors concluded that impairment in phonemic discrimination, as evidenced by choice of the phonemically similar item, was not responsible for their patients' comprehension deficits. This finding, however, is questionable in the light of a study of Gardner, Albert, and Weintraub (1975), who used a similar task that differed only by presenting target words in the context of a sentence as well as singly. These authors found that while semantic errors were the type of errors most frequently made by all aphasics, the posterior aphasics produced a significantly higher proportion of phonemic errors than did the anterior aphasics. In this context, reference may be made to the study of Boller and Green (1972), who found that patients with very severe comprehension deficits were nevertheless able to discriminate whole sentences spoken in their native language from sentences in a foreign language or phonemic jargon (cf. pp. 48–51). Clearly, even patients with extremely impaired comprehension retain some phonemic discrimination ability.

In order to explore some of the parameters of phonemic perception in greater detail, Blumstein (in press) presented synthesized consonant sounds (Lisker & Abramson, 1964), voiced or unvoiced, to normal controls, patients with RBD, and aphasics. The subjects were asked (1) to identify the auditory stimulus by selecting from two printed cards the one bearing the representation of the spoken sound and (2) to discriminate a pair of auditory stimuli which were either identical or distinguishable by a difference in voice onset time of 20 msec.

Normals and RBD patients exhibited equally good performance on the identification and the discrimination tasks, but the performance of aphasic patients was of three different types. Some aphasics displayed the same pattern as the normals and the RBD patients. A second group of aphasics was unable to identify the test stimuli but had normal ability to discriminate between them, showing discrimination peaks corresponding to the phoneme boundaries typically found in normal English-speaking subjects (Liberman, Cooper, Shankweiler, & Studdert-Kennedy, 1967). A third group showed impaired results on both the identification and discrimination tests. No subject exhibited abnormal discrimination coupled with normal identification.

Blumstein (in press) concluded that phonological processing may involve two distinct levels: a primitive, prelinguistic discrimination level which reflects the functioning of a set of "property detectors" sensitive to certain parameters of the acoustic signal, and a linguistic level which makes use of the information thus obtained to "encode" or "classify" the stimuli along linguistically relevant dimensions.

It seems difficult to draw definitive conclusions from the studies of phonemic discrimination ability in patients with comprehension deficits. It appears that some patients with comprehension deficits do not easily discriminate certain types of phonemic contrasts. For example, such patients have difficulty using the phonological features of place, in associating phonemes with a printed equivalent, and in matching words to pictures when alternative choices include only phonemically similar items. Each of these three difficulties have been interpreted as indicating an inability to use or to associate phonemic perceptions in a semantically or linguistically meaningful fashion, but the data base is quite limited. Studies have thus far involved only small numbers of subjects and have reported only the mean results for various aphasic subgroups. Furthermore, a number of studies have suggested that subjects may linguistically process ostensibly phonemic tasks, and that phonological processing itself may involve both prelinguistic and linguistic levels, so that some patients show deficits at one level, some at others, and some at both. It is certainly possible that there are patients (such as Naeser's pure word-deafness case) whose comprehension impairment is the result of defective phonemic processing. It seems reasonable to conclude, however, that impairments of phonemic discrimination that are so subtle or uncommon that they cannot account for gross differences in comprehension ability between aphasic groups cannot be said to provide a basis for the meaningful explanation of defective comprehension.

In contrast with researchers who have focused on systematically varying the phonemic aspects of the stimulus, some investigators have explored the roles of both phonemic and semantic errors in the speech of aphasics. Alajouanine and his associates (Alajouanine *et al.,* 1952, 1964), in a series of studies of patients with fluent jargonaphasia, noted that the speech of their patients tended to show two types of errors: "phonemic" jargon, characterized by strings of syllables bearing no relation to real words, and "semantic" jargon, in which real words were combined in such a manner as to produce meaningless utterances. Both types of errors were often exhibited by the same patient. However, the authors selected two groups of patients whose jargon was almost exclusively of one type or the other. After further study, the authors hypothesized that two separate systems are implicated in comprehension. The first is a sensorimotor, auditory–phonemic system responsible for the production and reception of phonemic units. An impairment of this system not only produces phonemic jargon but also affects auditory perception at the phonemic level, with impairment of phonemic discrimination, loss of the delayed auditory feedback effect (for an explanation of this effect, see Lee, 1950; Black, 1951), and deficits in the translation of auditory sequences into manual ones. The second, semantic system is thought to control the process of connecting thought and language, so a disturbance in this process results in the production of semantic jargon and in the impairment of semantic comprehension.

The hypothesis of Alajouanine *et al.* (1964) was partially confirmed by Gainotti *et al.* (1975). These authors found a high correlation between semantic paraphasia and semantic disorders of comprehension in their patients with Wernicke's aphasia. Patients with phonemic paraphasia, however, did not show an impairment in phonemic discrimination. It must be noted that Gainotti *et al.* tested phonemic discrimination by asking their patients only to point to one of six pictures, one of which, though incorrect, was phonemically similar to the stimulus word. It would be interesting to further test the hypothesis of Ala-jouanine *et al.* by giving patients who produce phonemic jargon a test of phonemic discrimination similar to those used by Blumstein *et al.* (1977), by Naeser (1974), and by Pizzamiglio and Appicciafuoco (1967). An attempt in this direction is a recent study by Basso, Casati, and Vignolo (in press). Phonemic identification was investigated in 50 aphasic patients by giving them a series of tape-recorded synthesized alveolar stop consonants, made up with different values of VOT (voice-onset timing) and by recording their ability to identify the acoustic boundary between the voiced /d/ and the unvoiced /t/ consonant. The findings pointed to disordered phonemic output as one of the dimensions of aphasia that are specifically associated with the phonemic identification defect in fluent as well as nonfluent aphasics, thereby supporting the hypothesis of Alajouanine *et al.* (1964).

Daujat, Gainotti, and Tissot (1974) tested Alajouanine's hypothesis in a slightly different way. In order to evaluate the relationship between measures of expression and comprehension, these authors classified three types of aphasics (Broca's and those Wernicke's with either phonemic or semantic paraphasia) according to the extent of their expressive deficits, and then correlated these results with the subjects' performances on three tests of comprehension. These tests all involved matching a spoken word with one picture in an array. In the semantic differentiation task, the other words in the array were semantically similar to the target word; in the phonemic discrimination task, the other words were phonemically similar to the target word; and in the semantic generalization task, the target word was to be matched with an associated word, and the other words had no relationship to the target. The authors found that the degree of expressive deficit was not highly correlated (though in some cases the correlations were significant) with comprehension on any of the tasks. Alajouanine *et al.* (1964), however, had not argued that the extent of expressive deficit per se was related to the type of comprehension deficit but rather that those patients who showed a pure type of expressive deficit (i.e., phonemic or semantic paraphasia) would show similar types of errors on comprehension tests. In addition, Daujat *et al.* (1974) found that the performance of their patients on the comprehension tasks was influenced by age, a factor which has not been analyzed in the other studies reviewed.

Gainotti *et al.* (1975) were also interested in finding out whether the results of their test would be different for patients with Broca's aphasia or Wernicke's (classified according to the phonemic—semantic jargonaphasia dichotomy), or for anomics. They found no difference in either the quantitative or the qualitative performance of their patients. Patients with Broca's aphasia had the same number and types of errors as those with Wernicke's aphasia. Gainotti *et al.* (1975) suggest that this finding may lend support to Pierre Marie's contention that "Broca's aphasia = Wernicke's aphasia + anarthria."

Both Blumstein (in press) and Alajouanine *et al.* (1964) have thus hypothe-sized that two separate processes are involved in comprehension: the first, a perceptual process responsible for phonemic discrimination; the second, a more semantic, or linguistic, process involved in relating speech sounds to their semantic meaning (or graphic representation, as in Blumstein's work). Ala-jouanine *et al.* apply their model to the production as well as to the reception of language. Blumstein, however, limits hers to reception, or at least she has not attempted to account for production errors. The former model, which was developed by observations of the speech output of selected patients, envisions relatively independent phonemic and semantic processes, while Blumstein's data seem to suggest that adequate phonemic discrimination in reception is a neces-sary prerequisite for linguistic analysis to occur. Gainotti *et al.* (1975) have called into question the model of Alajouanine *et al.* inasmuch as the former authors' patients with phonemic paraphasia did not show poor phonemic dis-crimination. At the same time, Gainotti *et al.*'s measure of phonemic discrimina-tion was really more akin to Blumstein's "identification" of speech sounds task and thus more linguistic than perceptual. It seems that by using a variety of tasks, one may demonstrate dissociated deficits in various patients, which suggests multiple processes in comprehension, but that the many differences in definitions and methodologies prevent a more precise comparison among the existing studies with respect to the role of phonemic versus semantic or more "linguistic" processes in the reception of language. It is even more difficult to compare these studies in regard to the relationship between comprehension deficits and the occurrence of phonemic versus semantic errors in language production.

SEMANTIC AND SYNTACTIC ASPECTS OF COMPREHENSION

A number of studies have attempted to deal directly with the semantic comprehension of aphasics. Schuell and her collaborators (Schuell & Jenkins, 1961; Schuell, Jenkins, & Landis, 1961) pointed out that difficulty in compre-hension of words is related to the frequency of their occurrence in English. A similar finding was reported by Rocheford and Williams (1965) in their study of naming by aphasics and by Howes (1957) in his work on the comprehension of normal subjects. Goodglass, Klein, Carey, and Jones (1966) amended this simple concept of the relative difficulty of various words by reporting that the order of difficulty in the production of words in five semantic categories (objects, colors, numbers, letters and actions) was different from their order of difficulty in auditory comprehension. Furthermore, they found that different types of aphasics showed different patterns of difficulty in comprehension for the five semantic categories. Wernicke's aphasics, for example, more frequently displayed impaired comprehension of the names of body parts than of the other categories. More recently, Goodglass, Gleason, and Hyde (1970) analyzed the relative difficulty level of different categories of words for different types of aphasics. The types of words included single names, tested with the Peabody Picture Vocabulary Test (Dunn, 1959); names in sequence, tested by a Pointing–Span Test; and directional prepositions, tested by asking the patient to recognize "the girl behind the car" among alternative pictures which showed a girl in front of a car, next to a car, etc. Finally, they presented a Preposition Preference Test, in which the patient was shown, for example, a picture of a man holding the door while a woman entered a room. The patient was asked to state which sounded best: "He is holding the door to the lady" or "He is holding the door for the lady." Scores were corrected for differences between groups in overall comprehension level by correcting the means of each test with a covariance adjustment for the scores on the remaining tests.

The findings of Goodglass *et al.* (1970) partially support the contention that aphasics' ability to comprehend a specific feature of language is related to their ability to produce that feature in speech (cf. Alajouanine *et al.*, 1964). The anomics, particularly poor at producing substantive nouns, were significantly worse than the other groups on the Peabody Picture Vocabulary Test. In contrast, however, the Broca's aphasics, who speak telegraphically and do not produce prepositions, did not exhibit impairment on tests requiring the comprehension of prepositions, although they were the most impaired group on the Pointing–Span Test. The Wernicke's aphasics were significantly worse than the other groups on the Preposition Preference Test. Finally, on the Test of Directional Prepositions there were no differences among the various groups of aphasics nor between them and a group of normal children.

The most important finding for our purposes was that patients who belonged to different aphasic subgroups showed qualitatively different patterns of impairment on tests of auditory comprehension. The authors used a discriminant function analysis to identify the critical patterns which appeared to distinguish the subgroups. When three discriminant functions were used to assign the individual subjects to the various groups, the global (7/8 correct) and Broca's aphasics (10/14 correct) were identified relatively accurately, but identification of the Wernicke's aphasics was poor (3/9 correct). These findings, assuming they can be replicated, provide strong support for the contention that auditory comprehension is not a unitary process.

In a related study, Smith (1974) questioned the extent to which aphasics who show production problems are free from impairment on tests of comprehending prepositions. She studied the performance of five aphasic subjects. Although Smith did not specify subtypes, her description of her subjects suggests that one was anomic and four were nonfluent aphasics. Smith modified the approach of Goodglass *et al.* (1970) by asking the subjects to carry out a spoken command that directed the subject to place 2 of 10 objects into a specified relationship

with one another (described by a critical preposition), while Goodglass *et al.*
simply asked the subject to point to the one of three sets of pictures, which
depicted several possible relationships, that corresponded to a spoken sentence.
In addition, Smith evaluated her subjects' accuracy in choosing the appropriate
objects as well as in placing them in the correct relationship with one another.
Thus she was able to compare subjects' performance in using the preposition
with their performance in selecting an object, reasoning that their performance
on prepositions alone had less meaning than when compared to their ability to
identify the objects.

In one respect, Smith's results repeated those of Goodglass *et al.* (1970); like
the anomics in the earlier study, on the Peabody test, her anomic subject clearly
made the most errors in identifying objects. The four other aphasics, however,
made more errors on tasks involving prepositions, which led Smith to conclude
that there was a correspondence between these subjects' performance in the
production and the comprehension of speech. It is not clear, however, whether
performance in carrying out a command to place 2 objects out of 10 in a
particular relationship to one another truly reflects auditory comprehension.
These four patients, all described as nonfluent, would probably not have been
capable of repeating the command. Furthermore, simply eliminating speech
from a task which requires listening and then performing a complex command in
a sequential order does not eliminate the influence of a possible deficit in
sequential repetition, a deficit which may be presumed to exist in patients with
nonfluent aphasia (Kim, 1976). In a sense, Smith's task is similar to the task
presented in the Token Test (Smith herself compares it to Head's Coin in Bowl
Test), and thus it is subject to the same problem in interpretation, that is, the
basis for failure is not clear (cf. the discussion of the Token Test, pp. 27–29). As a
result, the task of Goodglass *et al.* (1970), in which the subject merely pointed
to a picture that described a spoken sentence may be a more specific test of
comprehension of prepositions. Smith's idea of comparing the relative frequency
of errors in comprehending the various parts of an utterance is important, but it
is not clear whether the deficits she notes can be ascribed to a failure of
comprehension.

Several studies, which use a model analogous to that described in our review of
studies of phonemic discrimination, have explored what might be termed the
semantic discrimination ability of aphasics. Typically, such studies have reported
a tendency for aphasic subjects to mistakenly select the semantically related
alternative more often than the phonemically similar item, whether the target
word was presented alone (Gainotti *et al.*, 1975) or embedded in a sentence
(Gardner *et al.*, 1975).

Perhaps the most detailed investigation of semantic discrimination tasks was
carried out by Pizzamiglio and Appicciafuoco (1971). They presented a stimulus
word aloud and then showed a subject four pictures, including one that represented the stimulus, with the three incorrect alternatives consisting of the three

words most frequently associated with the target word in a normative study of word associations. Although normals and nonaphasic brain damaged subjects made few errors on this test, patients with Wernicke's, mixed, or global aphasia were quite impaired. Not one patient from these three groups did as well as the most poorly performing member of the two control groups. On the other hand, the Broca's and the amnesic (anomic) aphasics showed considerably more variability, several subjects scoring in the normal range. The results of the semantic discrimination test categorized subjects as aphasic or nonaphasic more accurately than the results of tests of either phonemic or syntactic discrimination but somewhat less accurately than results of the Token Test. In the sense that the Token Test's superior discrimination ability was due to its identification of the Broca's and the amnesic aphasics who scored well on the semantic discrimination task, it could reasonably be argued that while the Token Test might be superior for screening purposes, the semantic discrimination task may be a better measure of comprehension ability.

A subsequent attempt to cross validate these findings in an English aphasic population, however, found that while the semantic, phonemic, and syntactic tasks all produced significant group differences between aphasics and normals, only the latter two tests separated the aphasics from a group of patients with right hemisphere damage (Lesser, 1974). In view of the fact that the English and Italian normals attained the same level of performance, Lesser rejected the notion that English translation had made the semantic discrimination task more difficult. She was left to conjecture that right hemisphere brain damage may influence comprehension in terms of the selection of one word from a number of closely associated ones.

A recent approach to the study of semantic comprehension has involved the use of a word association test (Kent & Rosanoff, 1910) to determine to what extent a subject has available a normal pattern of associated words. Howes (1967) found Type A aphasics (corresponding approximately to anterior or Broca's aphasics) to display a normal pattern of word associations, although the subjects produced associates with greater latency than do normals. In contrast, Type B aphasics (corresponding to anomics and Wernicke's aphasics) tended to produce eccentric associations. Lhermitte, Desrouesne, and Lecours (1971) presented a series of word pairs which were either highly associated or unrelated to aphasics. The subject was simply asked to indicate whether or not the words were associated. Aphasics made errors on both types of word pairs, failing to identify some associates and mistakenly calling associates two words that were unrelated. In particular, the authors reported that aphasics with posterior lesions exhibited impairment similar to that of Howes' Type B patients, a deficit that Lhermitte *et al.* (1971) referred to as a widening of semantic boundaries.

Goodglass and Baker (1976) studied the associates elicited by the presentation of a single word, that is, the "semantic field" of the word. They classified aphasics into two groups according to their degree of comprehension deficit as measured by the Boston Diagnostic Aphasia Examination, and they compared the groups' performances on tests of semantic fields and of naming to that of normal controls and nonaphasic brain damaged patients. Subjects were shown a picture while they listened to a list of 14 words, 7 of which represented different types of associational relationships with the picture (including one word that correctly named the picture); 7 were unrelated. Performance was measured in terms of the latency of the subject's response and the number of errors (defined as a failure to respond within 5 seconds). It should be noted that false responses to unrelated words were quite rare. Thus, although there were a number of patients with poor comprehension (including some, presumably, with posterior lesions), there was no evidence of a "widening" of semantic boundaries.

In respect to both latency and error scores, the low comprehension aphasics were more impaired than any of the other groups. In terms of error frequency, there was no difference between the remaining groups, but all groups were significantly different from one another on the latency measure, with normals the quickest to respond, nonasphasics next, followed by high comprehension aphasics, and, slowest of all, the low comprehension aphasics. The latency scores could not be explained on the basis of a generalized slower tendency to respond in the brain damaged groups, since all groups were equally quick and accurate in responding to the word that actually identified the object pictured. Not only were the low comprehension aphasics thus more impaired in identifying associates of the picture, but their performance was qualitatively different from that of the other groups. In contrast to the others, they had particular difficulty in identifying words that were functionally (e.g., "eat") or contextually (e.g., "breakfast") associated with the picture (e.g., an orange). Thus, the aphasics with low comprehension appeared to know what the object was, but their knowledge of its semantic associates seemed constricted, and the constriction was related to particular types of associational relationships.

Goodglass and Baker (1976) then examined the relationship between constriction of semantic fields and naming ability. They found that the pictures low comprehension subjects failed to name had semantic fields that were considerably more constricted than those of the pictures the subjects named correctly. High comprehension aphasics showed the same tendency but at a level short of significance. This finding supports the notion that naming difficulties are related to constriction of associations or semantic fields. Note that the subjects clearly had some comprehension of the objects pictured, since in almost every case, they were able to identify the names when they were presented aloud. Thus failure to produce the name of the picture on confrontation seems to be related to a constriction of the semantic field surrounding the object. This complex associational structure appears to play an important role in determining the limits and nature of one's comprehension of the meaning of an object.

That this aspect of comprehension, that is, the ability to produce or recognize associates of a given word or picture, is related to the ability to produce names seems plausible. Naming ability may depend on several processes (Bisiach, 1966), but the use of associations is most certainly one of them. What seems somewhat more surprising is the relationship between comprehension, as measured by the standard techniques (in this case, the Boston aphasia battery), and constriction of semantic fields. In the Goodglass and Baker study, the patients with low comprehension showed considerable constriction of their semantic fields, and this constriction, in turn, was related to difficulty in producing names. Thus all three tasks seemed to represent a generalized capacity, with the low comprehension aphasics showing a global language deficit. Such a result is somewhat inconsistent with the notion of specific types of aphasic deficits. On the other hand, it must be remembered that in terms of their semantic fields, the low comprehension aphasics not only were more impaired than the other groups but showed a different pattern of impairment.

To make the problem even more complex, a recent report of Green and Howes (1975) has pointed out that the upper limits of the ability of an aphasic to extract semantic information may not be apparent in a standard experimental situation. These authors presented stimulus words aloud followed by a tachistoscopic presentation of a drawing of an object. The stimulus word represented one of five semantic relationships with the object pictured: the same specific name, the generic name, a contrasting coordinate name (e.g., "girl" with boy), an unrelated word, and a word phonemically similar to the name of the picture. Thus, the subject indicated, by matching the stimulus word with a particular picture, either correct comprehension, comprehension of the broad semantic field associated with the word, phonemic discrimination difficulty, or total lack of comprehension (i.e., by matching with an unrelated picture). The authors found one patient with severe comprehension impairment who showed no comprehension during the first 75 trials. However, with additional trials, the subject showed clearly differentiated patterns of responding to the various categories of pictures, indicating some ability to comprehend the meaning of words as well as a tendency to respond to semantically related words to a significantly greater extent than to unrelated words. While this finding needs replication, it suggests that brief experimental evaluations of severely impaired aphasics may not be sufficient to indicate their capacity for comprehending semantic information.

Of course, the comprehension of single words is a somewhat artificial task, in that the comprehension of a word in normal language usage is facilitated by the context in which the word is embedded. Gardner *et al.* (1975) studied the comprehension of single words in a more natural context by varying several aspects of the sentence in which the words were presented. They evaluated the performance of four groups of aphasics: anterior aphasics with little or no comprehension impairment; anteriors with comprehension deficits; two groups of posterior aphasics, with and without significant comprehension deficits; as well as normal controls. The critical stimuli were 24 target words of high frequency, each of which was to be matched to a picture in an array that included six other pictures with a semantic, phonemic, or no relationship to the target word. The target words were presented under five conditions: (*1*) the single word, spoken with normal speed and intonation; (*2*) the word embedded in a neutral sentence (one that provided no cues to the meaning of the target word); (*3*) the neutral sentence, spoken slowly; (*4*) a sentence with redundant information (other words that were semantically related to the target word; and (*5*) a sentence with a "detractor" word (one unlikely to be associated with the target word). They found that all aphasics tended to produce more semantic than phonemic errors, but that those with significant comprehension impairment produced more random errors in matching the target word with a picture. All four groups of aphasics, however, found the neutral sentence (condition 2) and the sentence with a detractor word (condition 5) more difficult than the other three conditions, which were not significantly different from one another.

Gardner *et al.* (1975) concluded that the comprehension of all aphasics was facilitated either by providing redundant information that afforded additional semantic cues to the patient or by slowing down the presentation of a nonredundant message, a factor which was also reported to improve comprehension in a patient with pure word deafness (Albert & Bear, 1974).

Several investigators have used a closer approximation to natural language by studying the comprehension of whole sentences in aphasics and normals, a procedure that permits the manipulation of syntactic structure as well as semantic elements. Parisi and Pizzamiglio (1970) used a technique proposed by Fraser, Bellugi, and Brown (1963), in which the subject is shown a pair of pictures while a sentence is read aloud. One of the two pictures is correctly described by the sentence (e.g., "The boy is pushed by the girl"), while the other is identical except for a single syntactic detail (e.g., a change of subject–object relationship: "The girl is pushed by the boy"). The authors also administered tests of phonemic and semantic discrimination, an aphasia battery, and the Token Test.

Results for the aphasics and normal controls (both adults and children) on the discrimination tests were not presented, but correlations with the results of the test of syntax were high (.68 for phoneme discrimination, .79 for semantic discrimination, and .72 for the Token Test). The overall results of the aphasics on the syntax test were such that the authors considered it to be of considerable diagnostic value in the evaluation of aphasics; only the Token Test was more accurate in identifying the aphasics. The results on the test of syntax by type of aphasic patient are most relevant to the present discussion. Wernicke's and global aphasics clearly performed more poorly than the Broca's aphasics; however, when test items were scaled in order of difficulty, the scores of the Broca's and Wernicke's aphasics were highly correlated ($r = .72$). There were some differences between the groups on individual items, including some differences in the ability of the two groups of aphasics to comprehend particular prepositions, a finding even more specific than that of Goodglass *et al.* (1970). The authors interpret the findings as evidence against theories that propose differing types of linguistic competence among Broca's and Wernicke's aphasics. Furthermore, they note a similarity between the order of difficulty of items for aphasics and the order of acquisition of various syntactic rules by children. In the words of Parisi and Pizzamiglio (1970), "these are very clear data supporting the broad Jacksonian concept of dissolution of linguistic functions and of regression to earlier developmental stages."

Lesser's (1974) cross validational study substantiated the findings for the test of syntax more satisfactorily than for the semantic discrimination task (discussed above). Only the Token Test and the auditory verbal comprehension (Oral Sentences) subtest of the Eisenson battery were as successful as the syntax test in discriminating the aphasic group from normal controls and from patients with right hemisphere brain damage. Lesser also found that the order of difficulty of the items for adult aphasics and normal children was correlated, as was the order of item difficulty between the Italian and English aphasic samples. She did find several items that differed in their degree of difficulty between the two languages, but she concluded that because the test included items that varied in their syntactic nature and level of difficulty, it had the potential of providing a detailed picture of some of the qualitative aspects of the performance of patients with impaired comprehension.

Shewan and Canter (1971) showed subjects four pictures, one of which corresponded to a sentence read aloud. The other three pictures differed from the stimulus sentence on one critical item. Increasing the number of variables studied by Parisi and Pizzamiglio (1970), Shewan and Canter varied not only syntactic structure but vocabulary level of difficulty and sentence length. Essentially, they were attempting to determine to what extent various aphasic subgroups would be differentially affected by changes in these three factors. Syntactic difficulty was varied by using either simple declarative sentences or one or two transformations, negative and passive; vocabulary difficulty was varied by selecting words at three different Thorndike–Lorge frequencies and two age levels on several picture vocabulary tests; and sentence length was manipulated by varying the number of key words (3 to 7) and the total number of syllables (7 to 15).

As expected, aphasics performed considerably more poorly than normals. Furthermore, the aphasic groups differed significantly among themselves; anomics, Broca's, and Wernicke's aphasics respectively displayed progressively greater impairment. When sentences were increased in difficulty by varying either the syntactic structure or the vocabulary level, the task was more difficult for all groups, but increases in sentence length had no effect on the aphasics' performance, a somewhat surprising finding. It may be that even the longest sentences were not sufficiently extensive to produce an effect. Certainly the question of the effect of sentence length on comprehension deserves further study, although a similar finding on Marie's Three Papers Test (Boller & Vignolo, 1966) also suggests that sentence length may not be a crucial factor in comprehension.

The critical finding, however, was that the effect of increasing the difficulty level of each of the three factors was essentially the same for all three groups of aphasics, leading the authors to conclude that no qualitative difference existed among them. Thus the authors reached essentially the same conclusion as did Parisi and Pizzamiglio (1970): there is no difference in the type of comprehension problem exhibited by different groups of aphasics. This finding differs from that of Goodglass *et al.* (1970), who found anomics to display relatively greater impairment in terms of vocabulary level on a test that required them to select the one of four pictures that corresponded to a spoken word rather than a whole sentence. It is not clear how the use of whole sentences as opposed to single words might obscure the differential effects of vocabulary level in various groups of aphasics. It may be that using whole sentences gives the anomics further cues, which improves their performance relative to the Broca's and Wernicke's aphasics, or it may be that the latter aphasics are adversely affected by the use of whole sentences. Further research using both approaches with the same subjects is needed to clarify this point.

Recent studies by Zurif and his co-workers are relevant to the study of comprehension in aphasia (Zurif, Caramazza, & Myerson, 1972; Zurif & Caramazza, 1976; Zurif, Green, Caramazza, & Goodenough, 1976). They ask their patients to judge how words in a sentence "go best together." The patient simply sorts the written words by pointing to them. This work is described in detail in a chapter in Volume 1 of this series (p. 261), and only the conclusions that are relevant to our present discussion will be summarized here. These authors have noticed that patients with Broca's aphasia have a tendency to treat functors inconsistently. Acting as if they do not know what role functors play in a sentence, Broca's aphasics, for example, may put two articles together or link an article and a verb. However, when functors are crucial in a given phrase, Broca's aphasics tend to treat them appropriately. In contrast, a group of "mixed aphasics" (i.e., Broca's aphasics with moderate comprehension disturbances) failed to place functors correctly regardless of their role in the sentence. Kurowski (cited in Zurif, Green, Caramazza, & Goodenough, 1976) found that patients who correctly order nouns and prepositions can also point correctly to the appropriate picture, while patients who fail in this task perform relatively poorly in choosing the correct pictorial representation of a sentence.

The findings of Kurowski thus suggest a relationship between the ability to place individually printed words into a grammatically ordered relationship and the ability to match a sentence with its pictorial representation. Von Stockert (1972) found that a Wernicke's aphasic, with severely impaired comprehension, was capable of placing cards on which were written several words (e.g., "the girl," "from Boston," "is pretty") in the correct grammatical order, while a patient with Broca's aphasia was not. Kremin and Goldblum (1975) found repetition disturbance to be correlated with deficits in constructing sentences in a task similar to von Stockert's.

It is difficult to correlate the findings of these studies, which deal with a similar task in very different ways. Kremin and Goldblum (1975) report a tendency (determined by means of a correlation) for patients who cannot repeat to fail the sentence construction task; such patients tend to have "motor and mixed" aphasia. The patient of Von Stockert's who performed most poorly on the sentence construction task was also a Broca's aphasic, and Zurif *et al.* (1976) found both Broca's and mixed aphasics did poorly on the task. Kurowski, on the other hand, found that patients who could construct grammatically ordered sentences could also match a sentence with its pictorial representation, the latter task being one that Broca's aphasics have been considered to carry out relatively well (Parisi & Pizzamiglio, 1970). Thus, there is some discrepancy in the findings in that it is not clear what types of patients can and cannot construct sentences in correct grammatical order. Smith (1974) found that Broca's aphasics could not place printed words in correct grammatical sequence, but her task involved copying sentences that were presented orally, rather than simply asking the subject to construct the sentences from only an internal model of how they should "best go together."

Furthermore, it is not clear how performance on the sentence construction task related to comprehension deficits. Von Stockert's patient with severe comprehension problems could, perform the task, but Kurowski's patients who could do the task also could relate sentences to pictures, a task which patients with poor comprehension could not carry out in the study of Parisi and Pizzamiglio (1970).

Finally, while both Broca's and mixed aphasics (i.e., Broca's with comprehension deficits) did poorly on the sentence construction task, those with mixed aphasia performed most poorly (Zurif *et al.,* 1976). The only possible conclusion would appear to be that, at present, the relationship between comprehension and the ability to construct sentences in correct grammatical sequence and comprehension is unclear.

A further aspect of comprehension of extended phrases or even paragraphs deals with the context in which the message is embedded. The work of Bransford and Johnson (1973) clearly demonstrates the extent to which the provision of an appropriate context facilitates the decoding of a complex verbal message To a group of normal subjects they read the following passage:

> If the balloons popped the sound wouldn't be able to carry since everything would be too far away from the correct floor. A closed window would also prevent the sound from carrying, since most buildings tend to be well insulated. Since the whole

operation depends on a steady flow of electricity, a break in the middle of the wire would also cause problems. Of course, the fellow could shout, but the human voice is not loud enough to carry that far. An additional problem is that a string could break on the instrument. Then there could be no accompaniment to the message. It is clear that the best situation would involve less distance. Then there would be fewer potential problems. With face to face contact, the least number of things could go wrong.

Both comprehension and retention of this passage were poor, but when subjects were provided an "appropriate context," as in Figure 1.2 (p. 48), their performance improved considerably.

The importance of context in relation to aphasia has been discussed (Goldstein, 1948), but little experimental attention has been paid to the effects of verbal context in the comprehension of aphasics. A study of Stachowiak, Huber, Kerschensteiner, and Poeck (in press) may represent one of the first attempts in this direction. These authors read a text of moderate complexity to three groups of patients: aphasics, patients with RBD, and normals. Comprehension was tested by asking the patients to point to the picture that accurately described the situation referred to in the text, which always contained one idiomatic, metaphorical expression. For example, the German sentence, "Da hat er sich eine schöne Suppe eingebrockt"—literally "He has prepared a nice soup for himself" and metaphorically, "He has made a nice mess for himself"—is used to describe the self-inflicted difficulties of an overworked clerk. The task consists of choosing among five alternative pictures: a man eating soup, a girl at a desk, a man in a shop, a man at a neat desk, and finally, the appropriate representation, a man at a desk piled with papers. There was no significant difference between the performance of the aphasics and normal controls, nor did the aphasics, subdivided into Broca's, Wernicke's, anomic, and global aphasics, differ among themselves. All aphasics were impaired on the Token Test, which clearly indicates the presence of language disturbance.

Like some of the tests used by Weisenburg and McBride (1935), Stachowiak *et al.*'s (in press) test appears to be heavily weighted with general intellectual and cultural factors, and, as a result, it may depress the performance of normal controls. On the other hand, the high redundancy of tests of this type may have a facilitative effect on the performance of the aphasics, so that they can no longer be reliably distinguished from normals. Stachowiak *et al.*'s (in press) conclusion that the ability to use contextual information to provide meaning is not impaired in aphasia is quite consistent with Gardner *et al.*'s (1975) report that aphasics can use redundant information to interpret single words, although the former authors state their conclusion more strongly.

"PARALINGUISTIC" ASPECTS OF COMPREHENSION

Many of the studies reviewed for this chapter reported the presence of comprehension deficits in a wide variety of aphasic patients when testing was carried out with isolated stimuli (such as single words) in a formal experimental situation. Because of the complexity of many of the experimental tasks and their sensitivity to comprehension deficits, patients with severe comprehension problems were often not included as subjects. In some instances, however, as experimental stimuli have approximated normal language usage, patients with comprehension deficits have been reported to perform closer to the level of normals (e.g., Stachowiak *et al.*, in press). These findings suggest that it might be possible to explore the performance of patients with severely impaired comprehension by systematically using verbal stimuli in situations approaching normal communication and by carefully noting the patient's response even when his actual language performance is quite defective. This approach is in keeping with Goldstein's (1948) observation that often patients who are unable to perform correctly in a test situation are able to perform normally on the same task in real-life situations. Sarno (1969) has also stressed this point. Evaluation of the lower limits of the aphasic's comprehension cannot be limited to the linguistic elements of the message but must involve the manipulation of very general aspects of the utterance. We shall refer to this borderline area of comprehension as its "paralinguistic" aspect.

Boller, in collaboration with Green (Boller & Green, 1972; Green & Boller, 1974), undertook a series of studies of patients with very severe comprehension deficits, primarily global aphasics and including several subjects with Wernicke's aphasia. Some reports—for example, that of Pick (1909, cf. above, p. 11), and, more recently, that of Goodglass *et al.* (1970)—have suggested that comprehension is not a unitary process. The general goal of Boller and Green's research was to learn whether comprehension occurs in successive stages, some of which might still be preserved in the population examined. Clinical experience with aphasics indicates that some patients with apparently very little comprehension will occasionally execute commands involving some whole body movements such as "Stand up" and "Sit down" and, curiously, "Take off your glasses" (Rubens, 1975). These tasks have been discussed in relation to apraxia (Geschwind, 1965, pp. 620–623) but are of relevance to the study of comprehension in aphasia as well.

Since severe global aphasics tend to give very few correct responses to test stimuli, initial efforts were directed toward observing global responses, such as reactions of amusement, surprise, or rejection. In the first phase of the research, Boller and Green (1972) set out to determine whether or not severe aphasics with very poor comprehension could distinguish their native language, English, from a foreign language and from semantic and phonemic jargon and to test the

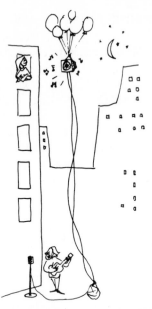

Figure 1.2 Appropriate context for the *balloon* passage. [Bransford & Johnson, 1973.]

hypothesis that aphasics perform relatively better in response to familiar questions and whole-body commands than to more complex items and other types of commands. The stimuli, 85 questions and commands presented in random order, consisted of:

1. Sentences in correct English: questions either requiring yes—no answers or requesting information, and commands. The items varied from familiar ("Stand up," "Do you have a headache?") to difficult ("If Sally is taller than Jane but smaller than Nancy, is Nancy smaller than Jane?") and involved both whole-body and other types of commands.

2. Questions in meaningful but grammatically incorrect English ("Do I wears a necktie?").

3. Sentences consisting of semantic jargon, that is, English words arranged in an order that make the utterance meaningless ("How would you bay the hair of querulous?").

4. Sentences consisting of phonemic jargon, or meaningless "words" with the phonetic characteristics of English, taken from Lewis Carroll's "Jabberwocky" (e.g., "Twas brillig and the slithy toves. . . .").

5. Sentences in correct French.

Two judges independently recorded and scored each subject's responses, including gestures and expressions as well as verbalizations.

Normal controls, who were included in the study, clearly discriminated commands and questions presented in English from those in jargon or French. Ungrammatical items were treated as if they were normal English. They reacted to meaningless sentences with expressions of surprise, amusement, or overt refusal ("No, I can't do that.")

The response of normals to meaningless items suggested the first step in the analysis of aphasics' responses. The number of refusals or quizzical responses were tabulated as a percentage of the total number of responses in each of the six categories. Figure 1.3 shows the mean percentage of such responses for 15 aphasics for each category of stimulus.

Phonemic jargon and French produced significantly more refusals or quizzical responses than did semantic jargon, which, in turn, produced significantly more refusals or quizzical responses than did the three categories of meaningful English. This pattern of response was exhibited by all patients except one with word deafness, who reacted with a stereotyped quizzical expression to all items in the battery.

Responses were then classified according to whether or not they were appropriate to a yes—no question (e.g., a nod, even if incorrect), a request for information (e.g., some extended verbal response), or a command (e.g., a gesture or motion). Two independent judges classified the responses with 96% agreement. Although the patient's percent of correct responses was low, the percentage of responses that were either correct or appropriate was nearly 50%, again suggesting some comprehension. Aphasic subjects, for example, responded with jargon significantly more often to questions requesting information than to yes—no questions or commands.

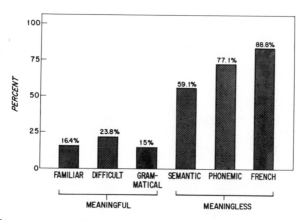

Figure 1.3 Mean percentage of refusal—quizzical responses made by aphasics on six categories of test items. [Boller & Green, 1972, pp. 382—394.]

There was no difference in the performance of the aphasics in response to familiar, difficult, and agrammatical but meaningful English utterances. Although patients tended to perform better on some commands than on others (for example, "Stand up" was performed correctly by 9 of 15 patients, but "Point to the chair" elicited only one correct response), there was no significant difference between the performance of aphasics in response to whole-body commands and to other commands.

In a subsequent study (Green & Boller, 1974), utterances were presented either by direct speech or by tape recorder, and within each of these conditions the sound was presented from either in front or in back of the subject. The syntactic structure of the utterance was also varied, such that presentations were made in the form of direct commands, indirect commands, or a direct command preceded by an introductory phrase. Responses were again classified according to their appropriateness as well as being scored as correct or incorrect.

Variations in the syntactic form of the stimuli affected the percentage of responses judged appropriate but did not influence the percentage of responses judged correct. Direct commands produced significantly more appropriate responses than indirect commands. Mode of presentation also played a significant role in the performance of aphasics. Patients consistently responded better, in terms of percentage of either correct or appropriate responses, to direct speech presentation than to the tape recorded version, although they showed no indication of diminished attention or uncooperativeness during the tape recorded administration. The position of the stimulus source (in front or in back of the subject) did not significantly affect aphasic performance, although the patients showed a tendency to respond more accurately when the stimulus was presented in front of them, as can be seen in Figure 1.4. The performance

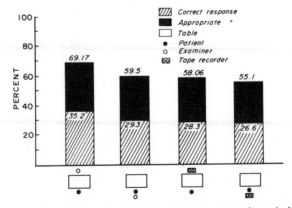

Figure 1.4 Percentage of correct and appropriate responses to test items in four conditions: Examiner in front of or behind patient, tape recorder in front of or behind patient. [Data from Green & Boller, 1974, pp. 133–135.]

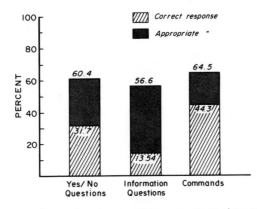

Figure 1.5 Percentage of correct and appropriate responses to three types of test items. [Data from Green & Boller, 1974, pp. 133–145.]

increment produced by the use of direct speech reflects primarily the performance of four patients whose degree of comprehension impairment was intermediate among the subjects of this study, all of whom were very severely impaired. The remaining subjects were far less affected by changes in the mode of presentation. Nevertheless, it seems important to realize that some patients can be considerably handicapped when required to communicate in the absence of a live interlocutor (as, for example, with a teaching machine or a telephone).

The use of the category of appropriateness in classifying aphasic responses seems an important contribution to the evaluation of the lower limits of comprehension ability. Yet it must be noted that classification of responses in terms of their appropriateness may not always correspond to classification in terms of correctness. As shown in Figure 1.5, initial examination of the results indicated that the aphasics exhibited significantly more correct responses for commands than for yes–no questions, which, in turn, elicited more correct responses than did the informational questions. When, however, responses were classified according to their appropriateness, the difference between responses to these three types of stimuli disappeared. Such a finding suggests that studies comparing the response of aphasics to various types of questions and commands should consider a number of response dimensions before drawing conclusions about the degree of comprehension shown by their patients.

CONCLUSIONS

The study of comprehension, long neglected in the history of aphasiology, has recently become an active field. Much early work in the study of comprehension involved the development of tests of comprehension ability. A number of comprehension subtests in various aphasia batteries and several single tests, such as the Token Test, were produced, all of which have been considered to be rather specific tests of comprehension. Little is known, however, about the specific processes that underlie the performance of patients on even the most sensitive of these tests, although current research has been concerned with identifying some of these processes.

Some recent work has focused on the study of phonological deficit as a major cause of auditory comprehension impairment. Studies have generally demonstrated that there is little relationship between performance on phonemic discrimination tasks and either performance on tests of comprehension ability or specific type of aphasic disturbance (Naeser, 1974; Blumstein *et al.*, 1977). Patients with comprehension difficulties, however, such as those with Wernicke's aphasia, have been found to have particular difficulty in matching spoken words with their pictorial equivalents when alternative pictures with phonemically similar names are simultaneously presented (Naeser, 1974). The latter finding has suggested the possibility that patients with comprehension impairment may have a specific disability in associating phonemic materials with their semantic equivalents. The likelihood that this finding can provide a major explanation of the phonemic basis of comprehension problems is lessened by the fact that when pictures with semantically related names have been included, patients with comprehension impairment have tended to select somewhat fewer phonemically similar incorrect alternatives (Gainotti *et al.*, 1975). One recent study did find, however, that aphasics made a high proportion of phonemic errors on such a task (Gardner *et al.*, 1975). In general, current research provides little basis for a phonemic explanation of comprehension deficits.

Semantic aspects of a linguistic utterance seem to be an important determinant of comprehension. Not only do patients with comprehension impairment have greater difficulty in matching spoken names with one picture in an array of semantically related pictures (Gainotti *et al.*, 1975); they seem to have particular difficulty in comprehending the meaning of specific types of semantic material (Goodglass *et al.*, 1970). Furthermore, they have been reported to be both slow and inaccurate in identifying associates of a particular word or picture; their knowledge of the semantic fields of words has been variously reported as erratic, widened (Lhermitte *et al.*, 1971), or reduced (Goodglass & Baker, 1976). In spite of this associational impairment, provision of redundant information, which offers additional semantic cues to the meaning of a particular word in a sentence, seems to improve comprehension (Gardner *et al.*, 1975).

In addition, it seems quite clear that manipulation of the syntactic aspects of an utterance critically influences the comprehension of aphasics. Indeed, Lesser (1974) found a syntax test to be more accurate than tests of semantic or phonemic discrimination in distinguishing aphasics from both normal controls and patients with RBD. The problem in regard to tests of syntax has been the consistent finding that all aphasics show evidence of impairment (Shewan & Canter, 1971). There is little basis for interpreting syntactic difficulties as a specific comprehension problem, since even aphasics with good comprehension ability show impairment on such tests, although patients with poor comprehension may tend to do worse than other aphasics.

An increasingly large number of studies have pointed out the importance of a series of more or less linguistic variables in determining performance on tests of comprehension. The context of the verbal utterance is clearly an important variable, as has been emphasized by Goldstein (1948) and by Sarno (1969). Not only does the inclusion of additional semantic cues help in the comprehension of single words within a sentence (Gardner *et al.,* 1975), but even aphasics with severe comprehension problems may exhibit normal performance when they are asked to match complex metaphorical utterances with a picture (Stachowiak *et al.,* in press). Patients with severe comprehension problems have been observed to respond more appropriately to direct speech than to tape recorded messages (Green & Boller, 1974) and to be able to discriminate (*1*) their own language from either a foreign language or from semantic jargon and (*2*) yes–no questions from commands and informational requests (Boller & Green, 1972). Thus the role of what we have termed "paralinguistic" factors is important to the overall level of comprehension, even in patients with severe impairment.

All of these conclusions lead to the consideration of an important question: how can comprehension be measured? On the basis of the present research on comprehension, it appears that a test of comprehension must involve the following stimulus elements: (*1*) a means of comparing a subject's response to single words with his response to more complete, "natural" utterances, the latter with and without redundant, associated cues as to the meaning of the utterances; (*2*) the presentation of utterances both independent of and within a context; (*3*) the presentation of utterances at both slow and natural speeds (cf. Albert & Baer, 1974; Gardner *et al.,* 1975); and (*4*) the presentation of numerous repeated trials (cf. Green & Howes, 1975). In addition, the subjects' responses should be evaluated in terms of both correctness and appropriateness (Boller & Green, 1972; Green & Boller, 1974). Just as these conclusions provide some clear direction for the future construction of tests of comprehension, it seems equally clear that current tests of comprehension ability fail to include several of the necessary features. Most current tests involve the presentation of both single words and more complete utterances. Little emphasis, however, has been given to the context in which the message is presented, except in the approach of Sarno (1969). In none of the tests has the speed with which the utterance is presented been systematically varied, and no one has attempted to present the same stimulus item on a number of trials. Only Sarno (1969) and Porch (1967) have made an attempt to evaluate the appropriateness of the subject's response. Thus, there appears to be no current test that adequately utilizes the results of research on auditory comprehension.

A second general question relates to the nature of the significant linguistic factors that underlie performance on tests of comprehension. Common sense suggests that the influence of factors such as short-term memory, general intelligence, and visual–spatial ability should be eliminated from measures of comprehension ability. However, the extent of the influence of such factors has been called into question. The influence of attentional or short-term memory factors may not be so critical as has been thought (Kreindler *et al.*, 1971; Gardner *et al.*, 1975). Phonemic factors, in spite of the opinion of Luria (1970), have not been found particularly important, except, perhaps, on tests requiring the association of spoken words with their semantic equivalents (Naeser, 1974). Semantic factors clearly influence performance on comprehension tests, but this influence may not be specific to aphasia, since Lesser (1974) found that patients with RBD also show impairment on a semantic discrimination test. Syntactic factors seem clearly associated with aphasic disturbance, but it is not clear that these factors specifically influence comprehension apart from other aphasic symptoms (Shewan & Canter, 1971). Phonemic, semantic, and, to a lesser extent, syntactic features of a message are varied in most tests of comprehension ability. Indeed, although these same tests fail to take into account most of the findings summarized in the preceding paragraph, they have emphasized phonemic and semantic aspects of the utterance in attempting to identify those patients with comprehension impairment. It would appear, therefore, that the primary approach of existing tests of comprehension ability has been to identify deficits that may not be specific to comprehension alone but rather may be related to all types of aphasic disturbance.

This possibility raises a third, more general question: Is comprehension a unitary function? Whether or not one can speak of comprehension as an isolated ability, it does appear that one can identify different levels of comprehension, a possibility discussed quite early by Pick (1909), although the precise nature of these levels is not certain. Blumstein (in press) has spoken of prelinguistic and linguistic levels of comprehension, while Boller and Green (1972; Green & Boller, 1974) have identified tasks that enable the examiner to quantify levels of comprehension in patients whose impairment is so severe that they appear totally lacking in comprehension ability. Research with normals also supports a view of comprehension as a multistage operation (Liberman *et al.*, 1967).

The question of whether or not comprehension is a unitary function is, however, more open to dispute. A number of studies of the comprehension of whole sentences (e.g., Parisi & Pizzamiglio, 1970; Shewan & Canter, 1971) have found that while patients with comprehension disturbance may do worse than other groups of aphasics, the pattern of their performance is not qualitatively different from that of the other patients. Furthermore, Poeck and his associates have consistently reported that different groups of aphasics do not differ from one another in their performance on the Token Test. On the other hand, on tests of the ability to comprehend different categories of single words (Goodglass *et al.*, 1970) or to identify associates of a particular word (Goodglass & Baker, 1976), patients with poor comprehension have been reported to produce responses that are qualitatively distinguishable from those of aphasics with relatively good comprehension ability. It is difficult to compare the results of these studies, since the former studies involve rather global (pointing to a picture) responses to complex utterances, while the latter involve more extensively categorized responses to simpler stimuli. In view of the fact, however, that those studies reporting qualitative differences between patients with high and low comprehension ability were all produced in the same laboratory, the burden of proof would appear to lie with those who oppose the notion of comprehension as a unitary function. The majority of existing studies support the contention that it is.

An important aspect of the previous question concerns the relationship between disturbances in the comprehension and production of speech. A number of investigators have argued that there is correspondence between the nature of the problems observed in each of these aspects of language. Thus, Alajouanine *et al.* (1964) have attempted to define groups of aphasics, not in terms of their comprehension and expressive deficits, but in terms of their phonemic and semantic impairments, contending that patients with phonemic problems will show phonemic paraphasia in speech and will have trouble with the phonemic aspects of the message in comprehension, while those patients with semantic problems will show, analogously, semantic paraphasia and semantic comprehension deficits. This argument is partially supported by the work of Gainotti *et al.* (1975). A number of other investigators have also reported correspondence between the nature of the deficits in comprehension and speech production (Goodglass *et al.*, 1970; Shewan & Canter, 1971; Kurowski, cited in Zurif *et al.*, 1976; Zurif and Caramazza, 1976). A few studies, however, have reported contrary findings. While Goodglass *et al.* (1970) found a relationship between the production and comprehension problems in anomic aphasics, they failed to find such correspondence in the performance of Broca's aphasics, although Smith (1974) later disputed this finding. Gainotti *et al.* (1975), in the study supporting the notion of a semantic production–comprehension equivalence, failed to obtain an analogous finding in regard to phonemic deficits. The approach of Zurif and his associates (e.g., Zurif *et al.*, 1976) seems a promising technique for evaluating sentence construction and its relationship to deficits in comprehension, but the results are thus far difficult to interpret. Again, the question remains open to dispute, but the evidence at present supports the notion that problems in the production and comprehension of speech are related.

Another question concerns the extent to which deficits of comprehension can be seen in all varieties of aphasic disorder. Clinical experience with aphasics has long suggested that some patients, particularly those with Broca's, transcortical motor, or anomic aphasia, show no comprehension deficits when tested either informally or with an aphasia battery. Actually, anomic patients do seem to have clear difficulties in matching words with pictures (Goodglass *et al.,* 1970; Gainotti *et al.,* 1975). Furthermore, it seems reasonable to argue that those transcortical motor aphasics with an isolated deficit in the spontaneous production of language cannot be considered truly aphasic according to our definition of the term. They do not have difficulty in the translation of words into thoughts but only of thoughts into words. The most difficult part of the question thus relates to the extent to which patients with Broca's aphasia show comprehension problems. They are generally deficient on the Token Test (Boller & Vignolo, 1966), and when ordering words in a sentence production task they treat unessential functors as if they lacked knowledge of their meaning (Zurif & Caramazza, 1976), but it is not clear that these deficits can be considered true failures of comprehension. Furthermore, the performance of individual Broca's aphasics may well provide exceptions to these generalizations, that is, some may not fail these tasks. Could the "pure anarthric" patients with verified destruction of Broca's area described by Hécaen and Consoli (1973) have performed such tasks as those of Zurif, the Token Test, or the test of semantic fields (Goodglass & Baker, 1976) without difficulty? If not, could their deficits be interpreted as failures of comprehension?

The question of the extent to which deficits of comprehension can be seen in all aphasic patients is a difficult one to answer. In some sense, our argument is circular, in that if we define aphasia as necessarily involving both expression and comprehension problems, we have, perforce, answered the question. In a more empirical sense, however, this circularity may not be the critical issue. More important is the extent to which patients with no apparent comprehension deficits in formal or informal testing show deficits on some of the new procedures which have not been widely applied to broad groups of patients yet which show signs of providing an extended picture of the nature of the deficit underlying the performance of aphasics on a variety of language tasks. If we can demonstrate that even patients with relatively pure Broca's or transcortical motor aphasia have difficulties with some aspects of these new tasks, then we still must answer the question of the meaning of these deficits. This question, in fact, is essentially the question of "What is comprehension?," a question we have explicitly avoided. Our approach rather, would be to defer judgment regarding the possible meaning of such hypothesized deficits until we have not only observed them but had an opportunity to study their relationship, in the patients in question, to other types of tasks.

The questions discussed above raise perhaps the most basic question of all: Is aphasia a unitary symptom complex, a single entity? If it were established that all aphasics have comprehension deficits and that these deficits are qualitatively similar, this would be a strong basis for presuming the existence of a unitary deficit. The trend of recent research has suggested that comprehension deficits may indeed be universal and that such deficits are not qualitatively distinguishable, a trend which supports the view that aphasia may be a single disorder. Such a tentatively expressed hypothesis need not rule out the contribution of specific functions to the varieties of aphasia. One might well imagine a general language factor, akin to Spearman's (1904) general intellectual factor, manifested in conjunction with a number of specific, related abilities, deficits in which might follow focal lesions within the language area. Obviously, existing data fall far short of being able to confirm such tenuous speculation.

ACKNOWLEDGMENTS

The authors are greatly indebted to Drs. Arthur L. Benton, Monroe Cole, Ennio De Renzi, and Eugene Green for their helpful criticisms on an earlier version of the manuscript and for supplying invaluable literature references.

REFERENCES

Abelson, A. R. 1911. The measurement of mental ability of backward children. *British Journal of Psychology, 4,* 268–314.

Alajouanine, T. 1968. *L'aphasie et le langage pathologique.* Paris: Baillière.

Alajouanine, T., Lhermitte, F., Ledoux, M., Renaud, D., & Vignolo, L. A. 1964. Les composantes phonémiques et sémantiques de la jargonaphasie. *Revue Neurologique 110,* 5–20.

Alajouanine, T., Sabouraud, O., & Ribaucourt, B. de. 1952. Désintégration anosognosique des valeurs sémantiques du langage. *Journal de Psychologie, 45,* 158–180; 293–330.

Albert, M. L. 1972. Aspects de la compréhension auditive du langage après lésion cérébrale *Langages, 7,* 37–51.

Albert, M. L., & Bear, D. 1974. Time to understand. *Brain, 97,* 373–384.

Assal, G. 1974. Troubles de la reception auditive du langage lors des lésions du cortex cerebral. *Neuropsychologia, 12,* 399–401.

Basso, A., Casati, G., & Vignolo, L. A. In press. Phonemic identification defect in aphasia. *Cortex.*

Basso, A., De Renzi, E., Faglioni, P., Scotti, G., & Spinnler, H. 1973. Neuropsychological evidence for the existence of cerebral areas critical to the performance of intelligence tasks. *Brain, 96,* 715–728.

Bastian, H. C. 1869. On the various forms of loss of speech in cerebral disease. *British and Foreign Medical Chirurgical Review, 43,* 209–236; 470–492.

Bastian, H. C. 1887. On different kinds of aphasia. *British Medical Journal, 2,* 931–937; 985–990.

Bay, E. 1962. Aphasia and non-verbal disorders of language. *Brain, 85,* 411–426.

Bay, E. 1969. The Lordat case and its import on the theory of aphasia. *Cortex, 5,* 302–308.

Benson, D. F. 1970. Fluency in aphasia: Correlation with radioactive scan localization. *Cortex, 3,* 373–394.

Benson, D. F., & Geschwind, N. 1971. The aphasias and related disturbances. In A. B. Baker & L. Baker (Eds.), *Clinical neurology.* Vol. 1. New York: Harper & Row. Ch. 8.

Benson, D. R., Sheramata, W. A., Bouchard, R., Segarra, J. M., Price, D., & Geschwind, N. 1973. Conduction aphasia. *Archives of Neurology, 28,* 339–346.

Benton, A. L. 1965a. Contribution to aphasia before Broca. *Cortex, 1,* 314–327.

Benton, A. L. 1965b. Johann A. P. Gesner on aphasia. *Medical History, 9,* 54–60.

Benton, A. L. 1967. Problems of test construction in the field of aphasia. *Cortex, 3,* 32–58.

Benton, A. L. 1973. The measurement of aphasic disorders. In *Aspectos Patologicos del Lenguaje. Actas de las Primeras Jornadas Internacionales del Lenguaje.* Lima: Peru.

Bisiach, E. 1966. Perceptual factors in the pathogenesis of anomia. *Cortex, 2,* 90–95.

Black, J. W. 1951. Effects of delayed side-tone upon vocal rate and intensity. *Journal of Speech and Hearing Disorders, 16,* 56–60.

Blumstein, S. E. In press. The Perception of speech in pathology and ontogeny. In A. Caramazza and E. Zurif (Eds.), *The acquisition and breakdown of language.* Baltimore: Johns Hopkins Press.

Blumstein, S. E., Baker, E., & Goodglass, H. 1977. Phonological factors in auditory comprehension in aphasia. *Neuropsychologia, 15,* 19–30.

Boller, F. 1968. Latent aphasia: Right and left "non aphasic" brain-damaged patients compared. *Cortex, 4,* 245–256.

Boller, F. In press. Comprehension disorders in aphasia: A historical review. *Brain and Language.*

Boller, F. In press. Johann Baptist Schmidt: A pioneer in the history of aphasia. *Archives of Neurology.*

Boller, F., & Green, E. 1972. Comprehension in severe aphasia. *Cortex, 8,* 382–394.

Boller, F., & Vignolo, L. A. 1966. Latent sensory aphasia in hemisphere-damaged patients: An experimental study with the Token Test. *Brain, 89,* 815–830.

Bransford, J. D., & Johnson, M. K. 1973. Considerations of some problems of comprehension. In W. G. Chase (Ed.), *Visual information processing.* New York: Academic Press.

Broca, P. 1861. Remarques sur le siège de la faculté du langage articulé, suivies d'une observation d'aphémie. *Bulletin de la Société d'Anatomie* (2ème série), *6,* 330–364. Reprinted in H. Hécaen & J. Dubois, 1969, *La naissance de la Neuropsychologie du Language (1825–1865),* Paris: Flammarion.

Brown, J. 1967. Physiology and phylogenesis of emotional expression. *Brain Research, 5,* 1–14.

Brown, J. 1972. *Aphasia, apraxia and agnosia.* Springfield, Ill.: Charles C Thomas.

Charcot, J. M. 1974. *Leçons du mardi à la Salpêtrière.* Paris: Centre d'étude et de promotion de la lecture, Retz.

Cole, M. 1968. The anatomical basis of aphasia as seen by Pierre Marie. *Cortex, 4,* 172–183.

Cole, M. F., & Cole, M. 1971. *Pierre Marie's papers on speech disorders.* New York: Hafner.

Daujat, C., Gainotti, G., & Tissot, R. 1974. Sur quelques aspects des troubles de la compréhension dans l'aphasie. *Cortex, 10,* 347–359.

Déjerine, J. 1891. Contribution à l'étude de l'aphasie motrice souscorticale et de la localisation cérébrale des centres laryngés. *Mémoires de la Société de Biologie, 43,* 155–162.

Déjerine, J. 1914. *Sémiologie des affections du système nerveux.* Paris: Masson.

De Renzi, E., Faglioni, P., & Scotti, G. 1970. Hemispheric contribution to exploration of space through the visual and tactile modality. *Cortex, 6,* 191–203.

De Renzi, E., & Vignolo, L. A. 1962a. Fattori verbali ed extraverbali della comprensione negli afasici. *Rivista di Patologia Nervosa e Mentale, 83,* 443–468.

De Renzi, E., & Vignolo, L. A. 1962b. The Token Test: A sensitive test to detect receptive disturbances in aphasics. *Brain, 85,* 665–678.

De Renzi, E., & Vignolo, L. A. 1966. Disturbi del linguaggio nei dementi. *Il Lavoro Neuropsichiatrico, 42,* 1–12.

Dunn, L. M. 1959. *Peabody Picture Vocabulary Test.* Minneapolis: American Guidance Series.

Eisenson, J. 1954. *Examining for aphasia.* New York: Psychological Corporation.

Finkelnburg, F. C. 1870. Niederrheinische Gesellschaft. Sitzung von 21 März 1870 in Bonn. *Berliner Klinische Wochenschrift, 7,* 449–450; 460–462.

Fraser, C., Bellugi, E., & Brown, R. 1963. Control of grammar in imitation, comprehension, and production. *Journal of Verbal Learning and Verbal Behavior, 2,* 121–135.

Gainotti, G., Ibba, A., & Caltagirone, C. 1975. Perturbations acoustiques et sémantiques de la compréhension dans l'aphasie. *Revue Neurologique, 131,* 645–659.

Gainotti, G., & Lemmo, M. A. 1976. Comprehension of symbolic gestures in aphasia. *Brain and Language, 3,* 451–460.

Gardner, H. 1975. *The shattered mind.* New York: Alfred Knopf.

Gardner, H., Albert, M. L., & Weintraub, S. 1975. Comprehending a word: The influence of speed and redundancy on auditory comprehension in aphasia. *Cortex, 11,* 155–162.

Gates, A. I. 1927. *The improvement of reading.* New York: Macmillan. Pp. 46–50.

Geschwind, N. 1965. Disconnexion syndromes in animals and man. *Brain, 88,* 237–294; 585–644.

Geschwind, N. 1967a. The varieties of naming errors. *Cortex, 3,* 97–112.

Geschwind, N. 1967b. Wernicke's contribution to the study of aphasia. *Cortex, 3,* 449–463.

Geschwind, N., & Fusillo, M. 1966. Color-naming defects in association with alexia. *Archives of Neurology, 15,* 137–146.

Geschwind, N., Quadfasel, F. A., & Segarra, J. M. 1968. Isolation of the speech area. *Neuropsychologia, 6,* 327–340.

Gesner, J. A. P. 1769–1776. *Sammlung von Beobachtungen aus der Arzneigelehrheit und Naturkunde.* Nordlingen (5 Vols).

Goldblum, M. C., & Albert, M. L. 1972. Phonemic discrimination in sensory aphasia. *International Journal of Mental Health, 1,* 25–29.

Goldstein, K. 1948. *Language and language disturbances.* New York: Grune & Stratton.

Goodglass, H., & Baker, E. 1976. Semantic field, naming and auditory comprehension in aphasia. *Brain and Language, 3,* 359–374.

Goodglass, H., Gleason, J. B., & Hyde, M. 1970. Some dimensions of auditory language comprehension in aphasics. *Journal of Speech and Hearing Research, 13,* 595–606.

Goodglass, H., & Kaplan, E. 1972. *The assessment of aphasia and related disorders.* Philadelphia: Lea and Febiger.

Goodglass, H., Klein, B., Carey, P., & Jones, K. 1966. Specific semantic word categories in aphasia. *Cortex, 2,* 74–89.

Grashey, H. 1885. Über Aphasie und ihre Beziehungen zur Wahrnehmung. *Archiv für Psychiatrie, 16,* 654–688.

Green, E., & Boller, F. 1974. Features of auditory comprehension in severely impaired aphasics. *Cortex, 10,* 133–145.

Green, E., & Howes, D. 1975. Semantic discrimination of words in receptive aphasia. Paper read at the 13th annual meeting of the Academy of Aphasia, Victoria, British Columbia, October 5, 1975.

Hartje, W., Kerschensteiner, M., Poeck, K., & Orgass, B. 1973. A cross-validation study of the Token Test. *Neuropsychologia, 11,* 119–122.

Head, H. 1926. *Aphasia and kindred disorders of speech.* Cambridge: Cambridge University Press.

Healy, W., & Bronner, A. 1927. *A manual of individual mental tests and testing.* Boston: Little, Brown.

Hécaen, H. 1969. Essai de dissociation du syndrome de l'aphasie sensorielle. *Revue Neurologique, 120,* 229–237.

Hécaen, H. 1972. *Introduction à la Neuropsychologie.* Paris: Larousse.

Hécaen, H., & Consoli, S. 1973. Analyse des troubles du langage au cours des lésions de l'aire de Broca. *Neuropsychologia, 11,* 377–388.

Hécaen, H., & Dubois, J. 1969. *La naissance de la Neuropsychologie du Langage (1825–1865).* Paris: Flammarion.

Howes, D. 1957. On the relation between intelligibility and frequency of occurrence of English words. *Journal of the Acoustical Society of America, 29,* 296–305.

Howes, D. 1967. Some experimental investigation of language in aphasia. In K. Salzinger and S. Salzinger (Eds.), *Research in verbal behavior and some neurophysiological implications.* New York: Academic Press. Also in H. Goodglass and S. Blumstein (Eds.), *Psycholinguistics in aphasia.* Baltimore: Johns Hopkins University Press, 1973.

Isserlin, M. 1936. *Aphasie.* In O. Bumke and O. Foerster (Eds.), *Handbuch der Neurologie.* Vol. 6. Berlin: Springer. Pp. 627–806.

Jackson, H. 1874. On the nature of the duality of the brain. *Medical Press Circular, 1.* Reprinted in 1915, *Brain, 38,* 80–86.

Jennett, B., & Plum, F. 1972. Persistent vegetative state after brain damage: A syndrome in search of a name. *Lancet, 1,* 734–737.

Kent, G. H., & Rosanoff, A. J. 1910. A study of association in insanity. *American Journal of Insanity, 67,* 27–96.

Kim, Y. C. 1976. Deficits in temporal sequencing of verbal material: The effect of laterality of lesion. *Brain and Language, 3,* 507–515.

Kinsbourne, M., & Warrington, E. K. 1963. Jargon aphasia. *Neuropsychologia, 1,* 27–37.

Kreindler, A., Gheorghita, N., & Voinescu, I. 1971. Analysis of verbal reception of a complex order with three elements in aphasics. *Brain, 94,* 375–386.

Kremin, H., & Goldblum, M. C. 1975. Étude de la compréhension syntaxique chez les aphasiques. *Linguistics, 154,* 31–46.

Kurowski, K. In preparation. MA Thesis, Dept. of Linguistics, Brown University. Quoted by Zurif, Green, Caramazza, & Goodenough, 1976.

Kussmaul, A. 1877. Disturbances of speech. In H. von Ziemssen (Ed.), *Cyclopedia of the practice of medicine.* Vol. 14. New York: William Wood. Pp. 581–875.

Lebrun, Y., & Hoops, R. (Eds.). 1974. *Intelligence and aphasia.* Lisse: Swets and Zeitlinger.

Lee, B. S. 1950. Effects of delayed speech feedback. *Journal of the Acoustical Society of America, 22,* 824–826.

Lesser, R. 1974. Verbal comprehension in aphasia: An English version of three Italian tests. *Cortex, 10,* 238–246.

Lesser, R. 1976. Verbal and non-verbal memory components in the Token Test. *Neuropsychologia, 14,* 79–85.

Lhermitte, F., Desrouesne, J., & Lecours, A. R. 1971. Contribution à l'étude des troubles sémantiques dans l'aphasie. *Revue Neurologique, 125,* 81–101.

Liberman, A., Cooper, F. S., Shankweiler, D., & Studdert-Kennedy, M. 1967. The perception of the speech code. *Psychological Review, 74,* 431–461.

Lichtheim, L. 1885. On aphasia. *Brain, 7,* 433–484.

Liepmann, H. 1905. Kleine Hilfsmittel bei der Untersuchung von Gehirnkranken. Reprinted in *Drei Aufsätze aus dem Apraxiegebiet*. Berlin: S. Karger, 1908.

Lisker, L., & Abramson, A. 1964. Across-language study of voicing in initial stops: Acoustical Measurements. *Word, 20,* 384–422.

Lordat, J. 1843. Analyse de la parole pour servir à la théorie de divers cas d'alalie et de paralalie (de mutisme et d'imperfection du parler) que les Nosologistes ont mal connus. *Journal de la Société de Médecine pratique de Montpellier, 7,* 333–353; 417–433. Reprinted in H. Hécaen & J. Dubois, 1969; *La naissance de la Neuropsychologie du Langage (1825–1865),* Paris: Flammarion.

Luria, A. R. 1947. *Travmaticheskaja Afaziji.* Moscow: Publishing House of the Academy of Medical Sciences of the USSR.

Luria, A. R. 1966. *Higher cortical functions in man.* New York: Basic Books.

Luria, A. R. 1970. *Traumatic aphasia.* The Hague: Mouton.

Marie, P. 1906. La troisième circonvolution frontale gauche ne joue aucun rôle special dans la function du langage. *Semaine Médicale* May 23rd, reprinted in P. Marie, 1926, *Travaux et Memoires,* Tome I, Paris: Masson, pp. 3–30. For translation, see M. F. Cole & M. Cole, 1971, *Pierre Marie's papers on speech disorders,* New York: Hafner.

Merritt, H. H. 1973. *A textbook of neurology.* Philadelphia: Lea & Febiger.

Meynert, T. 1866. Ein Fall von Sprachstörung anatomisch begründet. *Medizinische Jahruch der Zeitschrift ges Artze, 12,* 152–187.

Moutier, F. 1908. *L'aphasie de Broca.* Paris: Steinheil.

Naeser, M. A. 1974. The relationship between phoneme discrimination, phoneme perception and language comprehension in aphasia. Paper read at the 12th Annual Meeting of the Academy of Aphasia, Warrenton, Va., October 14, 1974.

Naeser, M. A. 1976. Untitled paper presented at the Symposium on Brain and Language, 9th Winter Conference on Brain Research. Summaries of symposia (BIS Conference Report No. 44). UCLA, Los Angeles, Brain Information Service/BRI Publications Office.

Ombredane, A. 1951. *L'Aphasie et l'Elaboration de la Pensée Explicite.* Paris. Presse Universitaire de France.

Orgass, B., & Poeck, K. 1966a. Clinical validation of a new test for aphasia: An experimental study on the Token Test. *Cortex, 2,* 222–243.

Orgass, B., & Poeck, K. 1966b. Ein neuer Aphasie-Test zur Diagnose von Sprachverständnisstörungen. *Nervenartzt, 37,* 124–126.

Orgass, B., & Poeck, K. 1969. Assessment of aphasia by psychometric methods. *Cortex, 5,* 317–330.

Orgass, B., Poeck, K., Hartje, W., & Kerschensteiner, M. 1973. Zum Vorschlag einer Kurzform des Token Tests zur Auslese von Aphasikern. *Nervenartzt, 44,* 93–95.

Parisi, D., & Pizzamiglio, L. 1970. Syntactic comprehension in aphasia. *Cortex, 6,* 204–215.

Pearson, G. H., Alpers, B. J., & Weisenburg, T. 1928. Aphasia: A study of normal control cases. *Archives of Neurology and Psychiatry, 19,* 281–295.

Peck-Swisher, L., & Taylor-Sarno, M. 1969. Token Test scores of 3 matched patient groups: Left brain-damaged with aphasia; right brain-damaged without aphasia; non brain damaged. *Cortex, 5,* 264–273.

Pick, A. 1909. *Über das Sprachverständnis.* Leipzig: Drei Vorträge.

Pizzamiglio, L., & Appiciafuoco, A. 1967. Test a scelta mutipla per la valutaziona dei disturbi di comprensione negli afasici. *Archivio di Psicologia, Neurologia e Psichiatria, 28,* 499–524.

Pizzamiglio, L., & Appicciafuoco, A. 1971. Semantic comprehension in aphasia. *Journal of Communication Disorders, 3,* 280–288.

Plum, F., & Posner, J. B. 1972. *The diagnosis of stupor and coma.* Philadelphia: Davis.

Poeck, K., Hartje, W., Kerschensteiner, M., & Orgass, B. 1973. Sprachvertändnisstörungen bei aphasischen und nichtaphasischen Hirnkranken. *Deutsche Medizinische Wochenschrift, 98,* 139–147.

Poeck, K., Kerschensteiner, M., & Hartje, W. 1972. A quantitative study of language understanding in fluent and non-fluent aphasia. *Cortex, 8,* 299–304.

Poeck, K., Orgass, B., Kerschensteiner, M., & Hartje, W. 1974. A qualitative study of the Token Test performance in aphasic and non-aphasic brain damaged patients. *Neuropsychologia, 12,* 49–54.

Porch, B. 1967. *The Porch Index of Communicative Ability.* Palo Alto: Consulting Psychologists Press.

Proust, A., 1872. De l'aphasie. *Archives générales de Médecine, 28,* 147–166; 303–318; 653–685.

Quadfasel, F. 1931. Ein Beitrag zum motorischen Verhalten Aphasischer. *Monatschrift für Psychiatrie und Neurologie, 80,* 151–188.

Rieger, C. 1889–1890. Beschreibung der Intelligenzstörungen in Folge einer Hirnverletzung und Entwurf zu einer allgemein andwendbaren Methode der Intelligenz Prüfung. *Verhandlunger der Physikalischen-medizinischen Gesellschaft zur Würzburg. 22,* 65–134; *23,* 95–150.

Rocheford, G., & Williams, M. 1965. Studies in the development and breakdown of the use of names. Part IV: The effect of word frequency. *Journal of Neurology, Neurosurgery, and Psychiatry, 28,* 407–413.

Rubens, A. 1975. Personal communication.

Sarno, M. T. 1969. *The functional communications profile.* In *Rehabilitation Monograph 42.* New York: New York University Medical Center, Institute of Rehabilitation Medicine.

Schmidt, J. B. 1871. Gehörs und Sprachstörung in Folge von Apoplexie. *Allgemeine Archiv für Psychiatrie, 27,* 304–306.

Schuell, H. 1965. *The Minnesota Test for Differential Diagnosis of Aphasia.* Minneapolis: The University of Minnesota Press.

Schuell, H., & Jenkins, J. J. 1961. Reduction of vocabulary in aphasia. *Brain, 84,* 243–261.

Schuell, H., Jenkins, J. J., & Jimenez-Pabón, E. 1964. *Aphasia in adults.* New York: Harper and Row.

Schuell, H., Jenkins, J. J., & Landis, L. 1961. Relationship between auditory comprehension and word frequency in aphasia. *Journal of Speech and Hearing Research, 4,* 30–36.

Shewan, C. M., & Canter, G. J. 1971. Effects on vocabulary, syntax and sentence length on auditory comprehension in aphasic patients. *Cortex, 7,* 209–226.

Smith, M. D. 1974. On the understanding of some relational words in aphasia. *Neuropsychologia, 12,* 377–384.

Spearman, C. E. 1904. "General Intelligence" objectively determined and measured. *American Journal of Psychology, 15,* 201–293.

Spellacy, F. J., & Spreen, O. 1969. A short form of the Token Test. *Cortex, 5,* 390–397.

Spreen, O. 1973. Psycholinguistics and aphasia: The contribution of Arnold Pick. In H. Goodglass and S. Blumstein (Eds.), *Psycholinguistics and aphasia.* Baltimore: Johns Hopkins University Press. Pp. 141–170.

Spreen, O., & Benton, A. L. 1969. *Neurosensory center comprehensive examination for aphasia.* University of Victoria, Dept. of Psychology, Victoria, British Columbia.

Stachowiak, F. S., Huber, W., Poeck, K., & Kerschensteiner, M. In press. Text comprehension in asphasia. *Brain and Language.*

Trabue, M. R. 1916. *Completion-test language scales.* New York: Teachers College Contribution to Education.

Van Dongen, H. R., & Van Harskamp, F. 1972. The Token Test: A preliminary evaluation of a method to detect aphasia. *Psychiatria, Neurologia, Neurochirurgia (Amsterdam)*, 75, 129–134.

Van Wagenen, M. J. 1920. Graded opposites and analogies test. *Journal of Educational Psychology, 11*, 241–263.

Vignolo, L. A. 1965. Evolution of aphasia and language rehabilitation. *Cortex, 1*, 344–367.

Vignolo, L. A. 1973. Afasia. In *Enciclopedia Medica Italiana*. Vol. 1. Firenze: Edizioni Scientifiche. Pp. 845–870.

Von Monakow, C. 1914. *Die Lokalisation in Grosshirn*. Wiesbaden: Bergmann.

Von Stockert, T. R. 1972. Recognition of syntactic structure in aphasic patients. *Cortex, 8*, 323–334.

Von Stockert, T. R. 1974. Aphasia *sine* aphasia. *Brain and Language, 1*, 277–282.

Weisenburg, T., & McBride, K. E. 1935. *Aphasia: A clinical and psychological study*. New York: Commonwealth Fund.

Wernicke, C. 1874. *Der aphasische Symptomenkomplex*. Breslau: Cohn & Weigart. For a translation, see C. Wernicke, 1968, The symptom complex of aphasia, *Boston Studies in the Philosophy of Science, 4*, 34–97.

Wernicke, C. 1908. The symptom-complex of aphasia. In A. Church (Ed.), *Modern clinical medicine*. New York: Appleton.

Wernicke, C. 1968. The symptom complex of aphasia. *Boston Studies in the Philosophy of Science 4*, 34–97.

Whipple, G. M. 1921. *Manual of mental and physical tests*. 3rd ed. Baltimore: Warwick and York. Pp. 79–80.

Whitaker, H. A., & Noll, J. D. 1972. Some linguistic parameters of the Token Test. *Neuropsychologia, 10*, 395–404.

Zurif, E. B., & Caramazza, A. 1976. Psycholinguistic structures in aphasia: Studies in syntax and semantics. In H. Whitaker and H. Whitaker (Eds.), *Studies in neurolinguistics*. Vol. 1. New York: Academic Press.

Zurif, E. B., Caramazza, A., & Myerson, R. 1972. Grammatical judgments of agrammatic aphasics. *Neuropsychologia, 10*, 405–418.

Zurif, E. B., Green, E., Caramazza, A., & Goodenough, C. 1976. Grammatical intuitions of aphasic patients: Sensitivity to functors. *Cortex, 12*, 183–186.

2 Bilingualism and Aphasia

Michel Paradis
McGILL UNIVERSITY

MODES OF RESTITUTION

In surveying the world literature on aphasia in polyglots, one is struck by the diversity of the modes of restitution of the patients' various languages. At least five basic patterns are encountered: synergistic, antagonistic, successive, mixed or selective.

Recovery is said to be synergistic when progress in one language is accompanied by progress in another. It is parallel when the languages are similarly impaired and restored at the same rate, and differential when impairment is of a different degree in each language and restitution occurs at the same or at a different rate (See Figure 2.1).[1]

Parallel recovery, which is what Pitres (1895) thought one ought to expect, seems indeed to be the more common (See Milner, 1964, p. 118; Brain, 1965, p. 118). Studies of 10 consecutive and unselected cases seen at the Neurological

---

[1] Figures 2.1–2.3 are meant to convey only a general notion of the kinds of phenomena reported in the literature. They do not illustrate any specific case, but the general shape that a curve might take in cases exhibiting a particular type of restitution. By *conventional proficiency rating* is meant a rough measure of the patient's approximation, during recovery, of an idealized maximum proficiency in his or her various languages prior to insult (which is itself seldom known with accuracy, as the patient is not typically tested *before* the aphasia). The reliability of these measures varies considerably from one report to the next, assessment being based sometimes on the author's commonsensical judgment alone, sometimes on detailed results of a battery of standardized tests.

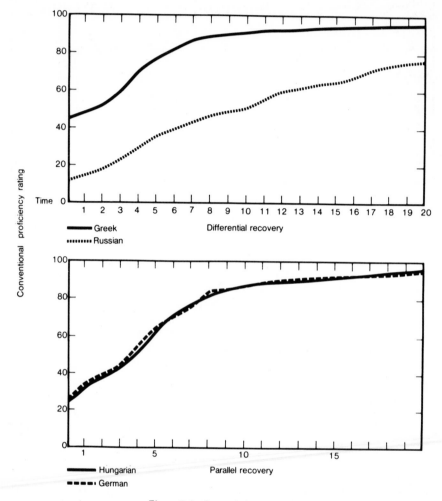

Figure 2.1 Synergistic recovery.

Institute of New York over a 3-month period by Charlton (1964) and of 33 randomly selected dysphasic patients observed by Nair and Virmani (1973) in India report that an average of about 90% of cases exhibited equal impairment with simultaneous restitution of all the languages that were familiar to the patients prior to insult. On the other hand, as Pitres also noted (p. 877), many examples of differential recovery can be found. It was to account for such exceptions that Pitres formulated a few concluding remarks that soon came to be known as *Pitres' rule*. Thus it is inaccurate to speak of a case as "contradicting" or, worse, "disproving" *Pitres' rule,* as some authors have done (L'Hermitte, Hécaen, Dubois, Culioli, Tabouret-Keller, 1966, pp. 315, 328), when the kinds of impairment are identical in all languages spoken by the patient and the recovery of these languages is parallel.

Of 138 cases reported in the literature and surveyed in the present study, 67 were found to follow a synergistic pattern of recovery, of which 56 were parallel and 11 differential. These numbers are not to be taken as representing valid ratios in an unselected population, since most of the published case reports are "interesting" rather than "typical," as pointed out by Charlton (1964). They are useful, nevertheless, in showing that the atypical cases do occur. Table 2.1 lists these cases and indicates type of aphasia and type and rate of recovery in languages spoken by each.

The reader may feel justified in doubting the validity of the linguistic evidence put forward by some of the earlier reports when he reads, for instance, that a patient was puzzled and did not seem to understand such simple questions as "Who are you born [sic] ?" This is no misprint or slip of the pen; the same sentence is found on two separate occasions (Pitres, 1895, pp. 892, 893). If the pronunciation of the examiner matched the grammar, many a nonaphasic might have been puzzled! Moreover, a number of "cases" discussed in the literature of those days are mere hearsay, often reported second or third hand (Bourdin, 1876; Scoresby-Jackson, 1867; Pitres, 1895). Nevertheless, some of these have been included in Table 2.1 because they have often been quoted and thus have become notorious. Some cases of polyglot reactions have been reported in which the patient was neither aphasic nor polyglot (Coppola, 1928)!

Recovery is said to be antagonistic when one language regresses as the other progresses (see Figure 2.2). Of the 138 cases reviewed here, 6 were found to follow such a pattern. For instance, when Minkowski's (1933) patient began to speak, he could express himself more easily in French because he could not find his words in Swiss dialect (his mother tongue and most fluent language before his accident) or in standard German. This condition lasted for a few weeks, during which time, the patient gradually regained normal use of dialect and of standard German, while his French regressed at the same rate.

Winterstein and Meier (1939) observed a Swiss—German female patient suffering from aphasia after a skull fracture. Upon recovery, she uttered her first words in Italian and spoke only this language for the first 4 or 5 days. Then she began to use French. With the improvement of her French, her Italian regressed and disappeared completely. As she began to regain German, two weeks after the accident, her French began to recede.

Shubert (1940) describes antagonistic recovery in a case of bilingual agraphia: The Georgian writing of the patient deteriorated at the same rate at which his Russian writing improved.

TABLE 2.1 Correlation of Patterns of Recovery with Characteristics of Language Recovered

	Parallel	Differential	Successive	Antagonistic	Mixed	Selective	Mother tongue				Most fluent				Surroundings				Type of aphasia
							F	L	B	W	F	L	B	W	F	L	B	W	
Alajouanine et al., 1949		+											+					+	T
Anastasopoulos, 1959	+	+					+		+		+		+		+		+		W X G
Bálint, 1923		+				+			+		+		+						W P R
Bianchi, 1886						+	+				+		+						D
Bonhoeffer, 1902						+	+		+		+				+		+		M X G
Bourdin, 1877										+						+			?
Brissot, 1910										+				+					T
Bychowski, 1919	+	+				+		+		+	+	+			+				M
Charlton, 1964 (1)	+																		N
(2)	+																		N
(4)	+																		M
(5)																			M
(6)	+					+	+		+		+		+						C
(7)						+													C
(8)				+								+	+		+		+		C
(9)	+								+				+		+		+		N
(10)	+							+				+							C
Chlenov, 1958 (1)						+	+		+		+		+		+		+		A
(2)				+									+						S X G
Dedić, 1926			+			+	+		+		+				+		+		C
Denès, 1914						+			+		+		+		+		+		M G
Dimitrijević, 1939																		+	M
Eskridge, 1896								+		+		+		+			+		D
Gerstenbrand, 1956						(+)		+	+	+		+	+	+			+		M

(continued)

	MWP	AWX	SAP	SG	S	M	?	S	SXG	S	G	SG	M	LGX	SM,B	SXG	SPR	?MW	W	?W	?W	?N	SXG	?C	?M	A	W	?	A	?MW	?L	A
Glonging & Gloning, 1965	+				+	+										+				+					+							
(2)A			+					+	+	+	+		+										+		+		+			+		+
(2)B	+				+				+				+										+									
(3)	+							+	+		+		+							+					+							+
(4)	+				+	+				+	+									+							+					+
Goldblum, 1928				+												+									+	+						+
Gorlitzer v. Mundy, 1959	+				+	+					+	+						+														+
Halpern, 1941													+							+	+											+
Halpern, 1949 (2)	+		+	+	+	+	+	+	+		+			+		+						+	+									+
Halpern, 1950 (oral)							+									+	+						+	+								
(written)	+	+		+		+	+	+		+		+		+		+	+						+								+	+
Hécaen et al., 1971							+									+	+						+	+								
Hegler, 1931	+			+		+	+				+			+			+						+									
Herschmann & Pötzl, 1920			+	+			+							+				+	+													+
Hinshelwood, 1902																																
Hoff & Pötzl, 1932											+				+				+	+												
Kauders, 1929	+	+		+			+	+	+	+				+				+	+	+			+							+	+	+
Lambert & Fillenbaum, 1959			+										+		+	+						+	+		+		+					
Ledinský & Mraček, 1958																																

TABLE 2.1 (continued)

Study	Parallel	Differential	Successive	Antagonistic	Mixed	Selective	Mother tongue				Most fluent				Surroundings				Type of aphasia
							F	L	B	W	F	L	B	W	F	L	B	W	
Leischner, 1943	+				+														S G
Leischner, 1948 (2)	+								+	+			+				+		S
(3)	+																		S
L'Hermitte et al., 1966 (1)	+																		M
(2)	+																		M
(3)	+																		S M A G
(4)					+		+												S
(5)								+											S
(6)		+														+			M
(7)		+																	M G
(8)											+								M
Luria, 1960	+									+*				+*					S, G
Lyman et al., 1938		+						+		+		+		+		+		+	X G
Minkowski, 1927 (1)			+			+				+				+				+	M X G
(2)			+			+				+		+				+		+	M
Minkowski, 1928				+	+			+		+		+		+		+			M
Minkowski, 1933		+		+		+	+	+				+				+		+	A W
Minkowski, 1949						+						+	+		+	+	+		A P G X M
Minkowski, 1964									+	+									M
Nair & Virmani, 1973 (1)	31					+			+	+									?
(2)						+													?
Oré, 1878						+	+		+		+		+					+	W X G

70

	S	S	W	M A	M A	S	S M G	?	?	?	?	?	?	A	?	D	?	M	A	M S	S M P	?	?	X G	E	M S	M S A	A	C G	M
Ovcharova et al., 1968	+	+	+	+												+														
(2)								+	+		+	+	+	+		+	+		+		+	+				+	+	+	+	
(3)	+	+	+	+												+					+									
Peter, 1864								+	+		+	+	+	+		+	+		+		+	+				+	+	+		
Peuser, 1974 (1)									+							+										+	+	+		
(2)											+	+	+	+	+			+		+	+		+						+	
Pick, 1903									+							+							+	+	+					
Pick, 1913											+	+	+	+	+			+		+	+									
Pitres, 1895 (1)									+							+	+		+						+	+	+			
(2)	+	+	+	+							+	+	+	+	+	+			+		+	+	+		+				+	
(3)		+														+		+			+				+	+	+			
(4)	+	+	+	+							+	+	+	+	+	+			+		+	+	+							
(5)		+						+	+	+	+	+	+	+	+		+	+		+			+		+					
(6)																+													+	
(7)																						+								
Pötzl, 1925	+						+									+					+	+	+	+						
Proust, 1872	+	+									+	+											+	+	+	+				
Reichmann & Reichau, 1919			+	+		+																							+	
Ribot, 1882																														
Riese, 1928																														
Rinckenbach, 1866																														
Salomon, 1914																														
Schulze, 1968																														
Schwalbe, 1920																														
Scoresby-J., 1867																														
Shubert, 1940																														
Simonyi, 1951																														
Smirnov & Faktorovich, 1949																														
(2)																														
(3)																														
Stengel & Patch, 1955																														
Stengel & Zelmanowicz, 1933																														

(continued)

TABLE 2.1 (continued)

Study	Parallel	Differential	Successive	Antagonistic	Mixed	Selective	Mother tongue F	Mother tongue L	Mother tongue B	Mother tongue W	Most fluent F	Most fluent L	Most fluent B	Most fluent W	Surroundings F	Surroundings L	Surroundings B	Surroundings W	Type of aphasia
Sträussler, 1912			+																A W
Veyrac, 1931			+			+													S
Wald, 1961 1		+		+			+	+			+	+			+	+			M
2					+		+	+	+		+		+		+		+		L M
3							+		+		+		+		+		+		M
4				+		+		+	+			+	+			+	+		M
5	+							+	+				+				+		?
6					+		+		+		+		+		+		+		M
Weisenberg & McBride, 1935				+	+			+	+			+	+			+	+		M
Winslow, 1868				+	+			+	+			+	+				+	+	?
Winterstein & Meier, 1939	+							+	+			+	+			+	+		W P R
Zaorski, 1952								+	+			+	+			+	+		M
Zierer, 1974	+																		M, S

Note: The question of the respective influences upon recovery of the mother tongue, the most fluent language at the time of insult, or the language of the environment not only was mentioned by Lambert and Fillenbaum (1959) but was discussed by eminent aphasiologists at the

1964 Ciba Symposium. Participants seemed to adhere to one or another of the following rules: the best preserved language is the one most needed, and the patient is likely to recover the language of the environment (Bay, 1964); the language first learned returns first (Ross, 1964); the language most practiced is retained best, irrespective of whether it was acquired first or last (Critchley, 1964); or disorganization is similar in every language that a patient was originally able to speak fluently (Hécaen, 1964). Because this question remains open and continues to be considered extremely important, this table includes data as described in the next three paragraphs.

Mother tongue: The language the subject acquired first. When two languages are learned simultaneously, the question of whether the mother tongue was recovered first (F) or last (L), best (B) or worst (W), is not appropriate since either of the languages recovered is a mother tongue.

Most fluent: The language that the patient spoke most fluently at the time of insult. This could be either the mother tongue or a language acquired later. In the case of a balanced bilingual, one who speaks both languages with equal fluency, this criterion does not apply.

Language of surroundings: The language spoken in the community in which the patient lived prior to insult and to which he or she is exposed during convalescence (i.e., the language of the hospital staff). This language may be the same as, or different from, both the patient's mother tongue and his or her most fluent language. When the hospital staff is bilingual or when all of the patient's languages—including that of the surroundings—are recovered in a parallel fashion, the question of whether the language of the surroundings was recovered first or last, best or worst, becomes irrelevant.

The *parallel, differential, successive, antagonistic, mixed,* and *selective* modes of restitution are defined in the introduction to this chapter.

Types of aphasia, or symptoms, as described by various authors, are as follows: A. amnestic; B. word blindness; C. central; D. word deafness; E. echolalia; G. agraphia; L. conduction (*Leitungsaphasie*); M. motor (Broca, expressive); N. nominal; P. paraphasia; R. perseveration; S. sensory (Wernicke, receptive); T. anarthria; W. word finding difficulties; X. alexia; ?. not mentioned, cannot be conclusively ascertained. A comma separating types of aphasia indicates a sequence in time.

"Motor" (M) and "Sensory" (S) are to be interpreted in the broadest possible sense. Some authors refer specifically to their patients as Broca or Wernicke aphasics, others speak of expressive or receptive aphasia. The syndromes covered by a particular label may vary over time: What one author calls, for example, *central aphasia* is not necessarily what another author means to indicate when he uses that term; similarly, not everyone is clear on what is meant by conduction aphasia (see discussion in De Reuck and O'Connor, 1964, pp. 251–252). It is therefore very difficult to assign a type of aphasia to some of the cases.

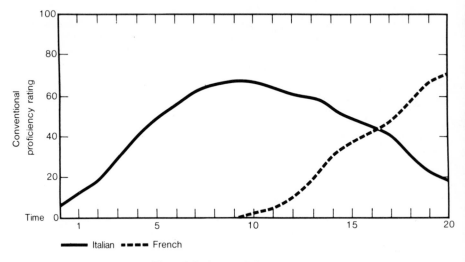

Figure 2.2 Antagonistic recovery.

Chlenov (1948) reports on a German who, after having suffered a trauma to the skull during the Spanish civil war, spoke only English at first. Then, while his native German improved gradually, his English regressed.

Wald (1958) relates the case of a Russian female patient who spoke only English for several days following an apoplectic stroke. During that period, she could understand questions put in Russian but would answer them only in English. Later, her Russian was restored and her English worsened.

Recovery is said to be successive when one language does not begin to reappear until another has been restored (see Figure 2.3). Eight such cases were reported by eight different authors. Rinckenbach (1866) describes the case of an Alsatian officer in the French army who regained some French only after he recovered German. Pick (1903) tells of a patient who began to recover German only after Czech was completely recovered. Reichmann and Reichau's (1919) patient relearned his East Prussian dialect only after his standard German had come back satisfactorily. Likewise, Schwalbe's (1920) patient began to recover German only when Hebrew had been completely restored. Veyrac's (1931) patient did not begin to understand her English mother tongue until she could speak French well again, 5 months after insult. In Ovcharova, Raichev, and Geleva's (1968) Case 2, the patient did not begin to recover Bulgarian until German was almost completely restituted (see also Bastian, 1875).

Reciprocal antagonism may occur after a period of successive restitution. Two or three days after a stroke, Minkowski's (1928) patient began to speak only French. Three weeks later, when he was speaking French quite fluently, the patient began to speak a little standard German and subsequently made slow but

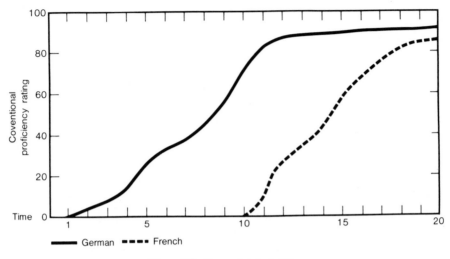

Figure 2.3 Successive recovery.

increasing progress in that language. Three months later, he was able to use some elements of Swiss dialect. Thus six months after insult, the patient spoke fluent and relatively correct French, his standard German was not quite as good as his French, and he could use only very little Swiss dialect. A month later, the patient had made more progress in German and in Swiss dialect, whereas his French had somewhat regressed (see Figure 2.4).

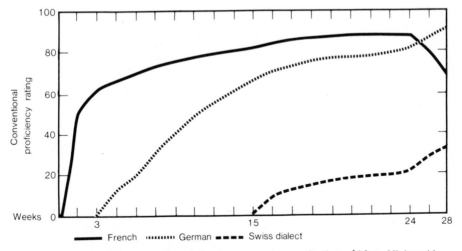

Figure 2.4 Reciprocal antagonism following successive restitution. [After Minkowski, 1928.]

Successive recovery may also be part of a selective restitution pattern. For example, Schulze (1968) describes a patient who recovered first his Bulgarian mother tongue, then German, and then Russian, but recovered neither French nor English.

Recovery is said to be selective when the patient does not regain one or more of his languages; 37 cases that followed a selective pattern of restitution were reported. Of these patients, seven are unambiguously reported as having lost their comprehension as well as their expression of one or more of their languages. Thus Minkowski's (1927) Case 1 lost the comprehension of French and Italian which he used to speak with his colleagues before his accident. Oré's (1878) patient is said to have recovered his dialect but to have remained unable to understand a word of French. Pitres' (1895) first three patients did not regain the use of their respective dialects although they did understand them, whereas his Case 4 recovered French and Spanish but lost even the comprehension of Italian. Case 5 recovered some French but no German, Basque, English, Spanish, or Arabic, all of which he spoke fluently before insult. This patient could recognize which language was being spoken but could not understand what was being said. Case 6 recovered French gradually but could not understand English or German. Case 7 slowly recovered his understanding, and then the use of, French. Four months later, he regained comprehension of his dialect but he could not speak or understand Arabic, Spanish, Italian, or English—not even "good morning!" Finally, Schulze's (1968) patient recovered successively Bulgarian, German, and Russian, but no longer understood French or English.

In the case of Veyrac's (1931) successive recovery, as we have seen, the patient did not begin to understand English again until she could speak French quite correctly.

Sixteen patients are reported to have retained comprehension, that is, they were able to understand what was said to them in at least one of their languages although they were unable to utter a word of it, and sometimes were unable even to repeat a word after several attempts (Bernard, 1885).

In another mode of recovery—probably the most interesting from a linguistic point of view—the bilingual's two languages are intermingled. It is of course not necessary to be recovering from aphasia to mix one's languages; bilinguals who use their two languages in equal proportions do this all the time, especially when speaking with other bilinguals. Pötzl (1930) refers the readers to what he calls the German—Polish—Jewish jargon of Eastern Europe as evidence of this phenomenon (see also Pick, 1915). Another example is the French-speaking Montrealer who works in an English milieu.

Herschmann and Pötzl (1920) hypothesize that two languages of more or less the same strength may struggle with one another for restitution and that this results in mutual interference. This type of interference may be experienced to some extent by nonaphasic polyglots. However, some types of mixing are not generally encountered among normal fluent bilinguals, and certainly not in a systematic way as is the case with some of the patients described. Intermingling has been observed at the levels of syntax, morphology, and phonology and in various ways in writing and reading.

Some patients—not too unlike healthy bilinguals—mix foreign words in their sentences: Pötzl's (1925) Case 2 mixed Czech words with his German mother tongue, which was by far his more fluent language; Minkowski's (1927) patient used expressions in standard German when speaking· Swiss dialect; Kauders' (1929) patient mixed French and English words with his German jargon; for the first 8 months, Halpern's patient mixed Hebrew words with his somewhat agrammatic and paraphasic German; after a second insult, Gloning and Gloning's (1965) Case 2 mixed German, Italian, and Serbocroatian; L'Hermitte *et al.*'s (1966) Case 4 at the outset suffered massive interference, in both syntax and vocabulary, from his English mother tongue on the French that he had been using regularly in his work for 30 years, at the level of syntax as well as vocabulary. Weisenburg and McBride's (1935) English professor of Romance languages often used French or Spanish constructions when speaking or writing English, and when questioned about them he usually failed to recognize that the form was incorrect for English.

Ovcharova *et al.* (1968) relate the case of a patient (Case 3) whose spoken Turkish was almost unimpaired but who spoke Bulgarian with a Turkish accent and used Turkish word order and grammatical structures. Moreover, this patient often replaced Bulgarian with Turkish phrases. Interestingly, whereas in the patient's spoken language, interference was unidirectional, in his written language, interference was reciprocal. He would substitute some Bulgarian (Cyrillic) letters in his Turkish writing, which was the more impaired. The latter phenomenon is by no means unique: Dedić's (1926) patient mixed Latin and Cyrillic value of letters in reading French; Florenskaja's (1940) patient would intermingle Russian and French writing and write "mama*chat*" for мамаша ('mother'); Gloning and Gloning's (1965) Case 3 exhibited polygraphic paragraphia by mixing Cyrillic and Latin letters, which was the more strange because the patient had only learned the Cyrillic alphabet and hardly knew how to read German (with Latin letters). As the condition of the latter patient worsened, he mixed German and Bulgarian words in an agrammatic jargon.

Schulze (1968) also reports contaminations between the Cyrillic and Latin alphabets in the writing of his patient. The same patient, made to repeat the word "consciousness" in English produced "conscious . . . *heit* . . . *ung*" (-*heit* and -*ung* are two German morphemes equivalent to the English "-ness,"), demonstrating interference at the level of bound morphemes—and this in a repetition task! Stengel and Zelmanowicz (1933) report an equally unusual case of inflexional substitution: Their patient spoke German but used Czech word endings.

Perhaps the most striking is the mixing within individual words which occurs in repetition or dictation tasks. Gloning and Gloning's (1965) Case 4 would say "heftag", a blend from Hungarian *heftö* and German *Montag* 'Monday'; "zwettö" from German *zwei* and Hungarian *ketto* 'two'; "Zwörpo" from German *Zwerg* and Hungarian *törpe* ("dwarf"). To the dictation of *schreiben* ('to write'), the patient wrote "schrini," from German *schreiben* and Hungarian *irni*. Similarly, Leischner's (1943) deaf–mute patient who jargonized with his hands sometimes blended Czech and German words in his writing. Under dictation, the patient wrote "ochor," a mixture of German *Ahorn* and Czech *javor* ('maple tree'); "mehrech" from Czech *mléko* and Germany *Milch*; ('milk'); "jahno" from German *ja* and Czech *ano* ('yes'); and "pkrgen" from Czech *pršeti* and German *regnen* ('rain').

Other forms of mixing are exemplified in various interferences with pronunciation: We have seen that Ovcharova *et al.* (1968) described a patient who spoke Bulgarian with a Turkish accent after insult; Stengel and Zelmanowicz's (1933) patient spoke German with a characteristic Czech intonation; Minkowski's (1927) patient used German intonations while speaking Swiss dialect; L'Hermitte *et al.*'s (1966) Case 8, at the beginning of his recovery, had lost the characteristic prosody of his Hungarian mother tongue; and Weisenburg and McBride's (1935) scholar (Case 4, mentioned above) not only made mistakes in pronunciation in all his languages but was unable to maintain the characteristic inflection of each. When writing words to dictation, the same patient sometimes slipped over from the English word to a similar word from one of his Romance languages (i.e., *correspondence → correspondance*).

The search for a pattern of restitution began with Ribot (1882) and Pitres (1895) who were interested to discover why one of several languages was preferentially recovered. On the basis of very little evidence (e.g., Hutchinson's (1799) account of a physician who had in early life renounced the principles of the Roman Catholic Church and who, during an attack of delirium preceding his death, "prayed only in the forms of the Church of Rome, all recollection of the prescribed formulae of the Protestant religion being obliterated"; Rush's (1812) sketchy descriptions of one case of yellow fever, one of temporary insanity, and one of trauma following a blow on the head, as well as his report of old Swedes who used to pray in Swedish on their death beds, after having presumably forgotten the language following 50 to 60 years of disuse), Ribot (1882, p. 183) concluded that the selective return of the mother tongue was merely a particular case of the law of regression, which states that the most recent formations of memory are the first destroyed and that the oldest acquisitions are the most stable and thus the most resistant to morbid dissolution. This was often to be cited as "Ribot's rule," also referred to as the "primacy rule" (Lambert & Fillenbaum, 1959), according to which the linguistic habits acquired in early childhood are more resistant to aphasic damage than those acquired subsequently, irrespective of their relative degree of fluency at the time of insult.

However, only two cases that unequivocally support this hypothesis have been reported (Winslow, 1868; Minkowski, 1964). The fact that in all other cases the mother tongue was in at least as current use as the more impaired language suggests that, rather than the primacy rule, the principle of *habit strength* stressed by Pitres (1895) and many of his followers may explain the nature of selective language recovery.

Reviewing a somewhat larger sample of cases than Ribot's, including eight of his own, Pitres (1895) noted not only that not all languages were restituted to an equal degree over the same period of time but that, in cases of selective restitution, it was not always the mother tongue that was recovered. Rather, more often, the patient would preferentially recover the language that was most familiar to him, which was in fact usually the mother tongue, but not necessarily so.

It has also been observed that sometimes the language preferentially recovered is neither the mother tongue nor the most fluent language but the language of the patient's milieu, that is, the language spoken by the hospital staff. However, no single characteristic of the language preferentially restituted seems to be the determining factor of its recovery: At least 27 patients have been reported as having clearly recovered their mother tongue first, but 27 recovered it last. Although 18 recovered first the language most familiar to them, 23 recovered first a less fluent language, in some cases the least familiar to them (Hegler, 1931; Smirnov & Faktorovich, 1949). Seven patients recovered the language of their surroundings, which was neither their mother tongue nor their most fluent language. On the other hand, six patients did not recover the language of their surroundings even though it was both their mother tongue and most fluent language. In all, 25 patients recovered the language of their surroundings, but 16 recovered a different tongue. Three patients preferentially recovered a language which was neither their mother tongue, nor their most fluent language, nor that of the surroundings. For many weeks after insult, a German-speaking patient in Germany could speak only Hebrew, which he had never used as colloquial speech (Schwalbe, 1920). Again in Germany, a German recovered French, which he had learned in his youth but had not much practiced since (Sträussler, 1912), and a colonel in the Austrian army recovered not German but the Italian which he had acquired as a youth (Hoff & Pötzl, 1932a,b). Grasset (1884) reports the case of a devout woman in her sixties who had never learned Latin but who attended numerous Catholic services conducted in Latin, and who, after a stroke, could utter only incoherent Latin phrases. It is therefore apparent that factors other than primacy, fluency, or usefulness are at play.

Other characteristics of the languages have been invoked as being responsible for their preferential recovery: the fact that a language was the last used before insult (Herschmann & Pötzl, 1920; Kauders, 1929; Hegler, 1931; Kainz, 1960) or the fact that a language was the first spoken to the patient upon his regaining consciousness (Bychowski, 1919). A number of other factors of restitution, which have emerged from several aphasiologists' attempts at ad hoc explanations of specific cases, will be discussed in the following paragraphs.

The Psychological Factor

Minkowski (1927) partially explains his first patient's preferential recovery of standard German over his more current, native Swiss dialect by the patient's close ("though proper!") relationship with his German-speaking landlady who visted him every day during his convalescence, as well as by his negative attitude toward his dialect-speaking relatives, whom he felt had neglected him, and toward a Swiss girl who had disappointed him in love several years previously. Another factor sometimes may be a patient's desire to improve his status by using high class, or standard, German. Minkowski's second patient, also a German Swiss, recovered French apparently as the result of strong motivation: He was teaching in a French university. Minkowski concludes that psychological factors, mostly affective, may interfere in the course of the development of an aphasia and determine the particular language of recovery.

In 1928, Minkowski presented a new case that reinforced the theory: After an apoplectic stroke, a 44-year-old native speaker of Swiss dialect, married to a German Swiss like himself and living in Alemanic Switzerland, recovered neither Swiss dialect nor standard German, but French, and thus could not be understood even by his wife. Having been initiated into the concepts of psychoanalysis, as he puts it, Minkowski asked the patient questions about his private life and discovered that his first and most passionate love had been a French girl with whom he had lived two of the happiest years of his life, when he was in his early twenties. Minkowski (1949) also relates the case of a Swiss patient who did not speak dialect for the first 4 months after insult and spoke only standard German. When he did begin to speak some dialect again, he would relapse into German every time his wife (with whom he had always gotten along poorly) voiced satisfaction at his progress. After having reviewed the above material, Minkowski (1965) concludes that psychosexual and psychosocial components of affective and emotional factors are capable, through a powerful psycho-neuro-biological dynamic force, of playing a decisive role in the struggle for the selection of the particular language to be used, and that language may very well be at times paradoxical and ill-adapted if called for by a special set of psycho-physio-pathological conditions.

Winterstein and Meier (1939) also attribute to psychological factors the fact that their German Swiss patient spoke only Italian (her third language) for the first few days of her recovery: Shortly before her accident, for a period of 6 weeks, she had enjoyed the visit of a girl friend who could speak only Italian.

According to Krapf (1955), the first language to be recovered is that which subjectively meets with the least resistance. Such resistance may originate in the patient's life history, for example, in his attitude toward a mother figure or in his relationships, during the period preceding the aphasia, with persons or groups of persons with whom contact is resumed later. In each of the five cases described by Krapf, the patient is inclined to use the language that is least likely to cause him anxiety, that provides him with the most security, and strengthens his super-ego. Krapf (1957) argues that restitution of the mother tongue may depend on the nature of the patient's relationship with his mother in infancy. Krapf (1961) reiterates that the preferential use of a language by a polyglot aphasic is a function primarily of the emotional significance of that language for the patient in terms of his past life history and his present life situation. The affective meanings to the patient of his various languages will influence their respective recoveries.

Gerstenbrand and Stepan (1956) also stress the role of the psychological antecedents of the patient: affective and instinctive factors are considered important. They agree with Krapf (1955a) that the patient tends to recover preferentially the language that is most likely to cause him minimal anxiety and to give him the greatest feeling of security. For their patient, Czech was linked with unhappy experiences whereas German was associated with security, calmness, professional success, and the good relationship he had with his second wife. German had endowed him with a way of warding off anything pertaining to his unhappy youth and first half of his life. Thus, because it was associated with a better life, German was preferentially recovered. Charlton (1964) concedes that one reason for preferring one language over another may be that it is associated with emotionally charged events, and, according to Jakobson (1964), "sometimes, particularly in women, it is the language with which in the past the strongest emotional experience was connected" that will prevail.

The Visual Factor

Minkowski (1927) had also noticed that a number of his patients would recover standard German over their current and usually more fluent native dialect. In addition to the possible psychological motivations already mentioned, another factor drew his attention: Standard German, which is learned in the school, can be written as well as spoken, whereas dialect is spoken only. At least in those days, dialect was rarely written or read. Minkowski's first patient volunteered the information that he found standard German easier because he could visualize the written word. In fact, this patient recovered some dialect when he was made to practice it through writing. Minkowski's second patient recovered French, also through reading and writing exercises, whereas Swiss dialect remained unavailable to him to the end of his life. This finding underlines the importance of the visual element of·language in the retrogression of aphasic symptoms: When the neurological correlates of reading and writing are not affected, as is often the case in Broca's aphasia, the visual element of language may facilitate the restitution of other elements of a standard language; it cannot be of any help in recovering a dialect that is spoken but not written.

Halpern (1941, 1949) reports two cases of patients who had studied Hebrew in the traditional fashion, from the written text, long before using it as a spoken language, and who preferentially recovered it over their native German and Russian, respectively. Halpern concludes that in some cases, restitution of a language is facilitated by the fact that it had been acquired through written form. A lesion to the temporal lobe will damage that part of the cortex which is the locus of acoustic engrams but will not interfere with the visual memory of words. A similar situation is reported by Hinshelwood (1902), who describes the case of an English scholar who recovered differentially, after word blindness that followed complete aphasia, each of his four languages: Greek, Latin, French, and English, in that order. The patient could read Greek correctly and with little difficulty, Latin not quite as correctly as Greek, and French not as well as Latin but much better than English. The two classical languages, which he had learned through reading and writing, were less affected (the Greek hardly at all) than the language he learned from both the written text and the spoken word (French) and less affected even than his English mother tongue, which he had learned by hearing and speaking long before he mastered it in written form.

In the cases of the two patients described by Halpern, there may be an additional factor at play. Hebrew is written without vowels; thus written signs do not correspond as closely to the spoken sounds as they do in European languages. Individual Hebrew words can be read only when the global meaning of the entire sentence is known. It is not possible to read Hebrew automatically and without reflecting, as it is possible to read languages like Russian or German. For example, if English were spelled without vowels, the sequence "rt" could stand for *rite, rote, rate, root, irate, rota, orate, aorta,* and so forth. Yet, in spite of this apparent difficulty, both of Halpern's patients read Hebrew easily and correctly, whereas their reading of German and Russian was deficient.

A third patient, described in more detail in Halpern (1950), recovered his English mother tongue first and no longer understood a word of Hebrew (cf. Ajuriaguerra & Hécaen, 1960; Hécaen & Angelergues, 1965). But in order to communicate again with his children he resolved to relearn the language and devoted his whole attention to this purpose. He had to look for the meaning of every word that he heard and to rehearse the word repeatedly during the day. Five months later, though his acoustic comprehension of the English spoken word was better than that of the Hebrew spoken word, his comprehension of writing was incomparably better for Hebrew than for English. Similarly, writing from dictation was considerably worse in English than in Hebrew. Yet, before his accident, the patient had been used to reading a great many English newspapers and books.

A third element may yet intervene. Professor Feigenbaum, head of the ophthalmology ward of the Rothschild–Hadassah Hospital of the University of Jerusalem (quoted as a personal communication by Halpern, 1941), has observed that patients with right hemianopia who speak both Hebrew and German generally read Hebrew, which is written from right to left, much more easily than they read German script, which is written from left to right.

Luria (1956) also notes that the degree of disturbance in the reading and writing of polyglot aphasics may vary as a function of the writing systems of various languages. Such systems range from those that are most phonetic, such as Russian and German, in which letters correspond closely to sounds, through those that are increasingly ideographic, in which letters, or characters, may correspond little or not at all to sounds: for example, in decreasing order of such correspondence, French, English, and Chinese. In patients who have lesions of the temporal lobe, in the auditory cortex, phonetic spelling suffers the most, whereas in patients with lesions of the occipito-parietal regions, ideographic writing is most impaired while phonetic writing may be preserved. Lyman, Kwan, and Chao (1938) reported such a case, in which a Chinese patient suffered alexia and agraphia following the removal of a cerebral tumor, which process caused a lesion limited to the left parieto-occipital region. Thanks to his intact auditory and motor speech functions, the patient's writing was less impaired in English than in his Chinese mother tongue. There have also been reports of cases of differential impairment of the reading and writing of *kana* and *kanji* in Japanese patients (Sasanuma & Fujimura 1971, 1972; Sasanuma 1975), *kana* being syllabic representations and *kanji* being ideogrammatic symbols derived from Chinese. Peuser & Leischner (1974) observed a case of dissociation between ordinary spelling and phonetic transcription in a German-English bilingual philologist.

In the same patient, alexia may be less severe than agraphia in such languages as French, where the same combination of letters will quite consistently yield the same pronunciation but where the same sound can be spelled in a multitude of ways. (Whereas in English, for example, the combination *ou* is pronounced in a variety of ways, as in the words *enough, through, though,* and *about,* in French the combination *eau* is always pronounced /o/, and *ou* always /u/. But the sound /o/ may be represented as in *p<u>o</u>t, b<u>eau</u>, cr<u>o</u>c, c<u>ô</u>ne, c<u>au</u>se, tr<u>o</u>p,* etc., and /so/ may be represented as in *sot(s), seau(x), sceau(x), saut(s),* etc.) Luria (1960) describes a patient, a 42-year-old French journalist, who could speak French, Polish, German, and Russian equally well before he was hit by a shell fragment in the left inferior parietal region. After an operation to remove a conglomeration of encapsulated bone fragments, performed 9 years later, the patient did not speak for 6 months but understood what was said to him. He then began to improve gradually but continued to have difficulties in speaking and reading, to an equal degree in all of his languages. However, in writing, he showed a marked differentiation: his Russian (which has a basically phonetic orthography) was almost undisturbed, but his French, which he must have known somewhat better than Russian, having been for many years on the staff of a French newspaper, contained a great many errors.

The Automaticity Factor

Freud (1891) considered degree of practice of a language one of only two factors that determined the character of speech disorders in the polyglot. (The other was age of acquisition of a language.) Bastian (1875) observed that, during recovery, immigrants were at first only able to express themselves in that language in which they were most automatically versed—namely, in their native tongue. According to Pick (1921), the order of recovery goes from the language that was most automatic to the language that was the least automatic at the time of insult. The most mechanized (*mechanisierten*) language is recovered first. Something acquired later to a high degree of automaticity can supersede something that is similarly automatic but that was acquired earlier. Practice (*Übung*) plays an important role. Bálint (1923) echoes this view: The automatization (*Automatisierung*) of some verbal material before aphasia may cause its reappearance during recovery. Bálint seeks to explain Schwalbe's (1920) patient's recovery of Hebrew by the fact that ritual prayers (said in Hebrew) had received the greatest practice. Dedić (1926) explains the fact that his patient recovered his Russian mother tongue faster and performed better in it by the fact that the speech mechanisms had been rehearsed more in that language. According to Dedić, words which are most often used in everyday life are best implanted ("*imprägniert*") in the speech center and are the first recovered. Kainz (1960) is of the same opinion: The language that is most mechanized at the time of insult seems to be the first, the most easily, and the most fully recovered. Or, as Quadfasel (1963) put it, improvement occurs first and most completely in "the language most automatized." In other words, Pitres' rule that the language most practiced before injury will be preferentially recovered is still considered applicable in most cases of differential restitution.

This pattern seems evidenced in other cases, among them Stengel and Patch's (1955) second patient, whose spontaneous speech and understanding of French and German, both of which he had once spoken fluently, were similarly impaired and to a greater extent than his speech and comprehension of English, his more currently practiced language. Ledinský and Mraček (1958) identify a group of polyglots for whom the first language to improve was the one each patient was using most frequently at the time of injury, and they describe one of the patients in that group at some length.

Leischner (1948) emphasizes relative degree of proficiency: When foreign languages have not been completely mastered, he suggests, they tend to be more impaired. According to Leischner, languages are restituted to a degree proportionate to their fluency prior to insult. However, some authors have claimed that preference is not decided by a patient's proficiency in a language (Krapf, 1955a). Charlton (1964) insists that all languages have an equal chance of coming back "however tenuous the grip on the second language." Gelb (1937) even claims that sometimes a foreign language, or better still, a classical language, may be recovered over the mother tongue, precisely because it is less automatic and demands a greater effort of reflection. Such mental effort may stimulate the injured mechanism where the mother tongue is insufficient.

The Severity Factor

Pötzl (1925) dealt again with the case that had been previously described in Herschmann and Pötzl (1920), and which would be further discussed in Pötzl (1930): the case of a Czech patient who had spoken only Czech until he moved to Vienna at age 14. There he learned to speak German fluently, used it at home as well as outside the home for the next 46 years, and became a balanced bilingual. At age 60 he suffered a mild stroke, followed by a quick recovery of both languages in the same manner and to the same extent; but after a second, more serious stroke 6 months later, the patient recovered only Czech. Thus it appeared to Pötzl that degree of severity had something to do with the mode of restitution. On the basis of this argument, as well as of his own experience, and in accordance with Pick (1921), Minkowski (1936) hypothesizes that there probably exists in the brain a functional substratum common to all languages stored therein, and that, particularly in conditions of global weakening in aphasia (though also to a certain extent in normal subjects; see Epstein, 1915), only a limited number of linguistic functions are available to the polyglot patient. The manner in which these functions are distributed among the different languages is governed, Minkowski suggests, by affective dynamics and by principles of biological economy as well as by reflex interferences, antagonistic innervations, and the like. By 1963, Minkowski is convinced that "if centres of speech are severely affected the polyglot is restricted, at least temporarily, to the use of one language instead of two or more" (p. 144), because in a severely damaged organism subjected to the "general neural physiopathological laws," it may not be functionally possible for two languages to coexist at an equal level (Minkowski, 1965).

Halpern (1949, 1950) concurs with the opinion that when the cortical structures connected with linguistic functions are severely damaged the patient adjusts to speaking one language only. Krapf (1957) claims to have demonstrated that the aphasic polyglot's choice of language of recovery is less free to the degree that the brain functions less well (see Krapf 1955a, b). Charlton (1964) concedes that, in a severe case, a patient may concentrate on one language in order to economize his resources; this is a psychological reaction of defense against the catastrophic impairment of an important faculty, a mechanism not needed in mild impairment. That this need not always be the case is evidenced by Zierer's (1974) patient, a 5-year-old child who had mastered German and Spanish and was considered a balanced bilingual. Twelve days after the surgical removal of a brain tumor, the young patient began to develop a motor aphasia, followed by a receptive aphasia, which gradually became total. As these symptoms evolved and the aphasia became progressively more severe, the patient showed increasing but parallel impairment in both languages which continued to be parallel until his comprehension and production had ceased entirely.

The Appropriateness Factor

Goldstein (1948) acknowledges that a number of functional factors determine the language preferentially recovered, but he seeks to learn why the patient's progress is determined in a particular situation by one or another of the factors observed by different authors and which we have discussed above. Indeed, progress seems determined by different factors at different times. The patient's behavior seems to reflect a kind of selection, which is determined by the fact that the patient will try to use that language which appears "the best for his purpose," the "most appropriate" to help him, by means of language, to come to terms with the situation with which he is faced at a given moment. This position amounts to declaring appropriateness the superseding factor since it controls which factor or set of factors will be allowed to operate in selecting the pattern of restitution. In fact, the language available may depend on the subject matter to be discussed (Bálint, 1923) or the ethnic origin of the interlocutor (Herschmann & Pötzl, 1920), in short, on the habitual use of a specific language in a given situation (Krapf, 1955b).

Bay (1964) also maintains that the best preserved language is that which is most needed, and Charlton (1964) tries to explain the selection of English, during a period of severe central aphasia, by a German patient—even when addressing his wife, with whom he had always spoken German before his illness—by the fact that the patient may have felt that the use of English, the language of the hospital environment, "offered the better means of communication and hope of assistance."

On the other hand, as we have seen, several cases have been reported in which the language most meaningful to the patient, which would have enabled him to communicate with those about him, including his relatives and the hospital staff, was more severely impaired or selectively lost while another, less immediately useful language, was recovered (See also Table 2.1, "language of the surroundings"). Similarly, van Thal (1960) reports the case of an Englishman who, after considerable spontaneous recovery following a cerebral vascular accident, complained that French words kept presenting themselves, and that he had to inhibit them consciously. He could not account for this: He did not know the language very well, did not use it in business, and did not seem to have had any memorable experiences during his short holidays in France (see also Adler, 1889, p. vii).

The Multiple Factors View

A number of other factors of preferential restitution have been invoked: the intellectual level of the patient (Leischner, 1948) and his degree of literacy, in particular the extent to which reading and writing played a role in his daily life (Anastasopoulos, 1959).

Very early, however, it became apparent that no single factor could explain all the different patterns of recovery and that in fact there are no fixed rules that hold for all cases, not even for all cases in which conditions have been similar (Weisenburg & McBride, 1935). Some authors came to consider the differential restitution of languages as not being rule-governed at all (Salomon, 1914).

Indeed there is no single law which governs the deterioration or improvement of the various languages of the polyglot aphasic (Wald, 1961), for no factor can be considered in isolation to be the cause of the individual picture. Rather, relative proficiency, the outer world conditions, the milieu in which one speaks, the differential use one makes of languages according to topic, as well as all the other factors that have been observed by various authors are to be taken into consideration (Goldstein, 1948). A combination of factors of a different nature work simultaneously (Minkowski, 1933). They may reinforce each other, for example, in Halpern's (1941) case, where affective factors (a dislike for German coupled with the religious and cultural appeal of Hebrew) supported the influence of a neurophysiological factor (an intact visual associative cortex favoring the restitution of the language that had been learned through reading), or there may be antagonism between them.

In the face of the extreme individual variability of clinical, psychopathological, neuropathological, linguistic, and social features of individual cases of aphasia in polyglots, as emphasized by Minkowski (1963), one is easily convinced that several factors interact—so many in fact that it may be impossible to disentangle them for the purpose of formulating a rule with any sort of predictive value. The conservative conclusion reached by Lambert and Fillenbaum (1959) is that the particular pattern of restitution depends in some complex fashion on "the order in which the languages were learned, the comparative levels of skill attained in each, and the affective value each language has for the individual." If we add to these the site and size of the lesion (Wald, 1961; Pötzl, 1930), the role of physiological factors (Winterstein & Meier, 1939), and the general biological condition of the patient (Minkowski, 1927) we have a very complex picture indeed.

THE SWITCH MECHANISM

Whatever the characteristics of the language that is preferentially recovered— whether it is the mother tongue, the most fluent language, that of the surround-ings, or the language which has particular emotional overtones—an important question remains: Why is one language restituted to the exclusion of all others? In some selective cases, although the patient is able to express himself quite adequately in one language, the aphasia is total for one or more of his other languages, in which he may not even understand "good morning" or "how are you?" For lack of a linguistic, psychological, or sociological explanation, aphasiologists have looked for a cortical correlate of selectivity in restitution. This problem has given rise to three basic theories: (*1*) The unrecovered language is not lost but inhibited; (*2*) there is a locus in the brain that acts as a switch mechanism which allows the patient to shift from one language to another; and (*3*) each language is stored in a different location in the brain.

The latter hypothesis has not found many supporters. Russell (1858) had alluded to Cardinal Mezzofanti's ability to hold his various languages distinct from each other to the point that it would almost seem as if his memory were divided into compartments, in which the several vocabularies could be stored apart. Russell however, was speaking metaphorically and made no attempt to correlate this psychological phenomenon with any particular part or parts of the brain. Scoresby-Jackson (1867), relates the story by Abercrombie who had it from Beattie, of an Englishman who, after a blow on the head, lost his knowledge of Greek and appeared to have lost nothing else. The author asks, "Where was that gentleman's Greek deposited that it could be blotted out by a single stroke, whilst his native language and all else remained?"

Pitres (1895) argues at length against Scoresby-Jackson's alleged hypothesis that, since the whole apparatus used to learn the mother tongue is contained, according to Broca, in the foot of the third frontal convolution, the rest of the convolution should remain available for the acquisition of other languages. Scoresby-Jackson himself had given this as "mere speculation," as one of three possible ways of explaining the function of the anterior part of the left frontal convolution, leaving it to physiology and pathology to confirm one or the other in the future. Yet Pitres thought the issue important enough to devote his third "rule" to it: "It is not necessary to postulate the totally hypothetical existence of new centres specifically assigned to each of the languages successively learned by polyglot subjects."

Although no one actually held this view, authors continued to argue against it and to refute it: Pötzl (1925) denies the existence of a separate center for each individual language; Minkowski (1927) insists that different languages are represented in common areas of the cortex; Veyrac (1931) agrees that there is no special locus in the brain devoted to foreign languages, and he is followed in this by Ombredane (1951); finally, Penfield (1953) categorically denies that there is a separate neuronal mechanism for each language set up in different speech areas of the cortex. When more than one language is learned, according to Penfield, the speech areas of the dominant hemisphere take them all on without geographical separation. Again 6 years later, Penfield and Roberts (1959) reaffirm that there is no evidence for the supposition that one anatomical area of the brain is used for one language and a separate area for another: the mechanism that is developed in the brain is the same whether one, two, or more languages are learned. More recent research confirms that there is no evidence for anatomical separation of languages within the brain (Minkowski, 1963; Gloning & Gloning, 1965).

The first hypothesis—that the unrecovered language is not lost but inhibited—is the more widely accepted and is consistent with the general laws of excitation, interference, and inhibition between neural phenomena of any kind (Minkowski, 1963). Pitres (1895) had already suggested that differential restitutions were not caused by organic destruction of physiologically specialized centres and that they seemed more likely due to functional disturbances. Selective impairment is not caused by damage to the stored language itself but by an incapacity to retrieve what is stored. Several facts argue in favor of this hypothesis. (*1*) In many cases, the patient retains comprehension though he is unable to utter a word in that language (see above, p. 76), and thus the cause of selective aphasia cannot be the destruction of the traces or engrams (Pick, 1921). (*2*) The loss of a language, sometimes of both comprehension and expression, is often only temporary, and after a certain period the language returns at a rate too fast to reflect relearning (Halpern, 1941). (*3*) Neurotic patients without gross cerebral lesions exhibit the same kind of polyglot reactions (Ghilarducci, 1892; Krapf, 1955b; Gerstenbrand & Stepan, 1956). (*4*) The unavailable languages do return during special states such as delirium (Eskridge, 1896) or epileptic fits, or under hypnosis (Ghiladucci, 1892).

Thus when one language does not return, it is not because the language as such has been forgotten but because it has been temporarily or permanently inhibited (Kainz, 1960). During a state of delirium or soon after an epileptic attack, various types of inhibition are suspended (as evidenced, e.g., in exaggerated reflexes) and hence it is not unreasonable to suppose that previously inhibited languages are similarly disinhibited under the same conditions. We may further suppose that during certain neuropathological conditions, only one language is enabled to function (for whatever reasons, chosen from among those previously spoken by the patient) and that others are inhibited by the same general neural process of inhibition that, under conditions of normal health, alternately inhibits one or the other language during speech.

The hypothesis that language A is inhibited while language B is in use, and that in some pathological states, this inhibition remains permanent, is compatible with, but independent of, the postulation of an anatomically localized mechanism that would enable switching from one language to another. The hypothesis has given rise to two interpretations, one localizationist, the other functionalist.

It appeared to Pötzl (1925) that there was a connection between damage to the left supramarginal gyrus and selective recovery, and Kauders (1929) agreed that this cortical area appeared to play the role of a distributing device (*Verteiler*), allowing transition from one language to the next. Pötzl (1930) further observed a correlation between injury to the posterior part of the Sylvian fissure and to the adjacent part of the parietal lobe and the patient's inability to use more than one language. He concluded that under normal conditions, this area facilitates the switching to the language required. This region, he insists, is not the center for a particular language, but has something to do with multilingualism and the gift of tongues. Hoff and Pötzl (1932a, b) were confirmed in that belief by a post mortem, microscopic examination of the brain of their patient (See also Pötzl, 1932). Leischner (1948) reached a similar conclusion: Based on seven published autopsy reports and on one personal observation, he deduced that superior linguistic capacities have an anatomo-physiological correlate in a highly developed configuration and increased surface of the posterior parts of the second and third temporal convolutions. Leischner also localizes the postulated switch mechanism in the supramarginal gyrus: damage to this region causes the patient either to speak only one language or to switch involuntarily from one language to another.

And yet, 15 years earlier, Stengel and Zelmanowicz' (1933) had already pointed out—based on their EEG findings, on specific neurological symptoms, and on kind of aphasia—that it was obvious that their patient, who spoke a mixture of Czech and German after insult, had a lesion in the *anterior* speech area. This was a clear exception to Pötzl's hypothesis. Since Pötzl's presentation of his theory, two sets of findings contradictory to his have been published, one that reports switching difficulties or mixing where the temporo-parietal region is intact (Minkowski, 1927; Stengel & Zelmanowicz, 1933; Gloning & Gloning, 1965: four polyglot reactions without posterior lesions; L'Hermitte *et al.*, 1966: two cases) and another that records instances of a damaged left temporo-parietal region without switching disturbances (Gloning & Gloning, 1965: five posterior lesions without polyglot reactions; L'Hermitte *et al.*, 1966; Schulze, 1968). In 1965, Kainz still felt that there must be in the dominant hemisphere a mechanism which permits switching from one language to another and which can be selectively damaged. However, this need not be an anatomically localized mechanism, as we shall see.

In fact, the capacity to switch need not be a faculty peculiar to the polyglot. It may be a more general function put to this particular use, a function served not by some mechanism specific to the polyglot, anatomically localizable, and nonexistent in the brains of persons who speak only one language. The decision to speak in English or in Russian is surely of the same order as the decision to speak at all or to remain silent, or the decision to wiggle one's little finger or to keep it still. The decision to switch from one language to another, just like the decision to speak in a particular language in the first place, is more economically explained by the functioning of a general neural mechanism than by a special mechanism for that specific purpose alone. There is no need to postulate an anatomical localization or even a specific functional organization, other than that which every speaker already possesses and which allows him, among other things, to switch registers within the same language.

Goldstein (1948) appears to be right in denying the validity of the assumption that ease of switching between languages depends on the localization of the lesion. Gloning and Gloning (1965) have established that there is no statistically significant correlation between a lesion in the angular or supramarginal gyrus, or in T_1, T_2, or T_3 and polyglot reactions, that is to say, selective restitution or mixing. Goldstein (1933) had already pointed out that, with any alteration of cerebral function, it becomes more difficult to make an abrupt change in one's style of mental processing (*attitude mentale*). The capacity for switching from one language to another can be maintained only if the faculty of abstraction is preserved. According to Jakobson (1955), aphasics with "similarity disorders," for example, lose their capacity for translation; hence, code switching of bilingual patients becomes totally impaired. Although they correlate interference problems with sensory aphasia, L'Hermitte *et al.* (1966) also argue against any connection between voluntary change of code and the lesion of any anatomical zone.

BILINGUALISM AND LATERALIZATION OF SPEECH FUNCTIONS

Halpern's (1949) third patient, described again at length in English in Halpern (1950), after recovering only English for the first 2 months after insult, painstakingly relearned Hebrew in order to be able to communicate with his children. Eventually, although his comprehension of spoken English remained better than that of Hebrew, the patient's comprehension of written Hebrew surpassed that of English, and he could also write Hebrew considerably better than English. As we have already seen (p. 82), Halpern attributed the restitution of Hebrew in this case partly to its triple visual significance (quasi-ideogrammatic spelling, without vowels; the presumed relationship between the patient's right hemianopia and his ability to read better from right to left; and the fact that he had learned Hebrew from books rather than colloquially), which may have caused the engrams to be preserved in the visual associative cortex. In addition, because the patient was definitely left-handed but had been urged in his childhood to write with his right hand, the author assumed that whereas the original language center was in the right hemisphere, the writing exercises may have led to some crossing and this, in turn, to the activation of an additional language center in the left hemisphere. It was the latter center that was damaged, presumably leaving the engrams for spoken English in the right temporal region intact. Minkowski (1963) attributes the restoration of Hebrew in this patient to relearning, made possible by an active participation of the preserved right hemisphere.

In a somewhat similar situation, Anastasopoulos (1959) is also led to assume that not all the speech functions of his patient were localized in the same hemisphere, and that some must have been mediated through the patient's originally nondominant hemisphere. Following a stroke at age 45, this patient suffered aphasia with severe word finding difficulties, alexia, and agraphia, but he retained excellent comprehension in all his successively acquired languages: Greek Pontin dialect, standard Greek, Russian, and Turkish. The patient did not make syntactic or other grammatical mistakes, but he had to search at length for the right word, which he would recognize immediately when told it, and he understood immediately and without difficulty whatever was said to him, even the most complicated utterances. Thus, considering the strong and obstinate alexia and agraphia of this patient, combined with the absence of word deafness in his speech disturbances, the author thinks it likely that, following a fall from a horse at age 7, which had caused the patient injury to the left side of the head, whatever language function was lateralized at that time, perhaps comprehension and some spontaneous speech, had remained in the left hemisphere, whereas written language and other language skills learned subsequently were established in the homologous parts of the healthy right hemisphere.

Bychowski (1919) also thinks that the right hemisphere played an essential role in the restoration of his patient's languages. According to him, Russian, the language of recovery, which was also that spoken around the patient and in which he received speech therapy, was probably relearned through the activity of the nondominant right hemisphere. The patient's Polish mother tongue and most fluent language before insult, as well as whatever German he knew, were not so exercised and remained impaired in the left hemisphere, at least until a Polish nurse joined the ward. Minkowski (1963) goes one step further in assuming that Polish was transferred to the right as well after that language had been practiced. In this event, however, one would have to assume that comprehension had always been stored there, since the patient understood Polish from the beginning of his recovery. Vildomec (1963) is of the opinion that, if Bychowski is right, it may be that the nondominant hemisphere is specialized to a certain degree for foreign languages. This does not necessarily follow. What does follow is that the nondominant hemisphere may share some language functions with the dominant hemisphere, particularly comprehension, or that it is capable of taking over some language functions when the dominant hemisphere has become inoperative. Although the latter occurs often in young children who suffer damage, it appears that by the age of 30 the brain has lost most of this kind of plasticity (cf. Penfield & Roberts, 1959).

A German-born sailor who was able to speak German, Danish, Norwegian, Dutch, and English, described briefly by Nielsen and Raney (1939) and again by Nielsen (1946), showed slight aphasic symptoms prior to the surgical removal of a tumor in the right temporal lobe. For 4 weeks after the operation, the patient was unable to spell simple words or to calculate or even to count correctly in Danish or Swedish, although he could still count in the other three languages. The authors report that his "concepts" had suffered considerably, and they are led to suppose that the right temporal lobe functioned to some extent in language before the operation. Since all defects disappeared after 5 weeks, they conclude that the left lobe had taken over all functions by that time.

Gorlitzer von Mundy (1959) reports the case of a 94-year-old patient who suffered an embolism in the left hemisphere that left him with a right hemiplegia and a selective aphasia: The patient, who for the past 40 years had spoken German in a German environment, could speak only Slovenian. The author tries to explain the pattern of restitution in the following manner. This patient, who spoke only Slovenian in his native village up to age 30, was both illiterate and ambidextrous. His cerebral hemispheres were symmetrical, including the speech areas. When he was 30, the patient was conscripted into an Austrian infantry regiment, where he served for 12 years. There he learned simultaneously to manipulate weapons with the right hand and to speak German, and thus, according to the author, German became localized in the left hemisphere. However, Slovenian remained in the speech centers of both hemispheres. Consequently, when the left hemisphere was damaged, the patient lost his German and the portion of Slovenian that was stored there but kept the Slovenian that was stored in his right hemisphere.

A number of recent studies have focused on the cerebral dominance for language in nonaphasic bilinguals. Kershner and Jeng (1972) concluded that in their 40 Chinese–English bilingual subjects, both languages were lateralized in the dominant hemisphere. In a dichotic listening experiment, Starck, Genesee, Lambert, and Seitz (1974) observed that children with bilingual or multilingual experience demonstrated greater cerebral asymmetry than children who spoke only one language and that learning a second or third language between the ages of 6 and 8 apparently enhances the development of cerebral asymmetry. In a similar experiment with Hebrew and English bilinguals, Obler, Albert, and Gordon (1975) report that although all their subjects showed a right ear effect (i.e., reported correctly more words provided through the right earphone than through the left, in both languages), the results show an asymmetry between the two languages when one looks at the degree of dominance (i.e., the right over left ratio) in each language. From the point of view of absolute difference, the balanced bilingual Americans showed stronger right ear effect dominance in English than in Hebrew, whereas the Israelis showed greater right ear advantage in Hebrew than in English. However, Hebrew scores showed less lateralization than English scores, and therefore the authors conclude that there might be a language-specific effect to the extent that the right hemisphere seems particularly suited for Hebrew. The authors also speculate that the first language might become lateralized to the left hemisphere, and that something about the process of learning a second language might involve significant participation of the adult learner's right hemisphere.

Hamers and Lambert (1974) report that in a tachistoscopic presentation of words in two languages in either the right or the left visual field, 2 subjects out of 15 showed a greater facility with words in one language on one side and with the other on the other side, while 3 other subjects showed a substantial left–right difference in the processing of one language and almost no left–right difference with the other. These last findings are consistent with Gorlitzer von Mundy's hypothesis, quoted earlier. Hamers and Lambert are fully aware that their investigation is a pilot study but think that, with more extensive sampling, additional examples might be found which deviate from the general pattern in which both languages are lateralized in the same hemisphere. The question of greater or lesser lateralization of language functions in bilinguals remains open.

After having examined 15 cases in which cerebral lesions had been verified by either autopsy or surgery, 11 from the literature and four of their own, Gloning and Gloning (1965) consider that it is not so much that polyglots are less lateralized than monoglots (i.e., their dominant hemisphere is equally committed to language functions), but, rather, that with people who speak two or more languages perfectly, the nondominant hemisphere must be involved to a greater extent in the speech function and consequently be subject to disturbances.

From the differential restitution patterns of their patients, whose symptoms varied qualitatively as well as quantitatively in the languages they spoke, Ovcharova *et al.* (1968) infer the need for a broader, more dynamic, and less lateralized organization of the speech functions in polyglots. Five years earlier, Vildomec (1963) had taken this argument one step further by assuming that, in subjects who are bilingual from infancy, the nondominant hemisphere co-operates in the act of speech more than it does in other bilinguals who have learned a second language after having mastered a first. This leads us to consider the different types of bilingualism that have been identified and the attempts that have been made to correlate them with various patterns of restitution.

TYPES OF BILINGUALISM

Weinreich (1953) reports having found the descriptions of three types of bilingualism in the literature: "Type A" (which was soon to be referred to as *coordinate*), in which the signs of each language—combining, in Saussurian terms, a unit of expression and one of content—are kept separate; "Type B (*compound*), wherein the signs combine one single unit of content with one unit of expression in each language (i.e., one signified for two signifiers); and "Type C" (*subordinate*), in which the meaning unit is that of the mother tongue, with its corresponding unit of expression that, in turn, has an equivalent unit of expression in the second language (See Figure 2.5).

The coordinate bilingual would presumably function as a native monolingual speaker of each language, always using the proper unit of expression to refer to the proper unit of content in each language. The compound bilingual would not function as a native speaker of either language since his units of content would represent a merging of the more or less closely related but not identical units of content of both languages. The subordinate bilingual would speak his mother tongue like a native but would use the unit of expression of the second language to refer to a more or less closely related unit of content of his mother tongue when speaking the second language; thus he would not function as a native speaker of that language.

In short, the coordinate bilingual possesses two sets of meaning units with their respective modes of expression; the compound bilingual possesses one set of merged meaning units with two modes of expression; and the subordinate bilingual possesses one set of meaning units—that of his mother tongue—with two modes of expression: one corresponding to his mother tongue and the other being a set of translation quasi-equivalents.

Weinreich never suggested that a bilingual should be all coordinate or all compound: The bilingual's two linguistic systems may stand in a variety of

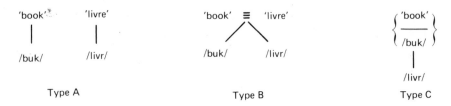

'book' 'livre'	'book' ≡ 'livre'	{ 'book' } { /buk/ }
/buk/ /livr/	/buk/ /livr/	/livr/
Type A	Type B	Type C

Figure 2.5 Types of bilingualism [after Weinreich, 1953]. A coordinate bilingual will not bring the same set of objects in response to the command "Bring me all the books which are on my desk" and "Apporte-moi tous les livres qui sont sur mon bureau." In the first case, he will bring textbooks, notebooks, and so on; in the second instance, he will bring only textbooks (*livres*) but not the exercise books (*cahiers*).

relationships with respect to each other, ranging from an idealized perfect coordinateness to total compoundness or subordinateness, with real individuals situated somewhwere on a continuum, sharing in various degrees parts of their linguistic systems with all three types. It is nevertheless useful to retain the theoretical distinction between coordinate, subordinate, and compound bilingualism, and it should be possible to ascertain by experimental investigation the extent to which, and possibly the areas for which, each bilingual is coordinate, subordinate, or compound.

Unfortunately, since Ervin and Osgood's study (1954), Types B and C, or compound and subordinate bilingualism, have been conflated into a single type referred to as *compound bilingualism.* Yet, from the differing composition of their respective semantic systems, it is clear that the two types of bilinguals will not behave linguistically in the same way. The meaning units of the compound share features of two languages, whereas those of subordinate are the meaning units of one language only. All other factors being equal, as we shall see, the two types should also be correlated to some degree with different contexts of acquisition.

Weinreich (1953) recognized that, besides semantemes, other parts of the linguistic system, such as phonemes, the tense system of verbs, word order, and the like, were also susceptible of merging or coexistence in varied proportions. It is therefore theoretically possible for someone to be coordinate at the level of syntax and semantics, but to have a compound phonology, that is a broadened system that serves for both languages (where /ɪ/ is neither the French /i/ nor the English /I/ but something in between that serves for both). In fact it is not difficult to find persons who have mastered a second language to the level of native fluency with flawless grammar and a rich vocabulary but who speak this language with a distinct foreign accent. Some patients were indeed so described.

Similarly, some individuals have mastered the phonology of a second language but will, if only occasionally, use a syntactic structure of their mother tongue (a phenomenon generally referred to as "interference"), or will use a word in the second language (pronounced as by a native speaker, in an otherwise grammatically well-formed sentence) with a meaning that correlates properly with a cognate in his mother tongue.

In compound bilinguals, such interference is bidirectional, the subject using now a structure of French while speaking English, now a structure of English while speaking French. The same person will say *je l'ai téléphoné* for *je lui ai téléphoné* from English 'I phoned him,' and '*since I am here' for 'since I have been here' from French *depuis que je suis là.* In subordinate bilinguals, the interference is always unidirectional, that is, from the mother tongue to the second language. Or, rather, we should say that to the extent that a subject shows interference unidirectionally, he is (called) subordinate at the level of phonology, syntax, or semantics as the case may be, and possibly to a different degree at each level; to the extent that the interference is bidirectional, the individual is compound; and to the extent that he keeps the two systems separate and behaves linguistically like a native speaker in each, he is coordinate.

It is conceivable that a single subject may demonstrate degrees of compoundness and of coordinateness and/or subordinateness in varied proportions at each level. The ratios can be quantitatively measured. Of course they are susceptible of change over time. But at a given moment, it should be possible to determine whether a subject's overall performance is more coordinate, or compound, or subordinate, and to what extent at each level.

Jakobovits (1968) introduced a new dimension into the compound–coordinate model: that of degree of bilingualism, or proficiency, which is not a function of the kind of bilingualism but of the amount of competence in each language. It is compatible with each of the three types of bilingualism described above, but, following Ervin and Osgood (1954) Jakobovits too collapses compound and subordinate into one, which he calls "compound." This conflation cannot be performed with impunity, since it blurs the important parameter of directionality of the interference at the various levels and confuses two distinct states of affairs.

For instance, compound bilingualism is assumed to come about as a result of (1) learning the second language in the same environmental setting as the first, and (2) using the first language as the direct channel of acquisition. Surely, all other factors being equal, (1) is apt to foster compound bilingualism, in which case it is irrelevant to speak of first or second language since both are learned together, typically by a child, as his two mother tongues, while (2) is more likely to promote subordinate bilingualism.

When "the second language represents a mere alternative channel for the overt manifestation of the same underlying system represented by the first language" (Jakobovits, 1968, p. 31) the speaker is not a compound but a subordinate bilingual. In a compound bilingual, the two linguistic systems are so fused and interdependent that there is no first or second language but a blend of the two, which as such deviates from the language of an idealized monolingual member of either linguistic community.

Ervin and Osgood (1954) had called attention to the fact that a foreign language learned in the school situation by a traditional method (vocabulary lists, grammar, translation) would typically yield subordinate bilingualism (which these authors call "compound" for lack of distinction between the two), and that a child growing up in a home where two languages are spoken more or less interchangeably by the same people and in the same situations would characteristically acquire compound bilingualism. Coordinate bilingualism would be facilitated by learning to speak one language—say, Japanese—with one's parents, for example, and the other language—say, English—in a school where the language of instruction as well as that of the student body is English.

Jakobson (1964) also explicitly distinguishes (without labeling) the three types of bilingualism and describes contexts of acquisition likely to foster each type. The child acquires a mixed language, or, at least, there is no strict delimitation between his two languages when each of his parents uses both languages indiscriminately in the child's presence (compound bilingualism); when the father speaks to the child in only one language, and the mother in only the other, both languages are perfectly mastered by the child, who thus acquires "real bilingualism" (coordinate); finally, in some cases, one of the two languages is the basic one and the other is superimposed (subordinate bilingualism). Milner (1964) declares having often witnessed in the Province of Quebec what Pick (1903) had observed in Prague, and Pötzl (1930) in central Europe: "a composite knowledge rather than two separate systems with the possibility of switching completely from one to the other" (p. 119).

A number of tests have been devised to assess the validity of the coordinate–compound distinction (cf. Lambert & Rawlings, 1969). It is unfortunate, however, that since Lambert, Havelka, and Crosby (1958) have shown experimentally that the context of acquisition has an influence on the type of bilingualism, "coordinate" has come to mean simply "acquired in different contexts." The two are not necessarily synonymous, even though there is a statistically significant tendency for the context to influence the kind of bilingualism. Other factors may be at work that either reinforce or, on the contrary, override this influence, such as individual preference for certain learning strategies. This is apparently the case in learning the mother tongue, irrespective of the similarities of context (see Bloom 1970, 1973).

Children learning two languages from the beginning seem to adopt one of at least two possible procedures in functionally separating their two incipient linguistic systems in the course of their dévelopmental progress: *chronic interference* (Burling, 1959) or *early achieved separation* (Imedadze, 1960).

One should realize that the context of acquisition, although it may have a strong facilitating influence, is neither a necessary nor a sufficient condition in determining the nature of the bilingualism of a given individual. Exposure to the same conditions does not ipso facto guarantee identity of product in a randomly selected case. Yet, neuropsychologists describe aphasic patients by labeling them "coordinate" or "compound" (the latter meaning either "compound" or "subordinate") solely on the basis of the way the two languages were learned (L'Hermitte *et al.,* 1966; Hécaen, Mazaro, Ramier, Goldblum, & Merienne, 1971). It is true that the more the learning contexts are separated, either in time, in cultural distinctiveness, or in distinctiveness of the setting of habitual usage, the more likely it is that bilingual coordinateness will develop (Lambert & Fillenbaum, 1959; cf. Lambert *et al.,* 1958), and one could make statistically valid predictions. The context of acquisition, however, cannot serve as the sole criterion for diagnosing coordinateness or compoundness in a bilingual patient.

Independent testing is needed, over and above the information about the context of acquisition, for, as Kolers (1963) pointed out, persons can hardly be categorized for life on the basis of how they originally learned their languages. Shifts from coordinate to compound bilingualism may occur over time (Stafford & Van Keuren, 1968) or from compound to coordinate (Fishman, 1964). Ervin and Osgood (1954) entertained that possibility, predicting that if a coordinate bilingual is required to translate in both directions, he will gradually transform his coordinate linguistic system into a compound system.

EVIDENCE OF TYPES FROM APHASIA

The correlation between type of bilingualism and patterns of recovery is complicated by the lack of standardization in anamneses. In the present state of the literature, we can hardly say with Diebold (1968) that "the most compelling evidence for differential dominance and the distinction between types of bilinguals comes from research into . . . aphasia" (p. 231). The evidence for the existence of distinct types of bilinguals might indeed possibly come from studies in polyglot aphasia, had we reliable systematic data in sufficient quantity. Unfortunately, this is as yet far from being the case: It is seldom possible to obtain a correct appraisal of the kind or even the degree of bilingualism of a patient prior to insult. The relatives are usually of very little help, for their assessment of the patient's bilingualism is generally quite subjective and lacks differentiation as to the various aspects of the patient's language: syntax, phonology, vocabulary, and the like. Evaluations are mostly given in global terms of greater or lesser overall fluency. Sometimes even this information cannot be elicited from the patient nor from anyone else. When they are reliable, the descriptions found in anamneses lack systematization and completeness. No two authors will give the same details about a case history: Items range from remarks on whether a patient masturbated a great deal as a youth (Minkowski, 1927) to detailed descriptions of aphasic symptoms in each of a patient's languages (e.g., Leischner, 1943; Gloning & Gloning, 1965).

Èven in reports within the last decade, the linguistic data and, particularly, details concerning the context of acquisition are given in a haphazard, unsystematic manner. Authors will give different items of information for different patients in the same paper. In L'Hermitte *et al.* (1966), for instance, in observation 1, we are given place of birth and the mode of acquisition of three of the patient's four languages; in observation 2, the mode of acquisition is given for none of the languages. We may assume that Ukrainian is the patient's mother tongue since he was born in Dnepropetrov, but no mention is made of Russian, although the patient was tested in that language. It could have been learned at home as a second mother tongue or at school around age 5. In observation 4, the authors specify that the patient (Geoffrey S.) was born in England *of English parents*. But in observation 3, although the patient's first name is given as Roland (a name that could either be French or German) and we are informed that he spoke French, we are not told what language(s) his parents spoke. Where did this patient learn French?—from his mother? from his French wife? in school? at work?

The above examples are given merely to illustrate the reportorial variability of the majority of published cases (See also van Thal, 1960). As the same details are not supplied in every case, the reports are difficult to evaluate, let alone to compare.

Most of this lack of standardization can be explained by the nature and characteristics of aphasia. The patient can scarcely be tested before insult, except possibly in cases of surgery; even then, by the time the patient is seen by the surgeon, he often has already shown signs of dysphasia. Nevertheless, it would be useful to standardize the available data, explicitly stating as "unknown" those items about which no information could be obtained, thus facilitating a more systematic approach to the collection and reporting of information. For purposes of comparison, a case report should contain at least the following information: Patient identification, age, sex, occupation, level of education; for each language, the age at which it was acquired, the way in which it was learned (at school, as a medium of instruction or as a second language, with direct or indirect method, from the environment with or without formal instruction and of what kind of instruction, whether reading and writing was learned and when), and the time until which it was used; the cause of the aphasia; a description of the aphasic symptoms and of the pattern of recovery; and, when available after autopsy or during surgery or from brain scans or other tests, the neuroanatomical findings.

From the information actually available it is not possible to correlate type of bilingualism with a particular pattern of restitution. In no case so far published has coordinateness, subordinateness, or compoundness been ascertained (beyond assumptions based on context of acquisition). In fact, there is some confusion as to the hypothetical expectations with respect to these types of bilingualism. Zierer's (1974) and Monteverde-Ganoza's (1974) claim that, in coordinate bilinguals, both languages suffer to the same degree directly contradicts Lambert and Fillenbaum's (1959) prediction that coordinate bilinguals are more likely to show aphasic damage in one language system, while compound bilinguals are more likely to show aphasic damage in all languages known. But then, Monteverde-Ganoza (1974) defines compoundness (*bilingüismo combinado*) as Weinreich's (1953) Type C bilingualism (subordinate) with dominance of the mother tongue, coordinateness (*bilingüismo coordinado*) being coordinated balanced bilingualism, that is, equal proficiency in both languages.

In their "Pilot Study," Lambert and Fillenbaum (1959) had set out to investigate whether there is any relationship between the nature of the aphasic disorder and learning contexts. By "nature of the aphasic disorder" we may assume the authors mean the pattern of restitution of the various languages; the nature of the aphasia (motor, sensory, conduction, etc.) is determined by the site and size of the lesion and could certainly not be influenced by the language learning contexts. A careful look at the data from all cases surveyed, including the 14 unpublished "Montreal cases" referred to in the "Pilot Study," does not reveal any particular relationship between the context, or even the age, of acquisition and the pattern of restitution (See Tables 2.1 and 2.2).

First of all, the Montreal patients do not collectively or severally show patterns significantly different from the rest of the cases in the literature. All languages are restituted eventually in proportion to their respective fluencies before the aphasia. Nine cases show differential restitution, three with mixing; four follow a parallel pattern, one after successive restitution; three show a successive pattern. All but perhaps 3 of the 14 Montreal patients learned their languages in "separated" contexts. There is therefore no basis for believing that they were compound bilinguals.

Only three patients (Cases 1, 13, 14) learned both languages in the same context (the home). The first patient's mother and father each spoke a different language to him when he was a child; both parents of the third patient spoke mainly English at home. It is not clear what pattern was followed in the second patient's home, but he attended school successively in both languages.

The other patients learned their second languages clearly in separate contexts: Yiddish at home, Russian at school as a medium of instruction, presumably from age 5, English from the environment and night school at age 16 (Case 2); French at home and English presumably at school as a second language as well as with sports companions, and later at work (Case 3); the second language was not learned until age 5 from a governess (Case 4); parents presumably spoke Ukrainian as well as French to the patient when he was a child, and he picked up English either at school as a second language or from the environment—the two languages tested after recovery were French and English (Case 5); Polish and presumably Yiddish as mother tongues, and German was learned at school, English from the environment, with or without formal instruction after the age of 20 (Case 6); English at home and French outside and in school as a medium of instruction (Case 7); French at home and not a word of English until age 13, at which time the patient went to English school (Case 8); French at home and English from the environment, mostly in the army (Case 9); Hungarian at home and German in school, presumably as a second language, English and French being learned in high school or later (Case 10); French at home, did not learn English until college (Case 11); French at home, picked up English from playmates, presumably around or after age 5 (Case 12).

The Canadian born French–English bilinguals recovered both languages in the order of their respective proficiencies before the aphasia, that is, in the same way as the New York patients (Charlton, 1964), who were immigrants and thus had the greatest possible separation of contexts of acquisition in time, place, and

TABLE 2.2 Correlation of Contexts of Acquisition and Use with Pattern of Recovery and Type of Aphasia

	Age	Sex	Occupation	Mother tongue(s)	Used currently until	Other languages	Age of acquisition	Context of acquisition	Used currently until	Cause of aphasia	Type of aphasia	Pattern of recovery
Anastasopoulos, 1959	45	M	farmer	GD GR	TI	R	5	1	U	V	W X G	D
						TU	U	U	U			
Bálint, 1923	60	M	various unsuccessful occupations	GR	TI	R	15	U	20	T	W P R	C
						G	20	U	TI			
						F	U	U	U			
Béhier, 1869			unknown	—	U	S	U	U	U	U	U	C
						F	U	U	U			
Bianchi, 1886	24	M	tradesman	—	TI	F	U	U	U	V	D	C
						E	U	U	U			
Bonhoeffer, 1902	56	M	nur.	P	TI	G	?Y	6	TI	T	M X G	D
						E	Y	U	TI			
Bourdin, 1877	U	F		F	TI	E		3	TI	U	U	C
Brissot, 1910	27	F		F G	TI	I	?16	3	?TI	V	T	P
						SP	12	3	?TI			
Bychowski, 1919	27	M	factory worker	P	TI	G	18	3	19	T	M	D
						R	24	6	TI			
Charlton, 1964 (1)	75	M	chemical engineer	HU	TI	F	?12	2	28	V	N	P
						G	?12	2	28			
						E	?28	7	TI			
(2)	62	F	unknown	R Y	TI	E	22	7	TI	C	N	P
(4)	54	M	plumber	SP	TI	E	U	U	TI	V	M	P
(5)	45	M	clothing manufacturer	G	TI	E	36	7	TI	A	M	P
(6)	41	M	actor & musician	E	TI	I	?36	U	U	V	C	C

Case	Age	Sex	Occupation									
(7)	60	M	restaurant worker	SP	TI	E	49	7	TI	O	C	P
(8)	76	M	businessman	G	TI	E	10	U	TI	V	C	C
(9)	40	F	unknown	SP	TI	E	?12	2	TI	C	N	P
(10)	60	M	executive	DA	TI	F	Y	2	23	V	C	P
Chlenov, 1948 (1)	43	M	salesman, then printer	G	TI	E	Y	2,6	TI	T	U	A
(2)	34	F	translator & English teacher	R	TI	SP	Y	2	TI	M	S X G	S
Cros, 1857	U	M	physicist	PA	TI	E	?12	2	TI	U	U	C
Dédić, 1926	33	M	army officer	R	TI	G	?12	2	TI	V	C	D
Denés, 1914	70	F	unknown	F	TI	F	?12	2	TI	V	M G L T	C
Dimitrijević, 1939	60	F	unknown	Y	TI	L	?12	?1	TI	V	M	C
Dreifuss, 1961	34	M	poet	BU	34	F	?5	U	TI	H	M S G L	C
Eskridge, 1896	23	M	coal miner	G	10	F	U	U	U	T	D	A
Florenskaja, 1940	U	F	unknown	BO	TI	SE	U	U	U	K	G	M
Gerstenbrand, 1956	56	M	autobody mechanic	R	TI	–	U	3	TI	V	M B	C*
Gloning, 1965 (1)	57	F	cook & housekeeper	CZ	TI	G	45	1	TI	O	M W P	D
(2A)	55	M	interpreter / travel agent	SL	TI	SE	28	3	46	V	A W X	D
(2B)	60	M	gardner	I	36	SP	25	7	TI	V	S A P	M
(3)	55	F	unknown	BU	26	SC	36	3	TI	V	S G	D M
(4)	50	M	woodcutter	HU	54	G	3	3,2	TI	E	S	P
Gorlitz v. Mundy, 1959	94	M	unknown	SL	TI	WH	30	6	TI	O	U	C
Halpern, 1941	24	M	unknown	G	TI	HE	20	7	TI	T	S	D

(continued)

TABLE 2.2 (continued)

Study	Age	Sex	Occupation	Mother tongue(s)	Used currently until	Other languages	Age of acquisition	Context of acquisition	Used currently until	Cause of aphasia	Type of aphasia	Pattern of recovery
Halpern, 1949 (1)	36	M		R	TI	HW, HE	8, 16	8, 7	TI, TI	T	S X G	D
(2)	42	M	teacher	E	TI	WH, HE	7, 22	8, 7	TI, TI	T	S G	
Hécaen, 1971	28	M	engineer	V	21	F	?19	U	TI	O	S G	P
Hegler, 1931	18	M	merchant	F	17½	E	16	U	U	V	M	C
Herschmann, 1920	60	M	businessman	CZ	TI	G	17½	7	TI	V	L G X	M
Hinshelwood, 1902	34	M	U (highly educated)	E	TI	AG	14	?2	U	V	S M B	D
Hoff & Pötzl, 1932	58	M	Colonel (Austrian)	G	TI	L, F	U, U	?2, ?2	U, U	V	S X G	C
Kauders, 1929	62	M	hotel doorman	G	TI	—	—	3	U	V	S P R	M
Krapf, 1955 (1)	38	M	sales clerk	CZ	TI	F, E	16, ?17	7, 7	TI	ψ	?T	M
(2)	37	F	unknown	G	TI	G	C	3	TI	S	U	C*
(3)	33	M	landowner	E SP	TI	SP	24	U	TI	T	U	D
(4)	U	M	unknown	G	TI	SP	26	7	TI	V	U	D
(5)	47	M	shipcaptain	ED	TI	SP	U	U	TI	V	U	S
Krapf, 1957 (1)	35	M	tradesman	E	TI	E	U	U	TI		U	M
(2)	50	M	unknown (refugee)	G	TI	SP	U	U	TI	?V	S	C*

Reference	Age	Sex	Occupation									
Lambert & Fillenbaum, 1959 (1)	30	M	electrician	FE	TI	R	5	1	19	T	?MW	D
(2)	49	F	housewife	Y	TI	E	16	8	TI	S	W	S
(3)	40	F	housewife	F	TI	E	U	?2,3	TI	V	W	M,D
(4)	50	F	housewife	F	TI	E	5	9	TI	V	?W	DM
(5)	40	F	housewife	UK	?Y	F	—	3,1	TI	V	?W	D
(6)	40	M	various occupations	P ?Y	TI	G	U	U	U	T	N	S,P
(7)	48	M	purchasing agent	E	TI	E	?3	1	TI	V	MS	P
(8)	30	M	foreman machine shop	F	TI	F	13	6	TI	T	M	D
(9)	60	M	various (including taxi driver)	F	TI	E	?C	3,1	TI	V	A	P
(10)	55+	M	customs broker	HU	TI	E	U	1	TI	V	W	S
(11)	64	M	journalist	F	TI	G	U	3,6	TI	V	?M	S
(12)	54	M	lawyer	F	TI	E	U	2	TI	V	ARXG	P
(13)	63	M	tram conductor	FE	TI	F	16+	2,7	TI	V	MW	D
(14)	40	F	housewife	EF	TI	E	5	2	TI	V	?LX	D,M
Lecours & Lhermitte	63	M	salesman	E	TI	F	5	?172	TI	V	T	?D
Ledinsky & Mraček	34	M	medical doctor	GR	10	CZ	18	3	TI	T	W	D,M
Leischner, 1943	64	M	artisan	z CZ	TI	G(W)	U	1,1	TI	V	SG	M
Leischner, 1948 (1)	50	M	medical doctor	G	TI	CZ	Y	1	U	V	S	C
(2)	71	M	lawyer	G	TI	L AG	?12	1	U	V	S	D
L'Hermitte et al., 1966 (1)	62	F	boarding house manager	R	?TI	F	?12	2	U	V	M	P

(continued)

TABLE 2.2 (continued)

	Age	Sex	Occupation	Mother tongue(s)	Used currently until	Other languages	Age of acquisition	Context of acquisition	Used currently until	Cause of aphasia	Type of aphasia	Pattern of recovery
(2)	66	M	head waiter	UK	?TI	R, G, P	U, U, U	U, U, U	U, ?TI, ?TI	V	MG	P
(3)	34	M	executive	G	TI	F	?–29	U	TI	O	SMAG	P
(4)	46	M	executive	E	TI	F	?12	2	TI	O	S	M
(5)	48	M	civil servant	SP	TI	F, G	?30, 8	2, U	TI, TI	S	SPN	P
(6)	40	M	factory manager	SP	TI	F, AR, H	4, U, U	1, 1, 9	TI, U, TI	V	M	P
(7)	30	M	medical doctor	AL	TI	F, E, I	?12, 18, 5	?2, 9, 1	U, TI, U	T	MG	P
(8)	37	M	dry cleaner	HU, G, F	17, TI, TI	G, F, F	9, 17, U	1, U, U	?TI, ?TI, TI	O	M	D
	42	M	journalist	CH	TI	P, G, R	U, U, U	U, U, U	?TI, ?TI, TI	T	SG	D
	42	M	financier			R, E	C	U	TI	O	XG	D

Luria, 1956

Lyman et al., 1938

Reference	Age	Sex	Occupation							T	MXG	SC
Minkowski, 1927 (1)	32	M	mechanic	SD	TI	G / F	5	1	TI	V	M	S C
(2)	54	M	professor, physics	SD	TI	—	U	U	TI	V	M	D, A
Minkowski, 1928	44	M	tradesman	SD	TI	G / F	5	1	TI	T	A W	A
Minkowski,i, 1933	46	M	carpenter	SD	TI	—	U	U	25	T	M A P G	D S
Minkowski, 1949	45	M	electrician	SD	TI	G / F	5	1,3	TI	V	M	D M
Minkowski, 1964	52	M	professor, psychology	G	32	G / F	30	7	TI	U	U	C
Nair & Virmani 1973 (1)	U	?M	lecturer, physics	UR	TI	SP	5	U	TI	U	U	C
(2)	U	?M	unknown	HI	TI	F	30	7	U	U	U	C
Nielsen & Raney, 1939	U	M	sailor	G	TI	E, PE, DA, N, SW, DU, E	U	U	?TI	O	G ?A	C
Oré, 1878	26	M	railroad worker	PA	?TI	F	75	1	?TI	T	?S	C
Ovcharova et al., 1968	76	M	chemical engineer	G	TI	HU, BU	10	1	?TI	V	S G	D
(2)	54	M	labourer	GY	TI	BU	30	7	?TI	V	S	S
(3)	21	M	miner	TU	TI	BU	—	3	?TI	V	S	D
Peter, 1864	U	M	civil servant	R	TI	F	9	1	?TI	V	W	C
Peuser, 1974 (1)	26	M	unknown	TU	TI	G	U	U	TI	V, S	A M	P
(2)	39	M	philologist	G	?TI	E	U	U	?TI	U	M	P
Pick, 1903	74	M	salesman	G	TI	CZ	U	U	TI	V	S	S

(continued)

TABLE 2.2 (continued)

	Age	Sex	Occupation	Mother tongue(s)	Used currently until	Other languages	Age of acquisition	Context of acquisition	Used currently until	Cause of aphasia	Type of aphasia	Pattern of recovery
Pick, 1913	33	M	unknown	CZ	TI	G	U	U	TI	M	MG S	P
Pitres, 1895 (1)	51	M	servant, soldier	PA	TI	F	12	3	TI	V	M T	C
(2)	25	M	baker	PA	TI	F	–	3	TI	V	?M	C
(3)	50	F	charwoman	BA	21	PA	15	3	21	V	?M	C
(4)	53	M	traveling salesman	F	TI	F	21	3	TI	V	M ?S	C
						SP	25	U	TI			
(5)	56	M	executive	F G	TI	–	25	U	TI	V	?S	C
						AG	?12	2	TI			
						L	?12	2	TI			
						BA	22	3	TI			
						E	?30	U	U			
						SP	?30	U	U			
(6)	36	M	cavalry officer	F	TI	–	?30	U	U	T	?M ?S	C
						E	U	U	U			
						G	U	U	U			
(7)	35	M	tradesman	F PA	TI ?15	E	15	11	TI	V	?M ?S	C
						SP	18	4	TI			
						AR	18	5	TI			
Pötzl, 1925 (2)	52	M	school teacher	G	TI	–	30	3	TI	T	A	M
						CZ	?51	U	TI			
Proust, 1872	U	F	unknown	I	U	F	U	U	TI	U	U	C

This is a continuation of a tabular listing of (polyglot aphasia) case references. The table is printed rotated on the page. Column headers are not shown on this page (the table is continued from a previous page). Values are transcribed as best read; question marks (?) are reproduced from the source.

	Age	Sex	Occupation									
Reichman & R., 1919	21	M	(farmer) soldier	PD	TI	G	18	6	TI	T	D	S
Riese, 1928	56	M	baker	P	TI	G	?12	2,3	TI	V	M	C
Rinckenbach, 1866	?60+	M	retired officer	G	?TI	F	U	U	U	V	W	S
Salomon, 1914	39	M	salesman	G	TI	F	11	2	U	V	M S	S
Schulze, 1968	55	M	professor	BU	TI	E	?15	U	U	A	S M P	S C
Schwalbe, 1920	70	M	unknown	G	TI	G, R	U	2	TI	V	?M ?S	S
Simonyi, 1951	72	F	unknown	G	TI	HE, HU	U	7	?TI	?V	E	P
Stengel & Patch, 1955	63	M	pharmacist	E	TI	G, F	U	U	TI	V	S L G	D
Stengel & Zelmanowicz, 1933	57	F	cook	CZ	TI	G	U	U	TI	T	M	P M
Sträussler, 1912	34	M	U (though upper middle class)	G	TI	F	Y	U	U	V	A W	S
Veyrac, 1931	65	F	dressmaker	E	21	F	31	7	TI	V	S	S
Weisenburg & McBride, 1935	49	M	professor, romance languages	E	TI	AG, L, F, SP, I, AR	U	U	24	V	M	P M
Winslow, 1868	?45	M	unknown	W	?15	E, G, F	?15	7	TI	T	U	C
Winterstein & Meier, 1939	35	F	unknown	SD	TI	E, G, F	5	1	TI	T	?M	M
Zaorski, 1952	40	M		P	TI	E, SP	12	2	20	T	M	A
Zierer, 1974	5	M	preschool child	G	TI	SP	19	10 3	TI	O	M, S	P

(continued)

TABLE 2.2 (continued)

Note: U. "unknown"; ?. "presumably", i.e., likely, given the context, though not necessarily so and not explicitly mentioned by author.

Languages: AG. ancient Greek? AL. Alsatian dialect; AR. Arabic; BA. Basque; BO. Bohemian; BU. Bulgarian; CH. Chinese; CZ. Czech; DA. Danish; DU. Dutch; E. English; F. French; G. German; GD. Greek dialect; GE. Georgian; GR. modern Greek; GY. Gypsy; HE. Hebrew; HI. Hindi; HU. Hungarian; I. Italian; K. Kazach; L. Latin; N. Norwegian; P. Polish; PA. Patois; PD. East Prussian dialect (*Plattdeutsch*); PE. Persian; R. Russian; SC. Serbocroatian; SD. Swiss German dialect (*Schweizerdeutsch*); SE. Serbian; SL. Slovenian; SP. Spanish; SW. Swedish; TN. Turkmanian; TU. Turkish; UK. Ukrainian; UR. Urdu; V. Vietnamese; W. Welsh; WH. written Hebrew; Y. Yiddish; Z. sign language (*Zeichensprache*) (this patient could also read and write.).

Used currently: Tl. until time of insult; 24. until age 24.

Age of acquisition: C. childhood; I. infancy; Y. youth; 46. age 46.

Context of acquisition: 1. at school as a medium of instruction; 2. at school as a foreign language; 3. from the environment, without formal instruction; 4. from the environment, with the help of a conversation manual; 6. in the army (and in prison: Bonhoeffer, 1902); 7. presumably from the environment, with or without instruction; 8. from the environment and night school; 9. from a governess (Lambert & Fillenbaum, 1959); Hebrew from mother, Italian from a friend (L'Hermitte *et al.*, 1966); 10. from a private teacher; 11. self-taught, from a book; *. see text for particular circumstances.

Cause of aphasia: A. cerebral abscess; C. cerebral atrophy; E. epileptic attack; H. Migraine headache; K. Korsakoff syndrone; M. tuberculous meningitis; O. tumor (-oma); ψ. psychosis; S. surgical intervention for various reasons; T. trauma (caused by a fall, bullet, grenade splinter, blow on the head, etc.); V. vascular accident (hemorrhage, thrombosis, or embolism).

Types of aphasia: A. amnestic; B. word blindness; C. central; D. word deafness; E. echolalia; G. agraphia; L. conduction (*Leitungsaphasie*); M. motor (Broca, expressive); N. nominal; P. paraphasia; R. perseveration; S. sensory (Wernicke, receptive); T. anarthria; W. word finding difficulties; X. alexia; ?. not mentioned, cannot be conclusively ascertained.

Pattern of recovery: A. antagonistic; C. selective; C*. context selective; D. differential; M. mixed; P. parallel; S. successive.

A comma in any column indicates a sequence in time.

For details about the restitution of specific languages see Table 2.1.

110

cultural background. Of the three immigrants, two (Cases 6 and 10) recovered all their languages in such a way that the hierarchy of proficiency was similar to that which obtained before insult. The third patient (Case 2) showed a somewhat stranger pattern of restitution: The first language that she recovered was not her Yiddish mother tongue, which she had continued to use at home before her operation, but a second language, Russian, which she learned in school and had hardly used over the last 30 years, and which was not even the language of the environment upon recovery. Two months later, all languages had recovered their previous status. Some of Pitres' cases are in every respect comparable to the typical Montreal cases. Henri B. spoke both Gascon patois and French indifferently from infancy to the time of admission to hospital, yet he recovered only French (See also Oré, 1878).

In fact, no one but Zierer (1974) has explicitly derived evidence for type of bilingualism from the pattern of restitution of a given patient. According to this author, parallel impairment in both languages is a confirmation that his patient had acquired a coordinate bilingualism. As we have already seen, this contradicts the general view that compound bilinguals would be expected to suffer more nearly equal losses in both languages and coordinate bilinguals to suffer more differential losses under aphasia (Osgood & Miron, 1963, reporting Wallace Lambert's contribution to a conference on aphasia; Lambert & Fillenbaum, 1959; Lambert, 1963). Hécaen *et al.* (1971) mention as unexpected the similar impairment and parallel recovery of their patient, whom they consider to be coordinate. Similarly, having observed that seven of their patients, whom they considered to be coordinate, showed equal deficit in both their languages, L'Hermitte *et al.* (1966) are led to suppose that type of bilingualism has no influence on the pattern of restitution of the bilingual aphasic's languages.

Perhaps Dimitrijević's (1940) explanation for the recovery by his patient of Bulgarian could be interpreted as an implicit acknowledgement of the effect of compound bilingualism. From infancy, the patient had spoken Yiddish at home and Bulgarian outside as well as in school, where Bulgarian was the only language used; thus Bulgarian became dominant through greater practice. At age 34, the patient moved to Yugoslavakia, where she learned to speak Serbian. She then stopped speaking Bulgarian to speak Serbian as well as Yiddish at home, and thus is said to have forgotten Bulgarian completely (*ganz verlernte*) after 25 years of disuse. The patient suffered a stroke followed by total aphasia. During her recovery, she spoke Yiddish and Bulgarian but could no longer speak Serbian, nor even repeat a Serbian word. The author interprets the recovery of this lost language, which had no particular affective significance for the patient, as due to the close association of the two languages (*assoziative Verknüpfung*) which had been learned and practiced together.

Vereshchagin (1966) describes a population of Russian–German subordinate bilinguals, in whom most German lexemes were associated indirectly through Russian to their corresponding concepts: in a naming task, German took considerably more time than Russian. This corresponds to the kind of bilingualism that Leischner (1948) described as a state in which each thought must first be elaborated in one's mother tongue and then, with more or less difficulty, be translated into the foreign language. The linguistic behavior of some patients during recovery might possibly be interpreted as evidence of this type of subordinate bilingualism: Charcot's (1887) patient who could speak French only after translating it from German or Spanish, or Mohr's (1905) patient who would always come up with the French word before he would find the German one. Veyrac (1931) reports the stranger case of a patient whose English mother tongue, after some 45 years of disuse, had become subordinate to her more current French: She would spontaneously translate into French, before answering them, all questions put to her in English. The patient would answer in French, and when specifically asked to answer in English, would quickly be at a loss for words, and would replace a missing word with a French one.

CONCLUSION

We have identified six basic patterns of restitution, each capable of entering in combination with one or more of the others over time or simultaneously with respect to the various lanaguges spoken by a given patient: A successive recovery may develop an antagonistic pattern (Minkowski, 1928), or a patient may recover some languages differentially and lose others selectively (Pitres, 1895; Wald, 1961). Yet, there seems to be no rule with predictive value as to how bilinguals recover their languages. At best, post hoc explanations can be given by determining what factor seems to have played a preponderant role in a particular case.

Various components in every individual state of bilingualism have been proposed as influencing factors in the particular pattern of recovery: age; modalities and sociological context of acquisition; context and modalities of usage; affective value attached to each language used; degree of proficiency in the various elements of the languages concerned (phonology, syntax, semantics, vocabulary, fluency, oral comprehension); and type of bilingualism. It is most likely that all these factors (and more) do interact. To what extent, in what proportion, and subject to what hierarchical organization cannot be determined on the basis of the evidence so far available. Too many heterogeneous factors are involved which interact with and support or cancel each other, and which are often, by their very nature, imponderable.

What then has been ascertained? Languages may be recovered in one or any combination of six basic patterns. Patients with little expressive difficulty in one language may be unable to utter or even to repeat a word of another language even though they may retain comprehension of it. They may lose one or several languages entirely, including comprehension, as though they had never spoken such language(s) before, but at the same time regain a satisfactory degree of comprehension and expression in one or several others. Selective loss of expression and/or comprehension of one or more of the patient's languages does not seem necessarily linked with type of aphasia: Selective restitutions have been reported in correlation with motor, sensory, amnestic, or central aphasias. For that matter, so have all other patterns of restitution. Comprehension and expression can be impaired not only selectively, but also differentially.

Wald's (1958, 1961) second patient is sometimes considered to have had two types of aphasia: conduction aphasia in Russian and motor aphasia in Yiddish, English, and German. (One may as well add a third: total aphasia in French, Latin, and Hebrew). In fact, what the evidence seems to show is that Yiddish, English, and German were simply more impaired than Russian, in that whereas the patient could produce some spontaneous speech in Russian, he could produce no expressive speech at all in Yiddish, English, or German. The patient's French, Hebrew, and Latin were even more impaired in that they had completely disappeared. The patient thus presents a case of selective restitution with regard to French, Hebrew, and Latin, which were totally inhibited, and of differential restitution with regard to the other languages. She retained some comprehension of separate words, simple sentences, and simple commands in Yiddish, English, and German, and, in addition, she could produce some spontaneous speech in Russian, although she could not repeat. Had the patient been able to produce some speech in any of her other more severely affected languages, she would most likely have exhibited the same symptoms of conduction aphasia as in Russian.

A more recent claim of mixed symptoms in polyglot aphasia was made by Albert and Obler (1975) at the Thirteenth Annual Meeting of the Academy of Aphasia. Their patient was observed to present symptoms of Broca's aphasia in English and of Wernicke's aphasia in Hebrew. This might again be a case of differential recovery: Word finding was defective in Hebrew as well as in English, and the patient would compensate by replacing the Hebrew words with Hungarian or English words. She is also reported to have produced phonemic paraphasias in both languages. It is unfortunate that the speech of the patient was not taped and that she has dropped out of sight. But perhaps, on closer examination of whatever data are available, the dissociation may reveal a difference of degree rather than of nature. It could also be that the apparent dissociation of aphasic symptoms reflects the patient's differential mastery of the various components of each language before the aphasia. Some speakers of foreign languages could easily pass for Broca or Wernicke patients! However, if indeed it turned out that this patient had motor aphasia in one language and sensory aphasia in the other, this would be the first clear case of differential *symptoms* (unless one wishes to treat all differential and selective restitutions as exhibiting different kinds of aphasia, a move that does not seem economical and which would require a theory other than that of inhibition as an explanation), and we would have to reconsider not only the whole issue of aphasia in polyglots but the theory of aphasia itself, and particularly the specialized role of Broca's and Wernicke's areas as cerebral correlates of language.

Modalities (reading, writing) can be differentially or selectively impaired and the nature of the impairment may be language specific, depending on the site of the lesion and, possibly, the modality of acquisition (auditory or visual). Prosody can be selectively impaired.

No localized "switch mechanism" could be found: Selective and mixed restitutions occur irrespective of the locus of the lesion. There is no need to hypothesize any special anatomical structure or function in the brain of the bilingual as differentiated from the monolingual. The same general neural mechanisms that make a speaker select /k/ and not /t/ in a given context can account for his selection of *Käse;* instead of *fromage.* The bilingual needs no different mechanism to allow him to choose to speak Czech at a given time, or German at another, than he needs to choose to speak at all or to remain silent: to say "it's a lovely day" or "it's a rotten day"; to say "John broke the window" or "the window was broken by John"; to say "I don' wanna go" to his sister and "I don't want to go" to his teacher. The nondominant hemisphere may play a role in the language of some bilinguals, but it is capable of doing so in monolinguals as well.

A glance at Tables 2.1 and 2.2 will convince the reader of the absence of obvious correlation between any given factor and pattern of restitution. These tables must be read with a great deal of caution. They are useful only in that they indicate general tendencies and account for a number of cases that have been reported in the literature, but they are not necessarily representative of a large random sample. They show what *does* happen but cannot serve to derive percentages of incidence. Moreover, very few patients lend themselves to being neatly categorized. As Figures 2.1–2.4 show, a patient's performance is rated against a conventional proficiency scale, which in general reflects the opinion of the neurologist as to what language was like before the aphasia. Respective degrees of fluency are very seldom known with any considerable accuracy. Too many details are missing in most reports (different details in each one) to make a comparison of all their results very fruitful. Information is so scarce or ambiguous sometimes as to force a quasi-arbitrary decision as to whether a given piece of data is to be placed in one cell or another in the table. Characteristically, it is not crystal clear what kind of aphasia symptoms represent nor what type of restitution occurred. The patient very often recovers two languages in a more or less parallel way, another one or two differentially, and another not at all or only in respect to comprehension. Thus Table 2.1 is only indicative of the pattern of recovery of some of the languages. The reader should refer to the text for a more explicit account and, eventually, to the articles themselves, once their English versions become available (Paradis, forthcoming).

It is to be hoped, however, that in future case reports, all the details mentioned above will be systematically specified, whenever ascertainable, in order that meaningful comparisons may lead the way to a better neurolinguistic understanding of both aphasia and bilingualism.

REFERENCES

Adler, Arthur. 1889. *Beiträge zur Kasuistik und Theorie der Aphasie* Breslau: Medicinischen Facultät der Universität Breslau.

Alajouanine, Th., Pichot, P., & Durand M. 1949. Dissociation des alternations phonétiques avec conservation relative de la langue la plus ancienne dans un cas d'anarthrie pure chez un sujet français bilingue. *L'Encéphale, 38,* 245–265.

Albert, Martin, & Obler, Loraine. 1975. Mixed polyglot aphasia. Paper presented at the Thirteenth Annual Meeting of the Academy of Aphasia, Victoria, British Columbia October 7, 1975.

Ajuriaguerra, J. de, & Hécaen, H. 1960. *Le cortex cérébral, étude neuro-psycho-pathologique.* 2ième éd. Paris: Masson and Cie. Pp. 192–194.

Anastasopoulos, G. K. 1959. Linkseitige Hemiplegie mit Alexie, Agraphie und Aphasie bei einem polyglotten Rechtshänder. *Deutsche Zeitschrift für Nervenheilkunde, 179,* 120–144.

Bálint, Aladar. 1923. Bemerkungen zu einem Falle von polyglotter Aphasie *Zeitschrift für die gesamte Neurologie und Psychiatrie, 83,* 277–283.

Bastian, Charlton. 1875. *On paralysis from brain disease in its common forms.* New York: Appleton.

Bay, E. 1964. General discussion. In A. V. S. De Reuck and Maeve O'Connor (Eds.), *Disorders of Language.* Boston: Little Brown.

Bernard, Désiré-Antoine-François. 1885. *De l'aphasie et de ses diverses formes.* Paris: A Delahaye et E. Lecrosnier. P. 191.

Bianchi, Leonardo. 1886. Un caso di sordite verbale. *Rivista sperimentale di Freniatria, 12,* 57–71.

Bloom, Lois. 1970. *Language development: Form and function in emerging grammars.* Cambridge: M.I.T. Press.

Bloom, Lois. 1973. *One word at a time: The use of single word utterances before syntax.* The Hague: Mouton.

Bonhoeffer, Carl. 1902. Zur Kenntnis der Rückbildung motorischer Aphasien *Mitteilungen aus den Grenzgebieten der Medizin und Chirurgie 10,* 203–224.

Bourdin, [Claude-Etienne]. 1877. Discussion sur l'aphasie (séance du 18 décembre 1876) *Annales médico-psychologiques, 17,* 229–230.

Brain, Walter Russell. 1965. *Speech disorders.* 2nd ed. London: Butterworths. Pp. 117–118.

Brissot, Maurice. 1910. *De l'aphasie dans les rapports avec la démence et les vésanies* (étude historique clinique et diagnostique, considérations médico légales). Thèse de doctorat, Universitéd Paris. Pp. 51–62.

Burling, R. 1959. Language development of a Garo and English speaking child. *Word, 15,* 45–68.

Bychowski, Z. 1919. Über die Restitution der nach einem Schädelschuss verlorenen Umgangssprache bei einem Polyglotten. *Monatschrift für Psychologie und Neurologie, 45,* 183–201.

Charcot, J. M. 1887. *Oeuvres complètes de J. M. Charcot.* Vol. 3. Paris: A. Delahaye & E. Lacrossier.

Charlton, M. 1964. Aphasia in bilingual and polyglot patients: A neurological and psychological study. *Journal of Speech and Hearing Disorders, 29,* 307–311.

Chlenov, L. G. 1948. Ob Afazii u Poliglotov. *Izvestiia Akademii Pedagogicheskikh NAUK RSFSR, 15,* 783–790.

Coppola, A. 1928. "L'afasia nei poliglotti e la simulazione nello "Sconosciuto" di Collegno." *Rivista di Patologia nervosa e mentale, 33,* 359–393.

Critchely, Macdonald. 1974. Aphasia in polyglots and bilinguals. *Brain and Language, 1,* 15–27.

Cros, Antoine. 1857. *Recherches physiologiques sur la nature et la classification des facultés de l'intelligence et sur les fonctions spéciales des lobules antérieurs du cerveau.* Thèse de Doctorat, Université de Paris.

Dedić, St. 1926. Zur Aphasiefrage. *Zeitschrift für die gesamte Neurologie und Psychiatrie 106,* 208–213.

Denès, P[rosper-August]. 1914. *Contribution à l'étude de quelques phénomènes aphasiques.* Travail de la clinique des maladies du système nerveux et du quartier des aliénés hospice général de Nantes, Thèse de Doctorat Paris: Ollier-Henry.

De Reuck, A. V. S., & O'Connor, Maeve (Eds). 1964. *Disorders of language* Boston: Little Brown. Pp. 116–121 and 248–250.

Diebold, Richard A., Jr. 1968. The consequences of early bilingualism in cognitive development and personality formation. In E. Norbeck, D. Price-Williams, and W. A. McCord (Eds). *The study of personality: An Interdisciplinary appraisal.* New York: Holt, Rinehart and Winston. Pp. 218–245.

Dimitrijević, D. 1940. Zur Frage der Sprachrestitution bei der Aphasie der Polyglotten. *Zeitschrift für die gesamte Neurologie und Psychiatrie, 168,* 277–281.

Dreifuss, F. E. 1961. Observations on aphasia in a polyglot poet. *Acta Psychiatrica Scandinavia, 36,* 91–97.

Epstein, Izhac. 1915. *La pensée et la polyglossie; Essai psychologique et didactique.* Paris: Payot.

Ervin, Susan M., & Osgood, C. E. 1954. Second language learning and bilingualism. *Journal of Abnormal and Social Psychology, 49,* (Supplement), 139–146.

Eskridge, J. T. 1896. Mind and word deafness after depressed fracture of the skull with subcortical hemorrhage—operation; complete recovery. *Medical News, 68,* 698–702.

Fishman, Joshua A. 1964. Language maintenance and language shift as a field of inquiry. *Linguistics, 9,* 32–70.

Florenskaia, J. A. 1940. Sluchai rasstroistva rechi pri organicheskom zabolevanii s korsakovskim sindromom. *Trudy Tsentral'nogo Instituta Psikhologii, 1,* 333–346.

Freud, Sigmund. 1891. *On aphasia: A critical study.* Authorized translation with an introduction by E. Stengel. New York: International University Press, 1953 (Zur Auffassung der Aphasien, 1891).

Gelb, A. 1937. Zur medizinischen Psychologie und philosophischen Anthropologie. *Acta Psychologica, 3,* 193–271 (see especially pp. 247–250).

Gerstenbrand, F., & Stepan, H. 1956. Polyglotte Reaktion nach Hirnschädigung; ein kasuistischer Beitrag. *Wiener Zeitschrift für Nervenheilkunde, 13,* 167–172.

Ghilarducci, F. 1892. Contribution au diagnostic différentiel entre l'hystérie et les maladies organiques du cerveau. *Archives de Neurologies, 24,* 287, 396–397.

Gloning, Ilse, & Gloning, Karl. 1965. Aphasien bei Polyglotten. Beitrag zur Dynamik des Sprachabbaus sowie zur Lokalisationsfrage dieser Störungen. *Wiener Zeitschrift für Nervenheilkunde, 22,* 362–397.

Goldblum, Zofja. 1928. Nach Trepanation aufgetretene motor[ische] Aphasie (Hypolalie) mit Restitution bei progressiv wachsendem Endotheliom im linken Zentrofrontallappen. *Schweizer Archiv für Neurologie und Psychiatrie, 22,* 227–268.

Goldstein, Kurt. 1933. L'Analyse de l'aphasie et l'étude de l'essence du langage. *Journal de Psychologie Normale et Pathologique, 30,* 430–496.

Goldstein, Kurt. 1948. Disturbances of language in polyglot individual's with aphasia. In *Language and language disturbances.* New York: Grune and Stratton. Pp. 138–146.

Gorlitzer von Mundy, V. 1959. Ein 94 jähriger mit einem deutschen sprachzentrum und mit warscheinlich 2 slowenischen Sprachzentren. *Wiener Medizinische Wochenschrift, 109,* 358.

Grasset, Joseph. 1884. Contribution clinique à l'étude des aphasies (cécité et surdité verbales). *Montpellier médical,* janvier (Observation II), 33–34.

Halpern, Lipman. 1941. Beitrag zur Restitution der Aphasie bei Polyglotten im Hinblick auf das Hebräische. *Schweizer Archiv für Neurologie und Psychiatrie, 47,* 150–154.

Halpern, Lipman. 1949. La langue hébräique dans la restitution de l'aphasie sensorielle chez les polyglottes. *Semaine des Hôpitaux de Paris, 58,* 2473–2476.

Halpern, Lipman. 1950. Observations on sensory aphasia and its restitution in a Hebrew polyglot. *Monatschrift für Psychiatrie und Neurologie, 119,* 156–173.

Hamers, Josiane F., & Lambert, Wallace E. 1974. Visual field and cerebral hemisphere preferences in bilinguals. Mimeograph, McGill University.

Hécaen, H. 1964. General discussion. In A. V. S. De Reuck and Maeve O'Connor (Eds.), *Disorders of Language.* Boston: Little, Brown.

Hécaen, Henry, & Angelergues, René. 1965. *Pathologie du langage.* Paris: Larousse.

Hécaen, H., Mazaro, G., Ramier, A., Goldblum, M. C., & Merienne, L. 1971. Aphasie croisée chez un sujet droitier bilingue. *Revue Neurologique, 124,* 319–323.

Hegler, C. 1931. Zur Aphasie bei Polyglotten. *Deutsche Zeitschrfit für Nervenheilkunde, 117,* 236–239.

Herschmann, H., & Pötzl, O. 1920. Bemerkungen über Aphasie der Polyglotten. *Neurologisches Zentralblatt, 39,* 114–120.

Hinshelwood, James. 1902. Four cases of word-blindness. *Lancet, 1,* 358–363.

Hoff, H., & Pötzl, O. 1932a. Schiefe Körperhaltung und schiefer Gang bei Kleinhirnerkrankung. *Jahrbücher für Psychiatrie und Neurologie, 48,* 217–262.

Hoff, H., & Pötzl, O. 1932b. Ueber die Aphasie eines zweisprechigen Linkshänders. *Wiener Medizinische Wochenschrift, 82,* 369–373.

Hutchinson, Benjamin. 1799. *Biographia medica; or, historical and critical memoirs of the lives and writings of the most eminent medical characters.* London: J. Johnson.

Imedadze, N. V. 1960. K psikhologicheskoi prirode rannego dvuiazychiia. *Voprosy Psikhologii, 6,* 60–68.

Jakobovits, Leon A. 1968. Dimensionality of compound–coordinate bilingualism. *Language Learning,* No. 3 (special issue), 29–49.

Jakobson, Roman. 1955. Aphasia as a Linguistic Problem. In H. Werner (Ed.), *On expressive language.* Worcester, Mass.: Clark University Press. Pp. 69–81. Reprinted in Sol Saporta (Ed.), 1961, *Psycholinguistics: A book of readings,* New York: Holt, Rinehart and Winston, pp. 419–427.

Jakobson, Roman. 1964. General discussion. In A. V. S. De Reuck and Maeve O'Connor (Eds.), *Disorders of Language.* Boston: Little, Brown.

Kainz, Friedrich. 1960. *Psychologie der Sprache.* Vol. 2. 2nd rev. ed. Stuttgart: F. Enke. Pp. 330–334.

Kauders, O. 1929. Über polyglotte Reaktionen bei einer sensorischen Aphasie. *Zeitschrift für die gesamte Neurologie und Psychiatrie, 122,* 651–666.

Kershner, John R., & Amy Gwan-Rong Jeng. 1972. Dual functional hemispheric asymmetry in visual perception: Effects of ocular dominance and postexposural processes. *Neuropsychologia, 10,* 437–445.

Kolers, Paul A. 1963. Interlingual word associations. *Journal of Verbal Learning and Verbal Behavior, 2,* 291–300.

Krapf, E. E. 1955a. Über das Sprachverhalten hirngeschädigter Polyglotten. *Wiener Zeitschrift für Nervenheilkunde, 12,* 121–133.

Krapf, E. E. 1955b. The choice of language in polyglot psychoanalysis. *Psychoanalytic Quarterly, 24,* 343–357.

Krapf, E. E. 1957. A propos des aphasies chez les polyglottes. *L'Encéphale, 47,* 623–629.

Krapf, E. E. 1961. Aphasia in polyglots. *Reports at the VIIth International Congress of neurology.* Vol. 1. Rome: Società Grafica Romana. Pp. 741–742.

Lambert, Wallace E. 1963. Psychological approaches to the study of language, Part II: On second-language learning and bilingualism. *Modern Language Journal, 47,* 114–121. Reprinted in Wallace E. Lambert, 1972, *Language, Psychology, and Culture,* essays selected and introduced by Answar S. Dil. Stanford: Stanford University Press. Pp. 179–196.

Lambert, Wallace E., & Fillenbaum, S. 1959. A pilot study of aphasia among bilinguals. *Canadian Journal of Psychology, 13,* 28–34. Reprinted in Sol Saporta (Ed.), 1961, *Psycholinguistics: A book of readings,* New York: Holt, Rinehart and Winston, pp. 455–459; and in Wallace E. Lambert, 1972. *Language, psychology and culture,* essays selected and introduced by Anwar S. Dil, Stanford, Calif.: Stanford University Press, pp. 71–79.

Lambert, W. E., Havelka, J., & Crosby C. 1958. The influence of language-acquisition contexts on bilingualism. *Journal of Abnormal and Social Psychology, 56,* 239–244.

Lambert, Wallace, & Rawlings, Chris. 1969. Bilingual processing of mixed-language association networks. *Journal of Verbal Learning and Verbal Behavior, 8,* 604–609.

Lecours, André Roch & Lhermitte, François. 1976. The "pure form" of the phonetic disintegration syndrome ("pure anarthria"): anatomoclinical report of a historical case. *Brain and Language, 3,* 88–113.

Ledinský, & Mraček. 1958. Vliv poranění temporálního laloku dominantní hemisféry na řečové funkce u polyglota. *Československá neurologie, 21,* 207–210.

Leischner, Anton. 1943. Die "Aphasie der Taubstummen." Beitrag zur Lehre von der Asymbolie. *Archiv für Psychiatrie, 115,* 469–548.

Leischner, Anton. 1948. Über die Aphasie der Mehrsprachigen. *Archiv für Psychiatrie und Nervenkrankheiten, 180,* 731–775.

L'Hermitte, R., Hécaen, H., Dubois, J., Culioli, A., & Tabouret-Keller, A. 1966. Le problème de l'aphasie des polyglottes: Remarques sur quelques observations. *Neuropsychologia, 4,* 315–329.

Luria, A. R. 1956. K voprosu o narushenii pis'ma i chteniia u poliglotov. *Fiziologicheskij Zhurnal, 2,* 127–133.

Luria, A. R. 1960. Differences between disturbance of speech and writing in Russian and French. *International Journal of Slavic Linguistics and Poetics, 3,* 13–22. (English version of Luria, 1956.)

Lyman, R., Kwan, S. T., & Chao, W. H. 1938. Left occipito-parietal brain tumor with observations on alexia and agraphia in Chinese and English. *Chinese Medical Journal, 54,* 491–516.

Milner, Brenda. 1964. General discussion. In A. V. S. De Reuck and Maeve O'Connor (Eds.), *Disorders of Language.* Boston: Little, Brown. Pp. 118–119.

Minkowski, Mieczyslaw. 1927. Klinischer Beitrag zur Aphasie bei Polyglotten, speziell im Hinblick aufs Schweizerdeutsche. *Schweizer Archiv für Neurologie und Psychiatrie, 21,* 43–72.

Minkowski, Mieczyslaw. 1928. Sur un cas d'aphasie chez un polyglotte. *Revue Neurologique, 49,* 361–366.

Minkowski, Mieczyslaw. 1933. Sur un trouble aphasique particulier chez un polyglotte. *Revue Neurologique, 59,* 1185–1189.

Minkowski, Mieczyslaw. 1936. Sur des variétés particulières d'aphasie chez des polyglottes. *Schweizerische Medizinische Wochenschrift, 66,* 697–704.

Minkowski, Mieczyslaw. 1949. Sur un cas particulier d'aphasie avec des réactions polyglottes, de fabulation et d'autres troubles après un traumatisme cranio-cérébral. *Comptes rendus du Congrès des Médecins Aliénistes et Neurologistes de France.* Clermont-Ferrand. Pp. 315–328.

Minkowski, Mieczyslaw. 1963. On asphasia in polyglots. In Lipman Halpern (Ed.), *Problems of dynamic neurology.* Jerusalem: Hebrew University. Pp. 119–161.

Minkowski, Mieczyslaw. 1964. Sur un nouveau cas d'aphasie avec des réactions polyglottes particulières. *Comptes rendus du Congrès de Psychiatrie et de Neurologie de Langue Française,* Marseilles. Paris: Masson. Pp. 1264–1274.

Minkowski, Mieczyslaw. 1965. Considérations sur l'aphasie des polyglottes. *Revue Neurologique, 112,* 486–495.

Mohr, Fr. 1905. Zur Behandlung der Aphasie. *Archiv für Psychiatrie und Nervenkrankheiten, 39,* 1003–1069 (see especially pp. 1023–1024, note 2).

Monteverde-Ganoza, Luisa A. 1974. Aspectos sicolingüísticos en la afasia de los bilingües. *Lenguaje y Ciencias, 14,* 1–9.

Nair, K. Rajasekharan, & Virmani, Vilma. 1973. Speech and language disturbances in hemiplegics. *Indian Journal of Medical Research, 61,* 1395–1403.

Nielsen, J. M. 1946. *Agnosia, apraxia, aphasia.* 2nd ed. New York: P. Hoeber. Reprinted 1962, New York: Hofner.

Nielsen, J. M., & Raney, R. B. 1939. Recovery from aphasia, studies in cases of lobectomy. *Archives of Neurology, 42,* 189–200.

Obler, Loraine, Albert, Martin, & Gordon, Harold. 1975. Asymmetry of cerebral dominance in Hebrew–English bilinguals. Paper presented at the Thirteenth Annual Meeting of the Academy of Aphasia, Victoria, British Columbia, October 7, 1975.

Ombredane, André. 1951. *L'aphasie et l'élaboration de la pensée explicite.* Paris: Presses Universitaires de France.

Oré, [Pierre-Cyprien]. 1878. Fracture du crâne . . . Désordres du mouvement et du langage . . . . *Bulletin de l'Académie de Médecine* (2e série), *7,* 1131–1138.

Osgood, Charles E., & Miron, Murray S. (Eds). 1963. *Approaches to the study of aphasia: A report of an interdisciplinary conference on aphasia.* Urbana: University of Illinois Press. Pp. 35–36, 135–137.

Ovcharova, P., Raichev, R., & Geleva, T. 1968. Afaziia u Poligloti. *Nevrologiia, Psikhiatriia i Nevrokhirurgiia, 7,* 183–190.

Paradis, Michel (Ed). Forthcoming. *Readings on aphasia in bilinguals and polyglots.* Montreal: Marcel Didier.

Penfield, Wilder, 1953. A consideration of the neurophysiological mechanisms of speech and some educational consequences. *Proceedings of the American Academy of Arts and Sciences, 82,* 199–214.

Penfield, Wilder, & Roberts, Lamar. 1959. *Speech and brain-mechanisms.* Princeton, N.J.: Princeton University Press.

Peter, Michel. 1864. De l'Aphasie. *Gazette hebdomadaire de médecine et de chirurgie, 1,* 358–361.

Peuser, G. 1974. Vergleichende Aphasieforschung und Aphasie bei Polyglotten. *Folia Phoniatrica, 26,* 167–168.

Peuser, G. and Leischner, A. 1974. Störungen der phonetischen Schrift bei einer Aphasiker. *Neuropsychologia, 12,* 557–560.

Pick, Arnold. 1903. Fortgesetzte Beiträge zur Pathologie der sensorischen Aphasie. *Archiv für Psychiatrie und Nervenkrankheiten, 37,* 468–487.

Pick, Arnold. 1913. Geheilte tuberkulöse Meningitis; zugleich ein Beitrag zur Aphasie bei Polyglotten. *Prager Medizinische Wochenschrift, 38,* 635–636.

Pick, Arnold. 1915. "Kleine Beiträge zur pathologie der Sprachzentren," *Zeitschrift für die gesamte Neurologie und Psychologie, 30,* 254–285.

Pick, Arnold. 1921. Zur Erklarung gewisser Ausnahmen von der sogenannten Ribotschen Regel. *Abhandlungen aus der Neurologie, Psychiatrie, Psychologie und ihren Grenzgebieter* (Beiheft 13 zur *Monatschrift für Psychiatrie und Neurologie*). Pp. 151–167.

Pitres, Albert. 1895. Etude sur l'aphasie chez les polyglottes. *Revue de Médecine, 15,* 873–899.

Pötzl, O. 1925. Uber die parietal bedingte Aphasie und ihren Einfluss auf das Sprechen mehrerer Sprachen. *Zeitschrift für die gesamte Neurologie und Psychiatrie, 96,* 100–124.

Pötzl, O. 1930. Aphasie und Mehrsprachigkeit. *Zeitschrift für die gesamte Neurologie und Psychiatrie, 124,* 145–162.

Pötzl, Otto. 1932. Zum gegenwärtigen Stand der Aphasielehre. *Wiener Medizinische Wochenschrift, 82,* 783–791.

Proust, Adrien. 1872. De l'aphasie. *Archives générales de médecine* (6e série), *19,* 303–318.

Quadfasel, Fred A. 1963. Discussion of clinical diagnosis and treatment of aphasia. In Charles E. Osgood and Murray s. Miron (Eds.), *Approaches to the study of aphasia.* Chicago: University of Illinois Press, P. 36.

Reichmann, Frieda, & Reichau, Eduard. 1919. Traubstummenlehrer: Zur Uebungsbehandlung der Aphasien. *Archiv für Psychiatrie, 60,* 8–42.

Ribot, Théodule. 1882. *Diseases of memory: An essay in the positive psychology.* London: Paul. Originally published 1881 as *Les maladies de la mémoire* (Paris: G. Baillère).

Riese, Walther. 1928. Po povodu odnogo słuchaia poligłoticznoi afazii. *Russko-Nemetskii Meditsinskii Zhurnal, 6,* 362–365.

Rinckenbach, J. 1866. Observation d'aphasie. *Archives générales de médecine, 8,* 105–106.

Ross, A. S. C. 1964. General discussion. In A. V. S. De Reuck and Maeve O'Connor (Eds.), *Disorders of Language.* Boston: Little, Brown.

Rush, Benjamin. 1812. *Medical inquiries and observations upon diseases of the mind.* Philadelphia: Kimber.

Russell, Charles Williams. 1858. *The life of Cardinal Mezzofanti; with introductory memoir of eminent linguists, ancient and modern.* London: Longman, Brown.

Salomon, Erich. 1914. Motorische Aphasie mit Agrammatismus und sensorisch Störungen. *Monatschrift für Psychiatrie, 35,* 181–208.

Sasanuma, Sumiko. 1975. Kana and kanji processing in Japanese aphasics. *Brain and Language, 2,* 369–383.

Sasanuma, Sumiko, & Fujimura, Osamu. 1971. Selective impairment of phonetic and non-phonetic transcription of words in Japanese aphasic patients: Kana vs. Kanji in visual recognition and writing. *Cortex, 7,* 1–18.

Schulze, H. A. F. 1968. Unterschiedliche Rückbildung einer sensorischer und einer ideokinetischen motorischen Aphasie bei einem Polyglotten. *Psychiatrie, Neurologie und medizinische Psychologie, 20,* 441–445.

Schwalbe, J. 1920. Über die Aphasie bei Polyglotten. *Neurologisches Zentralblatt, 39,* 265.

Scoresby-Jackson, R. E. 1867. Case of aphasia with right hemiplegia. *Edinburgh Medical Journal, 12,* 696–706.

Shubert, A. M. 1940. Dinamika dvuiazychnoi aleksii i agrafii pri travme golovnogo mozga. *Trudy Tsentral'nogo Instituta Psikhologii.* Moskva. Pp. 169–175.

Simonyi, Gustav. 1951. Echolalie im Rahmen der Aphasie bei Pickscher Atrophie. *Monatschrift für die Psychiatrie, 122,* 100–120.

Smirnov, B. L., & Faktorovich, N. Y. 1949. K voprosu ob afazii u poliglotov. *Nevropatologiia Psikhiatria, 18,* 26–28.

Stafford, Kenneth, & Van Keuren, Stanley R. 1968. Semantic differential profiles as related to monolingual–bilingual types. *Language and Speech, 11,* 167–170.

Starck, Richard, Genesee, Fred, Lambert, Wallace, and Seitz, Michael. 1974. Multiple language experience and cerebral dominance. Mimeograph, McGill University, November 1974.

Stengel, E., & Patch, I. C. 1955. "Central" aphasia associated with parietal symptoms. *Brain, 78,* 401–416.

Stengel, E., & Zelmanowicz, J. 1933. Über polyglotte motorische Aphasie, *Zeitschrift für die gesamte Neurologie und Psychiatrie, 149,* 292–311.

Sträussler, E. 1912. Ein Fall von passagerer systematischer Sprachstörung bei einem Polyglotten, verbunden mit rechtsseitigen transitorischen Gehörshalluzinationen. *Zeitschrift für die gesamte Neurologie und Psychiatrie, 9,* 503–511.

van Thal, Joan. 1960. Polyglot aphasics. *Folia Phoniatrica, 12,* 123–128.

Vereshchagin, E. M. 1966. K probleme oposredstvovannoi assotsiatsii leksem s poniatiiami v usloviiakh bilingvizma. *Voprosy Psikhologii, 3,* 96–104.

Veyrac, G.-J. 1931. *Etude de l'aphasie chez les sujets polyglottes.* Thèse pour le doctorat en médecine, Université de Paris.

Vildomec, Věroboj. 1963. *Multilingualism.* Leyden: A. W. Sythoff. Pp. 58–65.

Wald, Ignacy. 1958. Zagadnienie afazji poliglotow. *Postepy Neurologii Neurochirurgii i Psychiatrii, 4,* 183–211.

Wald, Ignacy. 1961. Problema Afazii Poliglotov. *Voprosy Kliniki i Patofiziologii Afazii.* Moskva. Pp. 140–176.

Weinreich, Uriel. 1953. *Languages in contact.* New York: Publications of the Linguistic Circle of New York.

Weisenburg, Theodore, H., & McBride, Katharina E. 1935. *Aphasia: A clinical and psychological study.* New York: Hofner. Pp. 160–182 (Case 4).

Winslow, Forbes. 1868. *On obscure diseases of the brain and disorders of the mind.* 4th Ed. London: Churchill.

Winterstein, O., & Meier, J. 1939. Schäderltrauma und Aphasie bei Mehrsprachigen. *Der Chirurg, 11,* 229–232.

Zaorski, Jan. 1952. Zagadnienie afazji u poliglotów. *Polski Tygodnik Lekarski i Wiadomosci, 7,* 202–203.

Zierer, Ernesto. 1974. Psycho-linguistic and pedagogical aspects in the bilingual education of a child of pre-school age. *Lenguaje y Ciencias, 14,* 47–64.

3

The Nature of Conduction Aphasia: A Study of Anatomic and Clinical Features and of Underlying Mechanisms

Eugene Green

BOSTON UNIVERSITY AND
BOSTON VETERANS ADMINISTRATION HOSPITAL

Davis H. Howes

BOSTON UNIVERSITY SCHOOL OF MEDICINE AND
BOSTON VETERANS ADMINISTRATION HOSPITAL

Probably every discipline has its enigma, its child that it would prefer not to recognize, and aphasiology is no exception. For a century now, conduction aphasia has been the one language disorder that has been shunted about, refused an identity, and, occasionally, rechristened with the hope of changing its character. Unlike the eponymous Broca's and Wernicke's aphasias, conduction aphasia will no doubt have to be forever content with a descriptive name, although the descriptor, as we shall see, is in some ways misleading. Moreover, like the characteristics of an unwanted child, the features of conduction aphasia, unless one is trained to look for them, can easily escape notice.

Why such a fate? Part of the difficulty is that the syndrome of conduction aphasia does not fit conveniently into any commonsense scheme of understanding or expressing utterances. One of its chief clinical features, a gross impairment of repetition, is for Stengel and Lodge Patch (1955) an impairment of "an activity which lacks any compelling biological purpose." And yet, for all this unfortunate reputation, the study of conduction aphasia has discovered new knowledge about the disorders of language and about normal mechanisms of speech as well. Just what that knowledge is and how it helps to illuminate the questions of linguistic structures and processes are the two principal concerns of this chapter.

123

IDENTIFYING THE DISORDER

The Syndrome

Conduction aphasia is an acquired disorder of language, attributable to focal lesions in the posterior area of the dominant cortical hemisphere which impair the ability of patients to express themselves in well formed utterances (Hécaen, 1972). Recent summaries (Brown, 1972; Benson, Sheremata, Bouchard, Segarra, Price, & Geschwind, 1973) that describe the syndrome of conduction aphasia emphasize a contrast between the defective speech and writing of patients and their relatively good comprehension. The spontaneous speech of a conduction aphasic is fluent, yet it is circumlocutory and inadequately structured. Not only is the syntax of utterances defective, but patients have difficulty in finding words appropriate to a context and in pronouncing words accurately. Similarly, defects of structure and gross misspelling characterize their spontaneous writing or writing to dictation (though copied work is often good). Failures in naming, reading aloud, and repeating are quite evident. Performances in naming tasks typically demonstrate an impaired ability to find words for presented objects, for body parts, and for colors. Oral reading is likely to be laborious and attended by the same errors that occur in spontaneous speech. Above all, the difficulty in repetition is remarkable. Despite self-criticism and repeated trials, patients characteristically fail to provide a suitable match for the examiner's model. In short, all forms of expression (except in such tasks as counting off numbers, the days of the week, or the months of the year) are severely impaired in conduction aphasia.

On the other hand, patients comprehend oral and written material satisfactorily. They read silently with understanding, carry on normal conversations, and respond appropriately to everyday questions and commands. The features of conduction aphasia distinguish it clearly from other aphasic disorders. Broca's aphasia, for example, is also a disorder in which comprehension remains largely intact, whereas speech output is dysarthric and agrammatic. But unlike the conduction aphasic, the speech of the Broca's aphasic is not at all fluent; his spontaneous speech is, in fact, worse than his repetition. In Wernicke's or sensory aphasia, there is fluent speech and poor repetition, but there is also a gross defect of comprehension that contrasts sharply with the conduction aphasic's intact ability to understand. Finally, conduction aphasia differs in its features from anomic aphasia, inasmuch as the anomic aphasic not only has good auditory comprehension, speaks fluently, but generally repeats without error. Dubois, Hécaen, Angelergues, de Chatelier, & Marcie (1964) emphasize, too, that the speech of the anomic aphasic contains none of the sound substitutions commonly found in the conduction aphasic's utterances. Detailed accounts of the contrasts between conduction aphasia and other aphasias appear in Goldstein (1948) and Brown (1972).

Unresolved Issues

To identify conduction aphasia and to contrast its symptoms with those of other aphasic disorders is not to say, however, that it is recognized everywhere as a distinctive form of linguistic deficit. The first analysis of conduction aphasia, made by Wernicke in 1874, met with the resistance of such contemporaries as Freud (1891), and even recent authors still feel the need to urge that it be recognized as one of the principal aphasic syndromes (Hécaen, Dell, & Roger, 1955; Geschwind, 1965). Benson *et al.* (1973) note that cases of conduction aphasia are frequent enough, and that they can be identified, for example, in 5% to 10% of new admissions to the aphasia ward of the Boston Veterans Administration Hospital. Yet the reluctance to recognize conduction aphasia as a well defined syndrome is due not so much to its relative infrequency as to a persistent uncertainty both about the anatomic lesions which underlie it and the nature and function of the mechanisms it disturbs. Luria (1966) asserts that conduction aphasia is a disorder "that has not received anatomical confirmation." Kinsbourne (1972) discusses some possible relations between focal lesions and the difficulties conduction aphasics have in repeating, yet he concludes that his findings "do not rely for their validity on any particular neuroanatomic hypothesis." And even studies like that of Benson *et al.* (1973), which suggest that there is a close correlation between focal lesions and the features of the syndrome, fail to demonstrate convincingly why it is that the same pattern of linguistic disorder should result from damage to different, though neighboring, areas of the posterior, dominant hemisphere of the cortex.

Moreover, from the pattern of linguistic disorder in conduction aphasia it is not immediately clear which mechanisms of speech suffer damage. The features of the syndrome—good comprehension, fluent but poorly structured spontaneous speech, impaired naming, severely disturbed repetition—indicate a disturbance primarily in some mechanism of speech output. But the nature of such mechanism and its components are by no means clearly understood; it is, indeed, hardly surprising, as Goodglass and Blumstein (1973) note, that analyses of conduction aphasia are likely to yield interpretations "totally different" from one another.

REEVALUATIONS OF THE DISORDER

Anatomic Findings

These continuing uncertainties about the nature of conduction aphasia have prompted the recent undertaking of two surveys (Howes & Green, 1972; Benson *et al.*, 1973), both of which aim to clarify issues and to investigate the possibility of deriving a cohesive set of clinicopathological findings from published cases. Benson *et al.* (1973) summarize twelve earlier reports of conduction aphasia and, in addition, supply evidence from three new cases. The findings in the literature are used by these authors to illustrate, for the first time in English, a consistent correlation between the sites of lesion and the clinical features of conduction aphasia. Thus most of the cases surveyed in this study report damage to "the posterior part of the superior temporal lobe and the inferior part of the supramarginal gyrus, the major abnormality involving the posterior portion of the perisylvian region both above and below the fissure." A few cases locate lesions either above the Sylvian fissure in the parietal operculum or wholly below, in Wernicke's area. In general, according to Benson *et al.,* conduction aphasia can result from damage to either or both of "two neighboring but different anatomical sites." Unfortunately, the authors' careful attention to neuroanatomy does not extend to behavioral features. Benson and his colleagues merely list the clinical findings in the earlier literature; they fail to integrate these findings into their discussion. The result is an unbalanced presentation, good on anatomical findings, less satisfying in describing the overall syndrome of conduction aphasia and in explaining the mechanisms related to it.

In 1972, we investigated the literature on conduction aphasia thoroughly, surveying and analyzing neuroanatomical and clinical features and the theories proposed to explain them. That study included thirty-three cases, sixteen of which provided neuroanatomical data from surgical intervention and postmortem examinations. The evidence in the present chapter includes all the clinical and anatomical findings we reported then as well as additional data; the current study is based on 52 cases, 25 of which include neuroanatomic accounts. Essentially, with regard to the neuroanatomic basis for conduction aphasia, the literature we here examined is in accord with that summarized by Benson *et al.* (1973). From reports of trauma, tumor, and vascular lesions, there emerges a consistent pattern of damage to the temporoparietal region of the dominant cerebral cortex. Thirteen cases involve an area extending from the temporal gyrus to the supramarginal gyrus. In nine cases, the temporal area is spared, and the principal damage is to the supramarginal gyrus. The remaining three cases involve the temporal area but spare the supramarginal gyrus (see Appendix A).

Partial damage to this area of cortex—for example, damage to the supramarginal gyrus that spares the temporal lobe—does not necessarily alter the clinical features associated with conduction aphasia. All 25 cases reporting neuroanatomic evidence share the principal clinical features in conduction aphasia of good comprehension, fluent speech, and impaired repetition. Moreover, there are no secondary features which might consistently subdivide conduction aphasics who have somewhat different lesions. For example, the records might have been expected to show that the speech of patients whose lesions spare the temporal gyrus contains fewer instances of neologism or jargon than that of other conduction aphasics. But a close reading of the reported clinical materials encourages no such distinction: The speech of Pick's patient (1898), who suffered gross damage in the first and second temporal gyrus, contained much jargon; but so did the speech of Pershing's (1900) case, whose lesion was in the supramarginal gyrus. Nor are there any other clinical signs of altered comprehension or speech output that subdivide conduction aphasics. In search of a clinical sign with which to distinguish patients, Benson *et al.* (1973) suggest that ideomotor apraxia—an inability to carry out motor activities (such as saluting) to commands that are fully understood—is present as a result of lesions implicating the parietal opercular region but sparing the temporal lobe. However, this suggestion cannot account for Caraceni's patient (1962) who had a tumor in the white matter of the parietal lobe yet no ideomotor apraxia, nor for Hoeft's patient (1957), who suffered gross damage in the temporal area yet did have some ideomotor apraxia. What the neuroanatomic evidence indicates instead is that the cortical area of the temporoparietal junction in the dominant hemisphere acts as a unit: Damage to this area may result in some differences in behavior among patients, such as the incidence of neologistic output or the presence of ideomotor apraxia, but the major clinical signs of good comprehension, fluent speech, and poor repetition recur consistently.

Clinical Features

The consistency of clinical features, moreover, applies to all 52 cases in the literature, not only to those that contain neuroanatomic evidence. Table 3.1, adapted from our 1972 analysis, divides the pattern of clinical features into major signs (those critical for identifying conduction aphasia) and secondary signs. The figures in Table 3.1 readily support the customary clinical view of conduction aphasia. (See Appendix B for details of each case.) In nearly 80% of the reported cases, auditory comprehension either remained within normal limits

TABLE 3.1 Reported Incidence and Degree of Severity of Major and Secondary Clinical Signs of Conduction Aphasia

Clinical Sign	Degree of severity				Number of reported cases
	Within normal limits	Mild	Moderate	Severe	
Major:					
Auditory comprehension	19	24	9	—	52
Spontaneous speech	—	26	18	7	51
Repetition	—	1	18	30	49
Secondary:					
Reading comprehension	6	9	15	8	38
Oral reading	—	9	22	17	48
Naming	—	8	15	23	46
Series speech	9	8	9	5	31
Writing	—	2	9	30	41

or suffered mild impairment. This finding, by the way, contrasts sharply with the patients' performance in reading comprehension, in which more than half exhibited considerable impairment. With respect to expressive speech, the difference between spontaneous speech and repetition is also plainly evident; nearly half the patients produced fluent, if mildly impaired, utterances, but almost all of them had moderate or severe difficulty in repetition. Furthermore, the severity of difficulty in repetition extends to naming and to oral reading. The variability in performance of spontaneous speech reflects not so much number of errors in grammar or pronunciation as rate of words produced; some patients' fluency of output was not markedly different from that of normal persons. Although the distribution of impairment among degrees of severity is greater in naming and in oral reading than in repetition, there is no significant difference among patients on their overall performance in these three tasks ($\chi^2 = 8.94$; $df = 4$; $p > .05$). Apparently in tasks requiring patients to attend with some care to specific words or phrases or to name specific objects and colors, the possibility of good performance decreases. Finally, most patients write very poorly, and it is only in series speech, that is, in listing the days of the week or the months of the year or in counting off numbers, that one finds wide differences in performance.

Linguistic Dysfunction

REPORTED CASES

The difficulties in the speech output of conduction aphasics have prompted, in more than half the 52 cases in the present study, some analysis of particular defects. Most of the emphasis has been on recording the incidence of errors in pronunciation, in word choice, and in the use of inflections and affixes. Words spoken clearly and that are recognizable but in which a patient has substituted an inappropriate sound for the one expected (e.g., /d/ for /m/ in /kədz/ "comes") or has deleted, transposed, or introduced sounds, count as instances of errors in pronunciation, or as literal paraphasias. In verbal paraphasias there is a reasonable substitution of words for those expected (e.g., a patient asked to repeat, *I saw a bear in the forest,* says, instead, "I saw a wolf in the forest"). Finally, in aphasic jargon the patient produces incomprehensible words or strings of words (e.g., "Well my /gupa/ wasn't too good"). Table 3.2, also adapted from our earlier (1972) study, presents data on the incidence of linguistic distortions in patients' speech as reported in the literature. Entries appear under spontaneous speech, repetition, naming, and oral reading; note that under grammatical errors, there is an entry for auditory comprehension, inasmuch as some patients were asked to analyze the inflections and affixes in utterances presented to them.

TABLE 3.2 Reported incidence and Degree of Severity of Different Forms of Linguistic Inadequacy

Form of inadequacy	Degree of severity				Number of reported cases
	Scant	Mild	Moderate	Severe	
Literal paraphasias in					
1. Repetition	2	4	12	11	29
2. Naming	1	5	8	7	21
3. Oral Reading	0	7	7	11	25
4. Spontaneous Speech	1	9	9	5	24
Verbal paraphasias in					
1. Repetition	6	6	10	4	26
2. Naming	8	5	6	4	23
3. Oral Reading	4	10	6	3	23
4. Spontaneous Speech	10	8	5	3	26
Jargon in					
1. Repetition	18	3	6	2	29
2. Naming	16	1	2	4	23
3. Oral Reading	20	2	0	3	25
4. Spontaneous Speech	15	7	2	2	26
Grammatical error in					
1. Repetition	2	2	6	4	14
2. Spontaneous Speech	1	0	9	8	18
3. Auditory Comprehension	1	4	8	4	17

Table 3.2 facilitates a closer analysis of impaired speech output in conduction aphasia, that is, an analysis of the different forms of linguistic inadequacy in patients' utterances. As one might expect, the several forms of linguistic inadequacy, to the degree that they are present, affect various speech tasks uniformly. Thus, literal paraphasias occur at a moderate or severe rate in repetition, naming, oral reading, and spontaneous speech. Verbal paraphasias occur more frequently in patients' repetitions (moderate or severe in 54% of cases reported) than in other speech tasks, but this difference is not statistically significant. Jargon is rare in speech output of all kinds. Somewhat more revealing is the incidence of grammatical errors, both in speech output and in patients' analysis of test items. Typically, patients cannot correct their own grammatical errors when they speak, nor can they adequately analyze grammatical features of test utterances.

What is significantly different among the linguistic inadequacies in aphasic speech, however, is their overall rate of severity. Literal paraphasias affect the speech of conduction aphasics much more severely, as Table 3.2 suggests, than do verbal paraphasias (χ^2 = 29.58; df = 3; $p <$ .001). And from inspection alone it is evident that jargon is less characteristic of speech output in conduction aphasia than any other linguistic inadequacy. Finally, literal paraphasias and grammatical errors are the most characteristic of speech output; there is no significant difference between them in rate of severity.

In sum, conduction aphasia is primarily an impairment of speech output in all its varieties that is marked most heavily with literal paraphasias and grammatical errors and that results from damage in the temporoparietal area of the dominant cortical hemisphere.

EXPERIMENTAL AND DESCRIPTIVE STUDIES OF DYSFUNCTION

The results discussed above are in substantial agreement with other studies directed at particular features of conduction aphasia. Boller and Vignolo (1966) investigated the frequency of literal paraphasias and verbal paraphasias in the repetitions of posterior aphasics. Their results showed that the repetitions of conduction aphasics contain many more literal paraphasias (to a significant degree) and fewer verbal paraphasias than did the repetitions of transcortical sensory aphasics (aphasics who repeat well but understand little). Alajouanine and Lhermitte (1964) found similar results in a test of naming ability in conduction aphasics: Literal paraphasias occurred far more frequently than verbal paraphasias in the names that patients gave to presented objects.

One recent advance in describing the expressive difficulties of conduction aphasics is made by Blumstein's phonological analysis (1973) of errors in spontaneous speech. Most literal paraphasias, as she shows, consist of sound substitutions (a patient may say /ræfs/ instead of the expected "laughs"); to a lesser degree, there are omissions of sounds, distortions that reflect particular phonological or morphological contexts (e.g., the progressive assimilation in /rof bif/ for "roast beef"), and excrescences. Further, Blumstein (1973) shows that a significant percentage of literal paraphasias in the speech of conduction aphasics are distortions of one distinctive feature. Thus, patients are more likely to pronounce "time" as /tain/, say, than as /tais/. From /m/ to /n/ is a shift in one distinctive feature of (+grave) to (−grave), which is a feature of place; from /m/ to /s/ would constitute a much more considerable shift. Blumstein (1973) says that altogether there is "a relative uniformity of error types and error directions" in conduction aphasics, and, what is more, in all aphasic groups. The profile of pronunciation errors that she draws up for conduction aphasics applies as well to Broca's and Wernicke's aphasics. Her results indicate that the greatest single difference among the three forms of aphasia is that in comparable speech samples, Broca's aphasics produce nearly four times as many literal paraphasias as conduction aphasics and nine times as many as Wernicke's aphasics. This is the only statistically significant difference found among the three groups of aphasics. It is particularly remarkable that the three groups show no difference in the kinds of literal paraphasias that they express.

It would be premature, however, to attribute this common pattern of phonological error to an impairment of a single mechanism. It is more likely that impairment of various processes that control speech output results in similar patterns of literal paraphasia. Indeed, Blumstein defines her analysis as an investigation, not of underlying processes, but of linguistic structures. Her argument is that the similarity of literal paraphasias in the speech of patients with different aphasic impairments results from a consistent distortion of sound patterns in a language, that is, to a systematic interference with the "hierarchical organization" of phonological structures. A minimal disruption to this hierarchy, regardless of the underlying processes impaired, results in similar patterns of literal paraphasia.

UNDERLYING PROCESSES

By and large, descriptions and analyses of clinicopathological features in conduction aphasia complement one another. Such congruence helps to lay the groundwork for an account of the underlying processes whose impairment results in the conduction aphasia syndrome. In our survey of the literature in 1972, we reviewed two long-standing interpretations of these processes, the first proposed by Wernicke (1874) and supported more recently by Geschwind (1965), the second advanced by Goldstein (1912, 1948) and revised by Hécaen et al., (1955). We summarized the two views as follows: Wernicke argued that conduction aphasia "results from an interruption of pathways connecting the posterior and anterior speech regions of the dominant hemisphere"; Goldstein held that it "results from disturbance of a central cortical system subserving inner speech." As these summary statements suggest, the Wernicke model relies heavily on an anatomical explanation; the Goldstein model is concerned with psychological processes. The present study undertakes a detailed analysis of each approach, including a review of recent work, in order to define some of the principal issues in the identification of the specific mechanisms whose impairment underlies conduction aphasia.

The Wernicke Model

THE DISCONNECTION THEORY

Wernicke's account of conduction aphasia was a remarkable achievement, for it preceded by some years the observation and reporting of actual cases with postmortem verification. What enabled Wernicke to predict the existence of conduction aphasia, that is, to identify it before this particular syndrome had been directly observed, was his theory of cortical organization and function in which he aimed to explicate the anatomical basis for man's ability to use language and to demonstrate how focal lesions could result in various forms of aphasic disorder. And, as we shall see, Wernicke's theory led him to foresee that one consequence of specific damage to the dominant, cortical hemisphere would be conduction aphasia.

The theory Wernicke proposed comprises a model of cortical centers that are connected to one another by fiber tracts whose combined functions underlie human language and consciousness. The centers themselves constitute two large areas of the cortex: The anterior, or motor, region contains mechanisms for directing movements necessary to produce speech sounds. The posterior center, in the first temporal gyrus, contains the auditory traces of word images. These two centers are connected directly and also by means of long fiber tracts with the perceptual traces of different kinds—tactile, visual, etc. This network is indicated in Wernicke's diagram shown in Figure 3.1.

Wernicke indicated just how the perceptual traces in the posterior region could innervate the mechanisms for producing speech sounds. In his view, these traces comprise images of different kinds: There are sound, or auditory, images of spoken words, stored in the first temporal convolution; there are also nonlin-

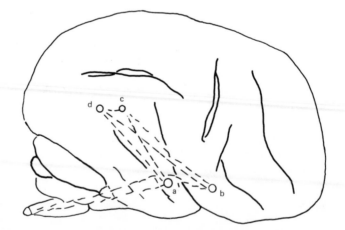

Figure 3.1 Wernicke's model of connections between traces of sensory and sound images and the mechanisms for articulatory gestures. a^1 is a site in the auditory association area for sound images; *b* is a site in the frontal region for articulatory gestures; *c* and *d* are sensory images in the posterior cortex.

guistic, sensory images of external stimuli (for example, visual and tactile images of objects) stored elsewhere (Wernicke was not certain of the anatomical sites of sensory images). Both kinds of perceptual traces—the sound images and the sensory images—function conjointly in normal brains to innervate the mechanisms for producing speech sounds. Wernicke regarded the sound images as especially valuable in the learning of new words or a new language, as instrumental in the development of accurate, articulatory gestures in the motor area. He believed, however, that once pronunciation is mastered the sensory images directly innervate the correct articulatory patterns, whereas the sound images merely have a subsidiary, regulatory function.

One immediate use that Wernicke made of this theory was to explain a variety of aphasic disorders. Damage to cortical centers results in such impairments as Broca's aphasia (a disturbance of the mechanisms for producing speech sounds in the frontal region) and sensory, or Wernicke's, aphasia (a disturbance of comprehension and speech attributable to damage in the auditory association center in the posterior region). Wernicke characterized conduction aphasia, however, as a disorder resulting from damage to the fiber tracts which connect the sound images of the posterior region to the mechanisms for producing speech sounds in the motor region. The consequence of such damage is that the patient's ability to comprehend and to speak remains intact, but his ability to choose words accurately is disturbed. The sound images of the posterior region cannot perform their regulative function, and the patient's speech becomes grossly paraphasic.

Wernicke's theory of speech processes and aphasic disorders was grounded in his knowledge of anatomy and physiology and in his own clinical observations. His analysis of conduction aphasia benefited considerably from this threefold approach, and though it has undergone change as a result of later findings in actual case studies, its influence has continued quite strong, even in current research.

MODIFICATIONS OF WERNICKE'S MODEL

a.   The Influence of Clinical and Anatomic Evidence

In many ways, subsequent changes have merely extended Wernicke's original analysis of conduction aphasia or have brought it into closer harmony with fresh evidence. Thus Lichtheim (1884) suggested that damage to the fiber tracts connecting the posterior sensory area to the frontal motor region should impair repetition, inasmuch as patients cannot use the sound images of the words they hear to control the mechanisms in the frontal area for producing speech sounds. As Geschwind (1963) points out, Lichtheim drew from Wernicke's theory an inference about impaired repetition that Wernicke himself failed to appreciate.

Wernicke had held that the fibers connecting the sensory area and the motor area came together in the insular cortex (located at the center of the hemisphere), a supposition that postmortem findings, however, did not confirm. Later, Geschwind (1965) revived a suggestion made by Wernicke (1908), after his original proposal, that the fiber tract connecting the posterior and anterior regions of the cortex might be the arcuate fasciculus. According to Geschwind (1965), "this tract runs from the posterior superior temporal regions, arches around the posterior end of the Sylvian fissure and then runs forward in the lower parietal lobe, eventually to reach the frontal lobe, and in particular Broca's area." Geschwind's suggestion is initially attractive, because it supports Wernicke's view of conduction aphasia as a disorder of language, the clinical symptoms of which result from damage to a fiber tract connecting the anterior and posterior regions of the cortex. Yet as Benson *et al.* (1973) and the present authors (Howes & Green, 1972) have shown, the lesions involved in most cases affect not merely fiber tracts but part of the sensory area or posterior superior temporal gyrus itself. Thus we need to examine closely whether conduction aphasia is a lesion primarily of fiber tracts or whether it implicates another center of cortical function that Wernicke overlooked.

In summary, Wernicke and those who have extended his research on conduction aphasia have clearly defined the features of the syndrome as consisting of poor repetition, fluent and paraphasic speech, and intact comprehension. They have also contended that the anatomic lesion underlying conduction aphasia most often implicates both the posterior third of the first temporal gyrus and the arcuate fasciculus, a fiber tract deep to the supramarginal gyrus.

b. Physiological

What has required most revision, however, is Wernicke's physiological account of the speech processes impaired in conduction aphasia. Although Wernicke (1874) argued plausibly that perceptual traces involved in the speech processes consist of distinguishable sound images and sensory images (separate images, for example, for the German *Tisch,* the English "table," and the sensory representation of the object itself), he also tried to maintain that "the actual sensory images of an object . . . are . . . able directly to innervate the representation of movement of a word directly [sic] . . . . The sound image seems simultaneously to be hallucinated, as it were, and thus exercises a continuous corrective function" on the mechanisms for producing speech sounds. Moreover, Wernicke asserted that the sensory images and sound images normally use different channels to affect the mechanisms for speech sounds in the frontal, motor region: There were also "direct connections between the visual and tactile sensory regions and the locus of representations of speech movements." The difficulty in all this, however, is that Wernicke had no anatomical evidence to show that sound and sensory images use different channels or fiber tracts, nor did Lichtheim (1884), who held the same views and offered an illustration of the possible pathways (see Figure 3.2), remarking, however, that there was a "want of demonstrative evidence" for them.

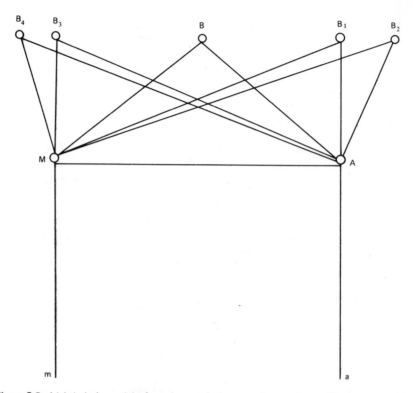

Figure 3.2 Lichtheim's model of cortico-cortical connections. *a* is an afferent branch that transmits acoustic impressions to *A*, the auditory center; *M* is the motor center from which efferent impulses to the organs of speech pass through the efferent branch *m*; B_1, B_2, B_3, and B_4 are parts of the cortex where "concepts are elaborated."

The postulation of separate channels to the motor region for sensory and sound images weakened Wernicke's theory in two ways. First, he had aimed to base his theory on anatomical evidence, yet his proposal had no demonstrable support. Second, the proposal prevented him from recognizing impaired repetition as a significant clinical sign of conduction aphasia. Wernicke had erroneously reasoned that a lesion in the fiber tract connecting the motor region and the cortical area for sound images (the lesion for conduction aphasia) would not prevent patients from using other pathways for purposes of speaking. Presumably, if their efforts were successful, the same pathways used for spontaneous speech could be used for repetition.

Freud's Revisions

The Wernicke model did not go long without criticism. Freud (1891) was among the first to explicate the shortcomings in Wernicke's model of sound and sensory images. Freud modified Wernicke's model in two ways and proposed a diagram different in some respects from Lichtheim's. From Figure 3.3, which is an adaptation of Freud's diagram, it can be seen that his schema was clearly an advance over the earlier models. Unlike Wernicke and Lichtheim, Freud connected the mechanisms for producing speech sounds directly to the mechanisms associated with sound images and to nothing else. Second, he emphasized a close bond between sound images and sensory images (for example, the bond in his diagram between visual associations to objects and sound images). In normal speech, he argued, the sound images of a word and the sensory images of the object for which it stands are closely allied: When one learns a new word he establishes a bond between these images that remains in force. In aphasic disturbances, however, the bond may be broken.

Even though his criticism suggested some valuable modifications in Wernicke's model, Freud failed to accept conduction aphasia as an actual syndrome, not even concurring in Lichtheim's analysis of it. For one thing, Freud had never seen a case that contained (all?) the features of conduction aphasia: intact comprehension, fluent but paraphasic spontaneous speech, and impaired repetition. Moreover, he regarded a lesion either in the temporal auditory association area or the tract between it and the motor center as responsible for sensory, or Wernicke's, aphasia. In Freud's view, a lesion directly in the sensory area or in the fiber tract would impair the innervation of articulatory movements in the motor area and would bring about gross disturbances in spontaneous speech and repetition. Conduction aphasia, if it could be demonstrated at all, Freud seemed to imply, would be a mild form of sensory aphasia; Wernicke's area, he suggested, "is probably so large that smaller lesions may lead to [somewhat different] clinical pictures." In one such clinical picture the disturbance in comprehension would be most severe; in another the repetition difficulty would be more pronounced, inasmuch as the lesion would disrupt the connections between sound images and the mechanisms for producing speech sounds.

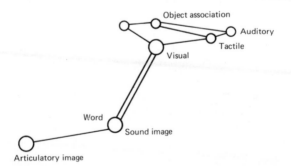

Figure 3.3 Freud's schema, showing a double bond between sound images and object associations and a single pathway between the double bond and the articulatory images.

Freud's analysis was important not only for its constructive review of Wernicke's model but also because it influenced the later studies of other aphasiologists, including Goldstein.

Goldstein's Theory of Central Aphasia

What Goldstein (1948) found particularly attractive was another idea of Freud's (1891), that there is a "unitary phenomenon as the center of language." This unitary phenomenon helped Goldstein develop his concept of "inner speech," a conceptual sphere central to language which, he claimed, is disturbed in conduction aphasia.

In his *Language and language disturbances*, Goldstein described the syndrome of *central aphasia* in this way: "Understanding is usually preserved best, repetition and spontaneous speech are always severely damaged . . . in some cases repetition is more severely damaged than spontaneous speech and vice versa. Reading and writing are always damaged, writing usually more than reading, . . . dictation in particular. Literal paraphasia is the most outstanding defect." Goldstein also reviewed the sites of lesion related to central aphasia, and, though he believed, as at first Wernicke had thought, that the insula was the region of cortex affected, he came to agree that "adjacent areas in the temporal and parietal lobe" were involved. Indeed, he went so far as to say that "the tractatus longitudinalis inferior suggests a particular role for repetition because it connects those parts of the temporal and frontal lobes which are certainly important for language." In short, Goldstein's clinicopathological account of central aphasia hardly differs, if at all, from what Wernicke and Lichtheim had proposed.

What does differ, however, is his interpretation of the processes disturbed, a difference in view that prompted him to describe the disorder as a *central* rather than a *conduction aphasia*. To understand the full significance of this change in name, we need to review briefly those aspects of Goldstein's theoretical framework which led him to reject the term *conduction* for the term *central*. The term *central* refers to a complex, cortical apparatus, the function of which is to relate external speech to nonverbal mental phenomena. By "external speech" Goldstein meant the vocal aspect of language, the speaking and hearing of utterances. By the phrase "nonverbal mental phenomena" he meant inner speech. Inner speech "belongs to the experiences which precede speaking, and is elicited by the hearing of speech." Moreover, these experiences of inner speech are not formless but involve an "organization . . . according to the 'inner speech form', in the selection of definite word structure, in the adaptation of the particular speech to the general and special situation in which it takes place, its dependence upon the environment, the listener, etc."

As for the complex, cortical apparatus itself, Goldstein regarded it as " 'underlying the concept of words'," an apparatus by means of which these concepts, described by him as "more or less fixed wholes," could affect the activity of speaking. In other words, Goldstein's apparatus is a kind of regulator that he once termed (1912) a *"Zwischenschaltung eines Vorstellungselementes"* 'an intermediary switch point of a concept-element'; it works as a control, analyzing and combining patterns of inner speech that normally influence what one says. Furthermore, inner speech and its underlying cortical apparatus are directed primarily at controlling expression and have only a tangential relationship to understanding; apparently, listening to others only serves to arouse the experiences of inner speech. In summary, Goldstein's model is primarily one of linguistic output: It proposes patterns of inner speech, mechanisms of motor speech, and a cortical apparatus to regulate expression.

In discussing possible impairments to his model for linguistic output, Goldstein argued that in central aphasia motor speech remains undisturbed, and the chief impairments are to inner speech itself and to the central, cortical apparatus. He reasoned as follows: Patients with central aphasia can speak easily enough; their effortless pronunciations in contrast to the Broca's aphasic indicate that motor speech is intact. On the other hand, patients with central aphasia cannot produce well formed words, phrases, or sentences. The organization of thoughts and experience identified with inner speech is disrupted, and the result is observable in impaired speech output. For example, the patient's inability to control his words fully is evident in the many literal paraphasias he produces.

Goldstein believed that not only impaired inner speech but damage to the central, cortical apparatus underlay aphasic impairment. Evidence of such damage is seen especially in the patient's impaired repetition; the defective cortical apparatus prevents him from matching patterns of inner speech to the models he has been given to repeat. On the other hand, the patient usually has less difficulty with spontaneous speech in which he can choose patterns and that he has found easy enough to produce. What is characteristic of all these performances of impaired speech output, however, is that the patient cannot integrate his words and phrases into complete structures. Instead of the simultaneous relationship among forms that is characteristic of normal speech output, the stream of speech in central aphasia suggests a fitful stringing together of bits and pieces, a form of speech quite imprecise in its structure.

Goldstein considered his theory an advance over the earlier notion of associations of sensory and sound images and their control of mechanisms for producing speech sounds. Although he agreed that there are sensory and speech images, he regarded them as ancillary, not basic, to thinking and language. These images might influence performance, but in no direct way, nor could they figure in the normal acts of repeating and speaking. In short, central aphasia was not just a disconnection between two cortical centers; it was due to an impairment of cortical spheres central to linguistic performance.

At the same time, Goldstein was also troubled that he could not establish a clear anatomical basis for inner speech. Inner speech was for him the central domain of language, and it may be that the very notion of centrality suggested to him that it ought to be located at the center of the dominant cortex, the insular region. Yet in his reviews of case studies, Goldstein found little evidence that lesions in the insula produce central aphasia.

Goldstein's contribution contains telling criticisms of earlier theories, yet it leaves unresolved a number of significant issues. His criticism, for example, that repetition is "not at all such a simple process" (1948) is well-taken, and surely his proposal of a central, cortical apparatus to help govern the act of repeating is valuable. On the other hand, his concept of inner speech remains insufficiently defined and his attempt to provide it with an anatomic basis unsuccessful. But to his credit, Goldstein (1948) acknowledged that "one can doubt the correctness of the interpretation."

Hécaen's Modifications of Goldstein's Model of Central Aphasia

Despite the weaknesses in Goldstein's model of central aphasia (the vague definitions of terms, the inadequacy of his neuroanatomical account of the disorder), his work has none the less helped initiate some of the best research nowadays, especially that of Hécaen and his colleagues. What the latter have done, in effect, is to delimit Goldstein's ideas, to elucidate them with the aid of valuable psycholinguistic concepts. Perhaps the most important aspect of Goldstein's work upon which they have focused is his concept of the central, cortical apparatus, instrumental in relating inner speech to the mechanisms of motor speech. The influence of this idea is plainly evident in Hécaen's view (1972) that in conduction or central aphasia (he prefers the earlier name) there is a disturbance of an active process, "a loss of the possibility of structuring thought into verbal form."

Two major studies (Hécaen *et al.*, 1955; Dubois *et al.*, 1964) undertake the revision of Goldstein's views and an outline of the psycholinguistic processes disturbed in conduction aphasia. The nature of the revision is evident in the discussion of the term "central." Although Goldstein had argued that a central feature of speech output is a cortical apparatus necessary to relate inner to external speech, he did not offer as elaborate an explication of that apparatus and its properties as Hécaen and his colleagues at the Saint-Anne Hospital in Paris have done. For the Saint-Anne group, the cortical apparatus is the central process for structuring thought into language, and within that process they include such components as matching, selecting, ordering, and regulating. Moreover, Goldstein had noted that language has an inner form of abstract structures as well as a vocal aspect, the articulatory features of pronunciation. The Saint-Anne group concur in this distinction between levels of language, but their emphasis is on language as an activity, as a double articulation of forms. For them, a speaker engages in two kinds of related linguistic articulation: The first articulation has to do with the structuring of thought into words, phrases, and sentences; the second articulation consists of producing the utterances themselves, of realizing them in phonic form. On the one hand, Goldstein's ideas have received some elaboration: There is agreement on a central function impaired. On the other, the Saint-Anne group have discarded a search for an anatomic basis of inner speech in the insular region and have instead focused on what they consider the central features of encoding: the first articulation of language and the processes for structuring it.

Their advances in delineating the features necessary to structure thought into verbal form are attributable to their close study of repetition and spontaneous speech. The analysis of breakdown in repetition clearly reveals that patients have difficulty in structuring an utterance that adequately matches a given model. Although the patients' overall comprehension of an utterance to be repeated remains intact, they find it difficult to grasp the syntactic relationships among the particular forms of the model utterances they are asked to repeat. These syntactic relationships, moreover, are ordered sequentially, each word and syllable preceding or following others in a string. To repeat adequately, one needs to appreciate just what the sequence of forms in a string is, and it is in this task that conduction aphasics fail. Often they will produce a phrase or a word, but there will be a gross defect in its structure. The patients' attempts to match models suffer from a defect in aligning structures; the output seems more like a loose ensemble of words or syllables than a well articulated utterance. Dubois *et al.* (1964) indicate, too, that patients' difficulties increase as a function of the amount of information they need to retain. Complex structures, or structures connected by a coordinating conjunction like "and," occasion considerable hardship; words of low frequency are harder to repeat than familiar ones. In a recent study Tzortzis and Albert (1974) demonstrate also how a difficulty in following the sequence of forms in a model prevents patients from repeating adequately. In carrying out a repetition task, patients are able to produce a string of words and numbers comparable to what there is in the model, but they cannot retain the proper order. In general, the results of repetition exercises show that patients are able to match models only partially: they often produce the same words contained in the model, but not in the same order.

The analysis of spontaneous speech underscores the same difficulty that conduction aphasics have in sequencing structures. In addition, it shows that there is often some inadequacy in selecting from several possibilities the word most appropriate to a context. Dubois *et al.* (1964) observe that this difficulty is due to differences in the information value of words in a string. If a patient begins an utterance with a preposition or an article, he may often omit the anticipated noun, the segment which bears information, and the result is a distorted utterance. Similarly, if patients do succeed in generating a noun, they find the task of selecting an appropriate verb—a segment that carries even more information than the noun—still more difficult, if not altogether impossible. Moreover, the control that patients exercise over the content words they manage to select is fragile indeed; a sign of this fragility appears in the distortions evident in the forms produced, in the literal paraphasias, omissions, and rearrangements of sounds that are characteristic of the words in their speech.

Finally, conduction aphasics are quite aware of their difficulties in structuring their thoughts. They often attempt to correct what they say; their efforts frequently result in slow, careful pronunciation of the syllables in a word. Moreover, patients seem to adopt strategies to circumvent many of their gross difficulties in spontaneous speech; they limit the types of sentences they produce and avoid sequences of content words, each of them contributing one after another to the meaning of an utterance.

By and large, the account of conduction aphasia presented by the Saint-Anne research group is the most satisfactory that we have. They identify the lesions underlying the disorder in the temporoparietal area; they clearly recognize that it is a center for speech encoding rather than a fiber tract that is damaged. Their analyses of the mechanisms disturbed—matching, selecting, sequencing—are certainly illuminating and complement the work done by others (see, for example, Mendilaharsu, 1958). The finding that repetition is more severely impaired than spontaneous speech is easy enough to explain, in their view, because in repetition patients must try to meet the demands of a model sentence, no matter how complex or how full of information it is. In spontaneous speech, on the other hand, patients can adopt strategies that limit the information they need to supply in utterances.

The very emphasis, however, that the Saint-Anne group places on the structuring of thought into verbal form should not suggest that impairments in the processes of encoding account in themselves for all the clinical features of conduction aphasia. Studies of particular cases, for example, indicate that patients have as much difficulty in identifying grammatical errors in presented items (see Table 3.2) as they do in avoiding such errors in their speech output. In an insightful footnote, Hécaen *et al.* (1955) suggest that the comprehension of conduction aphasics, although very good, might be disturbed in subtle ways. Secondly, the attention given to sequencing of forms is valuable, yet it does not in and of itself explain the possible interrelationships between thought and structuring or between structuring and the mechanisms controlling the second articulation of language, those which generate the phonic forms themselves. Goldstein attempted, however vaguely, some definition of inner speech; in the work of the Saint-Anne group, however, the problem of inner speech, or thought, has been held largely in abeyance. Moreover, the work of Blumstein (1973) on literal paraphasia implicitly addresses itself to questions of impaired encoding in conduction aphasia. Inasmuch as the patterns of distortion in the distinctive features of phonemes are the same for different forms of aphasia, it would seem reasonable to assume that in conduction aphasia these patterns of phonemic distortion are due to impairments in the processes of encoding. Yet the ways that impaired processes of encoding result in distortions of pronunciation have not been explicated.

STUDIES OF RECEPTIVE DIFFICULTIES IN CONDUCTION APHASIA

The recent work of the Saint-Anne group reveals a concern to extend the analysis of conduction aphasia, and to investigate possible receptive difficulties as well as expressive deficits. The Tzortzis and Albert study (1974), for example, argues that the inability of patients to sequence words correctly in a repetition task is due to "an impairment of their memory for sequences." Yet the idea that conduction aphasia entails subtle deficits of reception is not new. As Stengel and Lodge Patch (1955) suggested, the lesions common to conduction aphasia impair one's ability to attend to external stimuli. Patients understand messages, but they have difficulty in attending to the quality of the speech sounds themselves. Both forms of receptive deficit—difficulties with speech sounds and with sequences of words—clearly focus on structural properties of the speech signal, on features that identify the signal and the way in which it is ordered. A number of studies in the past decade have explored these receptive difficulties in detail and have offered accounts of the mechanisms disturbed.

Disturbances in Attending to Phonological Features of Utterances

Alajouanine and Lhermitte (1964) investigated the relationship between the sensitivity of conduction aphasics to the sounds of speech they hear and the phonological difficulties they have in repeating. To evaluate the ability of patients to recognize the phonological properties of test items, they devised several experiments easy enough for normals to carry out, but perhaps not for those with many literal paraphasias in their output. Their reasoning was that phonological difficulties in speaking reflect similar difficulties in listening. The results supported the hypothesis. Normals had no difficulty whatsoever with the various tests. Patients, however, had some difficulty (5.5% failure) in pointing at a correct picture from among a group of four whose names were either exact or near rhymes. They showed a marked impairment (21%) in discriminating correctly pronounced words from those that contained a literal paraphasia, either an inappropriate consonant or vowel. Finally, the presence of background noise prevented conduction aphasics from pointing at a correct picture (27% failure) within a group of four; this result differs sharply from the behavior of normals and of other patients with very few or no literal paraphasias in their speech.

Despite these results, however, Alajouanine and Lhermitte (1964) say of their patients that "their perceptual integration is intact." What they mean, in all likelihood, is that one can identify fine-grained variations in their ability to attend to speech signals, variations that distinguish them from other patients and from normals, but insufficient to interfere with the overall good processing of messages. Nevertheless, Alajouanine and Lhermitte regard errors on the tests they administered as symptomatic of another form of incapacity in conduction aphasia, an incapacity to derive from speech stimuli a coherent structure that can serve as a guide in pointing, discriminating, and repetition tasks.

Disturbances in Matching and Transposing Test Items

Alajouanine and Lhermitte (1964) also investigated the ability of conduction aphasics to transpose sequences of auditory and visual signals into corresponding articulations or gestures. For example, patients were asked to repeat or to tap keys in accordance with sequences (up to seven in a row) of syllables, pronounced as *ta* and *ti*. In addition, they were presented with visual sequences of dashes and dots, which they had to transpose either orally, as *ta* and *ti* syllables, or manually, by pressing the appropriate keys. Their success on visual transpositions exceeded by far their performances with auditory signals. Moreover, these same patients demonstrated little interference from delayed auditory feedback of their voices, when they were requested to recite numbers, the alphabet, the days of the week, the months of the year, a well remembered prayer or a poem; their performance differed altogether from the usual interruptions in normal behavior. From the results of all these tests (including those of auditory perception), Alajouanine and Lhermitte (1964) concluded that damage to some physiological mechanism underlies the patients' inability to organize and develop the coherent structures requisite for good performance. In effect, their conclusions accord with those of Hécaen *et al.* (1955).

More recent studies have addressed themselves to the psychological characteristics of this mechanism, the impairment of which prevents the development of a coherent linguistic structure that enables patients to repeat adequately. Shallice and Warrington (1970) and Strub and Gardner (1974), for example, investigated two possible deficits in the mechanism: severe limitations in a patient's capacity to store verbal material in short term memory or to retrieve verbal material already stored.

DEFICITS OF CAPACITY IN SHORT-TERM MEMORY

According to Shallice and Warrington (1970) the difficulty that conduction aphasics have in repeating or transposing auditory verbal material results from a deficit in short-term memory. Unfortunately, as they note, there is no general agreement on what short-term memory is, yet most studies assume that "auditory verbal span performance is primarily mediated by a single system." This single system thus constitutes short-term memory for Shallice and Warrington (1970), and it is this system, too, that suffers impairment in conduction aphasia. In their view, the deficit could be the result either of limited capacity in the system or of faulty retrieval mechanisms, and the purpose of their study is to show that the difficulties of patients do not reflect simply retrieval problems.

One way to investigate a deficit in capacity is to present paired sequences of verbal material: matching tests. The advantage of such tests is that they enable examiners to circumvent the impairments in patients' output and to focus directly on their capacity to store auditory material for a short term. In these tests, patients report only whether paired strings of numbers, letters, or words are the same or different, and in most accounts their performance is regarded as good (Warrington & Shallice, 1969; Kinsbourne, 1972; Strub & Gardner, 1974). Tzortzis and Albert (1974) report, however, that the performance of the conduction aphasics they tested was worse than that of sensory or motor aphasics. These mixed findings may result in part from the design of the tests. Whereas all the other examiners presented items in a given sequence no more quickly than a second at a time and introduced an interval of a second or two between the presentation of lists, Tzortzis and Albert (1974) presented their lists one immediately after the other. Differences even in small intervals have a telling effect; Warrington and Shallice (1969) note that their patient's ability to repeat improved as the interval between the test items grew.

Having reported these good results, however, Warrington and Shallice (1969) argue that they may simply reflect the patient's ability to perceive "at a pre-identification level in the auditory speech system," that is, that to match correctly one need not identify test items for what they actually are. If a patient actually had to identify the items and store them in short-term memory, he might have considerably greater difficulty.

This reservation about the usual matching tests led to the design of others that are more demanding as well as to the design of a probe test by Shallice and Warrington (1970). In his more difficult matching test, Kinsbourne (1972) found that his patients could determine whether paired lists of digits (up to eight digits in a list) were the same or not. To match so many numbers correctly was for him evidence enough that patients suffered no impairment in short-term memory capacity. Strub and Gardner (1974) had their patient fill the interval between list presentations by counting from one to five and found that he could still match with 90% success.

In a probe test, somewhat analogous to matching, Shallice and Warrington (1970) used a technique in which the patient had to decide whether a given letter had appeared in a sequence of five that he had heard seconds before. The test had three variations: The probe letter was given *a*) directly after the test list of five letters; *b*) after the patient had repeated the last letter in the list; and *c*) after a twenty second interval. Half the probe letters given to the patient had not appeared in the test sequences.

The purpose of the test was to determine whether patients suffered primarily from a deficit in storage capacity or in ability to retrieve items. Presumably, if the patient did well in this test, the evidence supporting a deficit in the retrieval mechanisms would be strengthened. Essentially, what the test requires is that the patient recognize the test items, rehearse them, and overcome interference effects. The results show that the patient performed best (with almost 100% success) when the probe letter was the same one as the fourth presented in the test sequence of five (the fifth was itself never directly tested), whereas the patient's success rate on letters in other positions (one through three) was no better than 60%. This discrepancy encouraged Shallice and Warrington (1970) to infer that the patient had suffered damage in short-term memory capacity, that his performance showed a diminished ability to retain material effectively. Yet this inference needs further study. The patient did very well, for example, in determining that a probe letter did not appear in a test sequence of five (77% correct under condition *c* with the longest latencies). Further, the patient had to rehearse letters; yet letters are likely to be confused, inasmuch as consonants often share similar vowel sounds (as in B, C, D, G and the like). Moreover, as Warrington and Shallice (1969) and Tzortzis and Albert (1974) show, patients do more poorly in matching letters than in matching words or digits. Finally, Shallice and Warrington (1970) seem to assume that rehearsal and recall are different, yet both are active processes, and it is just the ability to use auditory stimuli actively that most investigators regard as impaired in conduction aphasia.

DEFICITS IN RETRIEVAL OR PROCESSING

Strub and Gardner (1974) review the merits of the arguments for a deficit in short-term memory capacity and of those for a deficit in linguistic processing and retrieval. They cite the good performance of patients on matching tests as evidence against a purely mnestic incapacity. They also note that patients do not simply fail in recalling sequences of numbers, letters, or words; they produce the correct forms fairly often, but in the wrong order. In fact, the difficulties patients have in recall depend very much on the way in which stimuli are presented (visually or auditorily), on the length of the sequence, and on whether the task requires the patient to repeat or to transpose material (e.g., to point to items in an array after they have been presented visually). Table 3.3, based on evidence from Warrington and Shallice (1969), Kinsbourne (1972), Strub and Gardner (1974), and Tzortzis and Albert (1974), indicates the ways in which these various elements in tasks of transposition and repetition affect one another.

TABLE 3.3 Mean Scores in Tests of Transposition and
Repetition

Length of sequence	Items in a sequence	Number of cases	Overall sequence	Number of cases
		Transposition		
Oral response after visual presentation				
1	99%	6	—	—
2	95%	6	92%	4
3	91%	6	68%	5
4	68%	6	37%	4
5	25%	2	—	—
Pointing response after visual presentation				
2	98%	4	86%	4
3	81%	4	52%	4
4	74%	4	30%	4
Pointing response after oral presentation				
1	100%	3	—	—
2	80%	7	53%	5
3	66%	7	41%	5
4	50%	7	13%	5
		Repetition		
1	92%	6	—	—
2	70%	6	55%	5
3	60%	6	33%	5
4	48%	6	12%	5

As Table 3.3 plainly shows, the striking differences that the type of test
material and the number of test items in a sequence have upon the performances
of patients in transposing and repetition tasks underscore the great difficulty of
items presented orally. Visual stimuli are clearly easier for conduction aphasics
to process than are auditory stimuli. And obviously, too, the longer the
sequences, the poorer the performance. Repetition is the most difficult task, and
the ability to retrieve or recall items in a list is always better preserved than the
ability to present the overall sequences accurately. Pointing and oral responses
are largely analogous when the stimulus is visual (items in a sequence of three
fare somewhat better in oral response). When the stimulus is auditory, pointing
and oral responses are again analogous.

There are other, rather subtle, influences on the performances of conduction
aphasics. The effect of intervals between items presented on repetition has

already been noted. In addition, if the examiner reiterates test items before a patient repeats, performance is likely to improve (Warrington & Shallice, 1969). On the other hand, a patient may perform poorly in a visual-pointing task, if the array with stimulus materials differs in arrangement from the array of materials at which he has to point (Strub & Gardner, 1974). Finally, patients have less difficulty repeating high frequency than low frequency words.

For Warrington and Shallice (1969) the results of these tests merely give further support to their argument for an impaired capacity in short-term memory. They do not distinguish, as Strub and Gardner (1974) and Tzortzis and Albert (1974) do, between a better performance in recalling items of a sequence than in recalling an overall sequence itself. As Strub and Gardner (1974) conclude, the argument for a mnestic impairment cannot succeed merely on the evidence so far presented; in fact, it may well be that the breakdown of conduction aphasia affects a process that normally supports a cohesion and synthesis between short-term memory and linguistic function.

The simplest explanation for the receptive impairment of conduction aphasia is Kinsbourne's (1972). His view is that conduction aphasics cannot channel auditory stimuli well enough to direct the mechanisms in the frontal regions for producing the sounds of speech. The channel quickly becomes inefficient; it suffers from an overload. To support his view, Kinsbourne (1972) cites the greatly increased latencies in patients' responses, once they are asked to repeat or to transpose more than one item. What Kinsbourne says is probably correct, yet his observation avoids the issue of what in the channel or in the processes of transposing and repeating is affected. Moreover, he assumes that conduction aphasics discriminate the structure of speech without difficulty, a claim that contradicts the findings of Alajouanine and Lhermitte (1964) and of Strub and Gardner (1974).

The conclusion of Tzortzis and Albert (1974) that conduction aphasia entails a deficit in a memory for sequences has been amply demonstrated. On the other hand, it is hard to imagine that the receptive deficit in conduction aphasia is simply an inadequate memory for sequences. The findings suggest that a number of factors all contribute to the deficit of patients, not merely one.

The most satisfying discussion so far is that of Strub and Gardner (1974). In their view, the conduction aphasic retains an ability to identify words and utterances, but his capacity to analyze them so as to appreciate both their form and meaning suffers impairment. Like Kinsbourne (1972), they regard the disturbed ability as a decrease in efficiency. But what makes the Strub and Gardner model heuristic is their idea that in processing utterances, it is possible to distinguish between the "decoding for meaning" and the "selection and arragement of phonemes in their correct sequence." Any burden on this system, such as that introduced by infrequent words, unusual sound sequences, or a fast rate of presentation, may result in poor performance. Similarly, if the patient concentrates on the meaning of the forms in an exercise, he may be able to recall them on demand but probably in an incorrect sequence. One need only add that the selection and arrangement of phonemes ought to include the selection of such grammatical forms as affixes as well (see Table 3.2) and the processes disturbed in analyzing and synthesizing utterances heard will become easier to define. In short, there is for Strub and Gardner (1974) a split between form and meaning.

Moreover, in Strub and Gardner's view, the improved performance on matching is due to the relaxed demands on patients. They need only recognize an identity between sequences, not process them for such tasks as transposing and repeating. Finally, it is quite apparent that much of the work on the receptive difficulties of conduction aphasia has been confined to the study of sequences. Yet it is also evident that the difficulties patients have with utterances are selective, that they are better able to repeat commands, say, than questions, simple sentences more easily than complex structures. Surely, studies of patients' difficulties in repeating and transposing utterances ought to be undertaken.

CONCLUSION

From the comparison of case studies, the analysis of anatomic lesions, and the testing of hypotheses on the underlying mechanisms, there has developed since Wernicke's monograph of 1874 a fuller understanding of conduction aphasia. In some ways the brilliance of Wernicke's analysis still supports many of the findings made subsequent to his work. His desire to rest psychological studies on an anatomical basis has had salutary effects on the analysis of conduction aphasia. Clearly, it becomes more and more plausible to advance a theory of conduction aphasia that incorporates anatomical and clinical evidence and that sets forth a model to account for the mechanisms necessary to normal linguistic function. Briefly, conduction aphasia results from damage to a language center in the temporoparietal region that serves to synthesize meaning and form. Wernicke's suggestion is basically correct that in conduction aphasia there is a disruption to the linkages and workings of sound and sensory images (or, as they are called nowadays, auditory and other perceptual traces). The shortcomings in Wernicke's study of a disorder he had not even seen are minor, compared with the power of his insight. The work of the century following the publication of his monograph has been directed toward the modification of ideas in his model, and toward bringing them more into line with what can be empirically verified. This work is still not completed, but clearly Hécaen's analysis, as well as the valuable contributions of all those concerned with the structuring of thought into verbal output, have produced rich understanding.

Some issues and problems, however, have not received the attention they deserve. All of these—anatomical, clinical, and physiological—can aid our understanding of conduction aphasia, and a brief description of them may point the way to fruitful research.

One question that has gone unexamined in this chapter is whether the mechanisms in the minor hemisphere assume some linguistic functions after brain damage. This hypothesis, proposed by Kleist (1934), has recently found renewed support in the work of Kinsbourne (1971) and in Benson *et al.* (1973). Kinsbourne (1971) reports that a conduction aphasia patient, after a right carotid amobarbital (Amytal) injection, found himself unable to phonate, but that after an injection on the left side there was no change in the patient's performance. In short, the minor hemisphere may well be able to assume linguistic function after damage to the dominant hemisphere.

These results surely deserve further study. Moreover, they raise at least one question about interhemispheric linkages. Kinsbourne (1971) demonstrated that the minor hemisphere, without any sign of damage, assumed linguistic functions not only for a conduction aphasic, but also for a motor aphasic and possibly an anomic aphasic. Yet the output of all three aphasics was essentially different, as if the damaged hemispheres were still continuing to function. What is not clear, then, is the basis for the different performances by the three aphasics, if all were supposedly using intact minor hemispheres. Kinsbourne (1971) suggests that the minor hemisphere acts as a compensatory mechanism, not as a mechanism wholly in control. At any rate, the relationships between minor and major hemispheres surely deserve fuller analysis.

The clinical features of conduction aphasia are clearly marked, despite variations from case to case. Yet there is still considerable need for linguistic descriptions of aphasic performance. Table 3.2, which presents data on linguistic dysfunction, is not a satisfactory account. The literature contains only one careful analysis of phonological distortions in the spontaneous speech of conduction aphasics (Blumstein, 1973), and there is comparable analysis of such patients' failures in repetition and in oral reading. If the mechanism disturbed in conduction aphasia is one that does indeed structure thought into verbal form, then detailed analyses of breakdown in that mechanism might well assist in determining relative complexity in linguistic structures, and also in determining whether the structuring of utterances is an independent process or is a process that is affected by the nature of the speech act. In other words, if a patient is asked to repeat and to read aloud, is his ability to produce various linguistic structures affected by the nature of the task?

A century of work on conduction aphasia suggests that the mechanisms it affects are certainly integral to linguistic structures and functions. The studies of Alajouanine and Lhermitte (1964), Dubois *et al.* (1964), Shallice and Warrington (1970), and Strub and Gardner (1974) all present informal models of the mechanisms disturbed. Yet we still await a series of studies that will systematically investigate the factors that may contribute to the breakdown of mechanisms, and that will analyze the interrelationships between these mechanisms

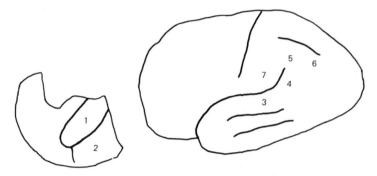

Figure A.1 Areas of the dominant cortical hemisphere implicated in cases of conduction aphasia.

and the ways in which damage to them affects patients' performance. If we can learn how these mechanisms work, we may again have a situation in which studies in aphasia cast valuable light on normal functioning of language.

APPENDIX A

Twenty-five cases of conduction aphasia, for which there is surgical or post-mortem evidence, are presented in Table A.1. The criterion for accepting these as cases of conduction aphasia was simply that they have been so identified in the literature and exhibit the three major clinical signs of Table 3.1.

Table A.1 presents a synopsis of each case and includes data on both the type of damage and on the extent to which it affects the dominant hemisphere. Fifteen of these cases are reported by Benson et al. (1973), and a comparison of Table A.1 with their findings will show close agreement. Even a cursory examination of the table demonstrates that the major site of damage is in the temporoparietal area.

Figure A.1 illustrates regions of the cortex, except for the insula, which have been implicated in cases of conduction aphasia.

APPENDIX B

Table B.1, below, records the performance of fifty-two conduction aphasics on tests of auditory and reading comprehension and on tests of spontaneous speech, reading aloud, repetition, and naming. Performances are rated from 1 to 4 according to degree of impairment exhibited (see footnote *a* to Table B.1 for detailed explanation of rating system). Qualitative comments in the literature, directed at the overall performance of patients in a task, generally took precedence over examples listed in evaluating impairments.

TABLE A.1 Surgical and Postmortem Reports of Lesions in Twenty-Five Cases of Conduction Aphasia

Author and date of case report	Type of lesion	Locus[a]							
		1	2	3	4	5	6	7	8
1. Lichtheim, 1884	infarct			1	2	2			1
2. Pick, 1898	infarct		2						1
3. Pershing, 1900	infarct					1		1	
4. Goldstein, 1911	tumor			1					1
5. Liepmann & Pappenheim, 1914	infarct	1		1	2	1	1		
6. Bonhoeffer, 1923	infarct		1		2	2	1		
7. Pötzl, 1925	infarct				2				
8. Hilpert, 1930	abscess				2	2			
9. Stengel, 1933	tumor			1	2		1		
10. Pötzl & Stengel, 1937	infarct	1	1		2	2			1
11. Goldstein & Marmor, 1938	infarct	1		2	1		1		1
12. Coenen, 1940	infarct	1		1	2		2		
13. Stengel & Lodge Patch, 1955	infarct			1	2	2	1	1	
14. Hécaen et al., 1955	tumor			1	2		1		
15. Hoeft, 1957	infarct			2	2				
16. Konorski et al., 1961	tumor			2					
17. Kleist, 1962	infarct		2	2	1		1		
18. Kleist, 1962	infarct	1	1	2	2				
19. Caraceni, 1962	tumor					2			
20. Warrington et al., 1971	tumor				2	2			
21. Warrington et al., 1971	tumor			2	2	2	1		
22. Brown, 1972	tumor					1	2		
23. Benson et al., 1973	infarct				2	1	2		
24. Benson et al., 1973	infarct				2	2	1		
25. Benson et al., 1973	infarct		1	2		1			1
Total cases of partial damage		5	4	7	2	5	9	2	6
Total cases of severe damage		0	1	8	16	9	3	0	0
Total damage (out of possible 50)		5	6	23	34	23	15	2	6

[a]Key to locus numbers: 1. Heschl's gyrus; 2. Planum temporale (posterior); 3. First temporal gyrus (posterior); 4. Supramarginal gyrus; 5. Supramarginal gyrus; 6. Angular gyrus; 7. Parietal operculum; 8. Insula.

Key to cell numbers: 1 = partial damage; 2 = severe damage. All 1s and 2s are summed separately to obtain column totals for partial and severe damage. Figures for total overall damage were obtained by multiplying each total for severe damage by two and adding that total column's total for partial damage.

TABLE B.1 Performance of Patients in Tests of Comprehension and Expression[a]

Author and date of case report[b]	Comprehension Tests		Expression Tests			
	Auditory	Reading	Spontaneous speech	Reading aloud	Repetition	Naming
Wernicke, 1874 (B)	1	4	3	4	—	4
Wernicke, 1874 (K)	1	—	3	2	—	3
Lichtheim, 1884	1	1	4	4	4	—
Pick, 1898	2	2	4	4	4	4
Pershing, 1900	2	4	4	4	—	4
Kleist, 1905	2	3	4	3	4	4
Goldstein, 1906	3	3	3	3	4	3
Lewy, 1908	1	3	3	2	3	4
Goldstein, 1911	1	—	2	3	2	3
Försterling and Rhein, 1914	2	2	2	2	4	4
Liepmann & Pappenheim, 1914	2	2	2	3	3	3
Stertz, 1914	2	2	2	4	4	4
Kleist, 1916	3	2	2	3	3	3
Isserlin, 1920	2	3	4	3	4	—
Bonhoeffer, 1923	3	2	2	3	3	4
Pötzl, 1925	1	—	2	4	4	2
Grubel, 1926	2	3	3	3	3	2
Hilpert, 1930	2	2	4	4	3	3
Klein, 1931	2	3	2	3	4	4
Stengel, 1933	3	3	2	3	4	3
Pötzl & Stengel, 1937	2	—	3	3	4	4
Goldstein and Marmor, 1938	3	4	3	4	4	4
Coenen, 1940	1	—	3	3	4	4
Conrad, 1948	2	—	2	3	3	4
Hécaen et al., 1955 (B)	2	4	3	4	4	3
Hécaen et al., 1955 (M)	1	—	3	4	3	4
Stengel & Lodge Patch, 1955 (W)	3	—	2	2	4	4
Stengel & Lodge Patch, 1955 (W)	3	—	2	2	4	4
Stengel & Lodge Patch, 1955 (E)	3	4	3	—	4	3
Hoeft, 1957	1	—	3	—	3	4
Konorski et al., 1961	2	—	2	—	4	2
Caraceni, 1962 (G)	2	3	3	4	3	3
Caraceni, 1962 (C)	2	4	3	4	3	4

(continued)

TABLE B.1 (continued)

Author and date of case report[b]	Comprehension Tests		Expression Tests			
	Auditory	Reading	Spontaneous speech	Reading aloud	Repetition	Naming
Dubois *et al.*, 1964 (R)	1	1	2	3	4	3
Dubois *et al.*, 1964 (W)	1	1	2	3	4	3
Luria *et al.*, 1967 (K)	3	—	—	3	3	3
Luria *et al.*, 1967 (B)	1	3	4	—	3	4
Marcie, 1967[c] (Ch)	1	2	2	2	4	—
Marcie, 1967 (Cl)	2	1	2	2	3	—
Marcie, 1967 (L)	2	4	2	3	4	—
Warrington *et al.*, 1967	2	4	3	3	3	2
Warrington *et al.*, 1971 (H)	2	—	3	2	3	2
Warrington *et al.*, 1971 (B)	2	1	2	2	3	2
Brown, 1972	1	3	2	4	3	3
Kinsbourne, 1972 (T)	1	3	3	3	4	4
Kinsbourne, 1972 (O)	2	3	2	3	4	—
Benson *et al.*, 1973 (1)	1	2	2	4	4	4
Benson *et al.*, 1973 (2)	1	3	2	4	4	4
Benson *et al.*, 1973 (3)	1	—	3	4	4	4
Tzortzis *et al.*, 1974 (1)	2	3	2	3	4	2
Tzortzis *et al.*, 1974 (3)	1	1	2	2	4	2
Strub *et al.*, 1974	2	—	2	3	4	3

[a]Numbers in cells indicate degree of impairment exhibited, according to the following rating scale: 1 = performance within normal limits; 2 = mild impairment (65% to 98% of trials correct); 3 = moderate impairment (35% to 65% correct); 4 = severe impairment (less than 35% correct).

[b]Multiple cases reported by one author are identified by final initial or by order of appearance.

[c]P. Marcie kindly provided us with three cases not generally available, for which we thank him.

Recorded samples of patients' performances were evaluated as follows: successes and failures in various tasks (e.g., naming of objects, colors, and numbers) were totaled, averaged, and the result rated for severity. Examples of spontaneous speech were analyzed for instances of paraphasia and grammatical error, but most reliance was placed, when possible, on whatever qualifying comment the case study offered. The results of this abstracting from case reports were compared with the descriptions in Benson et al. (1973), and there was more than 90% agreement on evaluations.

REFERENCES

Alajouanine, T., & Lhermitte, F. 1964. Les composantes phonémiques et sémantiques de la jargonaphasie. *International Journal of Neurology, 4,* 277–286. Reprinted in H. Goodglass and S. E. Blumstein (Eds. & Trans.), *Psycholinguistics and aphasia* (Baltimore: The Johns Hopkins University Press, 1973). Pp. 319–329.

Benson, D. R., Sheremata, W. A., Bouchard, R., Segarra, J. M., Price, D., & Geschwind, N. 1973. Conduction aphasia: A clinicopathological study. *Archives of Neurology, 28,* 339–346.

Blumstein, S. E. 1973. *A phonological investigation of aphasic speech* (The Hague: Mouton).

Boller, F., & Vignolo, L. A. 1966. Il Significato Dei Disturbi Della Ripetizione Nell'Afasia Di Wernicke. *Sistema Nervoso, 18,* 383–396.

Bonhoeffer, K. 1923. Zur Klinik und Lokalisation des Agrammatismus und der Rechts-Links-Desorientierung. *Monatsschrift für Psychiatrie und Neurologie, 54,* 11–42.

Brown, J. W. 1972. *Aphasia, apraxia and agnosia* (Springfield, Ill: Charles C Thomas).

Caraceni, T. 1962. "L'afasia di conduzione," *Rivista di Patologia Nervosa e Mentale 83,* 531–551.

Coenen, W. 1940. Klinischer und anatomischer Beitrag zur Frage der Leitungsaphasie. *Archiv für Psychiatrie, 112,* 664–678.

Conrad, K. 1948. Zur Problem der Leitungsaphasie. *Deutsche Zeitschrift für Nervenheilkunde, 159,* 188–227.

Dubois, J., Hécaen, H., Angelergues, R., de Chatelier, A., & Marcie, P. 1964. Etude neurolinguistique de l'aphasie de conduction. *Neuropsychologia, 2,* 9–44; Reprinted in H. Goodglass and S. E. Blumstein (Eds. & trans.) (1973) *Psycholinguistics and aphasia,* Baltimore: The Johns Hopkins University Press. Pp. 284–300.

Försterling, W., & Rein, O. 1914. Beitrag zur Lehre von der Leitungsaphasie nebst Bemerkungen über Lesen und Schrieben Aphasischer. *Zeitschrift für die gesamte Neurologie und Psychiatrie, 22,* 417–456.

Freud, S. 1891. *Zur Affassung des Aphasien.* Leipzig: Franz Deuticke. Translated in E. Stengel (1953), *On aphasia, a critical study* New York: International University Press.

Geschwind, N. 1963. Carl Wernicke, the Breslau School, and the history of aphasia. in *Brain Function,* Vol. III, No. 4, E. C. Carterette (Ed.), Berkeley: The University of California Press. Pp. 1–16.

Geschwind, N. 1965. Disconnexion Syndromes in Animals and Man, Part II. *Brain 88,* 585–644.

Goldstein, K. 1906. Ein Beitrag zur Lehre von der Aphasie. *Journal für Psychologie und Neurologie, 7,* 172–188.

Goldstein, K. 1911. Die amnestische und die zentrale Aphasie (Leitungsaphasie). *Archiv für Psychiatrie und Neurologie, 48,* 314–343.

Goldstein, K. 1912. Die zentrale Aphasie, *Neurologisches Zentralblatt, 12,* 739–751.

Goldstein, K. 1948. *Language and language disturbances* New York: Grune and Stratton.

Goldstein, K., & Marmor, J. 1938. A case of aphasia, with special reference to the problems of repetition and word-finding. *Journal of Neurology and Psychiatry, 1* (New Series), 329–339.

Goodglass, H., & Blumstein, S. E. 1973. *Psycholinguistics and aphasia* Baltimore: The Johns Hopkins University Press.

Grubel, R. 1926. Ein Beitrag zur Frage der Leitungsaphasie. *Archiv für Psychiatrie und Nervenheilkunde 76,* 410–430.

Hécaen, H. 1972. Studies of Language Pathology. *Current trends in linguistics,* Vol. 9, T. A. Sebeok (Ed.), The Hague: Mouton, Pp. 591–645.

Hécaen, H., Dell, M. B., & Roger, A. 1955. L'Aphasie De Conduction (Leitungsaphasie). *Encéphale 2*, 170–195.

Hilpert, P. 1930. Die Bedeutung des linken Parietallappens für das Sprechen. *Journal für Psychologie und Neurologie, 40*, 225–255.

Hoeft, H. 1957. Klinisch-anatomischer Beitrag zur Kenntnis der Nachsprechaphasie (Leitungsaphasie). *Deutsche Zeitschrift für Nervenheilkunde, 175*, 560–594.

Howes, D., & Green, E. 1972. Expressive aphasia from posterior cerebral lesions: A reevaluation of conduction or central aphasia. Unpublished paper given at the Academy of Aphasia, Rochester, New York.

Isserlin, M. 1920. Demonstrationen Hirnverletzter (Agrammatismus, subcorticale Aphasie und Leitungsaphasie, optische Agnosie). *Zeitschrift für die gesamte Neurologie und Psychiatrie, Referate 21*, 357–363.

Kinsbourne, M. 1971. The Minor Cerebral Hemisphere as a Source of Aphasic Speech. *Archives of Neurology, 25*, 302–306.

Kinsbourne, M. 1972. Behavioral analysis of the repetition deficit in conduction aphasia. *Neurology, 22*, 1126–1132.

Klein, R. 1931. Über leitungsaphasie. *Monatsschrift für Psychiatrie und Neurologie, 80*, 188–221.

Kleist, K. 1905. Über Leitungsaphasie. *Monatsschrift für Psychiatrie und Neurologie, 17*, 503–532.

Kleist, K. 1916. Über Leitungsaphasie und grammatische Störungen. *Monatsschrift für Psychiatrie und Neurologie, 40*, 118–199.

Kleist, K. 1934. *Gehirnpathologie*. Leipzig: Barth.

Kleist, K. 1962. *Sensory aphasia & amusia*. Translated by T. J. Fish and J. B. Stanton, Oxford: Pergamon Press.

Konorski, J., Kozniewska, H., and Stepien, L. 1961. Analysis of symptoms and cerebral localization of the audio-verbal Aphasia. *Proceedings of the VII International Congress of Neurology II*, (Rome: Societa Grafica Romana), Pp. 234–236.

Lewy, F. H. 1908. Ein ungewöhnlicher Fall von Sprachstörung als Beitrag zur Lehre von der sogenannten amnestischen und Leitungsaphasie. *Neurologisches Zentralblatt, 27*, 802–814, 850–861.

Lichtheim, L. 1884. Über Aphasie. *Deutsches Archiv für klinische Medizin, 36*, 204–268; Reprinted and translated in *Brain 7*, 433–484.

Liepmann, H., & Pappenheim, M. 1914. Über einen Fall von sogenannter Leitungsaphasie mit anatomischen Befund. *Zeitschrift für die gesamte Neurologie und Psychiatrie, 27*, 1–41.

Luria, A. R. 1966. *Higher cortical functions in man*. Translated by B. Haigh. New York: Basic Books.

Luria, A. R., Sokolov, E. N., & Klimkowski, M. 1967. Toward a neurodynamic analysis of memory disturbances with lesions of the left temporal lobe. *Neuropsychologia 5*, 1–10.

Mendilaharsu, S. A., Mendilaharsu, C., & Berta, M. 1958. Algunas consideraciones sobre la afasia central. *Acta Neurologica Latinoamericana, 4*, 11–23.

Pershing, H. T. 1900. A case of Wernicke's conduction asphasia with autopsy. *The Journal of Nervous and Mental Disease, 27*, 369–374.

Pick, A. 1898. *Beiträge zur Pathologie und pathologischen Anatomie des Zentralnerven-systems*. Berlin: Karger. Pp. 134–149.

Pötzl, O. 1925. Über die parietal bedingte Aphasie und ihren Einfluss auf das Sprechen mehrerer Sprachen. *Zeitschrift für die gesamte Neurologie und Psychiatrie, 96*, 100–124.

Pötzl, O., & Stengel, E. 1937. Über das Syndrom Leitungsaphasie-Schmerzasymbolie", *Jahrbucher für Psychiatrie, 53*, 174–207.

Shallice, T., & Warrington, E. K. 1970. Independent functioning of verbal memory stores: A neuropsychological study. *Quarterly Journal of Experimental Psychology, 22,* 261–273.

Stengel, E. 1933. Zur Lehre von der Leitungsaphasie. *Zeitschrfit für die gesamte Neurologie und Psychiatrie, 149,* 266–291.

Stengel, E., & Lodge Patch, I. C. 1955. 'Central' aphasia associated with parietal sympoms". *Brain, 78,* 401–416.

Stertz, G. 1914. Über die Leitungsaphasie. Beitrag zur Auffassung aphasischer Storungen. *Monatsschrift fur Psychiatrie und Neurologie, 35,* 318–359.

Strub, R. L., & Gardner, H. 1974. The repetition defect in conduction aphasia: Mnestic or linguistic?. *Brain and Language, 1,* 241–256.

Tzortzis, C., & Albert, M. 1974. Impairment of memory for sequences in conduction aphasia. *Neuropsychologia, 12,* 355–366.

Warrington, E. K., & Shallice, T. 1969. The selective impairment of auditory verbal short-term memory. *Brain, 92,* 885–896.

Warrington, E. K., Logue, V., & Pratt, R. T. C. 1971. The anatomical localisation of selective impairment of auditory verbal short-term memory. *Neuropsychologia, 9,* 377–387.

Wernicke, C. 1874. *Der Aphasische Symptomencomplex* Breslau: Cohn and Weigert. Reprinted and translated in *Boston studies in the philosophy of science,* Vol. IV. Dordrecht, Holland: D. Reidel.

Wernicke, C. 1908. The symptom-complex of aphasia. in *Diseases of the Nervous System.* A. Church (Ed.) London: Appleton.

4

The Limbic System
in Human Communication[1]

John T. Lamendella

SAN JOSE STATE UNIVERSITY

INTRODUCTION

Recent investigations into the neurological substrata of language processing have tended to emphasize two areas of empirical research: first, the pathology and symptomology of *language disorders*, and second, the *lateralization of language functions* to one or the other cerebral hemisphere (cf. Dingwall & Whitaker, 1974). Common to both interests has been an almost exclusive concern for the neocortical systems of the brain and for language and speech. Reasonable as this may seem, such a focus actually provides too narrow a theoretical foundation because grammatically organized, phonologically structured verbal encodings of messages constitute only one of many levels and types of human communication. There has been both a general failure to distinguish adequately among the many varieties of communication systems characteristic of our species and an unhealthy reliance on the term *language* as a catchall for widely divergent aspects of communication. The two most famous "language areas" of the brain—Broca's area in the frontal, and Wernicke's area in the temporoparietal region of the dominant hemisphere—are not language areas at all, but peripheral "speech" regions at best. The systems of Broca's area are involved in controlling the motor speech activity of the vocal tract articulators,

---

[1] This paper is an expanded version of a paper read before the Winter 1975 meeting of the Linguistic Society of America.

and the neural systems of Wernicke's area are involved in secondary auditory processing of incoming speech. No evidence exists that would allow us to associate these regions directly to the central processes that result in language formulation and language comprehension or to more basic underlying communication motives, strategies, and content. Furthermore, not every verbal aspect of communication is ipso facto deserving of the label "language." Anomic aphasics have difficulties applying lexical labels to objects in elicited and spontaneous naming situations (versus a more or less intact ability to use words in sentences). However, retrieving lexical labels as part of naming behavior cannot technically be called a language skill since such naming exists in the child long before the syntactic and morphological rules that are the definienda of language processing begin to regulate verbal production. Even though they are phonologically structured, the child's labels for objects during the naming stage are not used to communicate propositional messages. Although naming behavior is later assimilated into language production, we must bear in mind its distinctive character as a "prelanguage" capability.

If some scholars have used the term *language* too loosely, applying it to any and all aspects of human communication, the linguist has too often dealt only with *sentences*, which are formal constructs isolated from discourse, context, and the communicative interaction of speaker and hearer. This sharp focus is of limited usefulness even for the linguist's own goals,[2] but it is especially ill suited to understanding the way linguistic information processing is carried out by neural systems. This is true in part because the so-called extralinguistic and nonverbal aspects of communication aren't mere window-dressing that accompany sentences optionally but a fundamental ingredient of the process by which people decode and encode messages. Many propositional and symbolic components of communicative interactions are not expressed by linguistic means but rather by way of conventionalized manual gestures, body movements, facial expressions, and prosodic elements beyond phonology. These symbolic activities cannot be considered language in any strict sense, although from the point of view of the neural systems responsible for propositional communication, they are likely to be merely alternative output channels to language based on neural processes at the same level. Over and above these intentional nonverbal communication schemata, there are still other forms of nonpropositional multimodal behavior patterns that communicate. Some are output automatically under

[2] Many linguists have recently rejected the narrow goals promulgated by Chomsky's standard theory transformational grammar. Pragmatics, functionalism, relational grammar, and a concern for discourse structure have had the effect of broadening the linguist's horizons (cf. Kuno, 1972; Fillmore, 1975; Lakoff, 1974; Grossman *et al.*, 1975; Fauconnier, 1975). This shift has not yet been accompanied by a parallel refocusing within neurolinguistics that would clarify the status of a large number of communication phenomena that are too readily labeled "language."

specifiable internal and external conditions, and others are produced intentionally. Both are the product of neural elements other than the neocortical structures on which neurolinguists have focused their attention. The neurolinguist needs to maintain a broad view of communication phenomena so as not to exclude relevant facts from consideration. In addition, however, we must establish an explicit set of criteria capable of differentiating between the various categories and levels of language and nonlanguage phenomena. Only then will it become possible to understand how particular communication functions are carried out by particular neocortical and non-neocortical neural subsystems.

The obvious candidate for the level of brain activity likely to be responsible for the bulk of nonpropositional human communication is the *limbic system*. This forebrain network of cortical and subcortical structures has often been thought of only in relation to its regulation of emotion and motivation, but in fact its range of functional responsibilities is quite large and includes major segments of our social and communicative behavior. It is known that we share these structures homologously with other mammals, and that for nonhuman primates the limbic system comprises the level of neural activity that controls species-wide communication interactions. Up to some point in human ontogeny it is principally the infant's limbic system that controls instinctual behavior patterns for interacting with others in the environment. Furthermore, the majority of the limbic functions acquired by the child remain part of the adult communication repertoire as a neurobehavioral framework into which linguistic communication is embedded. There can be no doubt that the limbic system plays an important role in human communication of all types. Although there are huge literatures on both the limbic system and human communication, surprisingly little attention has been paid to the intersection of these two areas of research.

What I would like to do here is to help rectify this situation of neglect by presenting an overview of the limbic system and of research into its functional activity. I will summarize some tentative conclusions that may be drawn about social and communication functions of limbic subsystems for primates in general and how they are integrated with higher and lower levels of forebrain activity in humans. Undoubtedly, the limbic system has been neglected by nonspecialists both because of the great complexity of its anatomical and functional organization and because of our current low level of understanding of its activity as a unified system. Within the constraints of this paper it will be impossible to do more than present the general outlines of limbic anatomical and physiological makeup, as I wish to emphasize the role of this system in social and communicative behavior. I will discuss the evolution of the limbic system in our species, its development in human ontogeny, and several human clinical syndromes that have limbic etiologies, and I will conclude the chapter with a brief overview of the relationship between limbic and linguistic communication.

PHYLOGENETIC PERSPECTIVE ON THE LIMBIC SYSTEM

In the evolution of multicellular organisms, two major physiological systems developed to coordinate the activity of the individual's specialized subsystems. One is the *endocrine system*, which regulates basic metabolic activity of internal physiological systems by means of hormone messengers. The other is the *nervous system*, which served initially to coordinate interactions between sensory receptors and motor effectors. At some point, development of neural structures sensitive to the internal chemical environment of the body allowed the nervous system to control also the activity of the endocrine system based on sensory input and in concert with motor output. The prime example of such regulatory interaction takes place within the core brain structure called the *hypothalamus*, a complex of nuclei within the diencephalon division of the forebrain. It is out of systems capable of regulating internal chemical activity that there later evolved forebrain structures with a sensitivity to the external chemical environment, from which, in turn, the olfactory sensory system eventually developed. It is probably this evolutionary history that accounts for the close relationship existing in modern vertebrates between olfactory systems of the forebrain and visceral regulatory systems (Riss, Halpern, & Scalia, 1969). Among vertebrates, the sense of smell is tremendously important; for many species it is the principal means of acquiring information about the external world and the modality used to establish communication with members of social species. It is not surprising, therefore, that when systems evolved that allowed organisms to individually modify their species-specific response patterns to environmental stimuli, they developed to a large extent as elaborations of forebrain olfactory systems. The result was a new level of neural organization superimposed on striatal, midbrain, and hindbrain systems. This level of brain structure has traditionally been called the *rhinencephalon*, or "nose-brain," the second division of the vertebrate telencephalon (See Figure 4.1). Rhinencephalic systems contributed to the release of the higher vertebrates from the limited range of stereotyped responses available to the invertebrates and lower vertebrates. In primates, vision has supplanted smell as the major sensory input channel and is the primary basis for representing and processing external reality. Nevertheless, olfactory input still

Figure 4.1 *Two views of the human rhinencephalon.* (a) Ventromedial view of the right cerebrum; (b) The rhinencephalon as seen from above. *Abbreviations*: Amyg., amygdala; Ante. Comm., A.C., anterior commissure; Ante., anterior nucleus of thalamus; Bulb, olfactory bulb; Comm. Hipp., hippocampal commissure; Dent.G., dentate gyrus; Diag. Bd., diagonal band; Hab., habenula; Hap-ped., habenulopeduncular tract; Hipp., hippocampus; Iped., interpeduncular nucleus; Lat.St., lateral olfactory stria; Long. St., longitudinal stria; Mam., mammillary body; Med.St., medial olfactory stria; M.F.B., medial forebrain bundle; M.th., mammillothalamic tract; St.Med., stria medullaris; St.Term., stria terminalis; Subcal., subcallosal gyrus; Tract., olfactory tract; Tub., olfactory tubercle. [From Krieg, 1966, pp. 345, 346.]

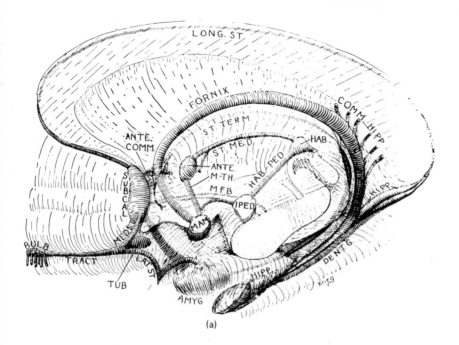

(a)

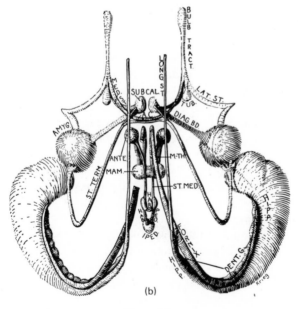

(b)

Figure 4.1

has a great capacity for influence in arousal, feeding behavior, fear and flight, sex, territoriality, and so on.

During the later 19th century, it was recognized (by Broca among others) that the rhinencephalon constitutes the greatest common denominator among the brains of the various types of mammals. It is relatively easy to trace the homologous realization of this level of brain organization among living species. Although a great many changes have occurred in the evolution of the vertebrate brain, rhinencephalic structures tend to maintain approximately the same functional interrelationships with each other. This is true even when they drastically change their relative position, as a result of, among other things, the pressure of the tremendously expanding neocortex of the *pallium* (the third subdivision of the vertebrate telencephalon). To understand the human rhinencephalon in relation to the brains of contemporary nonhuman vertebrates, it is helpful to realize that the primitive vertebrate forebrain was essentially cylindrical in shape, with the various zones like the hippocampus, septum, olfactory cortex, and so on, arranged like the staves of a barrel. The olfactory bulb, so prominent in the brains of lower vertebrates and most mammals as well, is like the bulging head of the barrel (Krieg, 1966). As one progresses up the phylogenetic scale, changes take place in the position of rhinencephalic components away from this basic structural plan. For example, the greater part of the hippocampus migrates far backward and downward, leaving in our species only a meagre rudiment (the *indusium griseum*) above the commissural fibers of the increasingly large corpus callosum (see (a) and (c) of Figure 4.2, and numbers 10 and 18 of Figure 4.3, for the location of the hippocampal rudiment above the corpus callosum). A second rhinencephalic component that has undergone drastic changes in position is the *amygdala*, a complex nuclear group derived partially from the *striatum* (the first division of the vertebrate telencephalon) and partially from the rhinencephalon. In the lower vertebrates the amygdaloid complex is located on the posterior surface of the cerebrum. As the neocortex expanded, the amygdala was pushed in an anterior direction and eventually was buried below the surface of the temporal lobe by the olfactory cortex as the latter was pushed back by neocortical expansion (see (b) of Figure 4.2). Figure 4.3 illustrates the realization of allocortical regions within the ascending primate scale and Figure 4.4 shows the modified recapitulation of this evolution as it occurs in human embryological development.

Beyond changes in position, the most striking differences between the rhinencephalon of higher and lower vertebrates result from the evolution in the higher forms of increasingly more complex types of *cortex* (Latin: 'bark, rind'). A cortical structure is the result of the migration of neurons during embryological development from tightly packed nuclear groupings of cell bodies and the horizontal distribution of these neurons into a superficial laminar array. The evolution of the various types of cortex occurred gradually, and there exist

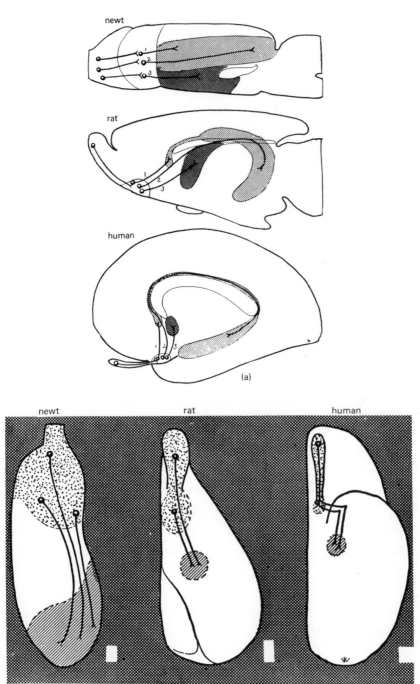

newt   rat   human

(b)

Figure 4.2 (Figure caption and part (c) on page 164)

newt

rat

human

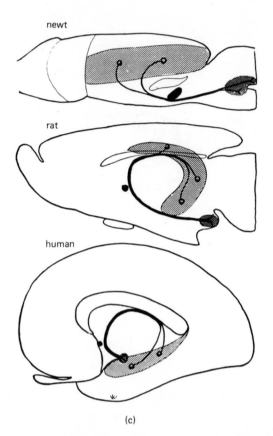

(c)

Figure 4.2 *The evolution of limbic system components.* (a) Medial view of the cerebrum of the newt, rat, and human, showing the evolution of the medial olfactory striae in relation to the hippocampus (lightly hatched) and septum (darkly hatched). 1, to anterior end of hippocampus (primordium hippocampi); 2, to hippocampus proper; 3, to septal nuclei. (b) Basal view of the cerebrum of the newt, rat, and human, showing the evolution of the lateral olfactory stria. The amygdala (lightly hatched area) shows a migration forward, ending up buried in the anterior portion of the temporal lobe in humans. (c) Medial view of the cerebrum of the newt, rat, and human, showing the evolution of the fornix in relation to the hippocampus (light hatching), mammillary body or its forerunner (dark hatching), and the anterior commissure (black). [From Krieg, 1966, pp. 341, 342, 350.]

several structures that are partially cortical and partially nuclear. (The *septum* in the human brain [see no. 12 of Figure 4.3] contains both a complex of *septal nuclei* and a *septal area*, a region of semicortex with a laminar structure.) In primates, the rhinencephalon contains an abundance of cortical structures, though none of the six-layered neocortex that has been called *isocortex* ("true" cortex in contrast to the *allocortex* or "other" cortex). Virtually all cortical structures other than the isocortex of the pallium are located within the limbic system and carry out limbic functions. The phylogenetically oldest type of

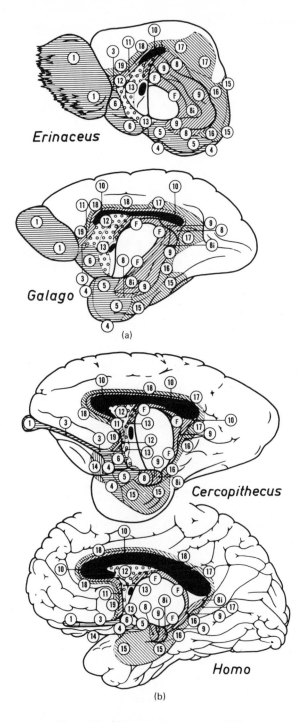

Erinaceus

Galago

(a)

Cercopithecus

Homo

(b)

Figure 4.3 (Figure caption on page 166)

cortex arose within the olfactory system and is found making up the *prepyriform* or *olfactory cortex* (see no. 4 of Figure 4.3). This type of cortex has basically a two-layered organization and is called *paleocortex*. The second major type of cortex arose within the complex of structures commonly known as the *hippocampus* (see nos. 7–11 of Figure 4.3), consisting of basically three layers and called *archicortex*.[3] An established finding within comparative neurology whose existence and implications have mostly been ignored is the notion of Dart (1934), corroborated by Abbie (1940, 1942), that all higher types of cortex, including the neocortex of the pallium, exist as derivatives of one of these two basic cortical types (Sanides, 1970; Stephan & Andy, 1970). The newer forms of

---

Figure 4.3 Allocortical regions in the ascending primate scale. Medial views of the telencephalon in (a) *Erinaceus* and *Galago* and (b) *Cercopithecus* and *Homo*, showing the position and shape of the various allocortical regions. [From Stephan & Andy, 1970, pp. 116–117.]
Legend
A. **Allocortex primitivus**
   I. *Palaeocortex*
      1. Bulbus olfactorius*
      2. Bulbus olfactorius accessorius*
      3. Regio retrobulbaris (= nucleus olfactorius anterior)*
      4. Regio praepiriformis (Area 51 of Brodmann)
      5. Regio periamygdalaris
      6. Tuberculum olfactorium
   II. *Archicortex* (Hippocampus, Formatio ammonis)
      7. Subiculum
      8. Cornu ammonis   Hippocampus retrocommissuralis
      9. Fascia dentata
     10. Hippocampus supracommissuralis   Taenia tecta of Rose
     11. Hippocampus praecommissuralis
     Structures with uncertain affiliation
     12. Septum*
     13. Diagonal band of Broca (Regio diagonalis)*
B. **Periallocortex**
   III. *Peripalaecortex*
     14. Formatio mesocorticalis insularis
       a. oralis (15 Brodmann)
       b. caudalis (16 Brodmann)
       c. temporalis
   IV. *Periarchicortex*
     15. Regio entorhinalis + perrirhinalis (28, 34, 35 Brodmann)
     16. Regio praesubicularis + parasubicularis (27 Brodmann)
     17. Regio retrosplenialis (26, 29, 30 Brodmann)
     18. Regio infraradiata ventralis (33 Brodmann)
     19. Regio subgenualis posterior (caudale 25 Brodmann, 14 b Vogt)

*Not classed as cortical structures by some authors.

---

[3] The histologist Ramón y Cajal (1968) identified seven layers within the hippocampus, an indication that the number of layers one finds within a given cortical region often depends simply on the criteria one brings to bear in distinguishing "sublayers" from "layers."

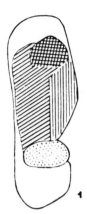
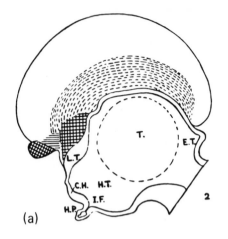

(a)

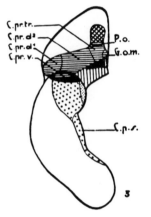
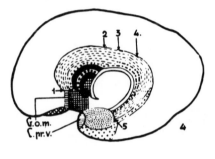

(b)

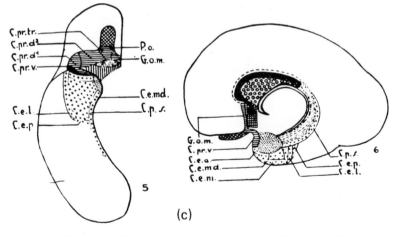

(c)

Figure 4.4   (Figure captions and parts (d) and (e) on page 168)

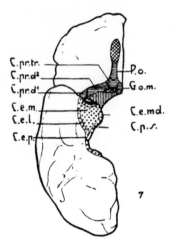
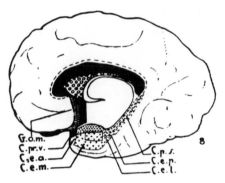

(d)

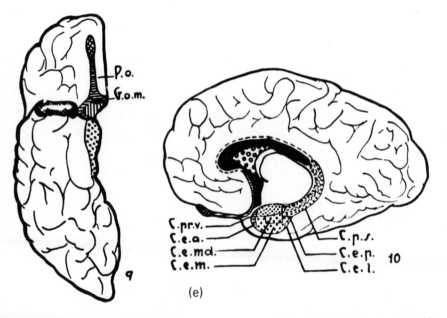

(e)

Figure 4.4 Embryological development of the human rhinencephalon. Diagrams 1 to 10 depict the olfactory areas in the telencephalon (i.e., rhinencephalon) of human fetuses at successive stages of development. All are drawn in the same size in order to show relative proportions of areas at different stages. *Stage 1*: (a) Diagrams 1 and 2—Ventral and median views of the human cerebrum at the end of the second month of fetal age. *Stage 2*: (b) Diagrams 3 and 4—Ventral and median views of the human cerebrum at the end of the third month. The four subdivisions of the hippocampal formation lie respectively between the numbers 1 and 2, 2 and 3, 3 and 4, 4 and 5. *Stage 3*: (c) Diagrams 5 and 6—Ventral and median views of the human cerebrum at the end of the fourth month. (d) Diagrams 7 and 8—Ventral and median views of the human cerebrum at the end of the sixth month. (e) Diagrams 9 and 10—Ventral and median view of the new-born human cerebrum. [From Macchi, 1951, pp. 248–252.]

BULBO-PEDUNCULAR EMINENCE
OLFACTORY BULB

PREPIRIFORM AREA

GYRUS OLFACTORIUS MEDIALIS
OLFACTORY PEDUNCLE; PREPIRIFORM AREA

PAROLFACTORY TUBERCLE

VENTRAL PAROLFACTORY AREA
BASAL PAROLFACTORY SPACE

MEDIAL PAROLFACTORY AREA

ENTORHINO-AMYGDALOID AREA
ENTORHINAL AND PRESUBICULAR CORTEX

CORTICAL AMYGDALOID NUCLEUS

HIPPOCAMPAL AREA
AMMON'S HORN

FASCIA DENTATA

PRIMORDIUM HIPPOCAMPI

SEPTUM PELLUCIDUM

ANTERIOR COMMISSURE
HIPPOCAMPAL COMMISSURE
CORPUS CALLOSUM

Abbreviation for all diagrams of Figure 4.4

A.A., anterior amygdaloid area
A.C.A., claustro-amygdaloid area
A.D., diagonal area
A.g.b., undifferentiated basal ganglia
A.I., intercalated area
Al., alveus
B., basal amygdaloid nucleus
B.n.s., bed nucleus of stria terminalis
C., central amygdaloid nucleus
C.A., anterior commissure
C.a., Ammon's horn
C.a.n., caudate nucleus
C.C., corpus callosum
C.E., entorhinal cortex
C.e., external capsule
C.e.a., entorhinal cortex, anterior field
C.e.l., the same, lateral field
C.e.m., the same, middle field
C.e.md., the same, medial field
C.e.p., the same, posterior field
C.H., chiasma opticum
C.p., pyramidal cells
C.p.s., presubicular cortex
C.pr.d¹., prepiriform cortex, subinsular zone
C.pr.d²., the same, gyrus olfactorius lateralis
C.pr.tr., the same, olfactory trigone
C.pr.v., the same, ventral zone
C.prp.i., undifferentiated prepiriform cortex
Cl.d., dorsal claustrum
Cl.f., claustrum falsum
Cl.v., ventral claustrum
E.T., epithalamus
F., fimbria
F.d., fascia dentata
F.H., hippocampal fissure
G.o.m., gyrus olfactorius medialis
G.P. or G.p., globus pallidus
H., hippocampus
H.P., hypophysis
H.T., hypothalamus
H.U., uncus of hippocampus
I., insula
I.F., infundibulum

I.L.C.a., Ammon's horn, lamina ventralis
II.L.C.a., the same, lamina dorsalis
III.L.C.a., the same, lamina terminalis
L., lateral amygdaloid nucleus
L.T., lamina terminalis
M., medial amygdaloid nucleus
M.a.p.s., germinative layer of palliostriatal angle
M.g., germinative layer of basal ganglia
M.p., germinative or periventricular layer
N., neopallial cortex
N.a., nucleus accumbens
N.c., cortical amygdaloid nucleus
N.C.A., anterior part of N.c.
N.C.P., posterior part of N.c.
P., putamen
P.H., primordium hippocampi
P.H.s., the same, pars supracallosa
P.l.n., lateral parolfactory (septal) nucleus
P.m.n., medial parolfactory (septal) nucleus
P.o., olfactory peduncle
P.sub., presubicular cortex
P.t., parolfactory tubercle
P.v.a., ventral parolfactory area
Pl.c., chorioid plexus
Pr.s., presubicular cortex
S.A., or S.a., fissura amygdaloidea
S.H.t., septo-hippocampal tract
S.I., innominate gray matter
S.p., septum pellucidum
S.t.tr., septo-tubercular tract
Sg., granular layer of fascia dentata
Sp., polymorphic layer of fascia dentata
St.c., cortical plate
St.g., germinative or periventricular layer
St.i., intermediate layer
St.m., marginal layer
Sub., subicular cortex
T., thalamus
V.L. or V.l., lateral ventricle
V.T., V.t., ventricle of temporal lobe

cortical organization differentiate ontogenetically, and they evolved phylogenetically in successive waves of condentric growth rings outward from the areas of
paleocortex and archicortex. There is a basically anterior *parapyriform moitié*
derived from pyriform paleocortex and tending to have motor/output functions
and a basically posterior *parahippocampal moitié* derived from hippocampal
archicortex with functions related to sensory/input processing (cf. Figure 4.5
and also Figure 4.7, in which the parapyriform moitié of limbic cortex is
distinguished from the parahippocampal moitié). Between the lowest levels of
allocortex and the isocortex there are a great many gradations of transitional
cortical types including *peripaleocortex, periarchicortex, juxtallocortex,* and
proisocortex, each more complex in organization and presumably able to carry
out more sophisticated information processing functions. As each higher type of
cortical organization arose phylogenetically the behavioral capabilities of the
species in question was altered based on elaborations of olfactory and visceral
regulatory functions.

   Many discussions of vertebrate evolution overemphasize the extent to which
telencephalization, the great expansion of the telencephalon division of the
forebrain, is viewable as a linear progression culminating in our species' great
quantity of neocortex. Actually, the process found various taxa pursuing different lines of specialization within the telencephalon. Thus, for example, amphibia
show a preponderance of paleopallial structures, and reptiles have developed
extensive archistriatal and archipallial structures. Birds show a neglect of dorsal
cortical areas and a tremendous development of the strio-amygdaloid complex,
extending to the elaboration of vocal communication functions in striatal and
midbrain regions rather than in the rhinencephalon or pallium. Mammals have
concentrated on elaborate cortico-thalamic mechanisms, neostriatum, and general cortex of the pallium (Kappers, Huber, & Crosby, 1936). Within primate
evolution, the olfactory bulb and directly related structures show a definite
regression in size, both relative and absolute. Contrary to what one might
suppose, however, the rest of the rhinencephalon shows a significant increase in
size and organizational complexity. From Figure 4.3, one might incorrectly
conclude that the human rhinencephalon as a whole has decreased in hominid
evolution; it must be realized that this impression results from the greatly
expanded neocortex visually overshadowing the still respectable expansion of
the rhinencephalon. The human hippocampus is four times as large as that of a
hypothetical basal insectivore of the same body size, and the combined volume
of the human septum, hippocampus, and schizocortical regions (the periarchicortex of Figures 4.2 and 4.7) is actually more than two times that of a gorilla
weighing approximately four times as much (Stephan & Andy, 1970). Humans
definitely rely less on olfaction than do other mammals or primates, and one
might puzzle over the fact that there are generally more fibers in human
rhinencephalic fiber tracts (e.g., five times more fibers making up the *fornix* in

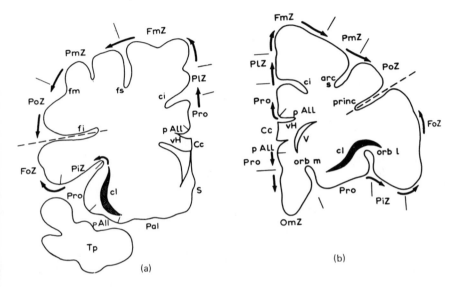

Figure 4.5 *Dual origin of the cortex.* Coronal diagrams of frontal lobe of man (a) and monkey (b). The arrows indicate the differential trends from the cingular proisocortex (Pro) medially and the insular proisocortex laterally. Because of the lesser vault of the frontal lobe of the monkey the plane at the level of the sulcus principalis does not pass through the paleocortex (Pal)—the last source of insulolimbic differentiation—but only through the caudoorbital claustrocortex (Pro). The paleocortex is present in the section through the human brain. The dashed line through sulcus frontalis inferior (fi) in man and sulcus principalis (princ) in monkey marks the basic medio/limbic borderline of the two prefrontal spheres. Sulci: arc, arcuatus superior; ci, cinguli; fm, frontalis medius; fs, frontalis superior; orbm, orbitalis medialis; orbl, orbitalis lateralis; Cc, corpus callosum; cl, claustrum; S, septum; V, ventricle. [From Sanides, 1970, pp. 138–139.]

Explanation of abbreviations in Figure 4.5

A I	primary auditory area	Pal	paleocortex
A II	secondary auditory area	pAll	periallocortex
All	allocortex primitivus	parK	parakoniocortex
FmZ	frontomotor zone	parM	paramotor area
FoZ	frontopercular zone	PiZ	parinsular zone
FpZ	frontopolar zone	PlZ	paralimbic zone
G	gustatory area	PmZ	paramotor zone
Gig	area gigantopyramidalis	PoZ	paropercular zone
H	hippocampus	pre Fr	prefrontal cortex
Ism	intermediate sensorimotor area	preM	premotor area
Ka	auditory koniocortex	proM	promotor area
Ks	somatic koniocortex	proK	prokoniocortex
lam. diss.	lamina dissecans	Prt	parietal cortex
Mpl	supplementary motor area	SmI	primary somatic area
MsI	primary motor area	SmII	secondary somatic area
OmZ	orbitomedial zone		

humans than other primates; Crosby & Humphrey, 1941.) Given the view of the rhinencephalon as possessing solely olfactory functions, the mystery deepened when it was discovered that structures like the amygdala and hippocampus are elaborated even in species such as the dolphin that have no sense of smell at all!

RESEARCH ON THE LIMBIC SYSTEM

Background

As more data on the functional activity of the rhinencephalic structures came to light during the early 20th century, the suspicion arose that the "nose-brain" might be involved in activity other than olfactory perception. Herrick (1933) suggested that the rhinencephalon might act as a nonspecific activator of all cortical activities, and Kleist (1934) saw these structures as the basis for emotional behavior, attitudes and drives, and as correlating visceral sensations to subserve the search for food and sexual objects. Several of these structures have more elaborate connections with the hypothalamus than with primary olfactory structures, and the important role of the hypothalamus in visceral regulatory activity and in the expression of behavior sequences of rage, pain, and so on, was becoming clear (e.g., from the work of Bard, 1928, on rage in decorticate cats). A major theoretical landmark was Papez's (1937), "A proposed mechanism for emotion," which established the role of a network of rhinencephalic structures in motivational behavior. The "Papez circuit," summarized in (a) of Figure 4.6 was an intuitively pleasing notion because it put together in a unified format much of the data on non-olfactory functions of the rhinencephalon, but especially because this hypothesis gave emotion a testable physiological basis. Emotion and motivation had long been a central concern within psychology but posed methodological problems for behaviorists loathe to deal with internal experience. Theories of emotion proposed up to this point (e.g., James, 1890; Cannon, 1927; cf. Reymert, 1928) had proven unsatisfactory for one reason or another, and since Papez (1937) the experimental work relating emotional behavior to these forebrain structures has provided a fruitful basis for empirical research.

Following Papez (1937), there was a drastic change in the view of the "olfactory brain," strengthened when Brodal (1947) substantiated Papez's claim that the hippocampus had nothing to do with olfactory perceptual processing. Also relevant to the developing understanding of the nature of these forebrain structures, Bard and Montcastle (1947) showed that mediobasal lesions affected the aggressiveness–tameness dimension of behavior in cats.[4] The result of the

---

[4] See Pribram (1969) for a discussion of theoretical developments following Papez's proposal.

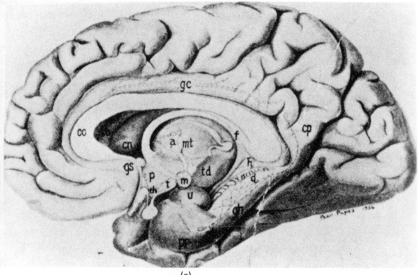

(a)

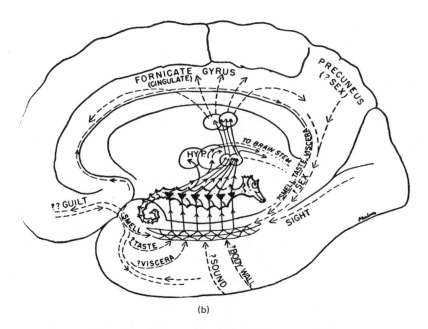

(b)

Figure 4.6 (Figure caption and part (c) on page 174)

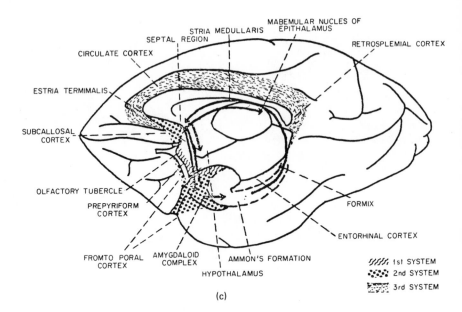

MABEMULAR NUCLES OF
EPITHALAMUS

STRIA MEDULLARIS
SEPTAL REGION
RETROSPLEMIAL CORTEX
CIRCULATE CORTEX

ESTRIA TERMIMALIS

SUBCALLOSAL
CORTEX

OLFACTORY TUBERCLE
PREPYRIFORM
CORTEX
FORMIX

ENTORHINAL CORTEX

FROMTO PORAL   AMYGDALOID   AMMON'S FORMATION
CORTEX   COMPLEX
HYPOTHALAMUS

//// 1st SYSTEM
.::. 2nd SYSTEM
:::: 3rd SYSTEM

(c)

Figure 4.6 Three "classic" proposals for defining the limbic system as a functional entity. (a) The original proposal of Papez (1937) that established the role of limbic structures in emotional behavior. Abbreviations: a, anterior nucleus; ab, angular bundle; cc, corpus callosum; cn, caudate nucleus; cp, posterior cingulum; d, dentate gyrus; f, fornix; gc, cingulate gyrus; gh, hippocampal gyrus; gs, subcallosal gyrus; h, hippocampus nudus; m, mammillary body; mt, mammillothalamic tract; p, pars optica of the hypothalamus; pr, pyriform area; sub, subcallosal bundle; t, tuber cinereum; td, mammillotegmental tract; th, hypophyseal tract; u, uncus. (b) The modified version presented by MacLean (1949). (c) The proposal of Pribram and Kruger (1954) that divided the rhinencephalon into three subsystems: (1) *rhinal system*: structures that have direct connections with the olfactory bulb; (2) *paleol system*: structures that have direct connections with the first system but none with the olfactory bulb; (3) *hippocampal-cingulate system*: structures that have direct connections with the second system but none with the bulb or first system. [From Papez, 1937, Copyright 1937, American Medical Association; MacLean, 1949; and Pribram & Kruger, 1954, reprinted by permission of the New York Academy of Sciences.]

mounting experimental evidence was to make even the term *rhinencephalon* inapplicable to human beings except within an embryological context. There was clearly another level of neural organization interposed between the homologous olfactory systems of lower species and the neocortical structures of higher species. During this period there was an emphasis on the endocrine and auto- nomic regulatory functions of the structures in the Papez circuit, and it is in this context that MacLean (1949) conceived the notion of the "visceral brain" (see (b) of Figure 4.6), asserting its basic function to be the regulation of instincts of self and species preservation. Meanwhile evidence was accumulating that the functional activity of these structures was actually much broader than visceral

174

control of emotional expression. A second major landmark in limbic research was Pribram and Kruger's 1954 paper in which three anatomically definable subsystems of the "olfactory brain" were distinguished, based on their patterns of anatomical connections to the olfactory bulb and to each other (see also Pribram, 1954, and note the summary in (c) of Figure 4.6). Along the way, Pribram and Kruger related their tripartite classification to the roles these structures played in other functional domains: arousal mechanisms beyond those of the brain stem reticular formation, learning, and social behavior. This still widely cited paper remains one of only a handful of attempts to make sense out of the functional organization of the limbic system in terms of the activity of subsets of its anatomical constituents.

The phrase *limbic system* was coined by MacLean (1952) to replace his earlier *visceral brain*, partly in recognition of the extensive involvement of these structures in nonvisceral activity. The term *limbic* itself was borrowed from Broca (1878), who had identified the ring of forebrain structures circling the mammalian brain stem as *"le grand lobe limbique"* (from the Latin *limbus* 'border, rim'; see White, 1965, for a partial history of terminology applied to limbic system structures from ancient to modern times). This shift in terminology helped establish the special status of these forebrain mechanisms as a general information processing system with a wide range of functional responsibilities including a major role in emotion, arousal, attention, habituation, social behavior, learning, and memory. The first indication of limbic involvement in communication functions came from Smith (1941), who showed that electrical stimulation of anterior cingulate cortex elicited vocal activity in monkeys.

Over the past 30 years, a great deal has been discovered about the anatomy and physiology of limbic system components, and a reasonable consensus has been reached as to which major structures should be included (see Figure 4.7), especially the long lists of functions associated with each of these structures. Nevertheless, serious disagreement remains as to which portions of the cortex, thalamus, basal ganglia, midbrain, and so on are actually part of the limbic system as opposed to merely being engaged in limbic-related activity. To some extent, this problem has been terminological and the result of a general lack of accepted criteria for establishing the limits of what should be included within a neural system. Unlike other levels of brain organization, limbic structures are not contiguous, in one identifiable lump and separate from other structures but are interspersed at various organizational levels over a large area of the mediobasal portion of the brain. The conceptual difficulties are compounded because there isn't just *one* limbic system, but a large number of different functional hierarchies deriving from the activity of the same structures but interacting in different ways. Depending on which functional domain an investigator deals with, a quite different view of the limbic system is likely to emerge. In a real sense, the limbic system (coupled with subordinate striatal, midbrain, and

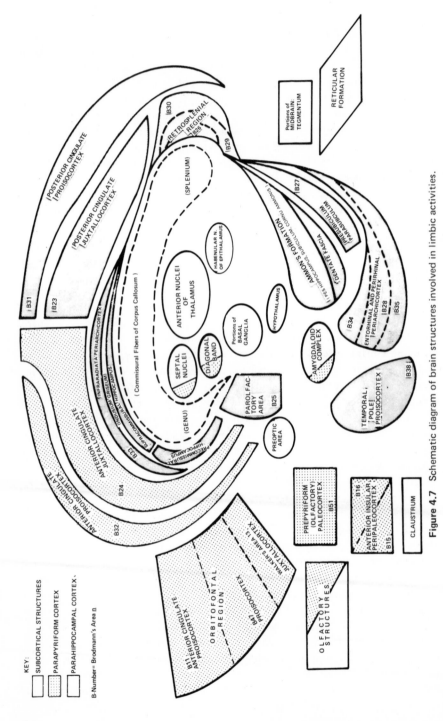

Figure 4.7 Schematic diagram of brain structures involved in limbic activities.

KEY:

☐ SUBCORTICAL STRUCTURES

▨ PARAPYRIFORM CORTEX

▢ PARAHIPPOCAMPAL CORTEX.

B-Number = Brodmann's Area ⛶

RETICULAR FORMATION

Portions of MIDBRAIN-TEGMENTUM

POSTERIOR CINGULATE |PROISOCORTEX

POSTERIOR CINGULATE |JUXTALLOCORTEX

IB31

IB23

RETROSPLENIAL REGION

IB30

IB26

IB29

IB27

(SPLENIUM)

PRESUBICULUM

PARASUBICULUM

HABENULAR N. OF EPITHALAMUS

ANTERIOR NUCLEI OF THALAMUS

AMMON'S FORMATION

(SUBICULUM) (CORNU AMMONIS)

(PRESUBICULUM)

DENTATE FASCIA

(Commissural Fibers of Corpus Callosum)

INFRARADIATA PERIARCH CORTEX

INDUSIUM GRISEUM

SUPRACOMMISSURAL HIPPOCAMPUS

Portions of BASAL GANGLIA

HYPOTHALAMUS

SEPTAL NUCLEI

DIAGONAL BAND

ANTERIOR CINGULATE JUXTALLOCORTEX

ENTORHINAL AND PERIRHINAL |PERIARCHICORTEX

IB28

IB35

B34

AMYGDALOID COMPLEX

(GENU)

PRECOMMISSURAL HIPPOCAMPUS

B33

B24

ANTERIOR CINGULATE PROISOCORTEX

B32

PAROLFACTORY AREA B25

PREOPTIC AREA

TEMPORAL, | POLE | PROISOCORTEX

IB38

B11 ANTERIOR CINGULATE ANTERIOSOCORTEX

ORBITOFONTAL REGION

WALKERS AREA 13

B47 PROISOCORTEX

JUXTALLOCORTEX

PREPYRIFORM (OLFACTORY) PALEOCORTEX

B51

B16

ANTERIOR INSULAR PERIPALEOCORTEX

B15

CLAUSTRUM

O L F A C T O R Y STRUCTURES.

176

hindbrain subsystems) constitutes an entire brain unto itself, so it is not surprising that it plays a role in most behavioral domains and has many different types of input/output relations with subordinate, superordinate, and auxiliary systems. In the higher mammals, neopallial systems have been superimposed on limbic systems, and the functional activity of the limbic system becomes absorbed into a higher level of metafunctional organization. The limbic system has to be viewed simultaneously in terms of its level-specific activity, in terms of its descending relations with subordinate systems, and in terms of its ascending relations with neocortical systems. Communication functions must likewise be viewed as they are distributed at various levels of neural organization, some having their homebase within the limbic system and others based at lower or higher levels but all needing to be understood in terms of the entire hierarchy.

Methodology

Like all other brain systems, the limbic system can be studied from a tremendous variety of observational, experimental, and clinical methodological approaches. A great many investigators have been concerned to discover the structure and function of subcortical limbic nuclei and especially their efferent and afferent fiber projections within and without the limbic system. Unfortunately, while this type of information has often been helpful in understanding the nature of functional interconnections among other brain structures, this has been less true for the limbic system. There seems to be no easy way to trace out a functional wiring diagram of limbic subsystems from a bare knowledge of this bewildering array of fiber systems. Taking into account the functions associable with individual limbic components, however, it is possible to describe the general patterns of information flow between a given pair of structures. Likely to help in this endeavor is the concern of some investigators for the pharmacological basis of the activity of given limbic fiber systems based on a knowledge of the neurotransmitter substances involved. For example, Lewis and Shute (1967) present evidence that the hippocampus receives the influence of the reticular formation via the septum and diagonal band, with cholinergic innervation (see also Domino, Dren, & Yamamoto, 1967). Also potentially revealing is the large body of data derived from electrophysiological recording of the activity of limbic structures under various conditions. Significant in this regard are the *theta rhythm of the hippocampus* (5–7 Hz), the *amygdala fast rhythm* (40–50 Hz), and the low seizure threshold of the amygdala and schizocortical regions (see, e.g., Isaacson, 1974; Eleftheriou, 1972).

The two main experimental methods employed in the attempt to discover the functions of limbic structures and the location of the structures carrying out given functions have been (*a*) *electrical stimulation* and (*b*) *tissue destruction* in conjunction with pre- and postsurgical testing and observation in a variety of mammals. The literature derived from stimulation studies is formidable in extent and abounds with conflicting results, unreplicated findings, and opposite effects from stimulation of the same structure. It has typically been the case that an abundance of different overt behavioral results are elicited by stimulation of the same subcortical limbic structure. For example, the list of specific behaviors elicited by amygdaloid stimulation is quite long, although it might be possible to reduce them to a few major categories (see Figure 4.8 for a summary of some of these results for the cat). It is often the case that the majority of these same behaviors may also be elicited by stimulating a number of other subcortical limbic structures, and almost never can one uniquely associate elicitation of a given behavior with the stimulation of one limbic structure.

The list of caveats for interpreting the results of stimulation studies is almost as long as the list of results! For example, the overt behavior produced depends very much on the stimulus parameters of intensity, duration, pattern, and frequency. The initial belief of many investigators that one could identify the

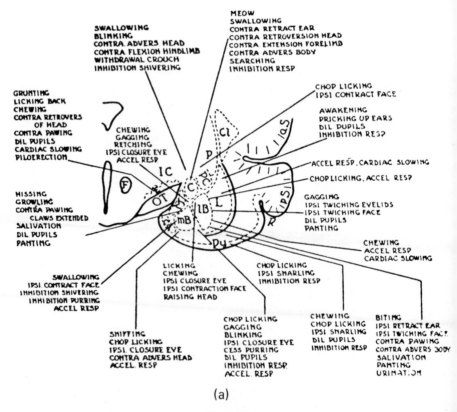

(a)

Figure 4.8

SELECTED STUDIES OF EFFECTS OF ELECTRICAL STIMULATION IN THE AMYGDALA OF THE CAT

Experimenters	Sites of stimulation tending to be in dorsomedial amygdala	Sites of stimulation tending to be in lateral and ventral amygdala
Egger and Flynn, 1963	Suppression of hypothalamically elicited attack behavior	Facilitation of hypothalamically elicited attack behavior
Fernandez de Molina and Hunsperger, 1959	Growling, hissing	Sniffing, retching
Gastaut, 1952; Morin et al., 1952	Increased blood pressure	Decreased blood pressure
Hilton and Zbrożyna, 1963; Zbrożyna, 1963	Defense reaction, including growling and extension of claws	Sniffing, searching
Kaada, 1951	Inhibition of knee jerk and of cortically induced movements	Facilitation of knee jerk and of cortically induced movements
Koikegami and Fuse, 1952	Increased amplitude of respiration	Decreased amplitude of respiration
Koikegami et al., 1952	Inhibition of gastrointestinal motility	Rise in body temperature
Kreindler and Steriade, 1964	Acceleration-desynchronization of neocortical electrical activity	Synchronization of neocortical electrical activity in the form of spindles and slow waves
MacLean and Delgado, 1953	Respiratory acceleration	Respiratory inhibition
Magnus and Lammers, 1956	Growling	Mastication
Norris, Jr., 1963	Arrest of eating and mousing, arousal	Effects other than arrest of activity or arousal
Shealy and Peele, 1957	Undirected rage	Cowering, sniffing, licking
Slusher and Hyde, 1961	Increased corticosteroid levels in adrenal vein	Decreased corticosteroid levels in adrenal vein
Ursin and Kaada, 1960	Growling and hissing	Cowering, flight, searching
Wood, 1958	Respiratory acceleration, growling and biting	Respiratory inhibition, searching
Yoshida, 1963	Rage	Sneezing, seeking
Zbrożyna, 1963	Inhibition of firing in short ciliary nerve, with dilation of sympathectomized pupil	Facilitation of firing in short ciliary nerve

(b)

Figure 4.8 *Behaviors elicited by electrical stimulation of the amygdala in the cat.* (a) Cross section through midregion of amygdala showing types of oral, facial and other behavior that result from stimulation. Note the divisions of the amygdala and its relationship to other brain structures. Abbreviations: *LB* and *mB*, lateral and medial parts of basal nucleus of amygdala; *L*, lateral nucleus; *C*, central nucleus of amygdala; *F*, fornix; *OT*, optic tract; *Py*, pyriform cortex; *R*, rhinal fissure; *Cl*, claustrum; *P*, pulvinar; *IC*, internal capsule; *Co*, cortical nucleus of amygdala; *E*, entopeduncular nucleus; *M*, medial nucleus of amygdala; *PC*, putamen-central amygdaloid complex; *aS*, anterior sylvian gyrus; *pS*, posterior sylvian gyrus. [From MacLean & Delgado, 1953, p. 92.] (b) Selected studies of effects of electrical stimulation in the amygdala of the cat. [From Egger & Flynn, 1967, p. 180.]

structure responsible for a function simply by noting the location of stimulation that elicited a given behavior or caused the arrest of that behavior has had to give way to much more cautious localization claims. In particular, the arrest of a behavior as a consequence of stimulation at a specific point has proven to be only very vaguely helpful in understanding the localization of function (see, e.g., Penfield & Roberts, 1959, on the vast extent of cortex that produces speech arrest upon stimulation). Even the active production of a behavior during stimulation is an insufficient basis for inferring localization of a function. As discussed by Rioch (1967), the fact that vocalizations are elicited by stimulation of anterior cingulate cortex in monkeys (Robinson, 1967b) does not automatically mean that this region is involved in controlling vocal activity. The actual site of stimulation is probably incapacitated during the application of the stimulus, and any overt behavioral response is produced by regions to which the stimulation site projects. It has often been found that while stimulation of a region elicits a given behavior, bilateral ablation of that same region has no effect on the behavior at all. Thus, Fedio and Ommaya (1970) found that left (but not right) anterior cingulate stimulation in humans produced verbal short-term memory deficits, but bilateral ablation of that same region failed to produce any memory deficits, and they concluded that the electrical stimulus had actually traveled elsewhere to trigger the lateralized effect.

Destruction of a region by one or another of various sorts of lesions and ablation techniques has tended to give more directly useful information concerning the localization of limbic functions, but here too there are many dangers for the unwary interpreter of results. For example, it is possible that when a structure that forms part of a series of structures in various combinations of inhibitory and excitatory interrelations is damaged or removed, the consequent change in the pattern of those interrelations may lead to the loss of a function. Clearly, that function is not necessarily localizable in the specific structure that was damaged.[5] A further difficulty in applying the results of lesion studies to the cortical regions of the limbic system is that real brains do not come equipped with dotted lines demarcating the various cytoarchetectonic fields of structurally distinct regions. If we are to make the best inferences about the functions carried out by specific regions, we need to know precisely how much and which portions of Brodmann's Areas 24 and 32 (see Figure 4.9 for Brodmann's classification of brain regions) were ablated, not that the *anterior cingulate gyrus*, a structurally complex region, was removed. Moreover, since the locations of specific cytoarchetectonic fields vary greatly among individual brains (see Whitaker & Selnes, 1975), and since very few lesion studies include a histological analysis, beyond serial sectioning to confirm the lesion, one must settle for summing up the results of many studies in order to extrapolate a correlation between structurally distinct regions and the location of lesions that produce a particular deficit. Worrisome, too, is the fact noted by Myers (1975b) that because of the extensive arterial supply to the anterior cingulate area in primates, it is extremely difficult to remove all of the cortical tissue buried within

[5] For example, the destroyed structure may no longer be inhibiting a second structure which, by its resumed activity, is now inhibiting a third structure which had previously served the function of exciting a fourth structure which was the one actually controlling the behavior.

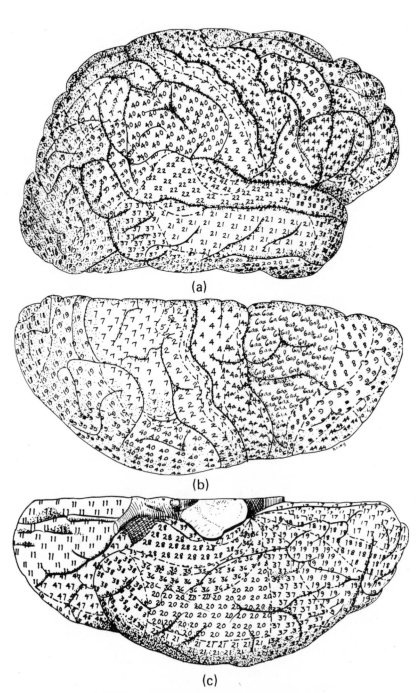

(a)

(b)

(c)

Figure 4.9 (Figure caption and part (d) on page 182)

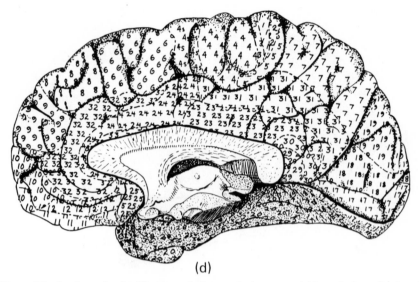

(d)

Figure 4.9 *Brodmann's classification of the cerebral cortex.* (a) lateral view; (b) dorsal view; (c) basal view; (d) medial view. [From Krieg, 1966, pp. 366–367.]

these fissures without causing extensive necrosis of underlying white matter. So, out of all the studies involving anterior cingulate lesions, only a fraction may be relied upon to have removed all of the tissue in question, and when we consider that, in turn, only some fraction of these involved the total removal of both Brodmann's Area 24 and his Area 32, it is not surprising that there are conflicting results, some investigators finding particular behavioral deficits in the vocal domain after ablation of cingulate cortex and others not.

No valid evidence of lateralized functional specialization has been found thus far for the limbic system, and it is generally necessary to remove a structure bilaterally in order to observe any functional deficits at all.[6] Probably the tremendously long lists of functions researchers attribute to a given limbic structure upon summing up the results of different studies are inflated and inaccurate. Donovick, Burright, Fuller, & Branson (1975) found that different behavioral results are obtained from the same septal lesions in different strains of laboratory mice. Also disturbing is the fact that, in this study, mice of the same strain showed different functional deficits after lesions of the same septal

---

[6] An extremely revealing, but difficult, technique is that of combining unilateral limbic lesions with sectioning of the corpus callosum and optic chiasm in such a way as to be able to control the hemisphere visual input arrives in. Where this has been done for the amygdala (e.g., Barrett, 1969), it has been found that the undamaged hemisphere produced a normal aggressive response to visual stimuli, but the hemisphere with the destroyed amygdala behaved with the tameness associated with amygdaloid lesions.

nucleus depending on whether their presurgical environment was "enriched" or "impoverished." Furthermore, it is known that the postsurgical environment is also relevant to the long term effects of a given lesion. If it is difficult to extrapolate results across subspecies of mice and from one individual mouse to another based on their particular experiences, it is all the more difficult to generalize from particular mice to species-wide characteristics of *Homo sapiens*. Where data on limbic functions does exist on human beings and other mammals, significant species differences have often been observed. For example, changes in delayed response performance following orbito-frontal cortex ablations are drastic in monkeys, only temporary in chimpanzees, and not seen at all in humans (Rosvold & Mishkin, 1961). On the optimistic side, however, it should be noted that quite frequently the same general patterns of limbic functioning have been found in humans as in other mammals, and thus there is some reason to hope that careful extrapolation of experimental results from other animals will prove reasonable.

Limbic Control of Social and Communicative Behavior in Primates

In all of us mammals, the limbic system is demonstrably involved in the control of multimodal behavior sequences that serve as signs for particular internal motivational states of fear, alarm, surprise, rage, and so on. These sign complexes are perceived and interpreted by other members of a species according to their own interests. Behavior patterns that are output automatically in particular motivational states constitute the overwhelming majority of messages in the communication repertoires of nonhuman primates and are easily observable in human behavior. Limbic structures are also implicated in the production and recognition of a second class of messages, those regulating social interaction that involves territorial concerns, expressions of dominance, mother–infant, and male–female interactions, and friendly, submissive, or aggressive displays. Perhaps the most production research on the role of limbic structures in mammalian social behavior has been carried out by R.E. Myers and his colleagues (Myers, 1969; Myers, 1972; Myers, 1975b; Franzen & Myers, 1973a; Myers & Swett, 1970; see also Kling, Lancaster, & Benitone, 1970; Pribram, 1962; Mirsky, Rosvold, & Pribram, 1957). From this work emerges the conclusion that it is essentially orbitofrontal cortex and, to a lesser degree, anterior temporal cortex that regulate instinctual social interactions. Bilateral lesions in these regions, but not in cingulate or visual association cortex, produce severe and lasting deficits in maternal protectiveness, aggressiveness, group cohesiveness, defense of territory, maintenance of hierarchical status, and sexual behavior (Myers, 1975b). Orbitofrontal and anterior temporal lesions also produce major dysfunctions in facial expressions and vocalizations that are output in emotional situations.

Probably because language is basically a vocal–auditory system, there has been a tendency to overestimate the importance of the vocal channel in the communication of other primates. Actually, vocalizations are merely one component of *multimodal sign complexes,* often serving merely to get the attention of other members of the species (cf. Altmann, 1967). Much of the research on the role of limbic structures in primate communication has been directed at vocal activity alone, and since Smith (1941), the role of anterior cingulate cortex and other limbic regions has been investigated by a number of researchers (e.g., Robinson, 1967a, 1967b; Jürgens & Ploog, 1970; Apfelbach, 1972). In this research there has often been a tendency to distinguish inadequately, in a formal way, between vocal activity in general, vocal components of multimodal sign complexes that are output automatically in particular motivational states, species-specific vocal components of social regulatory behavior, and the learned vocalizations of individuals (but an exception is Myers, 1975a). All four types of vocal activity may be expected to find a common neurological substratum in midbrain centers known to control the articulators, but beyond this, they are almost certainly realized quite differently in various limbic subsystems.

Much of the vocal call repertoire of squirrel monkeys may be elicited by limbic stimulation; such calls trigger appropriate responses from other members of the species. Figure 4.10 identifies the sites whose stimulation produced the cackling call of squirrel monkeys in a study by Jürgens and Ploog (1970). These sites were considered to form a "continuous system" running from the midbrain up to the temporal and cingulate cortex and outside of which no cackling calls could be elicited. However, it is doubtful that this is a useful way to look at the results of this study. As mentioned above, the actual site of stimulation is incapacitated during the application of the stimulus, and in order to understand the nature of the control of a specific call such as the cackling call, it would be necessary first to track down the regions to which all of these sites project. Thus it is very difficult to draw any firm conclusions about the location of the structures responsible for controlling the production of species-specific calls. As to which regions of the brain are responsible for the recognition (as opposed to production) of species-specific vocalizations, there is clear evidence that the primary auditory neocortex is involved since it has been shown that single cells in this area respond differentially to various types of calls in monkeys (Wollberg & Newman, 1972). Since auditory cortex is outside the limbic system proper, this at least opens the door to the claim that communication functions in other primates are not contained solely within the limbic system. The solution, I think, is to recognize that both for motor control of output and for sensory processing of input the limbic system acts together with nonlimbic systems that act in an auxiliary fashion.[7] It is legitimate to refer to the limbic system as the

---

[7] Perhaps in the case of auditory processing the posterior insular proisocortex, a region known to have auditory functions, is also involved.

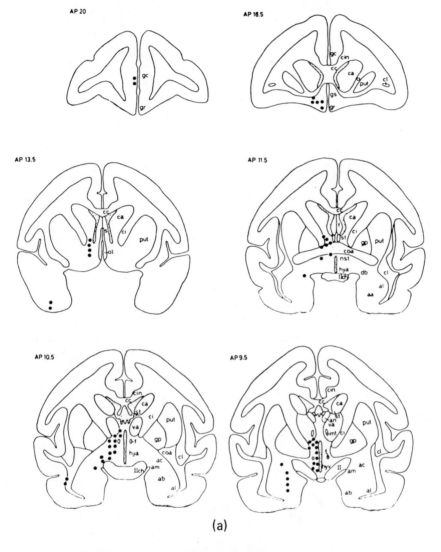

(a)

Figure 4.10 (Figure caption and parts (b) and (c) on page 186)

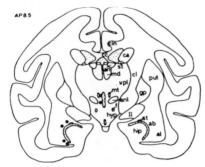

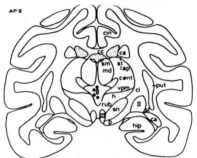

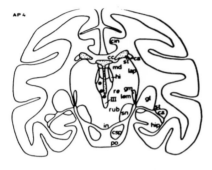

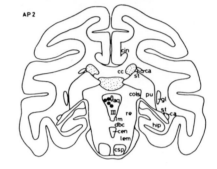

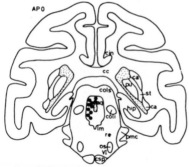

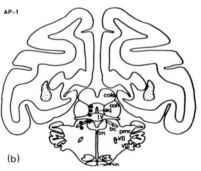

(b)

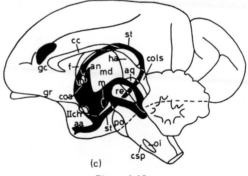

(c)

Figure 4.10

Abbreviations for Figure 4.10

a:	Nucl. accumbens	lm:	Fasc. longitudinalis medialis
aa:	Area anterior amygdalae	m:	Corpus mamillare
ab:	Nucl. basalis amygdalae	md:	Nucl. medialis dorsalis thalami
ac:	Nucl. centralis amygdalae	mt:	Tr. mamillothalamicus
al:	Nucl. lateralis amygdalae	nst:	Nucl. striae terminalis
amt	Nucl. medialis amygdalae	oi:	Nucl. olivaris inferior
an:	Nucl. anterior thalami	ol:	Fasc. olfactorius (Zuckerkandl)
anl:	Ansa lenticularis	os:	Nucl. olivaris superior
aq:	Substantia grisea centralis	p:	Pedunculus cerebri
bc:	Brachium conjunctivum	pmc:	Brachium pontis
ca:	Caudatum	po:	Griseum pontis
cc:	Corpus callosum	pp:	Nucl. praepositus hypoglossi
cen:	Nucl. centralis superior (Bechterew)	pro:	Area praeoptica
cent:	Centrum medianum	pu:	Nucl. pulvinaris thalami
ci:	Capsula interna	put:	Putamen
cin:	Cingulum	re:	Formatio reticularis tegmenti
cl:	Claustrum	rep:	Nucl. reticularis tegmenti pontis
coa:	Commissura anterior	rl:	Nucl. reticularis lateralis myelence-
coli:	Colliculus inferior		phali
cols:	Colliculus superior	rub:	Nucl. ruber
cr:	Corpus restiforme	s:	Septum
csp:	Tr. corticospinalis	sm:	Stria medullaris
db:	Fasc. diagonalis Brocae	sn:	Substantia nigra
dbc:	Decussatio brachii conjunctivi	st:	Stria terminalis
f:	Fornix	sto:	Stria olfactoria lateralis
gc:	Gyrus cinguli	tec:	Tr. tegmentalis centralis
gl:	Corpus geniculatum laterale	trz:	Corpus trapezoides
gm:	Corpus geniculatum mediale	va:	Nucl. ventralis anterior
gr:	Gyrus rectus	vpl:	Nucl. ventralis posterolateralis
gs:	Gyrus subcallosus		thalami
h:	Campus Foreli	vpm:	Nucl. ventralis posteromedialis
ha:	Nucl. habenularis		thalami
hi:	Tr. habenulointerpeduncularis	zi:	Zona incerta
hip:	Hippocampus	II:	Tr. opticus
hya:	Area hypothalamica anterior	IICh:	Chiasma nervorum opticorum
hyp:	Area hypothalamica posterior	III:	N. oculomotorius
hyv:	Area hypothalamica ventralis		Nucl. nervi oculomotorii
in:	Nucl. interpeduncularis	IV:	N. and Nucl. nervi trochlearis
lap:	Nucl. lateralis posterior thalami	VI:	N. abducens
lav:	Nucl. lateralis ventralis thalami	VII:	N. facialis
le:	Lemniscus lateralis	VIII:	N. acusticus
lem:	Lemniscus medialis	IX:	N. glossopharyngeus

Figure 4.10 *Elicitation of cackling vocalizations in squirrel monkeys by electrical stimulation of the brain.* Squirrel monkeys produce cackling calls in situations characterized by general aggressiveness and high excitement. Cackling is usually uttered by several animals simultaneously. For this study, all vocalizations consisting of a sequence of two or more elements at intervals of 81 ± 19 msec. and with a maximum intensity below 2000 cps were defined as cackling calls. (a) & (b) Diagrams showing the electrode positions yielding cackling calls in a series of representative frontal planes according to stereotaxic coordinates. These positions form a continuous system, illustrated in (c), outside of which no cackling calls can be elicited. This system runs from the caudal end of the periaqueductal grey and adjacent parabrachial nuclei (AP − 1) in a periaqueductal and periventricular position, respectively, throughout the midbrain and diencephalon (AP − 1 to AP 9.5). At the level of the inferior thalamic peduncle the system branches off in three components: the first component follows the inferior thalamic peduncle in a dorsal direction toward the anteromedial peduncle ventrolaterally into the central and basal nuclei of the amygdala (AP 10.5 to AP 8.5) and farther through the external capsule and uncinate fasciculus (AP 10.5) to the rostroventral temporal cortex (AP 13.5); the third component follows the anterior thalamic radiation along the ventromedial border of the internal capsule (AP 9.5 to AP 16.5) into the ventromedial orbital cortex (AP 16.5) and precallosal cingulate gyrus (AP 20). (c) General (sagittal) view of the cerebral system yielding cackling calls. [Adapted from Jürgens & Ploog, 1970.]

"homebase" for communication functions in primates even though both higher and lower levels of brain organization are involved in the overall behavioral complex in which limbic activity plays the dominant role.

Bilateral removal of cingulate cortex in monkeys has no effect on either the recognition or the production of vocal activity of the three nonlearned types mentioned above. We know that in our species, the control of complex intentional vocalizations has shifted upward to higher levels of neural organization, most notably Area 4, the primary motor neocortex; for phonologically structured output, control has shifted to Broca's area in the dominant hemisphere. These neocortical systems do not appear to be involved in the production of species-specific calls for monkeys, although stimulation of primary motor cortex in monkeys does elicit movements of laryngeal muscles (Jürgens, 1974; Hast, Fischer, Wetzel, & Thompson, 1974). Bilateral destruction, in monkeys, of the closest homologue of Broca's area does not interfere with the ability to produce vocal calls or vocal activity in general (Yamaguchi & Myers, 1975; Myers, 1972). The role of cingulate cortex in all of this is not clear. Although Sutton, Larson, Taylor, and Lindeman (1974) trained five monekys to give learned "long calls" for food rewards and then bilaterally ablated the homologue of Broca's area with no effect, cingulate and subcallosal lesions did result in a weakening or loss of the learned calls. One might therefore suspect that in monkeys the anterior cingulate cortex is part of a higher level of control, with a particular role in learned vocal activity. It is significant in this regard that Area 32 of the anterior cingulate gyrus is transitional in structure between the limbic cortex and the six-layered primary motor cortex that is the part of the pyramidal motor systems most closely associated with voluntary motor actions. Monkeys have only limited intentional control over vocalizations and it is very difficult to condition their vocalizations; manual behavior, which is under a higher degree of voluntary control, is easily conditioned (Yamaguchi & Myers, 1972; Myers, 1975a; Sutton *et al.*, 1973).

Another general issue in this same context is the extent to which there are critical periods for the phenotypic attainment of limbic functions and an ability to compensate for damaged limbic components. It has been shown that lesions in infant monkeys tend to spare some functions but not others (Molino, 1975; Harlow, Thompson, Bloomquist, & Schultz, 1970; Kling & Tucker, 1968; Kling & Green, 1967; Akert, Orth, Harlow, & Schlitz, 1960; Franzen & Myers, 1973b), an indication that the matter cannot be resolved by a simple "yes–no" answer. Franzen and Myers (1973b) showed that neonatal lesions and lesions made under the age of two (orbitofrontal cortex and anterior temporal cortex removals) in monkeys, left most vocal activity and social behavior patterns intact after a period of recovery. After the age of two, deficits tend to be permanent and increasingly severe.

HIERARCHICAL ORGANIZATION OF COMMUNICATION
FUNCTIONS OF THE FOREBRAIN

It would be very helpful to have some explicit understanding of the organization of the limbic system into subsystems that are relevant to particular domains of communicative activity. Unfortunately, with only a few exceptions, limbic researchers have dealt exclusively with the functions of single structures and have had almost nothing to say about the limbic system as a whole. Perusing the literature for such an understanding, one keeps finding out more than one would like to know about isolated structures such as the amygdala and one uncovers very little coherent discussion about the place of the amygdala in the larger system. A fairly extensive (but not exhaustive) foray into the limbic system literature has yielded only two serious proposals that claim to define the set of functionally relevant limbic subsystems. One is the already mentioned anatomically based classification of Pribram and Kruger (1954) into *rhinal, paleol*, and *hippocampal-cingulate* subsystems. MacLean (1973) has presented the other, most recently as part of his discussion of the "triune brain" notion, which posits

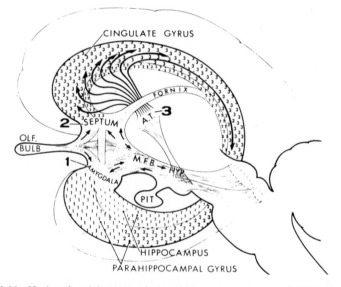

Figure 4.11 *MacLean's subdivisions of the limbic system.* MacLean (1973) discusses the functions of the limbic system according to the three main subdivisions shown in this diagram. The three main cortical regions in the limbic lobe are indicated by the small numerals 1, 2, and 3 (the smaller numerals overlie archicortex and the larger, mesocortex, i.e., transitional cortex). The principle pathways that link these three cortical regions with the brain stem are correspondingly labeled by the large numerals. [From MacLean, 1973, p. 14.]

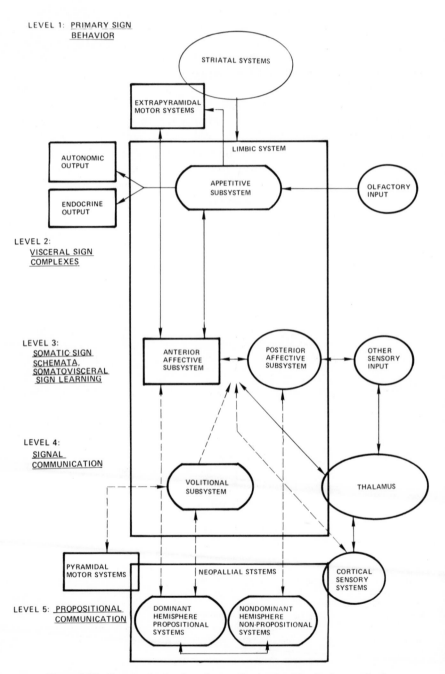

LEVEL 1: PRIMARY SIGN BEHAVIOR

STRIATAL SYSTEMS

EXTRAPYRAMIDAL MOTOR SYSTEMS

LIMBIC SYSTEM

AUTONOMIC OUTPUT

APPETITIVE SUBSYSTEM

OLFACTORY INPUT

ENDOCRINE OUTPUT

LEVEL 2: VISCERAL SIGN COMPLEXES

LEVEL 3: SOMATIC SIGN SCHEMATA, SOMATOVISCERAL SIGN LEARNING

ANTERIOR AFFECTIVE SUBSYSTEM

POSTERIOR AFFECTIVE SUBSYSTEM

OTHER SENSORY INPUT

LEVEL 4: SIGNAL COMMUNICATION

VOLITIONAL SUBSYSTEM

THALAMUS

PYRAMIDAL MOTOR SYSTEMS

NEOPALLIAL STSTEMS

CORTICAL SENSORY SYSTEMS

LEVEL 5: PROPOSITIONAL COMMUNICATION

DOMINANT HEMISPHERE PROPOSITIONAL SYSTEMS

NONDOMINANT HEMISPHERE NON-PROPOSITIONAL SYSTEMS

Figure 4.12   Communication functions at five levels of forebrain organization.

three levels in the evolution of the forebrain: the *reptilian forebrain*, the *paleomammalian brain* (which = limbic system), and the *neomammalian brain*. MacLean divides the limbic system itself into three subsystems: *a lower system fed by the amygdala* (see Figure 4.11, areas marked with the number "1"); *a subsystem connected by the septum* (see Figure 4.11, areas marked with the number "2"); and *a cingulate subsystem with strong visual input* (see Figure 4.11, areas marked with the number "3").

I would like to suggest a slightly different framework for viewing limbic organization, one that attempts to relate this organization directly to communication functions in human beings. To do this, it will be helpful to consider limbic activity in conjunction with a lower *striatal level*, as well as a higher *neopallial level* of forebrain organization, thus approximating MacLean's triune brain distinction. Figure 4.12 outlines a preliminary division of the limbic system into four subsystems, and sketches the functional relations of these subsystems at five levels of forebrain organization relevant to communication. In this section, we will discuss each of these four subsystems in turn, restricting the discussion mostly to the communication functions of each subsystem, its phylogenetic status, and its ontogeny in humans.

Striatal Systems (Primary Sign Behavior)

The first level of forebrain organization that has relevance to communication functions corresponds roughly to MacLean's reptilian forebrain and its highest-level component is the *striatum*, the first subdivision of the vertebrate telencephalon. Activity at this striatal level is characterized by reflexive, stereotyped responses to a limited range of stimuli related to basic matters of survival. As defined here, the striatal system is meant to incorporate not only the basal ganglia but subordinate midbrain and brain stem systems in what amounts to a hierarchical metasystem. The highest-level communication functions of reptiles and birds are carried out by specialized striatal systems, but in mammals there is only a minimal involvement of the striatum in communication activity, at a level that might be called *primary sign behavior*. In human ontogeny, the earliest behavior with even a marginal claim to the label "communicative" is the global crying of the neonate, triggered by the reticular formation as a total mobilization in response to any stimulus that produces discomfort. Crying is biologically adaptive for the helpless infant providing there is someone in the environment able to identify this behavior as a sign of internal discomfort and willing to do something about it. It is only in this sense that global crying is communicative. Notice that the vocal component of crying behavior is basically the acoustic byproduct of the forceful expulsion of air from the lungs through a constricted oral tract. This level of neural activity, however, may include systems located within the midbrain that are specifically charged with controlling phonation and vocalization. The midbrain has been shown to be a control center for vocalizations in a wide variety of mammals (Andrew, 1973; Kanai & Wang, 1962) and particularly in birds (Andrew, 1973; Lanerolle & Andrew, 1974; Brown, 1965). According to Kelly, Beaton, & Magoun (1946), it is the central part of the midbrain aqueductal grey and adjacent tegmentum beneath the superior colliculus that contains the systems integrating facio-vocal activity in mammals. It is significant that this striatal level of control over vocal activity functions in situations of discomfort and not in pleasurable states.

Limbic System

APPETITIVE SUBSYSTEM (VISCERAL SIGN COMPLEXES)

The first level of limbic activity corresponds roughly to what Pribram and Kruger identified as the *rhinal system*, based anatomically on the prepyriform cortex, septum, and diagonal band, but especially revolving around the activity of the hypothalamus as it receives olfactory and other input and regulates autonomic and endocrine activity related to self-preservation functions. This is the beginning of internal experience and primitive consciousness, or self-awareness, as the hypothalamic systems differentiate internal physiological states of the body based on its own receptor systems. The appetitive subsystem is the basis for internal *sensations* and associated *drive states* of hunger, thirst, pain, rage, and so on. The behavior controlled at this level is characterized by automatic response patterns more complex than the reflexes of striatally controlled activity. In respect to communication, the activity of this subsystem is marked in human development by the onset, at about two weeks after birth, of differentiated crying. Initially two sorts of cries are produced: a hunger cry and a general discomfort cry. Shortly thereafter, a rage cry and a pain cry are added to the repertoire of cries; each type can be identified by particular acoustic patterns and presumably by other characteristic somatovisceral behavior patterns as well (Ostwald, 1972; Ostwald & Peltzman, 1974; Wasz-Höckert et al. (1968); Bell & Ainsworth, 1972). Differentiated crying deserves to be called communication only in the same sense that global crying does, even though more than one implicational message is involved. These cries are not produced intentionally. Moreover, successful communication depends entirely on the ability of people in the environment to make correct inferences about the state of the infant. It is important to note that reticular formation control of behavioral response is inhibited in the case of differentiated crying and that control functions shift up to this level of limbic activity even while vocalizations may still be directly controlled by the same midbrain systems operating at the striatal level. Among adults, visceral sign complexes are both produced and recognized as signs of internal states at the lowest level of nonverbal limbic communication activity.

AFFECTIVE SUBSYSTEMS

Anterior (Somatovisceral sign schemata). The first subsystem at the second level of limbic activity corresponds to Pribram and Kruger's *paleol system* and as such has no direct anatomical connections with primary olfactory or endocrine and autonomic input/output, relying instead on connections to the appetitive structures on which it is superimposed. Revolving around the activity of the amygdala, the anterior affective subsystem is composed mostly of anterior structures with primarily motor/output processing functions; it is responsible for somatic output via the extrapyramidal motor systems. Functionally, this level of limbic activity is related to behavior sequences that foster species survival and it represents a more efficient means of implementing reactions to both internal appetitive states and external environmental stimuli than either striatal or appetitive limbic activity. Activity at the affective level was characterized by Pribram as involving the *Four F's:* feeding, fighting, flight, and reproductive behavior. It represents an advance in the internal organization of the schemata that control overt behavior, and it is particularly involved in predatory attack sequences, escape behaviors, defense postures, food seeking activity, and so on. This level of activity is characteristic of all mammals, but most of the nonmammalian vertebrates do not seem to have achieved this level of limbic organization.

In the human individual, this subsystem begins to function about one month after birth (see Bronson, 1965), and it is the means by which the infant is assimilated into a network of social relationships; that is, it controls a variety of instinctual interactions of the infant such as the establishment of the primary attachment with its mother and the special attention the infant pays to the human face and voice. This subsystem produces an abundance of sign behavior that communicates information about the affective state of the infant from which people may make more specific inferences. This level of limbic activity controls many involuntary oro–facial behavior sequences, facial expressions, agonistic vocalizations, and the standard set of primordial cries of our species. It is probably this subsystem that is responsible for the development in the human infant, about 6 or 8 weeks after birth, of a new class of comfort sounds that contrast sharply with the earlier discomfort vocalizations. Early cooing behavior and the beginnings of more complex vocal sequences are produced by the child when alone, for no apparent reason, but are more elaborate in structure in the company of other people.

This may be an appropriate point to emphasize the tentative nature of many of the conclusions drawn in this section. Conclusions which, it is hoped, are not contradicted by existing data but which still require explicit empirical verification. The major portion of the existing research on human communication fails to take into account neural systems of any sort, and the limbic system has been ignored even by those who have been concerned with the neural substrata of language processing. To understand the ontogeny of limbic communication functions and their integration with other realms of limbic activity, it will be especially important to have more data on the maturation of non-neocortical forebrain structures. Some general information exists on the myelinization of limbic fiber systems (see Flechsig, 1901; Yakovlev & Lecours, 1967), and it would certainly be useful to relate this data to EEG maturation during infancy (see Pretchl, 1968). In addition to observing communication activity in our species and in others, it will be important to relate data on the limbic system to the child's growth in general cognitive ability. There is every reason to think that the neural basis for many of the activities that define the substages of Piaget's (1952) *sensorimotor period* resides within limbic subsystems. Bringing together all of this information into a unified framework will be a monumental but necessary prelude to confirming hypotheses regarding the nature of communication systems in both the child and the adult.

Posterior (Somatovisceral sign learning). The second affective subsystem corresponds roughly to Pribram and Kruger's *hippocampal-cingulate system* and is based on the activity of the posterior cingulate juxtallocortex, the anterior temporal cortex, portions of the hippocampus, and related schizocortical regions. The cortical components of this limbic subsystem are basically derivatives of the parahippocampal moitié of posterior archicortex and have mostly sensory input processing functions. The system receives input from internal physiological systems by way of the septum as well as information about the external world through sensory (other than olfactory) modalities. It is therefore in a good position to integrate the two kinds of input and to assess the positive or negative reinforcement value of external phenomena for the individual. Possibly based on memory functions of the hippocampus, this level of limbic activity provides mammals with the ability to modify behavior as the result of experience and it is at this point that instrumental learning (operant conditioning) arises based possibly on the memory functions of the hippocampus. It is also at this point that one may legitimately talk about a new level of internal experience beyond the visceral sensations of the appetitive level, that is, emotions. Pribram (1967) has characterized emotion as an expression of the relationship between perception and action, between information processing of sensory input and motor control. In these terms, emotional experience is likely to be the result of the integrated activity of the two affective subsystems at the second level of limbic activity. The two affective subsystems together are the probable basis for communicative behavior regulating social interactions among mammalian species. For the human infant, the posterior affective subsystem is the direct basis not so much for overt communicative behavior as for learning about the affective content of other people's behavior. It is at this point in development that the child will cry when addressed in an angry voice and will be soothed by a pleasant tone. In adults, it is possible that the posterior affective subsystem continues to have the task of tracking the affective state of those with whom we interact.

VOLITIONAL SUBSYSTEM (SIGNAL COMMUNICATION)

The third level of limbic activity to be identified here was not distinguished by either Pribram and Kruger (1954) or MacLean (1973) and has generally been ignored by limbic researchers. The basis for inferring its existence is in data on the attainment by a variety of higher mammals of varying degrees of voluntary control over the implementation of limbic behavioral subroutines (see Vander-wolf, 1971). Anatomically, its organizational basis within the limbic system remains obscure, although some evidence exists that the hippocampus is involved (Isaacson & Pribram, 1976). Beyond this, it presumably involves the highest levels of limbic juxtallocortex and proisocortex, particularly the regions of the anterior cingulum transitional in structure to the primary motor cortex of Area 4 (the latter functions as an auxiliary element in limbic activity at this level).

Both phylogenetically and ontogenetically, it is the volitional limbic subsystem that is responsible for the inception of conscious behavior that is intentional in character. In human ontogeny, voluntary control over motor actions seems to develop about 3 to 4 months after birth, when the child begins to master complex action schemata as the means of satisfying affective needs such as the desire for a particular object. At some point, the infant achieves some limited control over affective output patterns themselves; for example, he learns to evince many of the overt signs of anger without really being angry. The child purposively implements components of multimodal sign complexes in order to communicate; this intentional use of signs satisfies the definition of *signal communication* (Morris, 1946). The first domain in which such signals are produced is probably that of manual gestures since the neocortical components of the pyramidal motor systems that control hand-arm activity mature first. Voluntary control over babbling vocalizations develops from about 6 months, based on a progressively maturing primary motor cortex, but the syllables of babbling are not used to communicate (Lamendella, in preparation). Only from about 9 months of age does intentional control of vocal activity arise with communicative functions as the child acquires and uses intonation contours and other prosodic features as components of somatic signal complexes (often called the *prosodic stage*; see Lamendella, 1975). At about 10 months, the child begins to imitate and repeat segmental speech sounds produced by those in the environment, an accomplishment other primates can match only to a very limited extent. This behavior provides further evidence of the increasing degree of voluntary control over vocal tract mechanisms that characterizes the maturational process of our species.

It is well known that investigators have been unable to train chimpanzees in the use of vocal communication systems, and that for this reason researchers have resorted to manual signing (Gardner & Gardner, 1969), geometric shape manipulation (Premack, 1971), and computer keyboard manipulation (Gill & Rumbaugh, 1974). All three of these techniques take advantage of the chimpanzee's relatively high degree of voluntary control over skilled manual activity. It is significant that one of the manual signing chimps, Bouee, has begun to substitute the species-specific chimp play vocalization in place of the sign "tickle" in sequences such as "Lynn tickle Bouee!" (Miles, 1975). Such behavior represents a logical "next step," an intermediate stage in the attainment of voluntary control over neocortically based vocal activity insofar as it is the intentional use of a previously existing automatic limbic vocalization. A progression on this same order is involved in human ontogeny, leading to the attainment of high-level vocal capabilities independent of limbic control.

The period from 9 to 12 months of age is also the time for the universal appearance of a curious set of "words" that, because of their frequent appearance in this context before they appear as babbling utterances, do not appear to be controlled by the neocortical motor systems that later output verbal and phonologically structured utterances. These "words" are as follows: (*a*) a *food–hunger vocalization,* "mam," showing up variously with such sounds as *mjam mjam, ma, am, mmm,* etc., for a given child; (*b*) a *"general want expresser"* (Carter, 1974), "uh uh," that has various phonetic forms, all of which revolve around the mid-central vowel [ə]; (*c*) a *surprise–wonder vocalization,* "-h-," manifested variously as *ho, ha, ah, aha,* . . . , in different children; and (*d*) a vocalization that is difficult to characterize but which may best be described as an *identification–recognition vocalization,* "-d-," found as *da, de, da da,* . . . , in various children (see Lamendella, in preparation, for further discussion). The obvious appetitive/affective nature of the first three forms suggests limbic involvement, but the place of these vocal forms in communication development is far from clear.

Neopallial Systems (Propositional Communication)

As neopallial systems arose phylogenetically, and as they develop in the human individual, they inhibit certain limbic functions and carry these functions out at a higher level in a novel fashion. Nevertheless, each limbic subsystem continues to exercise control over its sphere of human activity as a subordinate component of the higher neopallial metasystem. With the development of cognitive information processing in the human infant, from about 12 months of age, a new level of communicative competence is achieved as the child intentionally uses symbolic multimodal *gesture complexes* to communicate the content of propositional messages. These gesture complexes include subordinate limbic sign and signal behavior, and the difference between this stage and the preceding one is not so much in overt behavior as in the internal control schemata that organize overt actions. These gestural patterns and the verbal and linguistic systems that soon follow take their place within the hierarchy of forebrain communication functions, with each higher level built upon the foundation of the systems below it. Communication functions of the brain, therefore, are best viewed as distributed over this entire hierarchy. Patterns of overt verbal and nonverbal communication behavior must be parceled out among the various levels of internal functional systems according to what in the sender was responsible for producing them and what in the receiver is responsible for recognizing them.

A structure that has been claimed to play an important role in the functional hierarchy suspended from neopallial linguistic systems is the thalamus, which is part of the diencephalon division of the forebrain. At least the anterior nuclei of the thalamus are generally considered a proper part of the limbic system at the affective and perhaps volitional levels (Rose & Woolsey, 1948; Akert, 1961; Yakovlev & Locke, 1961). However, at issue here is the claim, originally formulated by Penfield and Roberts (1959), that speech itself is represented in the thalamus in a way going beyond the role of the thalamus as a relay station for sensory input to neocortical regions. Several investigators have claimed that the thalamus plays a major role in language and speech as part of the centrencephalic system postulated by Penfield. The data on which these claims are based are found in the clinical literature, especially in reports on surgery to relieve the symptoms of Parkinson's disease (see Figure 4.13). It is from the thalamus rather than from Broca's area or primary motor cortex that coherent words and phrases have been elicited by electrical stimulation (see Schaltenbrand, 1965; Schaltenbrand, Spuer, Wahren, & Rummler, 1971; and also p. 202 below). Given the unreliability of stimulation data as support for localization claims, these results in themselves might easily be explained away without attributing speech functions to the thalamus. Other thalamic stimulation results (Ojemann, Fedio, & Van Buren, 1968; Riklan, Levitta, Zimmerman, & Cooper, 1969; Ojemann & Ward, 1971) would be subject to the same criticisms. However, claims have been made that naming difficulties and various types of other speech dysfunctions occur after thalamectomy, particularly of the left (Allan, Turner, & Gadea-Cirja, 1966; Selby, 1967; Bell, 1968) as symptoms of thalamic tumors (Smyth & Stern, 1938; Cheek & Taveras, 1966); as symptoms of Parkinson's speech disorders (Boshes, 1966; Canter, 1963); and after thalamic hemorrhages (Penfield & Roberts, 1959; Fisher, 1961; Ciemins, 1970).

Speech disorders that have been noted under these conditions and which involve motor control of speech include dysfunctions of phonation, pitch, rate and rhythm of speech, anarthria (speech arrest), incomprehensible speech, and diminished voice volume. Naming difficulties (amnesic aphasia, anomia), mis-naming, and perseveration (continued repetition of the syllable of a correct object name during the application of the electrical stimulus) have also been

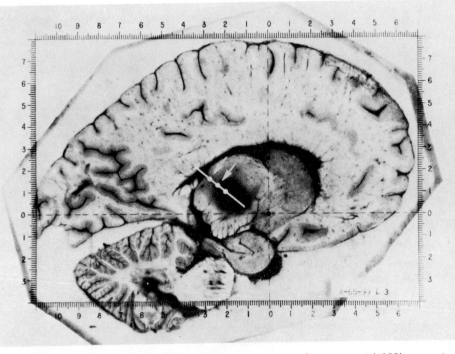

Figure 4.13 *Anomia produced during thalamic stimulation.* Ojemann *et al.* (1968) reported on the performance of patients with Parkinson's disease on a standard object-naming test while electrical stimulation was applied to the thalamus and medial parietal white matter. Stimulation in the left pulvinar nucleus of the thalamus and deep parietal white substance in the paracallosal region of both hemispheres produced *anomia* (name-finding difficulties). The photo below shows the left hemisphere of a right-handed patient sectioned 12 mm. from the mid-line. The lower section of the electrode tract is shown with three of the stimulus sites reconstructed. Anomia resulted from stimulation between the sites marked with arrows. The patient died of a massive right thalamic hemorrhage three weeks later, three days after coagulation in the right thalamus. [Photo from Ojemann, Fedio, & Van Buren, 1968, p. 117.]

noted. Naming difficulties involving the thalamus have typically been lateralized to the left; they have been caused particularly by stimulation of the left pulvinar nucleus and en passage fibers related to the centrum medianum and dorsal medial thalamic nuclei. Riklan *et al.* (1969) showed that ventrolateral thalamic stimulation produces naming difficulties. Assuming that these findings do not all result from chance occlusion of small vessels, the burr hole, the passage of the electrode, or damage to underlying white matter fiber tracts, there can be no doubt that the thalamus has a role to play in neocortical speech systems. (See Riklan & Levita, 1969, for a survey of research in this area, and also note Allison, 1966; Watkins & Oppenheimer, 1962; Botez & Barbeau, 1971; and Laitinen, 1966.)

It is not clear to me what it means to say that speech is "represented" in the thalamus, but it seems reasonable to believe that the thalamus is part of a hierarchy of speech control functions that is based in neocortical speech regions. The fact that naming difficulties have been found to be lateralized (naming being the highest-level verbal function that can be related to thalamic activity) suggests that some aspect of the neocortical speech systems is being accessed by thalamic projection systems, not that the thalamus per se is involved in naming.

A further complication in the parceling out of functional responsibilities for neopallial speech systems is the lateralization of functional capabilities taken over from the limbic system. Although I hesitate to strengthen the growing cult of the right hemisphere, the evidence indicates that the nondominant right hemisphere bears a special relationship to subordinate affective subsystems whereas the dominant left hemisphere acts in a mostly inhibitory fashion with respect to affective functions. Voluntary control over the output of propositional communication schemata and the elaboration of sensory input by verbally encoded conceptual information structures both appear to be primarily left-brain functions (but cf. Levy, Neves, & Sperry, 1971, and Butler & Norrsell, 1968, who suggest that the right hemisphere is capable of controlling certain output functions for language and speech). The right hemisphere appears to elaborate input that is generated by the limbic system in such a way that this input retains its immediateness and rich affective value. Various people have claimed that the right hemisphere is more "emotional" than the left; if this were true, there would have to be evidence of a qualitatively different right-brain interaction with the limbic system.

It has long been noted by clinicians that patients with left-sided cerebral lesions tend to be more emotionally volatile than patients with right-sided lesions; the latter tend to be curiously indifferent to their disorder and often deny its existence or make inappropriate jokes about it. Gainotti (1972) confirmed these informal observations, citing corroborative evidence from Terzian (1964) that pharmacological deactivation of the left hemisphere often leads to catastrophic-depressive reactions not found with deactivation of the right. If the left hemisphere acts to inhibit either right hemisphere elaborations of limbic functions or the limbic system itself, the emotional lability of patients with left-sided lesions would be explicable as the partial release of limbic functions from this inhibitory control. Patients with right-sided lesions, because of impaired limbic functions at the neopallial level, would tend to be less conscious of the emotional implications of their disorder and for this reason to be relatively indifferent toward it. The possibility of a disjunction between *conceptual awareness* in the left hemisphere and the representation of *emotional significance* in the right stands out clearly from the work of Sperry and Gazzaniga (1967), in which a picture of a nude was flashed to the right hemisphere of a split brain patient while objects to be named were flashed to the left. Although a sneaky grin crept across the patient's face, she was unable to conceptualize any reason for such a reaction (cf. discussion in Lishman, 1971). Gazzaniga (1970) describes a patient who seemed to have a different, violent personality whenever his right hemisphere was in control of behavior, thus supporting the hypothesis of differential interaction of left and right hemispheres with limbic functions (cf. Gazzaniga, 1972). There is some indication that integration of the two functional domains may take place via frontal lobe systems that may or may not be part of the limbic system proper, a notion perhaps testable in those many split brain patients in whom the genu of the corpus callosum has been left intact.

It is known that prosodic components of speech and emotional interjections often function as a running commentary on the affective import of the verbally encoded segmental content of speech. Further support for a claim that the right hemisphere is carrying out specialized limbic-related functions comes from a dichotic listening study of King and Kimura (1972) that demonstrated a left-ear superiority for processing laughter, coughing, crying, and other nonspeech vocalizations (see Van Lancker, 1975: Chs. 4 and 5). Milner (1967) found that patients with right (but not left) temporal lobectomies have significant deficits in the processing of tonal patterns. Although there is neither sufficient clinical nor experimental evidence to support a statement of exactly what the right and left hemispheres are doing with respect to limbic functions, there are strong indications that the two hemispheres process limbic input differentially. It may be that the right hemisphere is the mediator between the store of verbally encoded conceptual information in the dominant hemisphere and the motivational–appetitive mechanisms of the limbic system.

LIMBIC MANIFESTATIONS IN HUMAN CLINICAL SYNDROMES

Since we share much of our limbic system homologously with other mammals, a great deal can be discovered about the human limbic system from animal experimentation. Nevertheless, there clearly are species-specific, human adaptations of limbic functions that are not shared with other mammals or primates. The systems responsible are the product of the separate line of hominid evolution leading to *Homo sapiens*. This limits the applicability to humans of data on other species and puts a premium on the literature within clinical neurology that bears on the human limbic system. Clinical data is obviously less revealing than carefully controlled experimentation, if only because, with the exception of objectionable and unethical psychosurgery on otherwise healthy people, the bulk of such data is derived from patients already suffering some major neurological malfunction. Yet, if an appropriate degree of caution is exercised in extrapolating from such data to the normal operation of the limbic system in the healthy brain, much useful information can be gleaned. In this section, we will briefly review some of the clinical syndromes that involve the limbic system in order to indicate areas in which further investigation is likely to prove fruitful for understanding communication functions of the human limbic system and the relationship of the limbic system to neocortical language processing. In considering these disorders, we must distinguish clearly between those disorders with a specifically limbic etiology and those dysfunctions of other systems that result in abnormal functioning of the limbic system. With this division in mind, we will discuss the following categories of limbically based disorders: congenital and acquired arhinencephaly; temporal lobe epilepsy and bilateral and unilateral temporal lobectomies; Gilles de la Tourette's Syndrome; early infantile autism; prefrontal lobotomies, amygdalotomies, cingulotomies; and psychiatric illness.

Congenital and Acquired Arhinencephaly

Several cases have been reported in which rhinencephalon components failed to form during embryological development (e.g., Nathan & Smith, 1950; Dekaban, 1959; Yakovlev, 1959). The relatively minor degree of any behavioral abnormality produced by even very widespread congenital anatomical malformations within the rhinencephalon gives testimony to the capacity of the developing nervous system to compensate for the loss of otherwise important functional components. These observations in human beings are generally in accord with the results of lesions produced experimentally in neonatal and infant monkeys (see discussion on p. 188 above). More serious are those cases in which rhinencephalon components are damaged in adults (see Friedman & Allen, 1969). Gascon and Gilles (1973) described a case of "limbic dementia" in which there was wide destruction of limbic system structures, particularly the cortical regions and in the mediobasal temporal lobes, more on the right than the left. The patient became basically "affectless" and suffered the amnesic syndrome that is commonly associated with hippocampal lesions (Drachman & Arbit, 1966; Milner, Corking, & Teuber, 1968; Isaacson & Pribram, 1976).

Temporal Lobe Epilepsy (Limbic Epilepsy)

The involvement of limbic structures and limbic functions in temporal lobe epilepsy is clear. The focal regions that trigger seizures include the amygdala, schizocortical regions, and anterior temporal pole cortex, all components of the limbic system. Along with the hippocampus, these regions are known to have a low seizure threshold even in the normal individual. In childhood, a common symptom of temporal lobe epileptic seizures is an emotional "aura," in which the most common feeling is one of intense anxiety. This aura serves as a warning symptom and may be accompanied by particular visceral sensations, such as nausea. During seizures a great deal of oral behavior is produced, including drooling, spitting, hissing, muttering, lip smacking, and affective states such as anger or fear are experienced (Glaser, 1967). A characteristic symptom of adult temporal lobe epilepsy that is especially relevant to our present purpose is the compulsive utterance of incoherent or irrelevant words or phrases after the patient has lost contact with the environment. Serafetinides and Falconer (1963) distinguish five types of *speech automatisms* produced during seizures: (*a*) warning utterances, (*b*) recurrent utterances, (*c*) irrelevant utterances, (*d*) emotional utterances, and (*e*) perplexity utterances Such ictal speech automatisms may be repeated over and over, yet after the seizure the patient does not remember uttering them. Ictal speech automatisms tend to be associated with bilateral EEG abnormalities, but sometimes the abnormalities are predominantly right-sided (Chase, Cullen, Niedermeyer, Stark, & Blumer, 1967). It is significant that speech automatisms have been produced artificially by amygdaloid stimulation and by stimulation of overlying schizocortical regions (Driver, Falconer, & Serafetinides, 1964), making the anterior temporal pole the second site within the brain (the other being the thalamus, see above p. 197) from which articulate speech may be elicited. Chase *et al.* (1967) noted that although delayed auditory feedback disrupts normal voluntary speech activity, neither ictal speech automatisms nor emotional speech are interfered with. Their conclusion was that, unlike normal speech, the latter two types of speech production are totally "programmed" and therefore do not require continuous feedback for their continued implementation. Chase *et al.* (1967) also observed in temporal lobe epileptics a condition they called *ictal dysphasia*: patients had difficulties in expressing themselves with words while still conscious, although there seemed to be no impairment of either hearing or articulation. Such ictal dysphasias tend to be associated with presurgical EEG abnormalities that are predominantly left-sided.

Bilateral and Unilateral Temporal Lobectomies

Bilateral removal of the anterior temporal lobe may be performed as a means of relieving the symptoms of temporal lobe epilepsy. For some patients, however, bilateral temporal lobectomy produces many and in certain cases all (Maclowe *et al.*, 1975) of the symptoms of the Klüver–Bucy Syndrome previously identified in nonhuman primates (Klüver & Bucy, 1937). These symptoms include psychic blindness (agnosia), hyperoralism, hypersexuality, hypermetamorphosis (compulsive examination of objects), and loss of aggression. Milner (1967) reports that whereas left temporal lobectomy produces verbal short-term memory deficits, right temporal lobectomy produces deficits in the recognition of tonal patterns. Fedio and Van Buren (1971) have obtained the same lateralized results from electrical stimulation of the two temporal poles. These results are significant in the light of the close relationship between limbic activity and speech prosody (see p. 200 above).

Gilles de la Tourette's Syndrome

Tourette's syndrome is a poorly understood disorder whose symptoms typically begin to appear in adolescence. Its major symptoms are the involuntary production of facial and body tics, grunting and barking noises, and coprolalia (the compulsive utterance of obscenities) (Shapiro, Shapiro, Wayne, & Clarken, 1972; Shapiro *et al.*, 1973; Sweet, Soloman, Wayne, Shapiro, & Shapiro, 1973; Bruun & Shapiro, 1972).[8] The grunting and barking noises seem to be general mammalian noises almost certainly controlled by the limbic system. The utterance of obscenities represents one of the major interaction points between limbic and linguistic communication (see below, pp. 212–213). While there is no specific neurological evidence proving a limbic etiology for Tourette's syndrome, the nature of its symptoms make it plausible that the affective level of limbic activity is responsible for their production, possibly because the volitional subsystem is failing to inhibit the lower subsystems. In any case, there is no obvious explanation for exactly this mixture of symptoms as a consistent pattern across many patients.

Early Infantile Autism (Kanner's Syndrome)

Although disagreement as to the true nature of autism continues, particularly regarding its relationship to childhood schizophrenia, the syndrome as originally defined by Kanner (1943) seems identifiable as a unitary disorder. Early infantile autism becomes manifest in the first two or three postnatal months; it appears to be basically a disorder that on the one hand involves affect and its expression, and on the other is characterized by abnormal patterns of social interaction. Autistic children are aloof and indifferent to their surroundings. They fail to establish eye contact or to form the primary attachment with the mother. In contrast with their lack of affect, these children seem to be in a chronically high state of arousal, often showing a permanent condition of cortical desynchronization. They have a high pain threshold and high sensory thresholds in general; they sometimes appear to be deaf. Characteristically they will give one steryotyped response to several widely different stimuli. They reject novelty and demand sameness from the environment. Language development in these children is delayed or absent and when speech exists it has been called echolalic, metaphorical, irrelevant, and/or emotional. Kanner (1946) has noted that many repeated phrases of autistic children that seem irrelevant or metaphorical actually can be traced back to personal experiences that took place in contexts of intense emotionality.

Up to this point in time, no one has been able to correlate this package of symptoms with damage to particular neural structures and clinicians have tended

---

[8] Compulsive obscenities are also a symptom of *klasomania* and *v. Economo's encephalitis* (Bruun & Shapiro, 1972).

to focus on environmental factors as the cause. Rimland (1964), emphasizing the disorders of arousal and attention, claimed the reticular formation was the site of CNS dysfunction in autism. However, this account fails to explain the more striking disorders of affect and social interaction. Based on these symptoms, Schain and Yannet (1960) made the suggestion that it was the limbic system that was the organic base of autism. Deslauriers and Carlson (1969) strengthened this claim by applying the "two arousal system hypothesis" of Routtenberg (1968) which stresses the relationship between the arousal functions of the limbic system and reward/positive-incentive behavior. Since limbic subsystems are responsible for emotion, social interaction, arousal, the establishment of sensory thresholds, and the initiation and cessation of attention to novel stimuli, not to mention basic aspects of communication, it seems reasonable to view intrinsically or extrinsically triggered limbic malfunctions as the cause of early infantile autism.

Prefrontal Lobotomies, Amygdalotomies, Cingulotomies

A variety of limbic lesions are made purposefully in human beings for legitimate medical reasons, for example, as mentioned above, bilateral temporal lobectomies are performed in order to relieve epileptic symptoms. However, the overwhelming majority of limbic surgical procedures have been performed as questionable "psychosurgery" in order to make people more manageable, to remove violent or destructive tendencies, or to eliminate chronic depression (see Breggin, 1972). Thus, senior citizens in nursing homes, children who habitually run away from home, criminals, and patients in mental hospitals may, knowingly or unknowingly, willingly or unwillingly, have portions of their limbic systems bilaterally excised. Just as in other mammals, bilateral amygdalotomies in humans eliminate aggressive behavior and make the individual easier to manage in an institutional setting (Narabayashi *et al.*, 1963; Anderson, 1970; Vaernet & Madsen, 1970). Cingulotomies are performed for the same purpose, as well as for the relief of intractable pain or chronic depression (Meyer *et al.*, 1972). The effects of prefrontal lobotomies are perhaps more subtle to an outside observer, but are more personally devastating. These operations render the individual calm, but more specifically, the person's emotional reactivity and responsiveness are impaired, and he suffers a marked loss of self-awareness, judgment, and empathy.

Psychiatric Illness

It is in clinical psychology that one encounters some of the thornier aspects of the relationship between mind and body, for the line between a psychological disorder and a neurological disorder is often thin indeed. Whether produced congenitally or by environmental factors, whether based on biochemical abnormalities, actual tissue damage, or anomalous functional activity, many psychiatric disorders clearly involve the limbic system. The role of the limbic system in neurosis and psychosis has been explored most thoroughly by Smythies (1966), who summarizes his conclusions as follows:

> To conclude therefore we can postulate the following:
> 1. The neuroses represent quantitative disturbances of limbic control of the emotions and behaviour where the faulty patterns of feeling and behaviour are determined very largely by faulty conditioning and faulty setting of thresholds and generalizations in the way that we have described. There is no change in the normal ideation → emotion causal chain and no qualitative change in brain physiology.
> 2. In the psychoses there seem to be qualitative changes in brain physiology. Or rather that [sic] the quantitative changes in such systems as serotonin, nor-adrenaline and dopamine metabolism or the biochemical processes of methylation become so serious that homeostasis breaks down and the various vicious circles that we have described develop. The causal chain ideation → emotion reverses. In depression the disorder may be limited to the limbic system and in schizophrenia a more widespread disorder of brain function may be involved including the temporal lobe. This wider spread may occur for several reasons. The basic biochemical lesion, if there is such, may affect some widespread mechanisms. The emotions that become disordered may cause more widespread havoc. The delusions and behaviour manifest in the disease may result in greater cultural rejection, with consequent intensification of feelings of insecurity, rejection, suspicion, hatred, etc. [Smythies, 1966, p. 137]

The power of a limbic-related psychosis to override damaged neocortical systems is brought out clearly in a case described by Robinson (1972; 1975) of a patient who exhibited variable symptoms that are very difficult to account for. A male patient incurred a left-sided cerebral lesion which left him paralyzed on the right side of the body and also severely aphasic. The patient subsequently became manic-depressive and, when he was in the manic phase, both his paralysis and his speech disorder disappeared. When medication to control the mania was administered, the paralysis and speech disorder would reappear, only to disappear once more when medication was discontinued. Robinson concluded from this that speech is under the control of two separate systems, one for normal speech and another for speech under stress or in situations of strong emotion. It has long been recognized that Broca's aphasics show markedly improved speech competence during emotional and stressed speech (Jackson, 1932; Goldstein, 1948; Critchley, 1970). A disorder called *phrase fixation* results when an aphasic patient who has lost control over propositional speech fixates on one or more expressions, usually obscene words, which he repeats over and over. Rather than posit two distinct systems for speech we may consider the possibility that with strong arousal from the limbic system (perhaps operating through the right hemisphere—recall the discussion on pp. 199–200 regarding laterality of affect in cerebral lesions), whatever is blocking damaged left-hemisphere neocortical speech and motor systems from exercising normal control over behavior is overpowered or circumvented within the left hemisphere. It is also possible that powerful limbic activity may somehow provide the right hemisphere with the access to output functions for speech that is normally reserved to the left hemisphere. An understanding of what is actually going on here can only come from a better understanding of the interaction between the limbic system and linguistic systems of the neocortex. In the next section, we will explore this relationship briefly.

RELATING LIMBIC AND LINGUISTIC COMMUNICATION

As we have seen, the human limbic system is responsible for a variety of communication functions at three levels, these functions being superimposed on primary sign behavior at the striatal level. The most basic limbic communication activity exists within the *appetitive* subsystem and results in automatic sign behavior implying specific internal sensations and drive states. The *affective* level of limbic communication (also produced by preprogrammed circuitry) is related to emotion and motivational states, as well as to the regulation of social interactions characteristic of our species. It is with the third level of limbic activity, the *volitional* subsystem, that a new type of communication arises. At this point the conscious goals of the individual with respect to the environment and to other people become the basis for intentional signal behavior.

With the development of propositionally based symbolic activity by neocortical systems, new types of verbal and nonverbal nonlimbic communication appear, leading eventually to language and speech. However, limbic level communication patterns do not disappear at this point. The limbic communication systems continue to serve their special functional roles in concert with both higher and lower levels of neural organization. Speech is normally embedded within a matrix of behavior patterns regulated by the limbic system. In decoding a speaker's message, the addressee consciously and unconsciously attends to these nonlinguistic behaviors in order to extract the entire message. There are many questions about the relationship between linguistic and limbic communication that will not be answered without a good deal more effort by investigators in several fields; this will include not just the gathering of additional data, but the adoption of a productive theoretical framework within which to formulate both the questions and the answers. The conclusions drawn will depend to a large extent on the perspective from which the problem is approached.

Neurophysiological Framework

To understand limbic and linguistic communication from a neurological perspective, it is important to recognize that the various neural elements responsible operate together as part of the same neurofunctional metasystem, even while they exist as autonomous physiological systems with their own relationships to other (noncommunication) systems. Both phylogenetically and ontogenetically, the components of this metasystem appear as discrete neural structures with particular roles to play in communication behavior. As these structures become operational, they take their place at some level in the hierarchy of systems that make up the larger metasystem. It is worth mentioning that at higher levels there exist qualitatively different kinds of neuronal mechanisms: new types of neurons, more complex types of cortical organization, and so on. In all of these respects, the neural systems responsible for communication do not appear to be different from the many other such hierarchical metasystems within the brain. Certain aspects of the interaction of hierarchies of neural systems at different levels within the nervous system are illustrated hypothetically in Figure 4.14.

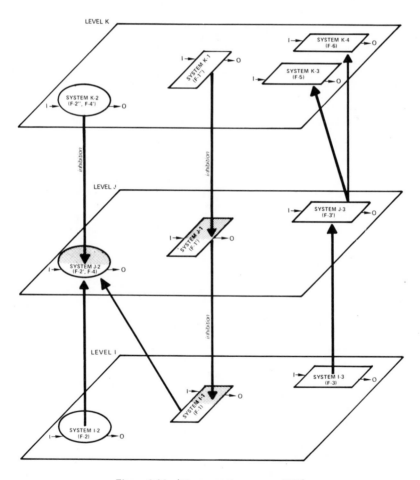

Figure 4.14 (Figure caption on page 208)

Specification of the anatomical and physiological relationships between neural elements cannot, by itself, tell us much about either limbic or linguistic communication. All we can describe from a neuroanatomical or neurophysiological perspective is neurons, groups of neurons, and the patterns of their anatomical connections and physiological interactions. Such a reductionist approach would eliminate the very (epi)phenomenon we are interested in describing. Because "communication" resides at a different epiphenomenal/descriptive level from such things as "axon" and "action potential," the neurophysiologist qua neurophysiologist can say nothing that directly illuminates the relationship between the limbic system and language. The neuronal activity actually producing overt behavior has to be translated into functional terms in order that the process of communication may be understood.

Figure 4.14 An illustration of some general principles underlying the organization of neural system. (*1*) The nervous system is organized anatomically into a series of increasingly more complex LEVELS (i $\Rightarrow$ j $\Rightarrow$ k in the diagram). (*2*) Each level consists of a number of *neurophysiological functional systems* definable in terms of their anatomical constituency, connections with other structures, and internal organization. Each system is responsible for a given domain of *functional activity* specifiable by the input/output relations of that system (I $\rightarrow$ System i-1 $\rightarrow$ 0) and its internal processing activity. (*3*) Each functional domain is realized in the mature nervous system as a *hierarchically organized* series of systems at increasingly higher levels, the hierarchy as a whole constituting a *functional metasystem* (System i-1 $\Rightarrow$ j-1 $\Rightarrow$ k-1 and the Functions F-1 $\Rightarrow$ F-1' $\Rightarrow$ F-1''). (*4*) A given system may form part of more than one functional hierarchy (System i-1) and/or carry out more than one function (System j-2). (*5*) In general, systems at a higher level in a hierarchy evolved later in *phylogeny* than lower level systems within the same hierarchy. For a given species, the hierarchical systems organization of the spinal cord and brain shows a high correlation with *stages of neural evolution*. (*6*) In general, systems at a higher level in a hierarchy become operational later in *ontogeny* than lower systems within the same hierarchy. The progressive maturation of higher level systems is responsible for the *developmental stages* observable in infancy and childhood. (*7*) For both phylogeny and ontogeny, new systems tend to first carry out old functions and new functions tend to be first carried out by old systems. (*8*) A higher level system within a hierarchy may stand in various different relations with lower systems: (a) it may simply be *added* into the information flow and work in concert with the lower system (System j-3); (b) it may *integrate* the activity of separate lower systems, thereby giving rise to new functional capabilities (System j-2); (c) it may *differentiate* the unified activity of a single lower system to produce novel functional organization at the higher level (Systems k-3 and k-4); (d) a higher system may be *superimposed* on a lower system. A higher system superimposed on a lower system may *inhibit* some subset of the lower system's functional activity, with the functions being re-translated at the higher level. Superceded lower systems tend to continue operating at this modified/reduced level of activity as a subordinate component of the functional metasystem (System j-1 is superimposed on i-1). (*9*) For a given functional hierarchy at any given moment, a particular level in the hierarchy may be said to be in *control* of input processing or the production of overt behavior within the functional domain of the hierarchy. Control functions undergo rapid shifts up and down the hierarchy based on a large number of variables. (*10*) If a higher system within a hierarchy is incapacitated by disease or trauma, a lower system may be released from its inhibitory influence and begin to function as it did before the higher system became operational. (*11*) In general, functional systems and functional hierarchies have a bilateral representation in the nervous system; however, in some species, there also exist forebrain systems that are lateralized to the left or right cerebrum.

Functional Framework

A second framework for considering the relationship between limbic and linguistic communication ignores the neurophysiological machinery for communicative behavior in favor of describing communication totally from a functional perspective. At issue here is the notion of "function" as it is used in information processing psychology (see Fodor, 1968; Lindsay & Norman, 1974). Many cognitive psychologists attempt to give abstract functional characterizations of the information processing activity that human beings engage in during perception and pattern recognition, memory storage and retrieval, problem solving, speech recognition, language formulation, and the like. All of these activities are dealt with as abstract functional processes, and no formal concern is given to the many different types of system that are capable of carrying them out. A computer program, a Martian, a chimpanzee, and a human being possessing internal systems of radically different design might be able to carry out some (or all) of the same communication functions.

For some purposes within psychology, it is not necessary or even helpful to tie one's theorizing to the neurophysiological level of description, especially when little may be known about the organization of the neural structures that perform the activity in question. At present, more is known from a functional point of view about how communication takes place than about the actual workings of the neural systems involved. On the other hand, investigating the nature of the physical mechanisms responsible could certainly help us to understand this functional domain. Knowledge concerning neural systems places needed constraints on models and theories constructed to describe and explain the information processing that produces human communication. It is questionable whether we could ever adequately describe internal human communication systems without taking into account the organization of neural systems. Clearly a mixture of the two perspectives—a neurofunctional framework—will provide the best all around basis for understanding the information processing involved in communication and the neural systems that perform it.

In considering limbic and language processing from a neurofunctional point of view, we see that the two domains tend to be complementary. Higher neocortical systems develop new functions that augment the older limbic functional repertoire, but there is also overlap, so that the same function may be carried out by more than one system, albeit in different fashions. Much need not be encoded propositionally because it is already being expressed through the limbic system, and some functions are implemented preferentially at one level rather than another. Figure 4.15 gives a first approximation to specifying the levels of communication functions within the human repertoire. Notice that for a given communicative interaction, each of these functions could occur in isolation or in combination with almost any subset of other functions. Verbal and linguistic

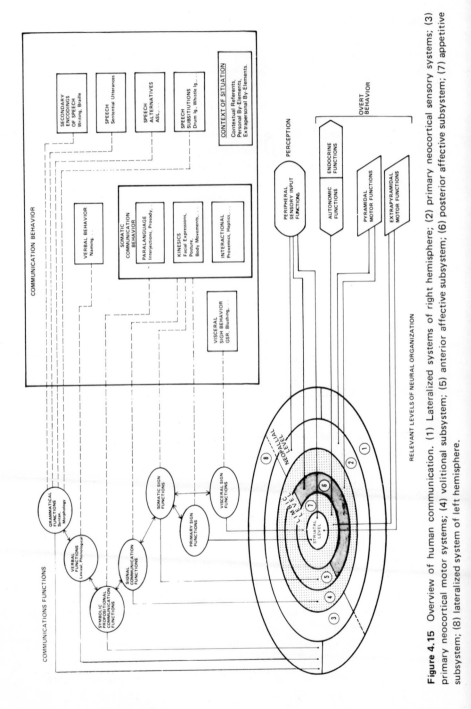

Figure 4.15 Overview of human communication. (1) Lateralized systems of right hemisphere; (2) primary neocortical sensory systems; (3) primary neocortical motor systems; (4) volitional subsystem; (5) anterior affective subsystem; (6) posterior affective subsystem; (7) appetitive subsystem; (8) lateralized system of left hemisphere.

behavior can be produced with almost no limbic accompaniment via prosody, sign, or signal behavior, and certainly communication behavior that is controlled by the limbic system can be produced without any verbal accompaniment. The normal condition is probably for the entire functional hierarchy to be represented in every communication interchange.

Behavioral Framework

A third perspective from which to consider the relationship between limbic and linguistic communication ignores both neurophysiology and functions to focus instead on *overt behavior*: classifying particular actions and correlating behavioral sequences with each other and with environmental circumstances. Although we must make empirical observations of human behavior under various conditions to establish a data base from which to formulate and validate theoretical claims, there is no justification for making behavioral taxonomies ends in themselves. The explanation for domains of human behavior such as communication will not be found in behavior alone, but in an understanding of the neurofunctional systems responsible for producing behavior. Unfortunately, the majority of work done within psychology, linguistics, and even neurolinguistics has avoided making claims about the organization of unobservable neurofunctional systems for language and other types of communication.

Communication behavior produced by the limbic system has been studied by scholars within speech science mostly under the heading of "nonverbal communication," approached in terms of several major subtypes: (*a*) *paralanguage*, (*b*) *kinesics*, and (*c*) *proxemics* and *haptics* (see Harrison, 1974; Knapp, 1972; Abercrombie, 1968; Key, 1975). Much effort has been spent in justifying the criteria by which given behaviors may be grouped into one or another category of nonverbal behavior (Figure 4.15 also gives a behavior-based classification of various communication activities). Because they are based solely on overt actions, these categories do not help us to understand limbic in relation to linguistic communication. Consider *paralanguage*. This class of nonverbal behavior is generally defined as involving all nonspeech vocalizations including prosodic elements beyond phonology. It includes in its scope many quite different communication phenomena: for example, symbolic propositional behavior that is particular to a given culture, and automatic appetitive and affective vocalizations (some found in all mammals, others in all primates, and still others species-specific in *Homo sapiens*). The hodgepodge category *paralanguage* fails to distinguish intentionally produced limbic or neocortical vocal activity from automatic limbic responses to internal physiological states or environmental conditions. Exactly the same overt vocalization can be a manifestation of many different underlying functions on different occasions. Moreover, examples of all of these same functional phenomena can be found under the label *kinesics*, a category generally taken to include facial expression, posture, body movements, gestures, and so on. The traditional distinction between paralanguage and kinesics obscures the fact that limbic communication is normally produced as multimodal behavior complexes with vocalizations, facial expressions, gestures, and the like systematically used as part of the same pattern. Within limbic communication, the vocal tract motor systems have no special status in respect to other forms of motor activity. It is also important to realize that many nonverbal behavior patterns are used to symbolically encode propositional messages as an alternate mode to speech, most likely based on the same neocortical systems. It would be more productive to categorize overt nonverbal behavior in terms of its organization by central neurofunctional systems than by arbitrary behavioral criteria such as whether it is vocal or nonvocal.

In a similar fashion, it is misleading to use overt behavior to define "verbal communication" or "speech" as a unitary phenomenon. Here too, it is the neurofunctional organization that produces overt speech behavior that should be the criterion. Utterances without any propositional content (such as might be produced by a parrot or by an epileptic during a seizure) must be distinguished from speech used by people to communicate propositional messages. It has long been known that aphasics in whom propositional speech is missing or severely disrupted often retain control over certain other forms of speech (Jackson, 1932; Head, 1926; Luria, 1970; Critchley, 1970; Bay, 1964). As discussed in Van Lancker (1975), there are a variety of different types of speech abilities arranged along a continuum from fully *propositional speech* to fully *automatic speech*. In between these two extremes there are a large number of different speech phenomena including memorized speech and songs, pause fillers, idioms, familiar and overlearned expressions such as greetings, conventionalized phrases, social formulas, and other types of holistic and recurring phrases—not to mention emotional speech. The closer a given type of speech is to the automatic end of the continuum, the more stable it tends to be with damage to left-hemisphere neocortical speech systems. Even though these forms of speech remain with left-hemisphere damage, this does not necessary mean (as has been claimed) that automatic speech behavior is coded by the right hemisphere and propositional speech in the left. These speech forms could just as well be bilaterally represented in neocortical systems as preprogrammed movement schemata for the vocal tract articulators. Different types of speech may even be "represented" in limbic, thalamic, basal ganglia, or midbrain motor systems. With one exception, the various types of automatic speech are devoid of content to one or another degree; they may lack referential meaning, propositional meaning, etc. The exception is emotional speech, which possesses *limbic content*.

Emotionally charged, vulgar, or obscene speech represents not just an interaction between the limbic system and linguistic systems, but the intersection of the two. Emotional speech results from limbic functions that have found linguistic expression, speech that while phonologically structured and possessing propositional content finds its major role in the expression of affect. Ordinarily, the affective state of the speaker shows up only "around the edges" of language in the form of prosodic patterns; the bulk of affective content is communicated by limbic sign and signal complexes. However, where a strong emotional content (positive or negative) is associated with components of the propositional message, the speaker may select words or constructions that are emotionally charged in that they have a special "tie-in" to the limbic system, perhaps via the right hemisphere (cf. above, pp. 199–200). The use of these words seems to give emotional release, and in this sense it is satisfying to sprinkle our speech with expletives. The recognition of emotionally charged words can also cause emotion to well up in the person addressed, and this is often precisely the intent of an insult. If someone calls you a dirty name, it is irrelevant whether your parents were really married or not; the insult was not aimed at the neocortex, but lower down. Whatever the nature of the connection between such words and their limbic content, if one uses a vulgar word too often without feeling the associated emotion, the connection between the word and the emotional charge may be lost and a new vulgar word must be invented.

Also interesting in this context is *speech under stress*, which even in a normal individual may resemble that of a Broca's aphasic. It is literally possible to become speechless with rage as control functions over behavior shift down from propositional, neopallial systems to limbic subsystems in interactional situations involving the Four F's. If one sits on a tack, it is likely to be the limbic system that will control the vocal and nonvocal reaction, and if words are uttered at all they are often limbically charged obscenities. Cultures differ widely in the extent to which they allow affective content to be given systematic expression during speech in the form of accompanying hand and body gestures, facial expressions, interjections, and prosodic patterns. Within a given culture the quantity of emotional expression also differs widely from individual to individual. American Sign Language seems to allow a great deal of freedom in expressing affective states and attitudes toward what is being said, and in this sense manual signing may be a more "gratifying" form of language than vocal speech. Many foreign language learners have felt the frustration of having failed to master the culturally conditioned expression of affect in a foreign language, and one can have a strong nonverbal "accent" even when phonology and grammar are under control. One reason why bilinguals might revert to a "mother tongue" under stress or strong emotion may simply be that this language has the best "tie-in" to limbic expression. Perhaps it is sometimes for this same reason that one language rather than another is less seriously disturbed in a bilingual aphasic.

There are a great many important topics that could benefit from a clearer understanding of the limbic system and the communication behavior it produces. Limbic information processing is of interest not merely as a nonverbal fringe to language, but because it lies at the heart of many theoretical issues currently under discussion in linguistics and psycholinguistics. Unquestionably, the limbic system has a strong claim on the attention of neurolinguists as they attempt to explain the neural systems responsible for human communication. Even though our species has developed high level neocortical systems for propositional and linguistic communication, as mammals, we are still the beneficiaries of a long evolutionary history that produced complex communication systems for appetite, affect, and social interaction. These more basic types of communication cannot be ignored if we hope to understand language and the functions it serves in human interaction.

ACKNOWLEDGMENTS

I would like to express my appreciation to K. Pribram for many valuable suggestions during various stages of preparing this chapter, and to R. E. Myers and W. O. Dingwall for their helpful comments.

REFERENCES

Abbie, A. A. 1940. Cortical lamination in the Monotremata. *Journal of Comparative Neurology* 72, 428–467.
Abbie, A. A. 1942. Cortical lamination in a polyprotodont marsupial, *Perameles nasuta*. *Journal of Comparative Neurology, 76*, 509–536.
Abercrombie, D. 1968. Paralanguage. *British Journal of Disorders of Communication, 3*, 55–59.
Adey, W. R., & T. Tokizane (Eds.) 1967. *Structure and function of the limbic system.* Amsterdam: Elsevier.
Akert, K. 1961. Diencephalon. In D. E. Sheer (Ed.), *Electrical stimulation of the brain.* Austin: Univ. of Texas. Pp. 288–310.
Akert, K., Orth, O. S., Harlow, H. F., & Schlitz, K. A. 1960. Learned behavior of rhesus monkeys following neonatal bilateral prefrontal lobotomy. *Science, 132*(3444), 1944–1945.
Allan, C. M., Turner, J. W., & Gadea-Ciria, M. 1966. Investigation into speech disturbances following stereotactic surgery for parkinsonism. *British Journal of Disorders of Communication, 1*, 55–59.
Allison, R. S. 1966. Perseveration as a sign of diffuse and focal brain damage. *British Medical Journal, 2*(5520), 1095–1101.
Altmann, S. A. (Ed.), 1967. *Social communication among primates.* Chicago: Univ. of Chicago Press.
Anderson, R. 1970. Psychological difference after amygdalotomy. *Acta Neurologica Scandinavica* (Suppl. 43), *46*, 94.
Andrew, R. J. 1973. The evocation of calls by diencephalic stimulation in the conscious chick. *Brain, Behavior, and Evolution, 7*, 424–446.
Apfelbach, R. 1972. Electrically elicited vocalizations in the gibbon, *Hylobates lar* (Hylobatidae), and their behavioral significance. *Zeitschrift für Tierpsychologie, 30*, 420–430.

Bard, P. 1928. A diencephalic mechanism for the expression of rage with special reference to the sympathetic nervous system. *American Journal of Physiology, 84*, 490–515.

Bard, P., and Montcastle, V. B. 1947. Some forebrain mechanisms involved in expression of rage with special reference to suppression of angry behavior. *Research Publications, Association for Research in Nervous and Mental Disease, 27*, 362–404.

Barrett, T. W. 1969. Studies of the function of the amygdaloid complex in *M. mulatta. Neuropsychologia, 7*, 1–12.

Bay, E. 1964. Principles of classification and their influence on our concepts of aphasia. In A. V. S. DeReuck and M. O'Conner (Eds.), *Disorders of Language*. CIBA Symposium. London: Churchill. Pp. 122–139.

Bell, D. 1968. Speech functions of the thalamus inferred from the effects of thalamotomy. *Brain, 91*, 619–638.

Bell, S., & Ainsworth, M. D. S. 1972. Infant crying and maternal responsiveness. *Child Development, 43*, 1171–1190.

Boshes, B. 1966. Voice changes in parkinsonism. *Journal of Neurosurgery, 24*(1), 286–288.

Botez, M. I., & Barbeau, A. 1971. Role of subcortical structures, and particularly the thalamus, in the mechanisms of speech and language. *International Journal of Neurology, 8*, 300–320.

Breggin, P. R. 1972. The return of lobotomy and psychosurgery. *Congressional Record, 118*(26).

Broca, P. 1878. Anatomie comparée de cerconvolutions cérébrales. Le grand lobe limbique et la scissure limbic dans le série de mammifères. *Revue d'Anthropologie, 1*, 385–498.

Brodal, A. 1947. The hippocampus and the sense of smell: A review. *Brain, 70*, 179–222.

Bronson, G. 1965. Hierarchical organization of the central nervous system. *Behavioral Science, 10*(1), 7–25.

Brown, J. L. 1965. Loss of vocalization caused by lesions in the nucleus mesencephalicus laterales of the Redwinged Blackbird. *American Zoologist, 5*, 693.

Bruun, R. D., & Shapiro, A. K. 1972. Differential diagnosis of Gilles de la Tourette's syndrome. *Journal of Nervous and Mental Disease, 155*(5), 328–334.

Buettner-Janusch, J. (Ed.) 1963. *Evolutionary and genetic biology of primates.* Vol. 1. New York: Academic Press.

Butler, S., & Norrsell, U. 1968. Vocalization possibly initiated by the minor hemisphere. *Nature, 220*, 793–794.

Cannon, W. B. 1927. The James-Lange theory of emotions: A critical examination and an alternative theory. *American Journal of Psychology, 39*, 106–124.

Canter, G. J. 1963. Speech characteristics of patients with Parkinson's disease. Part I. Intensity, pitch, and duration. *Journal of Speech and Hearing Disorders, 28*, 221–230.

Carter, A. L. 1974. *The development of communication in the sensorimotor period: A case study.* Unpublished PhD. dissertation, Univ. of California, Berkeley.

Chase, R. A., Cullen, J. K., Niedermeyer, E. F. L., Stark, R. E., & Blumer, D. P. 1967. Ictal speech automatisms and swearing: Studies on the auditory feedback control of speech. *Journal of Nervous and Mental Disease, 144*(5), 406–420.

Cheek, W. R., & Taveras, J. M. 1966. Thalamic tumors. *Journal of Neurosurgery, 24*, 505–513.

Ciemins, V. 1970. Localized thalamic hemorrhage: A cause of aphasia. *Neurology* (Mpls.), *20*, 776–782.

Critchley, M. 1970. *Aphasiology and other aspects of language.* London: Edward Arnold.

Crosby, E. C., & Humphrey, T. 1941. Studies of the vertebrate telencephalon. II. The nuclear pattern of the anterior olfactory nucleus, tuberculum olfactorum, and the amygdaloid complex in adult man. *Journal of Comparative Neurology, 74*(2), 309–352.

Dart, R. 1934. The dual structure of the neopallium: Its history and significance. *Journal of Anatomy, 69*(1), 3–19.

Dekaban, A. 1959. Arhinencephaly in an infant born to a diabetic mother. *Journal of Neuropathology and Experimental Neurology, 18*(4), 620–626.

Delafresnaye, J. F. (Ed.) 1967. *Brain mechanisms and consciousness.* Springfield, Ill.: Charles C. Thomas.

DeReuck, A. V. S., & O'Conner, M. (Eds.) 1964. *Disorders of language.* CIBA Symposium. London: Churchill.

DesLauriers, A. M., & Carlson, C. F. 1969. *Your child is asleep: Early infantile autism.* Homewood, Ill.: Dorsey Press.

DiCara, L. V. (Ed.) 1974. *Limbic and autonomic nervous systems research.* New York: Plenum Press.

Dingwall, W. O., & Whitaker, H. A. 1974. Neurolinguistics. *Annual Review of Anthropology, 3,* 323–356.

Domino, E. F., Dren, A. T., & Yamamoto, K-I. 1967. Pharmacologic evidence for cholinergic mechanisms in neocortical and limbic activiting systems. In W. R. Adey and T. Tokizane (Eds.), *Structure and function of the limbic system.* Amsterdam: Elsevier. Pp. 337–364.

Donovick, P. J., Burright, P. G., Fuller, J. L., & Branson, P. R. 1975. Septal lesions and behavior: Effects of presurgical rearing and the strain of mouse. *Journal of Comparative Physiology and Psychology, 89*(8), 859–867.

Drachman, D. A., & Arbit, J. 1966. Memory and the hippocampal complex. II. Is memory a multiple process? *Archives of Neurology, 15,* 52–61.

Driver, M. V., Falconer, M. A., & Serafetinides, E. A. 1964. Ictal speech automatisms reproduced by activation procedures: A case report with comments on pathogenesis. *Neurologyy, 14*(5), 455–463.

Egger, M. D., and Flynn, J. P. 1967. Further studies on the effect of amygdaloid stimulation and ablation on hypothalamically elicited attack behavior in cats. In W. R. Adey and T. Tokizane (Eds.), *Structure and function in the limbic system.* Amsterdam: Elsevier. Pp. 165–182.

Eleftheriou, B. E. (Ed.) 1972. *Neurobiology of the amygdala.* New York: Plenum Press.

Endröczi, E. (Ed.) 1972. *Limbic system, learning, and pituitary-adrenal function.* Budapest: Akadémiai Kiadó.

Fauconnier, G. 1975. Pragmatic scales and logical structure. *Linguistic Inquiry, 6*(3), 353–376.

Fedio, P., & Ommaya, A. 1970. Bilateral cingulum lesions and stimulation in man with lateralized impairment in short-term verbal memory. *Experimental Neurology, 29*(1), 84–91.

Fedio, P., & Van Buren, J. M. 1971. Cerebral mechanisms for perception and immediate memory under electrical stimulation in conscious man. Unpublished ms. Bethesda: Surgical Neurology Branch, National Institute of Neurological Disease and Stroke.

Fields, W. S. (Ed.) 1961. *Pathogenesis and treatment of cerebrovascular disease.* Springfield, Ill.: Charles C Thomas.

Fillmore, C. 1975. On the problem of characterizing linguistic abilities. Proceedings of the NYAS Conference on the Origins and Evolution of Language and Speech (to appear).

Fillmore, C., Lakoff, G., & Lakoff, R. (Eds.) 1974. *Berkeley studies in syntax and semantics.* Vol. 1. Berkeley: Univ. of Calif., Dept. of Linguistics and Institute of Human Learning.

Fisher, C. M. 1961. Clinical syndromes in cerebral hemorrhage. In W. S. Fields (Ed.), *Pathogenesis and treatment of cerebrovascular disease.* Springfield, Ill.: Charles C Thomas. Pp. 318–338.

Flechsig, P. 1901. Developmental (mylogenetic) localization of the cerebral cortex in the human subject. *Lancet 2*, 1027–1029.

Fodor, J. A. 1968. *Psychological explanation.* New York: Random House.

Franzen, E. A., & Myers, R. E. 1973a. Neural control of social behavior: Prefrontal and anterior temporal cortex. *Neuropsychologia, 11*, 141–157.

Franzen, E. A., & Myers, R. E. 1973b. Age effects on social behavior deficits following prefrontal lesions in monkeys. *Brain Research, 54*, 277–286.

Friedman, H. M., & Allen, N. 1969. Chronic effects of complete limbic lobe destruction in man. *Neurology* (Mpls.), *19*, 679–690.

Gainotti, G. 1972. Emotional behavior and hemispheric side of the lesion. *Cortex, 8*(1), 41–55.

Gardner, R. A., and Garnder, B. T. 1969. Teaching sign language to a chimpanzee. *Science, 165*, 664–672.

Gascon, G., & Gilles, F. 1973. Limbic dementia. *Journal of Neurology, Neurosurgery, and Psychiatry, 36*, 421–430.

Gazzaniga, M. S. 1970. *The bisected brain.* New York: Appleton.

Gazzaniga, M. 1972. One brain—two minds? *American Scientist, 60*, 311–317.

Gill, T. V., & Rumbaugh, D. M. 1974. Mastery of naming skills by a champanzee. *Journal of Human Evolution, 3*, 483–492.

Glaser, G. H. 1967. Limbic epilepsy in childhood. *Journal of Nervous and Mental Disease, 144*(5), 391–397.

Glass, D. C. (Ed.) 1967. *Neurophysiology and emotion.* New York: Rockefeller Univ. Press.

Goldstein, K. 1948. *Language and language disturbances.* New York: Grune and Stratton.

Grossman, R. E., San, L. J., & Vance, T. J. (Eds.) 1975. *Papers from the Parasession on Functionalism.* Chicago: Chicago Linguistic Society.

Harlow, H. F., Thompson, C. I., Bloomquist, A. J., & Schultz, K. A. 1970. Learning in rhesus monkeys after varying amounts of prefrontal lobe destruction during infancy and adolescence. *Brain Research, 18*, 343–353.

Harrison, R. P. 1974. *Beyond words: An introduction to nonverbal communication.* Englewood Cliffs, N.J.: Prentice-Hall.

Hassler, R., & Stephan, H. (Eds.) 1966. *Evolution of the forebrain: Phylogenesis and ontogenesis of the forebrain.* Stuttgart: Georg Thieme Verlag.

Hast, M. H., Fischer, J. M., Wetzel, A. B., & Thompson, V. E. 1974. Cortical motor representations of the laryngeal muscles in *Macaca mulatta. Brain Research, 73*, 229–240.

Head, H. 1926. *Aphasia and kindred disorders of speech.* Cambridge: Cambridge Univ. Press.

Herrick, C. J. 1933. The functions of the olfactory parts of the cortex. *Proceedings of the National Academy of Sciences of the United States of America, 19*(1), 7–14.

Isaacson, R. L. (Ed.) 1968. *The neuropsychology of development.* New York: Wiley.

Isaacson, R. L. 1974. *The limbic system.* New York: Plenum Press.

Isaacson, R. L., & Pribram, K. H. (Eds.) 1976. *The hippocampus.* Vols. 1 and 2. New York: Plenum Press.

Jackson, J. H. 1932. On the nature of the duality of the brain. In J. Taylor (Ed.), *Selected writings of John Humphrey Jackson.* London: Hodder and Stroughton. Pp. 129–145.

James, W. 1890. *The principles of psychology.* New York: Holt.

Jürgens, U. 1974. On the elicibility of vocalizations from the cortical larynx area. *Brain Research, 81*, 564–566.

Jürgens, U., & Ploog, D. 1970. Cerebral representation of vocalization in the squirrel monkey. *Experimental Brain Research, 10*(5), 532–554.

Kanai, T., & Wang, S. C. 1962. Localization of the central vocalization mechanism in the brain stem of the cat. *Experimental Neurology, 6*(5), 426–434.

Kanner, L. 1943. Autistic disturbances of affective contact. *The Nervous Child,* 2(3), 217–250.

Kanner, L. 1946. Irrelevant and metaphorical language in early infantile autism. *American Journal of Psychiatry, 103,* 242–246.

Kappers, C. U. A., Huber, G. C., & Crosby, E. C. 1936. *The comparative anatomy of the nervous system of vertebrates including man.* (2 Vols.) New York: Macmillan.

Kelly, A. H., Beaton, L. E., & Magoun, H. W. 1946. A midbrain mechanism for facio-vocal activity. *Journal of Neurophysiology, 9*(3), 181–189.

Key, M. R. 1975. *Paralanguage and kinesics.* Metuchen, N.J.: Scarecrow Press.

King, F. L., & Kimura, D. 1972. Left-ear superiority in dichotic perception of nonverbal sounds. *Canadian Journal of Psychology, 26*(2), 111–116.

Kleist, K. 1934. Gehirn-Pathologie vornehurlich auf grund der Kreigesfahrungen. in *Handbuch der ärzlichen Enfahrungen in Weltkrieg.* Vol. 4. Leipzig: Barth.

Kling, A., & Green, P. C. 1967. Effects of neonatal amygdalectomy in the maternally reared and maternally deprived Macaque. *Nature* (London), *213*(5077), 742–743.

Kling, A., Lancaster, J., & Benitone, J. 1970. Amygdalectomy in the free-ranging vervet (*Cercopithecus aethiops*). *Journal of Psychiatric Research, 7,* 191–199.

Kling, A., & Tucker, T. J. 1968. Sparing of function following localized brain lesions in neonatal monkeys. In R. L. Isaacson (Ed.), *The neuropsychology of development.* New York: Wiley. Pp. 121–145.

Klüver, H., & Bucy, P. C. 1937. "Psychic blindness" and other symptoms following bilateral temporal lobectomy in rhesus monkeys. *American Journal of Physiology, 119,* 352–353.

Knapp, M. L. 1972. *Nonverbal communication in human interaction* New York: Holt.

Koch, S. (Ed.) 1962. *Psychology: A study of a science.* Vol. 4. New York: McGraw-Hill.

Kuno, S. 1972. Functional sentence perspective: A case study from Japanese and English. *Linguistic Inquiry, 3*(3), 269–320.

Krieg, W. J. S. 1966. *Functional neuroanatomy.* (3rd ed.) Evanston, Ill.: Brain Books.

Laitinen, L. 1966. Thalamic targets in the stereotaxic treatment of Parkinson's disease. *Journal of Neurosurgery, 24,* 82–85.

Laitinen, L. V., & Livingston, K. E. (Eds.) 1972. *Surgical approaches in psychiatry.* Baltimore: Univ. Park Press.

Lakoff, G. 1974. Pragmatics in natural logic. In C. Fillmore, G. Lakoff, and R. Lakoff (Eds.), *Berkeley studies in syntax and semantics.* Vol. 1. Berkeley: Univ. of Calif., Dept. of Linguistics and Institute of Human Learning. Pp. X1–X45.

Lamendella, J. T. 1975. Maturational stages in the development of communication systems by the child. Paper presented to the California Linguistics Assoc. Conference.

Lamendella, J. T. In preparation. *The early growth of language and cognition: A neuropsychological approach.*

Lanerolle, N. de, & Andrew, R. J. 1974. Midbrain structures controlling vocalization in the domestic chick. *Brain, Behavior, and Evolution, 10,* 354–376.

Levy, J., Neves, R. D., & Sperry, R. W. 1971. Expressive language in the surgically separated minor hemisphere. *Cortex, 7*(1), 49–58.

Lewis, P. R., & Shute, C. C. D. 1967. The cholinergic limbic system: Projections to hippocampal formation, medial cortex, nuclei of the ascending cholinergic reticular system, and the subfornical organ and supra-optic crest. *Brain, 90*(3), 521–540.

Lindsay, P. H., & Norman, D. A. 1972. *Human information processing.* New York: Academic Press.

Lishman, W. A. 1971. Emotion, consciousness and will after brain bisection in man. *Cortex, 8*(2), 181–192.

Luria, A. R. 1970. *Traumatic aphasia*. The Hague: Mouton.

Macchi, G. 1951. The ontogenetic development of the olfactory telencephalon in man. *Journal of Comparative Neurology, 95*(2), 245–305.

MacKeith, R., and Bax, M. (Eds.) 1968. *Studies in infancy*. Clinics in Developmental Medicine, No. 27. London: Heinemann.

MacLean, P. D. 1949. Psychosomatic disease and the "visceral brain:" Recent developments bearing on the Papez theory of emotion. *Psychosomatic Medicine, 11*(6), 338–353.

MacLean, P. D. 1952. Some psychiatric implications of physiological studies on frontotemporal portion of limbic system (Visceral Brain). *Electroencephalography and Clinical Neurophysiology, 4*(4), 407–418.

MacLean, P. D. 1958. Contrasting functions of limbic and neocortical systems of the brain and their relevance to psychophysiological aspects of medicine. *American Journal of Medicine, 25*, 611–626.

MacLean, P. D. 1973. *A triune concept of the brain and behavior*. Toronto: Toronto Univ. Press.

MacLean, P. D., & Delgado, J. 1953. Electrical and chemical stimulation of frontotemporal portion of limbic system in the waking animal. *Electroencephalography and Clinical Neurophysiology, 5*, 91–100.

Maclowe, W. B., Mancall, E. L., & Thomas, J. J. 1975. Complete Klüver-Bucy syndrome in man. *Cortex, 11*, 53–59.

Meyer, G., McElhaney, M., Martin, W., & McGraw, C. P. 1972. Stereotactic cingulotomy with results of acute stimulation and serial psychological testing. In L. V. Laitinen and K. E. Livingston (Eds.), *Surgical approaches in psychiatry*. Baltimore: Univ. Park Press. Pp. 39–58.

Miles, L. 1975. The use of sign language by two chimpanzees. Paper presented to the Linguistic Society of America, San Francisco.

Millikan, C. H., & Darley, F. L. (Eds.) 1967. *Brain mechanisms underlying speech and language*. New York: Grune and Stratton.

Milner, B. 1967. Brain mechanisms suggested by studies of the temporal lobes. In C. H. Millikan and F. L. Darley (Eds.), *Brain mechanisms underlying speech and language*. New York: Grune and Stratton. Pp. 122–145.

Milner, B., Corking, S., & Teuber, H. L. 1968. Further analysis of the hippocampal amnesia syndrome: 14-year followup study of H.M. *Neuropsychologia, 6*, 215–234.

Minkowski, A. (Ed.) 1967. *Regional development of the brain in early life*. Oxford: Blackwell.

Mirsky, A. F., Rosvold, H. E., & Pribram, K. H. 1957. Effects of cingulectomy on social behavior in monkeys. *Journal of Neurophysiology, 20*, 588–601.

Molino, A. 1975. Sparing of function after infant lesions of selected limbic structures in the rat. *Journal of Comparative Physiology and Psychology, 89*(8), 868–881.

Morris, C. 1946. *Signs, language, and behavior*. Englewood Cliffs, N.J.: Prentice-Hall.

Myers, R. E. 1969. Neurology of social communication in primates. *Proceedings of the Second International Congress of Primatology, 3*, 1–9.

Myers, R. E. 1972. Role of prefrontal and anterior temporal cortex in social behavior and affect in monkeys. *Acta Neurobiologiae Experimentalis, 32*, 567–579.

Myers, R. E. 1975a. Comparative neurology of vocalization and speech: Proof of a dichotomy. *Proceedings of the NYAS conference on the origins and evolution of language and speech* (to appear).

Myers, R. E. 1975b. Neurology of social behavior and affect in primates: A study of prefrontal and anterior temporal cortex. In K. J. Zülch, O. Creutzfeldt, and G. C. Galbraith (Eds.), *Cerebral localization: An Otfrid Foerster symposium*. Berlin: Springer-Verlag. Pp. 161–169.

Myers, R. E., & Swett, C., Jr. 1970. Social behavior deficits of free-ranging monkeys after anterior temporal cortex removal: A preliminary report. *Brain Research, 18*, 551–556.

Narabayashi, H., Nagato, T., Saito, Y., Yoshida, M., & Nagahata, M. 1963. Stereotaxic amygdalotomy for behavioral disorders. *Archives of Neurology, 9*, 1–16.

Nathan, P. W., & Smith, M. C. 1950. Normal mentality associated with a maldeveloped "Rhinencephalon." *Journal of Neurology, Neurosurgery, and Psychiatry, 13*(3), 191–197.

Noback, C. R., & Montagna, K. W. (Eds.) 1970. *The primate brain.* New York: Appleton.

Ojemann, G. A., Fedio, P., & VanBruen, J. M. 1968. Anomia from pulvinar and subcortical parietal stimulation. *Brain, 91*, 99–116.

Ojemann, G. A., & Ward, A. 1971. Speech representation in ventrolateral thalamus. *Brain, 94*, 669–680.

Ostwald, P. F. 1972. The sounds of infancy. *Developmental Medicine and Child Neurology, 14*, 350–361.

Ostwald, P. F., & Peltzman, P. 1974. The cry of the human infant. *Scientific American, 230*(3), 84–90.

Papez, J. W. 1937. A proposed mechanism of emotion. *Archives of Neurology and Psychiatry, 38*, 725–743.

Penfield, W., & Roberts, L. 1959. *Speech and brain mechanisms.* Princeton, N.J.: Princeton Univ. Press.

Piaget, J. 1952. *The origins of intelligence in children.* New York: International Univ. Press.

Premack, D. 1971. Language in chimpanzee? *Science, 172*, 808–822.

Prechtl, H. F. R. 1968. Polygraphic studies of the full-term newborn infant. II. Computer analysis of recorded data. In R. C. MacKeith and M. C. O. Bax (Eds.), *Studies in infancy.* Clinics in Developmental Medicine, No. 27. London: Heinemann. Pp. 22–40.

Pribram, K. H. 1954. Concerning three rhinencephalic systems. *Electroencephalography and Clinical Neurophysiology, 6*, 708–709.

Pribram, K. H. 1962. Interrelations of psychology and the neurological disciplines. In S. Koch (Ed.), *Psychology: A study of a science.* Vol. 4. New York: McGraw-Hill. Pp. 119–157.

Pribram, K. H. 1967. Emotion: Steps toward a neuropsychological theory. In D. C. Glass (Ed.), *Neurophysiology and emotion.* New York: Rockefeller Univ. Press. Pp. 3–40.

Pribram, K. H. 1969. The neurobehavioral analysis of limbic forebrain mechanisms: Revision and progress report. *Advances in the Study of Behavior, 2*, 297–332.

Pribram, K. H., & Kruger, L. 1954. Functions of the "olfactory brain." *Annals of the New York Academy of Sciences, 58*, 109–138.

Ramón y Cajal, C. 1968. *The structure of Ammon's Horn.* Springfield, Ill.: Charles C Thomas.

Reymert, M. L. (Ed.) 1928. *Feelings and emotions.* Worcester, Mass.: Clark University Press.

Riklan, M., & Levita, E. 1969. *Subcortical correlates of human behavior.* Baltimore: Williams and Wilkins.

Riklan, M., Levita, E., Zimmerman, J., & Cooper, I. S. 1969. Thalamic correlates of language and speech. *Journal of Neurological Sciences, 8*(2), 307–328.

Rimland, B. 1964. *Infantile autism.* New York: Appleton.

Rioch, D. 1967. Discussion of causal mechanisms. In S. A. Altmann (Ed.), *Social communication among primates.* Chicago: Univ. of Chicago Press. Pp. 185–192.

Riss, W., Halpern, M., & Scalia, F. 1969. Anatomical aspects of the evolution of the limbic and olfactory systems and their potential significance for behavior. *Annals of the New York Academy of Sciences, 159*, 1096–1114.

Robinson, B. W. 1967a. Neurological aspects of evoked vocalizations. In S. A. Altmann (Ed.), *Social communication among primates*. Chicago: Univ. of Chicago Press. Pp. 135–147.

Robinson, B. W. 1967b. Vocalization evoked from forebrain in *Macaca mulatta*. *Physiology and Behavior, 2*, 345–354.

Robinson, B. W. 1972. Anatomical and physiological contrasts between human and other primate vocalizations. In S. Washburn and P. Dolhinow (Eds.), *Perspectives on human evolution*. New York: Holt. Pp. 438–443.

Robinson, B. W. 1975. Limbic influences on human speech. *Proceedings of the NYAS Conference on the Origins and Evolution of Language and Speech* (to appear).

Rose, J. E., & Woolsey, C. N. 1948. Structure and relations of limbic cortex and anterior thalamic nuclei in rabbit and cat. *Journal of Comparative Neurology, 89*(3), 279–349.

Rosvold, H. E., & Mishkin, M. 1961. Non-sensory effects of frontal lesions on discrimination learning and performance. In J. F. Delafresnaye (Ed.), *Brain mechanisms and consciousness*. Springfield, Ill.: Charles C Thomas. Pp. 555–576.

Routtenberg, A. 1958. The two-arousal hypothesis: Reticular formation and limbic system. *Psychological Review, 75*, 51–80.

Sanides, F. 1970. Functional architecture of motor and sensory cortices in primates in the light of a new concept of neocortex evolution. In C. R. Noback and W. Montagna (Eds.), *The primate brain*. New York: Appleton. Pp. 137–208.

Schain, R. J., & Yannet, H. 1960. Infantile autism: Analysis of 50 cases and a consideration of certain neurophysiologic concepts. *Journal of Pediatrics, 57*(4), 560–567.

Schaltenbrand, G. 1965. The effects of stereotactic electrical stimulation in the depth of the brain. *Brain, 88*, 835–840.

Schaltenbrand, G., Spuer, H., Wahren, W., & Rummler, B. 1971. Electro-anatomy of the thalamic ventro-oral nucleus based on stereotactic stimulation in man. *Zeitschrift für Neurologie, 199*, 259–276.

Selby, G. 1967. Stereotactic surgery for the relief of Parkinson's disease. Part 2. An analysis of the results in a series of 303 patients (413 operations). *Journal of Neurological Sciences, 5*, 343–375.

Serafetinides, E. A., & Falconer, M. A. 1963. Speech disturbances in temporal lobe seizures: A study in 100 epileptic patients submitted to anterior temporal lobectomy. *Brain, 86*, 333–346.

Shapiro, A., Shapiro, E., Wayne, H., & Clarken, J. 1972. The psychopathology of Gilles de la Tourette's Syndrome. *American Journal of Psychiatry, 129*(4), 427–434.

Shapiro, A., Shapiro, E., Wayne, H., & Clarken, J. 1973. Organic factors in Gilles de la Tourette's Syndrome. *British Journal of Psychiatry, 122*(571), 659–664.

Sheer, D. E. (Ed.) 1961. *Electrical stimulation of the brain*. Austin: Univ. of Texas Press.

Smith, W. K. 1941. Vocalizations and other responses elicited by excitation of the Regio Cingulares in the monkey. *American Journal of Physiology, 133*(2), 451–452.

Smyth, G. E., & Stern, K. 1938. Tumours of the thalamus: A clinico-pathological study. *Brain, 61*, 339–374.

Smythies, J. R. 1966. *The neurological foundations of psychiatry: An outline of the mechanisms of emotion, memory, learning, and the organization of behavior with particular regard to the limbic system*. New York: Academic Press.

Sperry, R. W., & Gazzaniga, M. S. 1967. Language following surgical disconnection of the hemispheres. In C. H. Millikan and F. L. Darley (Eds.), *Brain mechanisms underlying speech and language*. New York: Grune and Stratton, Pp. 108–121.

Stephan, H., & Andy, O. J. 1970. The allocortex in primates. In C. R. Noback and W. Montagna (Eds.), *The primate brain*. New York: Appleton. Pp. 109–135.

Sutton, D., Larson, C., Taylor, E. M., & Lindeman, R. C. 1973. Vocalization in rhesus monkey: Conditionability. *Brain Research, 55*, 225–231.

Sutton, D., Larson, C., & Lindeman, R. C. 1974. Neocortical and limbic lesion effects on primate phonation. *Brain Research, 71*, 61–75.

Sweet, R., Soloman, G. E., Wayne, H., Shapiro, E., & Shapiro, A. K. 1973. Neurological features of Gilles de la Tourette's Syndrome. *Journal of Neurology, Neurosurgery, and Psychiatry, 36*(1), 1–9.

Taylor, J. (Ed.) 1932. *Selected writings of John Humphrey Jackson.* London: Hodder and Stoughton.

Terzian, H. 1964. Behavioral and EEG effects of intracarotid sodium amytal injection. *Acta Neurochirugica, 12*, 230–239.

Vaernet, K., & Madsen, A. 1970. Stereotaxic amygdalotomy and basofrontal tractotomy in psychotics with aggressive behavior. *Journal of Neurology, Neurosurgery, and Psychiatry, 33*, 858–863.

VanBuren, J. M. 1963. Confusion and disturbance of speech from stimulation in vicinity of the head of the Caudate Nucleus. *Journal of Neurosurgery, 20*(3), 148–157.

Vanderwolf, C. H. 1971. Limbic-diencephalic mechanisms of voluntary movement. *Psychological Review, 78*(2), 83–113.

VanLancker, D. 1975. *Heterogeneity in language and speech: Neurolinguistic studies.* UCLA Working Papers in Phonetics No. 29.

Washburn, S. L., & Dolhinow, P. (Eds.) 1972. *Perspectives on human evolution.* New York: Holt.

Watkins, E. S., & Oppenheimer, D. R. 1962. Mental disturbances after thalamolysis. *Journal of Neurology, Neurosurgery, and Psychiatry, 25*, 243–250.

Wasz-Höckert, O., Lind, J., Vuorenkoski, V., Partanen, T., & Valanne, E. (Eds.) 1968. *The infant cry: A spectrographic and auditory analysis.* Clinics in Developmental Medicine, No. 28. London: Heinemann.

Whitaker, H. A., & Selnes, O. A. 1975. Anatomic variation in the cortex; Individual differences and the problem of the localization of language function. *Proceedings of the NYAS Conference on the Origins and Evolution of Language and Speech* (to appear).

White, L. E. 1965. A morphologic concept of the limbic lobe. *International Review of Neurobiology, 8*(1), 1–34.

Wollberg, Z., & Newman, J. D. 1972. Auditory cortex of squirrel monkey: Response patterns of single cells to species-specific vocalizations. *Science, 175*(4018), 212–214.

Yakovlev, P. I. 1959. Pathoarchitectonic studies of cerebral malformations. III. Arhinencephalies (Holotetencephalies). *Journal of Neuropathology and Experimental Neurology, 18*(1), 22–55.

Yakovlev, P. I., & Lecours, A. R. 1967. The myelogenetic cycles of regional maturation of the brain. In A. Minkowski (Ed.), *Regional development of the brain in early life.* Oxford: Blackwell. Pp. 3–70.

Yakovlev, P. I., & Locke, S. 1961. Limbic nuclei of thalamus and connections of limbic cortex. III. Cortico-cortical connections of the anterior cingulate gyrus, the cingulum, and the subcallosal bundle in monkey. *Archives of Neurology* (Chicago), *5*, 364–400.

Yamaguchi, S. Y., & Myers, R. E. 1975. Failure of discriminative vocal conditioning in rhesus monkey. *Brain Research, 37*, 109–114.

Zülch, K. J., Creutzfeldt, O., & Galbraith, G. C. (Eds.) 1975. *Cerebral localization: An Otfrid Foerster symposium.* Berlin: Springer-Verlag.

5

A Model of Individual Differences in Hemispheric Functioning[1]

Curtis Hardyck

UNIVERSITY OF CALIFORNIA, BERKELEY

INTRODUCTION

Study of the differential functioning of the human cerebral hemispheres has progressed to a point where statements can be made with reasonable certainty about the nature of cerebral specialization for most individuals. Given the type of experiment where verbal material is presented in such a manner as to insure stimulation of nerve pathways leading to only one hemisphere, it is a reasonable expectation that, in an unselected sample, comprehension of verbal material will be superior in the left hemisphere as compared to the right for most individuals. Similarly, when spatial ability tasks are used, also with an unselected sample, the expectation is that spatial processing will be done more efficiently in the right hemisphere than the left, for most individuals.

Within this specialization, substantial individual differences exist. If people are categorized on the basis of handedness, the results of experiments on hemispheric specialization are sharpened: The right-handed will show greater hemispheric specialization than the left-handed, as indicated by the magnitude of between-hemisphere differences for verbal and spatial problems. If the categorization of handedness is extended to include family history of handedness, the differences between the right-handed with no family history of left-handedness and the left-handed with a positive family history of left-handedness are further intensified, the right-handed individuals showing marked hemispheric specialization and the left-handed little or no specialization of hemisphere function.

[1] This work was aided by a grant from the Spencer Foundation.

223

These individual differences present continuing problems of explanation in the construction of models of cerebral functioning. It does not seem an exaggeration to say that the differences in cerebral organization shown by the majority of left-handed do not fit into most models of cerebral functioning. The observed differences found in the left-handed are frequently used to demonstrate the pattern of cerebral functioning characteristic of the right-handed majority, while the relationship of these differences in the left-handed to models of hemisphere function is usually not delineated.

Approaches to explanation have varied. Semmes (1968) candidly states that her model does not offer a satisfactory explanation for bilateralized cerebral organization. Levy (1973) argues that the left-handed represent an evolutionary retrogression in the development of cerebral specialization—a position which implies that the cerebral organization characteristic of the left-handed will eventually disappear, given the normal processes of evolutionary selection. Beaumont (1974) suggests that the "non-right-handed" (his term) possess a more diffuse cerebral organization than the right-handed. Again, the question of relationships among these differing patterns of cerebral organization is not dealt with directly.

In this chapter, the models of hemispheric functioning proposed by Semmes, Levy, and Dimond and Beaumont (Beaumont, 1974) will be reviewed briefly. Following this discussion, a proposed model of individual differences in hemispheric functioning as related to familial handedness will be presented and evaluated. A set of propositions developed from this model will be examined for their ability to account for published research work on hemispheric specialization. In the review and in the development of the model, a high degree of relationship between familial handedness and cerebral organization is assumed.

As a leitmotif in our examination of models of hemisphere function, the commentary of Teuber (1974) on the problems of hemispheric specialization and interaction seems especially useful.

> With so much current agreement of principles, it deserves to be stressed how little we know about the fundamental questions of what, how and whence. Yet we need to know (1) *what* it is that characterizes the specific functions of the right and left hemispheres in the normal adult; (2) *how* the commissures act in providing information transfer, between the hemispheres, and in constraining, or modulating, the activities in the parallel halves of the brain, in such a way that a functional asymmetry arises and is maintained; (3) last, one should reopen the question of *whence* the asymmetries arise in phylogeny and ontogeny. For man, one should ask whether it is not after all a genetic predisposition that produces somewhat dissimilar hemispheres in the course of embryonic development and, if so, is this bias initially limited to one hemisphere, determining the fate of the other only secondarily? Or do we start with a double but opposite bias of the two sides? It is remarkable that these latter questions, those pertaining to the ontogeny of hemispheric specialization, have hardly been touched upon at all in the past and current work on our two hemispheres. [p. 71]

Teuber's points offer a succinct categorization of basic problem areas and will be referred to frequently in this discussion.

MODELS OF HEMISPHERIC FUNCTIONING

Semmes

Semmes' (1968) paper on hemispheric specialization is an attempt to systematize a number of observed clinical and research findings on sensory and motor capacities and their hemispheric representations. Her specific views are as follows:

> Focal representation of elementary functions in the left hemisphere favors integration of similar units and consequently specialization for behaviors which demand fine sensorimotor control, such as manual skills and speech. Conversely, diffuse representation of elementary functions in the right hemisphere may lead to integration of *dissimilar* units and hence specialization for behaviors requiring multimodal coordination, such as the various spatial abilities. [p. 11]

The Semmes model is based on the results of studies of brain function in somesthesis on patients with penetrating brain injuries. The results of these studies indicated that responses were different for the right and the left hand over several lesion locations.

Semmes' model is consistent with much of the existing data, including the findings of many studies done since her account was published. There is little question about the accuracy of her classification of hemisphere functions. However, the model is limited to a general specification of types of processes that occur within hemispheres and does not offer any guidelines as to the functions of the commissures and the basis for asymmetries. The model is based primarily on the high degree of cerebral lateralization characteristic of right-handed individuals who have a negative family history of left-handedness. Semmes comments that her model does not offer satisfactory explanations of either the bilateral speech organization found in many left-handed or of those cases of left-handedness where speech is completely lateralized in the left hemisphere. Her model does account for the relatively rare mirror image individual who is left-handed, and has speech localized in the right hemisphere.

Levy

In the model of hemispheric functioning proposed by Levy (1973, 1974), based on her studies of commissurotomy patients and the studies of Sperry and others (Gazzaniga, Bogen, & Sperry, 1967; Levy, 1969; Levy, Nebes, & Sperry, 1971; Nebes, 1971; Sperry, 1968a,b, 1973, 1974; Sperry, Gazzaniga, & Bogen, 1969), the optimally functioning individual is right-handed (presumably with no family history of left-handedness, although the question of familial handedness is not dealt with specifically) and has a high degree of lateralization of functions. The left hemisphere in these individuals is specialized for language, speech and calculation—types of analytical processing in which a high degree of precision and specification is required. The right hemisphere processes spatial relationships, interprets music, recognizes patterns, and, in general, processes those aspects of perception which are most efficiently treated globally. The organization of the hemispheres can be represented diagrammatically as follows:

Left hemisphere	*Right hemisphere*
Speech	Spatial
Language	abilities
Writing	Nonverbal
Calculation	ideation

Right-handed

In contrast, the left-handed individual has a high probability of having language functions located in both the right and left hemispheres. This bilateralization of language, according to Levy, limits the capacity of the right hemisphere to process spatial information. Cerebral organization of these left-handed individuals can be represented as follows:

Left hemisphere	*Right hemisphere*	
Speech	Speech	Spatial
Language	Language	abilities
Writing	Writing	Nonverbal
Calculation	Calculation	ideation

Left-handed

Evidence for these models of organization comes from studies (Levy, 1969; Miller, 1971; Nebes, 1971; Nebes & Briggs, 1974) showing that left-handed individuals do less well on nonverbal intelligence tasks and on tests of certain types of spatial ability that are thought to measure right hemisphere function. The subject samples used in these studies have been small, drawn from highly select populations, and unselected on familial handedness. Attempted replications have not been successful (Fagan-Dubin, 1974; Hardyck, 1976; Hardyck, Petrinovich, & Goldman, 1975; Kutas, McCarthy, & Donchin, 1975; Newcombe & Ratcliff, 1973).

In evaluating the Levy model, the following comments seem justified: The left-handed in the Levy model are treated as an undifferentiated group. However, studies of handedness and hemispheric functioning (see Hardyck & Petrinovich, 1977, for review of such studies) strongly indicate that bilateralization of function in left-handedness may cover a wide range of localization, from a complete left side lateralization of speech and right side lateralization of spatial ability through bilateral localization of both speech and visual functions to complete lateralization of speech in the right hemisphere and spatial ability in the left hemisphere—a mirror image of the usual right-handed localization pattern. If the clinical studies of Hécaen and Sauget (1971) are examined in relation to the Levy model, other deficiencies become apparent, since Hécaen *et al.* find the strongly left-handed with no family history of left-handedness to be identical in cerebral localization with the right-handed with no family history of left-handedness. The moderately left-handed with a positive family history of left-handedness are those individuals most likely to show bilateral cerebral organization of both spatial and verbal functions. Compounding the problem is the evidence (again from Hécaen & Sauget, 1971) indicating that the right-handed with a family history of left-handedness are more likely to recover from dysphasia following a left-side lesion than are either the right-handed with a negative family history of left-handedness or the left-handed with a negative family history of left-handedness.

The types of tasks used by Levy (1969) and by Nebes (1971) have been limited to certain kinds of spatial ability—no work has yet been reported on other aspects of right hemisphere function. For example, there are studies (on right-handed only) (Geffen, Bradshaw, & Wallace, 1971; Rizzolati, Umilta, & Berlucchi, 1971) showing that facial recognition ability is superior in the right hemisphere, yet no studies have been reported testing for possible facial recognition deficit in the left-handed.

The Levy model offers statements as to *what* occurs in each hemisphere. The studies (Gazzaniga *et al.*, 1967; Levy, 1969; Levy *et al.*, 1971; Nebes, 1971; Sperry, 1968a,b, 1973, 1974; Sperry *et al.*, 1969) on commissurotomy patients and on normal subjects have added a great deal to knowledge of hemispheric specialization. However, when the question of *how* the commissures work is raised, the Levy model has little to offer. In the Levy model, each hemisphere seems largely responsible for its own specialized functions, and interhemispheric transfer is given little importance. Functions appear to be organized in a competitive rather than a cooperative mode, as suggested by the model for the left-handed, where spatial abilities are displaced by the more dominant speech functions. In this respect, the Levy model seems overly dominated by the commissurotomy studies.

Dimond and Beaumont

The model of hemispheric functioning proposed by Dimond and Beaumont (Beaumont, 1974) is based on an extensive amount of experimental work (Beaumont, 1974; Beaumont & Dimond, 1973, 1975; Dimond, 1970a,b,c, 1971,

1972; Dimond & Beaumont, 1971a,b, 1972a,b,c,d,e, 1973, 1974a,b) and differs in many ways from other models. Dimond and Beaumont argue that the brain works as a unit, with specialized abilities located within hemispheres, but with the capability of sharing functions and distributing workloads between the hemispheres. The results reported in their extensive series of experimental studies are consistent with results reported by others and with the divisions of hemispheric specialization proposed by Semmes (1968) and by Levy (1973).

Cerebral function in the Dimond and Beaumont model is essentially the same as in previously discussed formulations—the right hemisphere is seen as specialized for analysis and processing of spatial information and the left hemisphere as having language and serial, analytic processing ability. The uniqueness of the Dimond and Beaumont model is in its emphasis on the functions of the cerebral commissures and on hemispheric interaction. Dimond and Beaumont postulate that the hemispheres of the brain function as two computers, similar in many ways, but each with specialized abilities. In the Dimond and Beaumont model, the *how* of commissural transfer is developed in more detail than in other models. The hemispheres are both capable of processing stimuli separately where appropriate, or of sharing a workload where necessary. Such abilities as color naming, incidental learning, paired-associate learning, and matching may be shared interhemispheric tasks, not the private province of one hemisphere as in the Levy model. Commissural transfer of information in the Dimond and Beaumont model serves to share workload and ease demands placed on a particular hemisphere.

The Dimond and Beaumont model of handedness and cerebral function (Beaumont, 1974) is developed in considerable detail. Many of these authors' studies included handedness as a variable, and effects of handedness were assessed, although familial and nonfamilial handedness were not differentiated.

Dimond and Beaumont argue that the effect of handedness is related to one of three possibilities, "an increased laterality effect, a decreased laterality effect, or no effect at all" (Beaumont, 1974, p. 109). They group their experimental studies evaluating handedness (13 studies in their 1974a account) by these possible effects; no effects due to handedness; larger interhemispheric differences for "non-right handers" (their term) and smaller interhemispheric differences for non-right-handed. They found mode of response—verbal or manual— to be evenly distributed throughout the tasks and to produce no significant effects related to handedness. They conclude that their groupings show discernible task differences: Tasks on which the non-right-handed show larger hemispheric differences were "higher level" cognitive tasks such as speed of subtraction, a Stroop-type interference task, normality of word association, and paired-associate learning. Tasks which are categorized as "lower level" cognitive tasks and on which smaller hemispheric differences are present for the non-right-handed are fatigue effects on digit identification, speed of translation of letters from English to Greek, addition, and color naming.

From these results, Dimond and Beaumont draw the following conclusions:

It is proposed therefore, that the level of complexity and the order of integration demanded by the task, interacting perhaps to some degree with modality of response, mediates the differential effects of handedness. Tasks requiring more processing are associated with greater interhemispheric differences in the more sinistral, the additional effect of the response mode being to reduce interhemispheric differences in the non-right-hander.

Before proceeding to develop this into a general model, we must reintroduce our second conceptual factor. During discussion of the various experiments, much reference has been made to the idea that the brain of the left-hander might be less lateralized than that of the right hander. We saw that this view, at least with respect to verbal functions, was a current one in the literature and it has assumed a great deal of power in our own explanations of the effects observed. Many of our experimental results—the majority—certainly support such a view of the differential cerebral organization of the left and right hander. None suggested the contrary.

This being the case, it is important to note that the greater diffusion observed in the sinistral does not apply to verbal functions alone. The experiments supporting the concept most clearly do not all involve verbal material, nor do they exclusively involve vocal responses. . . . The greater diffusion of the system of the non-right-hander is therefore considered to be a general characteristic. [Beaumont, 1974, p. 110]

The characterization of the left-handed as possessing a more diffuse cerebral organization that requires more cerebral processing time on higher level cognitive tasks seems, at first, similar to the Levy model, at least in the sense of suggesting a possible handicap for the left-handed. However, Dimond and Beaumont go on to state: "In simple terms, the diffuse system, that of the left-hander, carries an advantage for complex, integrative operations, but a disadvantage for rapid simple communication." (1974, p. 112). A graphic representation of the cortical organization of the right- and left-handed is given by Dimond and Beaumont and is reproduced here as Figure 5.1.

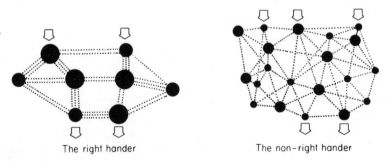

The right hander   The non-right hander

Figure 5.1 The cortical organization of the right- and left-handed. [From Dimond and Beaumont, 1974a.]

In the Dimond and Beaumont model of handedness and cerebral functioning, the left-handed differ from the right-handed, not in hemispheric specialization, but in *degree* of organization. (By contrast, the Levy model would argue that the left-handed differ in *type* of organization.) The Dimond and Beaumont argument that the left-handed are more diffuse in cortical organization and take longer to process high level cognitive tasks suggests not that the left-handed are deficient in *ability,* as in the Levy model, but that they are deficient in *speed* of processing and solving problems.

The Dimond and Beaumont model of handedness and cerebral organization seems to accord better with data on the relationship of intellectual functioning and handedness (Hardyck *et al.*, 1976) than the Levy model. However, two critical comments can be made.

The Dimond and Beaumont grouping according to hemisphere differences assumes the generality of the hemispheric specialization hypothesis, irrespective of differences in cerebral organization—a reasonable assumption in view of the large number of studies showing hemisphere differences. However, the rationale for task classification is not obvious, at least not from the descriptions of the tasks. For example, paired-associate learning tasks appear in both the lack-of-differences grouping and the greater-difference groupings. There is no obvious reason why one of these tasks is more appropriately classified as a "higher level" cognitive task than the other. In the absence of any psychometric evidence to support the categorization, it can be argued that the classification is too arbitrary to be useful.

A second and more serious criticism can be made of Dimond and Beaumont's formulation that the left-handed are diffuse in cortical organization as compared to the more efficiently organized right-handed. The model implies that this diffusion of organization in the left-handed requires more processing time for complex cognitive tasks, as compared to time required by the right-handed. This seems to contradict the authors' argument that the diffuse system of the left-handed has an advantage for complex integrative operations.

The notion of increased processing time in the left-handed seems questionable in view of the lack of evidence, in other data, for such handedness differences. If there is an increased processing time, it would be expected that the right-handed would have a speed advantage on IQ tests, especially on timed tasks. The alternative would be to argue that the capacity of the diffuse system to handle complexity somehow compensates for the increased speed of the right-handed, obscuring any differences. As an explanation, it is possible, but there is no evidence to support it.

The notion of diffuse organization seems contradicted by some of the results reported by Dimond and Beaumont themselves as well as by findings of other investigators. Faster reaction times to a discrimination task would not seem to be a characteristic expected of a more diffuse organizational system. However, Dimond and Beaumont (Beaumont, 1974) report that the left-handed are faster, regardless of hemisphere, at color naming (1972) and at vigilance tasks (1973). Results of other studies are supportive of this finding. Cohen (1972) found left-handed subjects faster overall in a letter-classification task. Provins and Jeeves (1975) found the left-handed to have faster overall reaction times to tones, regardless of ear. Finally, it should be pointed out that Dimond and Beaumont do not develop the relationship between the postulated greater diffuseness of functioning and the hemispheric differences reported for the tasks they classify as measuring higher-level cognitive functioning.

A PROPOSED MODEL OF HEMISPHERIC FUNCTIONING

Theoretical Formulation

Looking over the Semmes, Levy, and Dimond and Beaumont models, it seems quite reasonable to introduce this discussion with the comment that these formulations have some difficulty in integrating the differences in hemispheric organization found in the familial left-handed.[2] In the Semmes model, the only left-handed who are consonant with the model are the mirror-image left-handed who have speech functions located in the right hemisphere and spatial ability in the left. However, the clinical and surgical studies, including those patients examined with Wada's (Wada & Rasmussen, 1960) technique, indicate that the mirror-image left-handed are relatively rare. The Levy model characterizes the left-handed as a possible evolutionary retrogression, owing to some failure to develop full lateralization. In Dimond and Beaumont's formulations, the left-handed are more "diffusely organized" than their right-handed brethren. In these formulations, it is difficult to integrate the left-handed and their differing cerebral organization into any general model of human cerebral functioning. The majority of the left-handed stand aside, as it were, while models that are consonant with patterns of organization found in the right-handed are developed and tested, frequently by comparison with groups of left-handed. Such an approach seems to ignore the increasing body of experimental data on the left-handed. Although it is parsimonious to postulate one type of cerebral

[2] It is perhaps evident by now that familial handedness is a variable of fundamental importance in the model proposed in this chapter. Ideally, this should be extensively documented. Unfortunately, familial handedness is a neglected variable, and relatively few investigators have bothered to determine family history in relation to handedness. I consider it to be an extremely powerful variable that can be defined and documented and that has great potential for organizing and systematizing research findings in hemisphere function. The documentation for the importance of familial handedness that is available has been carefully assessed (see Hardyck & Petrinovich, 1977, for a detailed review of handedness, including its relationship to hemispheric functioning). In the initial presentation of the model, no detailed documentation will be provided. In the section to follow, six specific propositions concerning hemisphere functioning are drawn from the model, and existing research evidence is presented as it relates to those propositions.

organization for all people, the evidence suggests that this is incorrect. In this context, Marshall's (1973) quote of George Eliot seems appropriate: "I say nothing against Mr. ——'s theory; if we are to have one regimen for all minds, his seems to me as good as any other."

It seems a reasonable supposition that "one regimen for all minds" is not adequate to account for current experimental results. While attempts to design a unitary system of hemisphere function are clearly preferable to a fragmented or typological approach, it also seems obvious that some allowance must be made for a range of individual differences. It may also be that existing approaches that do not allow for the incorporation of differing patterns of cerebral organization have come about as a result of the types of questions asked in hemisphere function studies.

An examination of existing experimental work provides a detailed illustration. Table 5.1 summarizes 37 studies of hemispheric function and specialization. Only three of these studies discuss efficiency of hemispheric specialization in relation to results obtained when problems are presented to both hemispheres simultaneously (Dimond & Beaumont, 1972c, 1974b; Beaumont & Dimond, 1975). The great majority of studies ask one of two related types of questions:

1. What are the special abilities of the left hemisphere as compared with the right hemisphere?
2. What is the relative computing or problem solving power of the left hemisphere for a given type of problem as compared to the power of the right hemisphere for the same problem?

Experiments formulated with these questions in mind provide some information about the relative specializations of the hemispheres, but they offer no information about interhemispheric cooperation and facilitation. To use a deliberately extreme analogy, this approach can be likened to a handicap race in which an individual is asked to cover a given distance as fast as possible, first with one leg immobilized, and then with the other leg immobilized. This procedure will tell us on which leg a person can hop faster, has better balance, and falls down less often. It is not especially useful in assessing how a person uses both legs cooperatively in walking and running.

Such an analogy is absurd, especially since the evidence for specialization within cerebral hemispheres is clearly positive. However, the cooperative aspects of the analogy are not necessarily so absurd, since examination of problem solving abilities within one hemisphere as compared to the other does not provide any information about how the hemispheres may work together or about how the commissures work in providing information transfer.

As an introductory argument, the existence of two types of human cerebral organization, representing extremes of a continuum, is postulated. The first, most frequently occurring type, is highly lateralized for specialized kinds of

TABLE 5.1 Studies in Differences in Hemispheric Functions Associated with Handedness[a]

Author	Sample	Results
Dichotic listening studies		
Bryden (1970)	152 RH, 82 LH school children, grades 2, 4, & 6	RE score increased with age for RH and decreased for LH
Curry (1967)	25 RH, 25 LH	RE better for RH; RE-LE difference not significant for LH
Curry & Rutherford (1967)	12 RH, 12 LH	Degree of between-ear-difference less for LH
Cyr, Daniloff, & Berry (1971)	18 RH, 18 LH college students	No differences found between RH and LH
Dee (1971)	33 strongly LH, 37 moderate LH, 49 strong RH	Strongly LH+, strongly RH-:RE dominant; moderate LH: slightly LE dominant
Hines & Satz (1974)	30 R−, 30 R+, 30 LH college students, no history taken	No differences found between RH and LH
Knox & Boone (1970)	11 RH, 11 LH matched college students	RE better for RH, LE better for LH; differences increased as task difficulty increased
Satz, Achenbach, Pattishall & Fennell (1965)	52 RH, 41 LH hospital employees	RE-LE difference less for LH
Zurif & Bryden (1969)	20 R−, 10 L+, 10 L− college students	RH significantly better in RE. L+ had slightly LE preference. L− had significant RE reference. Order of report in dichotic listening: R+ reported RE first; L+ reported LE first. L+ only group not to show clear dominance.
Visual field studies		
Bryden (1965)	20 RH, 20 LH college students, family history taken	RH better at detecting right visual field differences, L+ more left-dominant
Bryden (1973)	22 RH, 22 LH college students	RH subjects superior in RVF, LH+ more accurate in LVF. Interhemispheric differences less for LH
Hines & Satz (1971)	11 R−, 3 R+	R− better at right visual field detection
Hines & Satz (1974)	30 R−, 30 R+, 30 LH, no history given	No differences found between RH and LH

(continued)

TABLE 5.1 (continued)

Author	Sample	Results
McKeever & Gill (1972)	13 R−, 7 R+, 9 LH	RH subjects superior in right visual field; LH showed no differences
McKeever, VanDeventer, & Suberi (1973)	24 R−, 24 R+, 14 L+, 9 L− college students	R− superior on RVF tasks, L+ better on LVF word recognition than L−
McKinney (1967)	49 RH, 58 LH high school students	No differences found between RH and LH
Orbach (1967)	47 RH, 45 LH college students	RH recognized more English and Hebrew words in RVF; LH recognized more English words in RVF, more Hebrew in LVF
Zurif & Bryden (1969)	20 R−, 10 L+, 10 L− college students	RH significantly better in RVF; L+ have slight LVF preference
Verbal task studies		
Beaumont & Dimond (1973)	12 RH, 8 LH college students	No differences for handedness in inter- or intrahemispheric paired associate learning
Buffery (1974)	32 RH, 32 LH college students	Inter- and intrahemispheric differences less pronounced for the left-handed
Cohen (1972)	5 RH, 5 LH college students	RVF performance superior for RH subjects; LH subjects showed smaller interhemispheric differences in reaction time
Dimond (1971)	20 RH, 2 LH college students	For RH subjects, word pairs presented interhemispherically had better accuracy in right hemisphere for interhemispheric comparisons
Dimond & Beaumont (1972b)	18 RH, 18 LH college students	Interhemispheric differences in color naming smaller for LH subjects. LH subjects showed more blocks to functioning
Dimond & Beaumont (1974b)	18 RH, 12 non RH college students	LH subjects superior over all others on task; RH subjects better at left hemisphere recognition

Study	Subjects	Results
Kershner (1974) (Ocular-manual laterality)	20 RH, right eye dominant (lateralized); 20 RH, left eye dominant (crossed)	Lateralized superior at word recognition; Crossed superior at form perception
Lomas & Kimura (1976)	24 RH, 24 LH college students	Manual activity with right hand interfered with speech for RH subjects; no effect with left hand activity. LH subjects showed interference with speech with manual activity with either hand
McKeever, Gill & VanDeventer (1975)	20 RH, 20 LH college students	RH significantly faster RT to letter stimuli in RVF; LH overall show smaller RVF advantage. L— significantly faster in RVF; L+ show zero visual field differences
Moscovitch & Catlin (1970)	7 RH, 2 mixed college students	Interhemispheric differences in reaction time less for mixed subjects
Nonverbal task studies		
Beaumont & Dimond (1975)	20 RH, 20 non-RH college students	LH subjects superior in shape matching over all conditions
Davidoff (1975)	24 RH, 24 LH college students	RH subjects saw LVF stimulus as lighter. LH subjects reported no difference
Efron (1962)	20 RH, 20 LH college students	RH subjects reported simultaneity of light flashes when right hemisphere stimulus appeared first. LH subjects reported simultaneity when stimuli appear simultaneously
Groberg, Dustman, & Beck (1969)	24 RH, 20 LH college students	No differences found between RH and LH
Kutas & Donchin (1974)	7 RH, 4 LH college students	Readiness potentials prior to hand motor activity greater in contralateral hemisphere in RH for both right and left hand. LH subjects showed contralateral potentials for right-hand activity, but not for left-hand activity

(continued)

TABLE 5.1 (continued)

Author	Sample	Results
Petersen & Lansky (1974)	RH, LH architecture students	LH students made fewer errors in designing a maze
Provins & Jeeves (1975)	10 RH, 10 LH college students	RH had faster reaction times to RE presentations of tones. LH subjects faster over all.
Varney & Benton (1975)	102 college students grouped into 6 categories of handedness and familial handedness	RH superior at tactile perception of direction with left hand. LH subjects had equal accuracy with either hand; R— showed clear LH superiority. R+ had equal accuracy with either hand; L— equally accurate with either hand; L+ showed greater right hand accuracy

[a]The following abbrevations are used in this table:

RH	Right handed	+	Family history of left-handedness
LH	Left-handed	—	No family History of left-handedness
RVF	Right visual half-field	RE	Right ear
LVF	Left visual half-field	LE	Left ear

processing within each hemisphere, with little ability for such specialized processing inhering in the other. In this type of organization such skills as language and corresponding long-term memory are located almost completely within the left hemisphere, which is specialized for such processing. Skills such as spatial ability and pattern recognition (with appropriate memory), for example, are located primarily within the right hemisphere, also specialized for such processing. The hemisphere specialized for a given type of activity can accept data, carry out whatever processing is necessary, and output an appropriate response. In such an organization, interhemispheric transfer is limited to functions which may be carried out as shared hemispheric activities. Complete lateralization is not assumed—a hemisphere specialized for language will also have some spatial ability, and interhemispheric communications of these abilities is possible.

A second type of organization, occurring much less frequently, can be characterized as bilateral, with multiple specializations present in each hemisphere. In this type of cerebral organization, skills that in the proposed first type of organization are highly lateralized are here present in each hemisphere. For example, processing of language skills and of spatial abilities can be done in either hemisphere. It is not argued that the two hemispheres are identical, but that much duplication of functions and specialized abilities, including memory, is present in each hemisphere. This organization is characterized by a high degree of interhemispheric transfer of information between the corresponding specialized areas. For example, verbal processing carried out in one hemisphere can be sent to the corresponding verbal processing center in the other hemisphere. These two extremes of cerebral organization are represented as the end points of a continuum of human cerebral organization.

Given these two postulated types of cerebral organization, it is argued that under conditions where problem solving ability of a given type is assessed on a hemispheric basis, the most extreme between-hemispheres differences will be found in those persons whose hemispheres are highly specialized for particular kinds of processing. The smallest between-hemisphere difference will be found in persons who are bilateralized, where hemispheric functions are duplicated, and specializations for multiple types of data processing are present in each hemisphere.

These hypothesized differences in the two proposed types of hemispheric specialization are detectable only under experimental conditions in which input to the cortex is highly restricted. Under normal conditions of information processing, where visual and auditory input are unrestricted, equal flow of information to both hemispheres occurs, and responses to problems will be identical in outcome. If solutions to a given set of problems can range in power, individual solutions will range similarly, regardless of type of cerebral organization.

It is specifically proposed that hemispheric specialization in humans is organized on a continuum that ranges through the two extremes presented above—

from an organization where each hemisphere is highly specialized in the sense of being equipped to carry out, within itself, particular kinds of processing activities to an organizational system where each hemisphere has multiple processing capabilities.

It is further proposed that familial handedness is highly, though imperfectly, correlated with the proposed models of cerebral organization; that the right-handed individual with no family history of left-handedness is the most appropriate representative of the extreme lateralization model; and that the left-handed individual with a positive family history of left-handedness is the most appropriate representative of the multiple specialization-bilateral model of cerebral organization. Between these two groups are the right-handed with a positive family history of left-handedness, who will display the characteristics of bilateral organization characteristic of the left-handed, but to a lesser degree. These three groups form a continuum of cerebral organization from one extreme of hemispheric specialization to the other.[3]

A definition of familial handedness can be only provisional at this time, since studies of the genetics of handedness (Annett, 1964, 1967, 1974; Falek, 1959; Hudson, 1975; Levy & Nagylaki, 1972; Trankell, 1950) have not resulted in a model that will predict handedness with any accuracy.

Familial left-handedness is defined as the presence of left-hand preference in at least three members of a biologically related family spanning at least two generations. Left-handedness is defined as encompassing the range from moderately strong left-hand preference through ability to use either hand for a variety of tasks.

This definition avoids misclassification of the left-handed who appear as isolated cases in families where all other members are right-handed. Allowing the ambilateral cases to be classified as left-handed seems appropriate in view of the studies of Benton, Myers, and Polder (1962) and Satz, Achenbach, and Fennell (1967), which show that the right-handed tend to be strongly right-handed, and the findings of Hécaen and Sauget (1971) that the familial left-handed have less extreme hand preferences than the nonfamilial left-handed.

---

[3] Left-handed individuals with no family history of left-handedness constitute a unique subgroup. On the basis of clinical lesion studies (Hécaen & Sauget, 1971) and several studies of hemisphere function, the left-handed with no family history of left-handedness seem to be identical in lateralization with the right-handed with no family history of left-handedness. As Levy (1973) and Satz (Satz et al., 1969; Satz, 1972) have pointed out, a relatively minor cerebral insult is sufficient to change a right-handed individual to left-handed and the reverse. However, as Satz (1972) has pointed out in his model of "pathological left-handedness," any study seeking equal numbers of right- and left-handed subjects will contain a higher proportion of pathologically left-handed relative to right-handed because of the differential frequencies of handedness in the population. The model proposed by Satz is a powerful one, and the implications for studies of cerebral function generated by it increase the importance of considering familial handedness.

Hypothesized differences in cerebral organization associated with these handedness differences will be discussed primarily in terms of the groups that define the ends of the continuum since there is at present insufficient data to adequately characterize the large center group of right-handed individuals with a positive family history of left-handedness. The study of Shankweiler and Studdert-Kennedy (1975), which used multiple regression methods to investigate a hypothesized continuum of cerebral lateralization, is one of the few studies to deal with cerebral organization as other than a simple dichotomy.

The right-handed with no familial left-handedness are hypothesized to be highly lateralized for certain types of problem solving. Evidence for this is plentiful. The right-handed invariably do better at handling verbal material within the left hemisphere, and they are better at solving spatial problems within the right hemisphere. The evidence, to be reviewed in more detail later, suggests that there is a fairly high degree of specialization. Left hemisphere solutions of spatial problems are not as good as right hemisphere solutions, and right hemisphere solutions of verbal problems are not comparable in power to those of the left hemisphere. Under normal conditions of information input, it is assumed that the hemisphere best able to process a problem carries out the operations necessary to solve that particular problem and outputs the result.

For the familial left-handed, differences in ability between the hemispheres are much less extreme. Few differences in power of problem solving ability have been noted. However, there are certain limits on the amount of information that can be presented tachistoscopically to retinal hemifields and on what can be retained in short-term memory operations. Hemispheric differences in computing power, given multiple specializations, seem reasonable.

If a cerebral organization with multiple specializations in both hemispheres does operate under the restrictions of reduced computing power within any one hemisphere, the problem of how such a system reaches an equivalent level of problem solving ability must be solved. It is argued that the bilaterally organized individual—the familial left-handed individual—achieves exactly the same range of quality of solutions to problems as does the highly lateralized and specialized right-handed individual, despite the lack of extreme hemispheric specialization. The bilaterally organized individual achieves the same high level of solutions to problems that the lateralized individual attains by employing both hemispheres to work on problems in a parallel manner and then combining the two efforts in order to reach a solution equivalent to one that a single, highly specialized hemisphere could produce. The process can be characterized as follows: Individuals with a highly lateralized form of cerebral organization will solve a given type of problem by processing it in the hemisphere specialized for that type of problem, checking it and rechecking it until a satisfactory answer is reached. An individual with a bilateralized type of cerebral organization will solve a problem by having the two hemispheres do overlapping parts of the problem in parallel, sharing data and cross-checking until a satisfactory answer is reached. Measures of outcome, in terms of successful solutions, for both lateralized and bilateralized individuals will be identical.

These models of cerebral organization can be represented pictorially, with the same type of diagram used to illustrate the Levy model. For the right-handed individual with no family history of left-handedness, cerebral organization here is identical to that in the Levy model:

Left hemisphere	*Right hemisphere*
Speech	Spatial
Language	abilities
Writing	Nonverbal
Calculation	ideation

Right-handed

The corresponding model of organization for the left-handed with a family history of left-handedness is as follows:

Left hemisphere		*Right hemisphere*	
Spatial	Speech	Speech	Spatial
abilities	Language	Language	abilities
Nonverbal	Writing	Writing	Nonverbal
ideation	Calculation	Calculation	ideation

Left-handed

Certain other considerations should be specified. It is assumed that organization of motor functions does not differ as a result of differences in lateralization. It is further assumed that in the majority of people, whether they are laterally specialized or bilateral, motor speech is controlled by the left hemisphere. There is some evidence that the familial left-handed may have the potential for bilateral motor control (Jones, 1966) but the amount of information on the problem is not sufficient for other than speculation.

It is also assumed, in the absence of any data to the contrary, that the efficiency of callosal transmission between hemispheres does not differ between the proposed types of cerebral organization. Moreover, the evidence for differences in hemispheric abilities seems to be sufficient evidence for concluding that raw sensory data is not transmitted by the corpus callosum. If basic sensory information were transmitted, we would expect no differences in measures of hemispheric specialization where time to solution is not a variable.

Finally, it should be emphasized that even in the highly lateralized individual, lateralization is far from absolute. In studies of hemispheric specialization, there are no instances where the left hemisphere failed completely at a task or where the right hemisphere was totally unable to respond. Differences in cerebral specialization are a matter of degree.

Experimental Evidence

In the section to follow, six propositions derived from the present model will be stated and examined for goodness of fit to existing experimental data.

I. Given the proposed differences in cerebral organization postulated to exist for the right-handed with a negative family history (hereafter R−) and the left-handed with a positive family history of left-handedness (hereafter L+), it is expected that the magnitude of interhemispheric differences will be most pronounced for the R−, less evident for the right-handed with a history of familial left handedness (hereafter R+) and least evident for the L+.

Of the studies of hemispheric functioning and handedness reviewed, six studies find no difference in hemispheric function attributable to handedness (Beaumont & Dimond, 1973; Cyr, Daniloff, & Berry, 1971; Groberg, Dustman, & Beck, 1969; Hines & Satz, 1974 [2 studies]; McKinney, 1967), and 18 studies find interhemispheric differences less extreme for the left-handed (Beaumont & Dimond, 1975; Bryden, 1973; Buffery, 1974; Cohen, 1972; Curry, 1967; Curry & Rutherford, 1967; Davidoff, 1975; Dimond & Beaumont, 1972b; Efron, 1962; Knox & Boone, 1970; Lomas & Kimura, 1976; McKeever & Gill, 1972; McKeever, Gill, & VanDeventer, 1975; Moscovitch & Catlin, 1970; Provins & Jeeves, 1975; Satz, Achenbach, Pattishall, & Fennell, 1965; Varney & Benton, 1975; Zurif & Bryden, 1969). No studies were found to report larger between-hemisphere differences for the left-handed.

Family history has not been taken in enough studies to allow any firm conclusions in this regard. In those studies where such history was taken (Hines & Satz, 1971; McKeever, VanDeventer, & Suberi, 1973; McKeever, Gill, & VanDeventer, 1975), the R+ group is, as predicted, a group intermediate in hemispheric differences between the R− and L+ groups.

As an illustration, the study by McKeever, Gill, and VanDeventer (1975), which examined visual field reaction time differences to single letter stimuli, offers an interesting demonstration of the differences in cerebral organization associated with familial handedness. Their right-handed subjects showed a statistically significant advantage in vocal reaction time to letters projected to the left hemisphere as compared with letters projected to the right (36.9 msec). Their left-handed subjects had a difference on only 13.6 msec favoring the left hemisphere. When the left-handed subjects were divided into familial and nonfamilial left-handed, the nonfamilial left-handed were found to have a significant left hemisphere advantage (21.3 msec) while the familial left-handed had no left hemisphere advantage at all (−0.57 msec). While the number of subjects is quite small, the data are an impressive illustration of differences in cerebral organization associated with familial handedness.

The evidence, considered over all studies, is strongly in favor of the predicted differences between R− and L+ groups. No studies report a larger between-hemispheres difference for the left-handed, whereas 18 report smaller between-hemispheres differences for the left-handed as compared to the right-handed. The difference seems even more impressive when the lack of selection for familial handedness is taken into account. Given a reasonably high probability of selecting both left-handed with no family history of left-handedness in the L groups and right-handed with a positive family history of left-handedness in the R groups, the number of studies that report consistently smaller between-hemisphere differences for the left-handed is quite impressive. It can be argued that if many of the existing studies were replicated with stricter selection for familial handedness, both the magnitude and the number of differences between the handedness groups would increase.

II. It is argued that the bilaterally organized individual (L+) can accept input data, carry on processing, and output a response within the same hemisphere. The R− individual has less ability to do this, owing to a higher degree of lateral specialization. It follows from this that when reaction time is taken as a measure of response to simple problem solving, the average reaction time taken over both hemispheres should be faster for L+ individuals, since input, memory access, computation, and output response can all be done within the hemisphere where the data were first received. The highly lateralized individual (R−) will show the fastest absolute reaction time when data is input to a hemisphere specialized for that type of processing. The slowest absolute reaction time should occur for the R− individual who receives data in a hemisphere with little specialized processing capability for that type of data. As problems increase in difficulty, the between-hemisphere differences for the R− group should increase.

For example, if a study such as that of Rizzolati, Umilta, and Berlucchi (1971) on hemispheric specialization for facial recognition and recognition of verbal material were to be repeated with groups selected for familial handedness, the following predictions could be made.

1. The R− individual will recognize faces and respond in the shortest absolute time interval when test stimuli are presented to the right hemisphere.
2. The R− will recognize verbal material and respond in the shortest absolute time interval when test stimuli are presented to the left hemisphere.
3. Reaction times will be at a maximum for the R− when he is asked to respond to face-recognition tasks with the left hemisphere and to verbal recognition tasks with the right hemisphere.

4. Interhemispheric differences in reaction times, regardless of type of task, will be minimal for the L+ individual.
5. Reaction time computed as an average for *both* hemispheres over all tasks will be faster for the L+.
6. As the difficulty of a task increases, the R− will make fewer errors than the L+, provided the task is directed to the hemisphere specialized for that type of task.

Evidence for statements (1), (2), (4), and (5) can be found in current research work. Hemispheric differences in right-handed (R) individuals in processing verbal material as compared with spatial material has been well documented (Buffery, 1974; Cohen, 1972; Geffen *et al.*, 1971; Gross, 1972; McKeever & Huling, 1971; McKeever *et al.*, 1973; Moscovitch & Catlin, 1970; Rizzolati *et al.*, 1971; Shannon, 1974; Wilkins & Stewart, 1974). For predictions (4) and (5), four studies (Cohen, 1972; Dimond & Beaumont, 1972b, 1973; Provins & Jeeves, 1975) found the left-handed to have faster reaction times to tasks regardless of hemisphere. Cohen found her left-handed faster in both hemispheres at a letter classification task of shape versus identity (aA vs. AA) task than the R subjects. Dimond and Beaumont (1972b) reported identical right and left hemisphere reaction times for the left-handed in a color naming task. They found the fastest absolute reaction time in the right-handed responding to right hemisphere presentation, with left hemisphere reaction time for the R subjects equal to that for the left-handed. Provins and Jeeves (1975) found the left-handed to react faster to judgments of tones regardless of hemisphere, and found the largest interhemisphere differences in reaction time for the right-handed. The only surprising aspect of these studies is the tendency for the left-handed to have faster overall reaction times, regardless of hemisphere, than the right-handed, even though the right-handed can be assumed to have an advantage from greater lateral specialization. The simplest hypothesis possible is that the tasks used in the studies reported are not demanding enough to show differences in processing ability and that more complex judgments would produce the expected differences, given the conditions specified in statement (6).

III. A bilaterally organized individual receiving identical nonsymmetrical patterns of stimulation to each hemisphere will make more accurate judgments of identity than an individual who is highly lateralized. It is assumed that bilateral organization will allow more direct interhemispheric comparison of data, regardless of the type of data. By contrast, a highly lateralized individual given identical patterns of stimulation to both hemispheres will have a higher error rate, because of difficulty in accepting data and carrying out preliminary processing in a hemisphere that lacks specialized processing ability for that type of data. It is argued that, for the lateralized individual, when stimulation is complex, information must be transferred to the hemisphere specialized for processing that particular type of data before interhemispheric comparisons can be made. Because of the difficulty of putting data into a form suitable for transmission from one hemisphere to another, this increases the possibility of error.

As an illustration, the experiment by Dimond, Gibson, and Gazzaniga (1972) an intra- and interhemispheric matching of word pairs will be used. In their study using only right-handed subjects, they found no differences in the number of correct matches in intrahemispheric comparisons, regardless of hemisphere. However, when interhemisphere comparisons were made, the error rates increased. Dimond *et all.* suggest that errors of transmission across the corpus callosum account for these errors.

Although there is no specific evidence that can be brought to bear on their explanation, some questions can be raised about the notion of "errors of transmission." If this refers to loss of accuracy in the transmission of sensory data, then this type of synaptic or neural loss should be detectable in other kinds of measures and should have shown up in other kinds of experiments. The studies of Davis and Schmit (1971) and Moscovitch and Catlin (1970) reported time differences but little that could be ascribed to error in information transmission. A more reasonable argument would be to suggest that, given the lateral specialization characteristic of R subjects, the data as presented could not be accepted and computed in sufficient degree to allow for errorless comparison. If the study were to be repeated with R− and L+ groups, the prediction to be made is that fewer errors will be made by the L+ group in the interhemispheric condition. The groups will not differ in rates of error for intrahemispheric comparisons.

The only experimental data relevant to this point is provided by Beaumont and Dimond (1975), who found the left-handed to be superior at interhemispheric matching of relatively simple shapes. No experiments have been reported to date on interhemispheric matching of verbal stimuli in the left-handed.

IV. A bilaterally organized individual receiving mirror-image patterns of stimulation in both hemispheres simultaneously will make more errors of judgment in comparisons of identity than a laterally organized individual. This proposition is based on the experimental evidence indicating that visual information transmitted across the corpus callosum is reversed. Under conditions of simultaneous presentation, mirror image patterns would appear identical, resulting in confused judgments of similarity. Under such conditions the individual with greater ability to make interhemispheric comparisons will make more errors of judgment. The person who is laterally organized for a given type of stimulus processing will make fewer errors of judgment since his comparisons are made in only one hemisphere, which is specialized for that type of processing.

Specific experimental data on this point is lacking, since the majority of studies of similarity-difference have been done as intrahemispheric comparisons (Egeth, 1971; Egeth & Epstein, 1972).

However, evidence from animal studies (Mello, 1965a,b; Noble, 1966) indicates that interhemispheric transfer of information is mirror imaged. In the pigeon, the optic fibers from each eye cross completely in the optic chiasma, terminating in the tectum on the opposite side of the brain, and perceptual integration occurs in the wulst (Cuénod, 1974). This characteristic of the unoperated pigeon permits its use as an analogue to the split-brain organism. In Mello's studies (1965a,b) the pigeon showed interocular transfer, but only to the mirror image of the stimulus, not to its original form. This suggests that visual information is reversed as a result of transfer across the corpus callosum. Noble (1966) suggests that such reversals may be a generalized feature of callosal transmission. In his studies, the monkey, after sectioning of the optic chiasma, learned to discriminate different shapes. Nonmirror shapes were correctly discriminated by the untrained eye, as were up–down differences. However, left-right mirror-image stimuli could not be differentiated.

As mentioned earlier, human experimental data is lacking. Corballis, Miller, and Morgan (1971) argue against the mirror-image hypothesis of callosal transmission but report data only on right-handed individuals.

The clinical literature on reading disabilities is of interest here, since speculations about the relationship of left-handedness to confusion of reversible letters such as *b d*, *p q*, are common in reading literature (Frith, 1974; Hildreth, 1949). Similar speculations exist about the role of mirror writing and handedness. Much of the reading disability work should be replicated, but the relationship occurs sufficiently often to warrant investigation in groups systematically assessed for familial left-handedness.

V. Under experimental conditions where interhemispheric integration of information is necessary to solve a problem, the most efficient performance will be achieved by the L+. The next level of performance will be achieved by the R+. The highest error rate on such tasks will be in the R−.

This proposition is similar to *III*, in assuming that bilaterality of organization has unique advantages for certain types of problems just as high lateralization does for others. Under conditions where data given to each hemisphere must be transformed to equivalent forms to achieve solutions to a problem, that organization most capable of efficient transformation and interhemispheric exchange will achieve superior performance. The inability of the highly lateralized individual to do well on such tasks is the result not of any lack of ability to perform the task but of an inability to transform and send the information to the hemispheric region suitable for such analysis. As an example, it is expected that when given an embedded figures task (Gottschaldt, 1926) under conditions where the figure to be identified is presented to one hemisphere and the embedding context to the other hemisphere, the R− person will have difficulty in performing. The basis of the difficulty lies in the inability of a hemisphere highly specialized for nonspatial tasks to transform the data for transmission to the other hemisphere without error. If the task is performed within the hemisphere specialized for such analysis, the performance will be much improved. The difficulty R− subjects have in performing the task interhemispherically lies in the lack of suitable specialization in both hemispheres for spatial processing. By contrast, the L+ subjects, who have spatial processing centers within each hemisphere, will be able to perform such a task much more easily.

Experimental data appropriate to this proposition are relatively sparse; only two experiments are directly applicable. Dimond and Beaumont (1974) found the left-handed to be superior at a paired-associate learning task where one member of each pair was presented to each hemisphere. In another experiment, Beaumont and Dimond (1975) found the left-handed to show superior performance at matching abstract shapes when pairs were presented, one to each hemisphere.

VI. A bilaterally organized system with a high degree of interhemispheric transfer will be disrupted in function if any part of the bilateral system is disrupted, but will show faster and more complete recovery than a unilaterally organized system.

The clinical literature relevant to this topic has been summarized by a number of investigators (Branch, Milner, & Rasmussen, 1964; Gloning, Gloning, Haub, & Quatember, 1969; Goodglass & Quadfasel, 1954; Hécaen & Piercy, 1956; Hécaen & Sauget, 1971; Luria, 1970; Penfield & Roberts, 1959; Subirana, 1958). About 24% of right-handed individuals with left-side cortical lesions develop language disorders as compared to 6.7% of right-handed with right-side lesions (data taken as a median percentage over all studies where data are roughly comparable and summing over all categories of verbal disorders—oral language, reading, writing, etc.). The left-handed with left-side cortical lesions show language disorders in 22.4% and for right-side lesions 13.7%.

These between-hemisphere differences are not as extreme for visual measures: For the right-handed, the percentage of visual disorders for left-side lesions is 7.1% and for right-side lesions, 10.8%. For the left-handed, the percentage of disorders for left-side lesions is 7.8% and for right-side lesions, 10.1%.

Another way of examining these differences is by comparing the number of findings of statistically significant differences for type of disorder and lesion site in right- and left-handed persons. For the right-handed, disorders in relation to lesion site are almost always statistically significant—for example, language disorders occur frequently with left-side lesions and rarely with right-side lesions. For the left-handed, the most usual finding is lack of significance in relation to lesion site—disorders that are significantly often associated with one hemisphere seem to occur at no more than chance level. Hécaen and Sauget (1971) assessed 50 types of symptoms in relation to lesion site—right or left hemisphere—on right- and left-handed patients. They reported 47 out of 50 between-hemisphere differences on right-handed patients as statistically significant at a probability of .05 or less. The corresponding number of significant differences for the left-handed patients was 4 out of 50.

The evidence supports the view that the left-handed have greater bilaterality of functional process and memory, both verbally and visually, than do the great majority of the right-handed. However, as the study of Hécaen and Sauget (1971) indicates, both the family history of left-handedness and the behavioral tendency to left-handedness must be carefully assessed, since there are striking differences between the familial left-handed and the nonfamilial left-handed. There are no differences in the verbal performances of the familial left-handed who have suffered either right or left cortical lesions—the frequency of language difficulties is virtually identical for right- and left-side lesions. For the non-familial left-handed, the frequency of language difficulties of all types is always greater with left-side lesions.

Studies of experimentally produced disruption of function in normal subjects are few in number. Kinsbourne and Cook (1971) and Hicks (1975) reported depressed performance levels on such tasks as dowel balancing and sequential typing when R subjects had to carry on continuous speech during these tasks. Lomas and Kimura (1976) report results of experimentation where speech interference was noted in R subjects during sequenced finger tapping with the right hand, but not with the left hand. By contrast, L subjects showed speech interference with both right and left hand sequenced tapping. Lomas and Kimura were concerned with investigating motor functions of the left hemi-sphere and their relationship to speech. However, their results seem interpretable as an experimentally produced analogue to the effects of brain injury on speech production. It would be of interest to prolong the Lomas and Kimura study, to see if changes occur over time. If the analogy to brain injury is correct, the expectation is that the left-handed would achieve normal speech levels during the sequencing task more quickly than the right-handed. There is a possibility that the left-handed would show a higher level of recovery of performance (regardless of time) than the right-handed, but such a prediction is much more speculative.

ANATOMICAL AND PHYSIOLOGICAL CONSIDERATIONS

Anatomical evidence related to handedness is, unfortunately, in short supply. Geschwind and Levitsky (1968), in an analysis of 100 brains, found the area behind Heschl's gyrus to be larger on the left in 65% of the brains examined and larger on the right in 11%. Whitaker and Selnes (1975), on the basis of a study of anatomical variation, suggest that the range of existing variations in cortical organization is such that every individual may be unique. Unfortunately, specific studies of handedness in relation to these differences have yet to be done.

Electrophysiological studies do offer some support for differences associated with handedness. Laterality preferences and interhemispheric EEG phase rela-tionships have been reported (Giannitrappani & Darrow, 1963; Giannitrappani, Darrow, & Sorkin, 1964).

The most detailed evidence for bilateralization is presented by Kutas and Donchin (1974) in a study of slow cortical potentials associated with voluntary movement. In their study, subjects squeezed an electric dynamometer at each of three force levels, using right and left hands. For the right-handed subjects, the potentials were consistently larger in the hemisphere contralateral to the hand used. In contrast, the left-handed subjects showed larger contralateral potentials when responding with the right hand but not with the left. The authors interpret their findings as supporting the hypothesis of reduced cerebral asymmetry in the left-handed.

SEX DIFFERENCES

The question of sex differences in relation to handedness is an intriguing one, especially since studies of handedness consistently suggest that left-handedness is less frequent in women (Hardyck & Petrinovich, 1977). However, this difference is so small (about 1%) that the possibility that sampling fluctuations are responsible should not be discounted.

In general, investigators of sex differences in cortical organization have argued that females tend to be less lateralized than males (Kimura, 1969; Levy, 1972; McGlone & Davidson, 1973; Harshman & Remington, 1975; Harshman, Remington, & Krashen, 1975). Harshman *et al.* (1975), in an extensive reanalysis of dichotic listening data, argue for the hypothesis of less lateralization in females. A notable exception to this position is taken by Buffery and Gray (1972) who argue that males are more bilateralized than females for visuo-spatial abilities.

A model of hemispheric functioning should account for sex differences if any claim of comprehensiveness is to be made. Unfortunately, the magnitudes of the effects found for sex differences are so small as compared to the magnitudes of the effects predictable by familial handedness that their stability has yet to be firmly established. It may be that there are consistent sex differences in cortical organization, but the data at present are too scanty to warrant any firm statement, at least in the context of the areas of concern here.

EPILOGUE

It is difficult to assess the usefulness of one's own model, but it does seem safe to say that the proposed model has three advantages, not unique but present to perhaps a greater degree than in existing models of cerebral function.

1. The continuum of functioning proposed encompasses, within one framework, the known variations of human cortical functioning, from the highly lateralized to the highly bilateralized and allows for the known ranges and kinds of individual differences.

2. The model is consistent with the vast majority of published research on hemisphere function and specialization, including experimental work on normally functioning subjects and clinical studies of lesion damage.
3. It is possible to make more specific predictions that can be experimentally tested on the basis of this model than on the basis of existing models of function. For many of the model's propositions, it is possible to predict interactive effects among the groups as defined.

Two issues remain, the question of mechanisms and the question of origin. There seems to be no way in which systematic differences in cerebral organization could develop other than genetically. There are proponents of nongenetic explanations of handedness such as Collins (1970), but his arguments fail to deal with the problem of explaining the relationships between cerebral organization and handedness. The genetic model of handedness proposed by Levy and Nagylaki (1972) is intriguing and undoubtedly the most advanced and systematic of the genetic models. However, this model has recently been critically evaluated by Hudson (1975), who found it unable to account for observed distributions of handedness in three sets of data. The Levy–Nagylaki model argues that only half the population of familial left-handed should have bilateral representation of function. In view of the large number of studies which report that interhemispheric differences for the left-handed are less pronounced than for the right-handed, this aspect of the model seems suspect. If the Levy–Nagylaki model were correct on this point, the expectation would be that results on unselected left-handed individuals would be much more variable and inconsistent than those reported in current published work. Failure to take family history into account should increase error variance within the left-handed but not to such an extent that L differences would be completely masked. To obtain results similar to most of those published, it would be necessary to assume that for the L+ showing bilaterality and the L+ showing no bilaterality of function (within the Levy–Nagylaki model), a majority of studies had somehow managed to sample more of the bilateral L+ groups. If the occurrence of bilateral organization is actually 50% within the L+ groups, such a result would be most unlikely to occur on the basis of chance sampling. While the mechanism is undoubtedly genetic, models offering an adequate fit to experimental data seem to be lacking in some respects.

The question of advantage can only be speculative. It is tempting to agree with Dimond and Beaumont (1974b) in their speculation that left-handedness may be an evolutionary advantage. However, it is doubtful that any trait offering an evolutionary advantage would remain relatively stable in humans from the time of *Australopithecus* to the present (Hardyck & Petrinovich, 1977). The hypothesis of deficiency in the left-handed does seem refutable, since there is little evidence of substance indicating that left-handedness and the associated patterns of cerebral organization are associated with any type of deficit. Whatever the origin may be of the differing patterns shown by the left-handed, there is little basis for judging left-handedness a handicap and more than a little reason to view it as an asset.

ACKNOWLEDGMENTS

I wish to express my gratitude to Jon Feshbach, Juan Pascual-Leone, Lewis Petrinovich, Leo Postman, and Anne Singer, who commented on earlier drafts of this paper. I am much indebted to Hilary Naylor for her valuable comments and suggestions for revision. I retain responsibility for errors, omissions, and inconsistencies.

REFERENCES

Annett, M. 1964. A model of the inheritance of handedness and cerebral dominance. *Nature, 204*, 59–60.

Annett, M. 1967. The binomial distribution of right, mixed and left handedness. *Quarterly Journal of Experimental Psychology, 19*, 327–333.

Annett, M. 1974. Handedness in the children of two left-handed parents. *British Journal of Psychology, 65*, 129–131.

Beaumont, J. G. 1974. Handedness and hemisphere function. In S. J. Dimond and J. G. Beaumont (Eds.), *Hemisphere function in the human brain.* New York: Wiley.

Beaumont, J. G., & Dimond, S. J. 1973. Transfer between the cerebral hemispheres in human learning. *Acta Psychologica, 37*, 87–91.

Beaumont, J. G., & Dimond, S. J. 1975. Interhemispheric transfer of figural information in right and non-right handed subjects. *Acta Psychologica, 39*, 97–104.

Benton, A. L., Meyers, R., & Polder, G. J. 1962. Some aspects of handedness. *Psychiatric Neurology Basel, 144*, 321–337.

Branch, C., Milner, B., & Rasmussen, T. 1964. Intracarotic sodium amytal for the lateralization of cerebral speech dominance. *Journal of Neurosurgery, 21*, 399–465.

Bryden, M. P. 1965. Tachistoscopic recognition, handedness, and cerebral dominance. *Neuropsychologia, 3*, 1–8.

Bryden, M. P. 1970. Laterality effects in dichotic listening: Relations with handedness and reading ability in children. *Neuropsychologia, 8*, 443–450.

Bryden, M. P. 1973. Perceptual asymmetry in vision: Relation to handedness, eyedness, and speech lateralization. *Cortex, 9*, 419–435.

Buffery, A. W. H. 1974. Asymmetrical lateralization of cerebral functions and the effect of unilateral brain surgery in epileptic patients. In S. J. Dimond and J. G. Beaumont (Eds.), *Hemisphere function in the human brain.* New York: Wiley.

Buffery, A. W. H., & Gray, J. A. 1972. Sex differences in the development of spatial and linguistic skills. In C. Ounsted and D. C. Taylor (Eds.), *Gender differences: Their ontogeny and significance.* London: Churchill-Livingstone.

Cohen, G. 1972. Hemispheric differences in a letter classification task. *Perception and Psychophysics, 11*, 139–142.

Collins, R. L. 1970. The sound of one paw clapping: An inquiry into the origin of left-handedness. In G. Lindzey and D. D. Thiessen (Eds.), *Contributions to behavior-genetic analysis: The mouse as prototype.* New York: Appleton.

Corballis, M. C., Miller, A., & Morgan, M. J. 1971. The role of left–right orientation in interhemispheric matching of visual information. *Perception and Psychophysics, 10,* 385–388.

Cuénod, M. 1974. Commissural pathways in interhemispheric transfer of visual information in the pigeon. In F. O. Schmitt and F. G. Worden (Eds.), *The neurosciences: Third study program.* Cambridge: M.I.T. Press.

Curry, F. W. 1967. A comparison of left-handed and right-handed subjects on verbal and nonverbal dichotic listening tasks. *Cortex, 3,* 343–352.

Curry, F. W., & Rutherford, D. R. 1967. Recognition and recall of dichotically presented verbal stimuli by right and left-handed persons. *Neuropsychologia, 5,* 119–126.

Cyr, D., Daniloff, R., & Berry, R. 1971. The perception of clicks embedded in sentences as a function of handedness and mode of presentation. *Journal of Auditory Research, 11,* 251–259.

Davidoff, J. B. 1975. Hemispheric differences in the perception of lightness. *Neuropsychologia, 13,* 121–124.

Davis, R., & Schmit, V. 1971. Timing the transfer of information between hemispheres in man. *Acta Psychologica, 35,* 335–346.

Dee, H. L. 1971. Auditory asymmetry and strength of manual preference. *Cortex, 7,* 236–245.

Dimond, S. J. 1970a. Hemispheric refractoriness and control of reaction time. *Quarterly Journal of Experimental Psychology, 22,* 610–617.

Dimond, S. J. 1970b. Reaction time and response competition between the right and left hands. *Quarterly Journal of Experimental Psychology, 22,* 513–520.

Dimond, S. J. 1970c. Cerebral dominance or lateral preference in motor control. *Acta Psychologica, 32,* 196–198.

Dimond, S. J. 1971. Hemisphere function and word registration. *Journal of Experimental Psychology, 87,* 183–186.

Dimond, S. J. 1972. *The double brain.* London: Churchill-Livingston.

Dimond, S. J., & Beaumont, J. G. 1971a. The use of two hemispheres to increase brain capacity. *Nature, 232,* 270–271.

Dimond, S. J., & Beaumont, J. G. 1971b. Hemisphere function and vigilance. *Quarterly Journal of Experimental Psychology, 23,* 443–448.

Dimond, S. J., & Beaumont, J. G. 1972a. Hemispheric control of hand function in the human brain. *Acta Psychologica, 36,* 32–36.

Dimond, S. J., & Beaumont, J. G. 1972b. Hemisphere function and color naming. *Journal of Experimental Psychology, 96,* 87–91.

Dimond, S. J., & Beaumont, J. G. 1972c. On the nature of the interhemispheric transfer of fatigue in the human brain. *Acta Psychologica, 36,* 443–449.

Dimond, S. J., & Beaumont, J. G. 1972d. Processing in perceptual integration between and within the cerebral hemispheres. *British Journal of Psychology, 63,* 509–514.

Dimond, S. J., & Beaumont, J. G. 1972e. A right hemisphere basis for calculation in the human brain. *Psychonomic Science, 26,* 137–138.

Dimond, S. J., & Beaumont, J. G. 1973. Differences in the vigilance performance of the right and left hemispheres. *Cortex, 9,* 259–266.

Dimond, S. J., & Beaumont, J. G. 1974a. Different personality patterns of the human cerebral hemispheres. In S. J. Dimond and J. G. Beaumont (Eds), *Hemisphere function in the human brain.* New York: Wiley.

Dimond, S. J., & Beaumont, J. G. 1974b. Hemisphere function and paired-associate learning. *British Journal of Psychology, 65,* 275–278.

Dimond, S. J., Gibson, A. R., & Gazzaniga, M. S. 1972. Cross field and within field integration of visual information. *Neuropsychologia, 10,* 379–381.

Efron, R. 1962. The effect of handedness on the perception of simultaneity and temporal order. *Brain, 86,* 261–284.

Egeth, H. 1971. Laterality effects in perceptual matching. *Perception and Psychophysics, 9,* 375–376.

Egeth, H., & Epstein, J. 1972. Differential specialization of the cerebral hemispheres for the perception of sameness and difference. *Perception and Psychophysics, 12,* 218–220.

Fagan-Dubin, L. 1974. Lateral dominance and development of cerebral specialization. *Cortex, 10,* 69–74.

Falek, A. 1959. Handedness: A family study. *American Journal of Human Genetics, 11,* 52–62.

Frith, U. 1974. A curious effect with reversed letters explained by a theory of schema. *Perception and Psychophysics, 16,* 113–116.

Gazzaniga, M. S., Bogen, J. E., & Sperry, R. W. 1967. Dyspraxia following divisions of the cerebral commissures. *American Medical Association Archives of Neurology, 16,* 606–612.

Geffen, G., Bradshaw, J. L., & Wallace, G. 1971. Interhemispheric effects on reaction time to verbal and nonverbal visual stimuli. *Journal of Experimental Psychology, 87,* 415–422.

Geschwind, N., & Levitsky, W. 1968. Human brain: Left-right asymmetries in temporal speech region. *Science, 161,* 186–187.

Giannitrappani, D., & Darrow, C. W. 1963. Differences in EEG time relationships in right and left handed individuals. *Electroencephalography and Clinical Neurophysiology, 15,* 721–727.

Giannitrappani, D., Darrow, C. W., & Sorkin, A. 1964. Asleep and awake interhemispheric EEG phase relationships in left and right handed subjects. *American Psychologist, 19,* 480–481.

Gloning, I., Gloning, K., Haub, G., & Quatember, R. 1969. Comparison of verbal behavior in right-handed and non right-handed patients with anatomically verified lesion of one hemisphere. *Cortex, 5,* 43–52.

Goodglass, H., & Quadfasel, F. A. 1954. Language laterality in left-handed aphasics. *Brain, 77,* 521–548.

Gottschaldt, K. 1926. Uber den Einfluss der Erfahrung auf die Wahrnemung von Figuren I: Uber den Einfluss gehaufter Einpragung von Figuren auf ihre Sichbarkeit in umfassenden Konfigurationen. *Psychologische Forschung, 8,* 261–317.

Groberg, D. H., Dustman, R. E., & Beck, E. C. 1969. The effect of body and head tilt in the perception of vertical: Comparison of body and head tilt with left and right-handed male and female subjects. *Neuropsychologia, 7,* 89–100.

Gross, M. M. 1972. Hemispheric specialization for processing of visually presented verbal and spatial stimuli. *Perception and Psychophysics, 12,* 357–363.

Hardyck, C. 1977. Handedness and part-whole relationships: A replication. *Cortex,* in press.

Hardyck, C., & Petrinovich, L. 1977. Left-handedness. *Psychological Bulletin,* in press.

Hardyck, C., Petrinovich, L., & Goldman, R. 1976. Left-handedness and cognitive deficit. *Cortex, 12,* 266–278.

Harshman, R. A., & Remington, R. R. 1975. Sex, language and the brain. Part I. A review of the literature on adult sex differences in lateralization. Unpublished manuscript, Dept. of Linguistics, University of California, Los Angeles.

Harshman, R. A., Remington, R. R., & Krashen, S. D. 1975. Sex, language and the brain. Part II. Evidence from dichotic listening for adult sex differences in verbal lateralization. Unpublished manuscript, Dept. of Linguistics, University of California, Los Angeles.

Hécaen, H., & Piercy, M. 1956. Paroxysmal dysphasia and the problem of cerebral dominance. *Journal of Neurology, Neurosurgery, and Psychiatry, 19*, 194–201.

Hécaen, H., & Sauget, J. 1971. Cerebral dominance in left-handed subjects. *Cortex, 7*, 19–48.

Hicks, R. E. 1975. Intrahemispheric response competition between vocal and unimanual performance in normal adult human males. *Journal of Comparative and Physiological Psychology, 89*, 50–60.

Hildreth, G. 1949. The development and training of hand dominance. *Journal of Genetic Psychology, 75*, 197–220, 221–254, 255–275; 1950, *76*, 39–100, 101–144.

Hines, D., & Satz, P. 1971. Superiority of right visual half-fields in right-handers for recall of digits presented at varying rates. *Neuropsychologia, 9*, 21–25.

Hines, D., & Satz, P. 1974. Cross-modal asymmetries in perception related to asymmetry in cerebral function. *Neuropsychologia, 12*, 239–247.

Hudson, P. T. W. 1975. The genetics of handedness—A reply to Levy and Nagylaki. *Neuropsychologia, 13*, 331–339.

Jones, R. K. 1966. Observations on stammering after localized cerebral injury. *Journal of Neurology, Neurosurgery, and Psychiatry, 29*, 192–195.

Kershner, J. R. 1974. Ocular-manual laterality and dual hemisphere specialization. *Cortex, 10*, 293–301.

Kimura, D. 1969. Spatial localization in right and left visual fields. *Canadian Journal of Psychology, 23*, 445–458.

Kinsbourne, M., & Cook, J. 1971. Generalized and lateralized effects of concurrent verbalization on a unimanual skill. *Quarterly Journal of Experimental Psychology, 23*, 341–345.

Knox, A. W., & Boone, D. R. 1970. Auditory laterality and tested handedness. *Cortex, 6*, 164–173.

Kutas, M., & Donchin, E. 1974. Studies of squeezing: Handedness, responding hand, response force, and a symmetry of readiness potential. *Science, 186*, 545–548.

Kutas, M., McCarthy, G., & Donchin, E. 1975. Differences between sinistrals' and dextrals' ability to infer a whole from its parts: A failure to replicate. *Neuropsychologia, 13*, 455–464.

Levy, J. 1969. Possible basis for the evolution of lateral specialization of the human brain. *Nature, 224*, 614–615.

Levy, J. 1973. Lateral specialization of the human brain: Behavioral manifestations and possible evolutionary basis. In J. Kiger (Ed.), *The biology of behavior*. Corvallis: Oregon State Univ. Press.

Levy, J. 1974. Psychological implications of bilateral asymmetry. In S. J. Dimond and J. G. Beaumont (Eds.), *Hemisphere function in the human brain*. New York: Wiley.

Levy, J., Nebes, R. D., & Sperry, R. W. 1971. Expressive language in the surgically separated minor hemisphere. *Cortex, 7*, 49–58.

Levy, J., & Nagylaki, T. 1972. A model for the genetics of handedness. *Genetics, 72*, 117–128.

Lomas, J., & Kimura, D. 1976. Intrahemispheric interaction between speaking and sequential manual activity. *Neuropsychologia, 14*, 23–33.

Luria, A. R. 1970. *Traumatic aphasia*. The Hague: Mouton.

Marshall, J. C. 1973. Some problems and paradoxes associated with recent accounts of hemispheric specialization. *Neuropsychologia, 11*, 463–470.

McGlone, J., & Davidson, W. 1973. The relation between cerebral speech laterality and spatial ability with special reference to sex and handedness. *Neuropsychologia, 11*, 105–113.

McKeever, W. F., & Gill, K. 1972. Visual half-field differences in masking effects for sequential letter stimuli in the right and left-handed. *Neuropsychologia, 10*, 111–117.

McKeever, W. F., & Huling, M. 1971. Bilateral tachistoscopic word recognition as a function of hemisphere stimulated and interhemispheric transfer time. *Neuropsychologia, 9*, 281–288.

McKeever, W. F., VanDeventer, A. D., & Suberi, M. 1973. Avowed, assessed, and familial handedness and differential hemispheric processing of brief sequential and non-sequential visual stimuli. *Neuropsychologia, 11*. 235–238.

McKeever, W. F., Gill, K. M., & VanDeventer, A. D. 1975. Letter versus dot stimuli as tools for "splitting the normal brain with reaction time." *Quarterly Journal of Experimental Psychology, 27*, 363–373.

McKinney, J. P. 1967. Handedness, eyedness and perceptual stability of the left and right visual fields. *Neuropsychologia, 5*, 339–344.

Mello, N. K. 1965a. Interhemispheric reversal of mirror-image oblique lines after monocular training in pigeons. *Science, 148*, 252.

Mello, N. K. 1965b. Mirror-image reversal in pigeons. *Science, 149*, 1519.

Miller, E. 1971. Handedness and the pattern of human ability. *British Journal of Psychology, 62*, 111–112.

Moscovitch, M., & Catlin, J. 1970. Interhemispheric transmission of information: Measurement in normal man. *Psychonomic Science, 18*, 211–213.

Nebes, R. D. 1971. Handedness and the perception of part–whole relationships. *Cortex, 7*, 350–356.

Nebes, R. D., & Briggs, G. G. 1974. Handedness and the retention of visual material. *Cortex, 10*, 209–214.

Newcombe, F., & Ratcliff, G. 1973. Handedness, speech lateralization and ability. *Neuropsychologia, 11*, 399–407.

Noble, J. 1966. Mirror-images and the forebrain commissures of the monkey. *Nature, 211*, 1263–1266.

Orbach, J. 1967. Differential recognition of Hebrew and English words in right and left visual fields as a function of cerebral dominance and reading habits. *Neuropsychologia, 5*, 127–134.

Penfield, W., & Roberts, L. 1959. *Speech and brain mechanisms*. Princeton, N.J.: Princeton Univ. Press.

Petersen, J. M., & Lansky, L. M. 1974. Left-handedness among architects: Some facts and speculation. *Perception and Motor Skills, 38*, 547–550.

Provins, K. A., & Jeeves, M. A. 1975. Hemisphere differences in response time to simple auditory stimuli. *Neuropsychologia, 13*, 207–211.

Rizzolati, C., Umilta, C., & Berlucchi, G. 1971. Opposite superiorities of the right and left cerebral hemispheres in discriminative reaction time to physiognomical and alphabetical material. *Brain, 94*, 431–442.

Satz, P. 1972. Pathological left-handedness: An explanatory model. *Cortex, 8*, 121–135.

Satz, P., Achenbach, K., & Fennell, E. 1967. Correlations between assessed manual laterality and predicted speech laterality in a normal population. *Neuropsychologia, 5*, 295–310.

Satz, P., Achenbach, K., Pattishall, E., & Fennell, E. 1965. Order of report, ear asymmetry, and handedness in dichotic listening. *Cortex, 1*, 377–396.

Satz, P., Fennell, E., & Jones, M. B. 1969. Comments on: A model of inheritance of handedness and cerebral dominance. *Neuropsychologia, 7*, 101–103.

Semmes, J. 1968. Hemispheric specialization: A possible clue to mechanism. *Neuropsychologia, 6*, 11–26.

Shankweiler, D., & Studdert-Kennedy, M. 1975. A continuum of lateralization for speech perception? *Brain and Language, 2*, 212–225.

Shannon, B. 1974. Lateralization effects in reaction time to simple sentences. *Cortex, 10*, 360–365.

Sperry, R. W. 1968a. Mental unity following surgical disconnection of the cerebral hemispheres. In *The Harvey lectures, series 62*. New York: Academic Press.

Sperry, R. W. 1968b. Hemisphere deconnection and unity in conscious awareness. *American Psychologist, 23*, 723–733.

Sperry, R. W. 1973. Lateral specialization of cerebral function in the surgically separated hemispheres of man. In F. J. McGuigan and R. J. Schoonover (Eds.), *The psychophysiology of thinking*. New York: Academic Press.

Sperry, R. W. 1974. Lateral specialization in the surgically separated hemispheres. In F. O. Schmitt and F. G. Worden (Eds.), *The neurosciences: Third study program*. Cambridge: M.I.T. Press.

Sperry, R. W., Gazzaniga, M. W., & Bogen, J. E. 1969. Interhemispheric relationships: The neocortical commissures; syndromes of hemisphere disconnection. In P. J. Vinken and G. W. Bruyn (Eds.), *Handbook of clinical neurology*. Vol. 4. Amsterdam: North-Holland Publishing.

Subirana, A. 1958. The prognosis in aphasia in relation to cerebral dominance and handedness. *Brain, 81*, 415–425.

Teuber, H. L. 1974. Why two brains? In F. O. Schmitt and F. G. Worden (Eds.), *The neurosciences: Third study program*. Cambridge, Mass.: M.I.T. Press.

Trankell, A. 1950. *Vänsterhänthet hos barn i skolåldern*. Helsingfors.

Varney, N. R., & Benton, A. L. 1975. Tactile perception of direction in relation to handedness and familial handedness. *Neuropsychologia, 13*, 449–454.

Wada, J. A., & Rasmussen, T. 1960. Intracarotid injection of sodium amytal for the lateralization of cerebral speech dominance: Experimental and clinical observations. *Journal of Neurosurgery, 17*, 266–282.

Whitaker, H. A., & Selnes, O. A. 1975. Anatomic variation in the cortex: Individual differences and the problem of the localization of language functions. *Conference on origins and evolution of language and speech*. New York: New York Academy of Sciences.

Wilkins, A., & Stewart, A. 1974. The time course of lateral asymmetries in visual perception of letters. *Journal of Experimental Psychology, 192*, 905–908.

Zurif, E. B., & Bryden, M. P. 1969. Familial handedness and left–right differences in auditory and visual perception. *Neuropsychologia, 7*, 179–187.

6

Variability and Constraint
in Acquired Dyslexia

John C. Marshall

UNIVERSITY OF NIJMEGEN

Freda Newcombe

THE CHURCHILL HOSPITAL, OXFORD

INTRODUCTION

Acquired dyslexia as the sole, or even salient, symptom of cerebral damage is undoubtedly rare (Casey & Ettlinger, 1960; Gloning, Gloning, & Hoff, 1968). As Holmes (1950) points out, however, "its main interest does not lie in its rarity, but in the light its study may throw on the anatomical and physiological organization of certain functions of the brain, and their relation to some features of aphasia." Recent case reports (Ajax, 1967; Geschwind & Fusillo, 1966; Greenblatt, 1973), in the tradition of Déjérine (1892), have clearly advanced our understanding of the anatomical substrate of the reading process. To Holmes' remark we would add Poppelreuter's (1917) observation that the *psychology* of normal reading skills may be illuminated by study of the patterns of impairment to which these skills are subject (and vice versa). It is indeed notable that recent, apparently competing, theories of word recognition (Baron, 1973; Meyer, Schvaneveldt, & Ruddy, 1974) in normal subjects seem to be closely paralleled by recent taxonomies of acquired dyslexia as outlined on the basis of patients' predominant error-types (Marshall and Newcombe, 1973). It is, however, in precisely this latter area—the specification of error-types—that data have been most conspicuously lacking.

The approach we shall adopt here constitutes a preliminary attempt to explore this area; we shall be concerned primarily with the psycholinguistic nature of dyslexic errors and with the additional dysphasic symptoms which seem to accompany the component features of an error taxonomy. Finally, we shall make some tentative observations on the course of remission of acquired dyslexia. In addition to the remedial implications which may eventually be derived from longitudinal studies (Newcombe & Marshall, 1973), we note the theoretical point that the construction of taxonomies of impairment may be complicated by differences between the acute and chronic phases of aphasic conditions (Brown, 1972).

A distinction has traditionally been made between pure word-blindness—attributed to a disconnection between visual cortex and language areas—and dyslexia accompanied by dysgraphia, usually in the setting of a more generalized disturbance of language functions. The pure syndrome is as rare as its qualifying adjective suggests, and it is doubtful whether there has been a more convincing or elegant presentation than that of Déjérine (1892). The patient, an intelligent and cultivated businessman of 68, developed total word-blindness, including inability to read musical symbols, after a stroke. He had a homonymous hemianopia but no other neurological signs. Intelligence, understanding of spoken language, and his own spontaneous speech were unimpaired. He could write to dictation but could not read what he had written. The symptom persisted unchanged for 4 years until another stroke led to his death after a 10-day illness during which he was aphasic and agraphic. The first lesion involved the lingual gyrus, the fusiform gyrus, the cuneus, the occipital pole, and the splenium of the corpus callosum; the later lesion included the angular gyrus and inferior parietal lobe. Further evidence that an isolated reading disorder can be specific to the visual modality was provided by Holmes (1950) whose patient could generally decipher letters traced on his hand and who could recognize at once words spelled aloud to him. For Charcot's (1889) patient, reading was "only possible with the aid of ideas furnished by movements executed by the hand in the act of writing . . . and even after placing his hands behind his back and telling him to read, one sees that he traces the letters with his index finger on the nail of his thumb." The patient himself commented, "I can read printing less well than writing, because in writing it is easier for me to mentally reproduce the letter with my right hand, whereas it is more difficult to reproduce the printed characters."

There have been other individual case reports of circumscribed dyslexia (see Benson & Geschwind, 1969, for a review), but it is sometimes difficult to evaluate the "purity" of the defect because of the limited evidence about language functions other than reading or writing. Vocabulary and spoken language may be intact (Ajax, 1967), but slight word-finding or object-naming difficulties are sometimes mentioned (Charcot, 1889; Holmes, 1950; Greenblatt, 1973), and one case, often cited as "pure" (Broadbent, 1872) had a fairly severe nominal defect. Impairment in recent memory has also been reported (Lyman, Kwan, & Chao, 1938; Greenblatt, 1973).

The nature of the errors made by these patients is obscure. Déjerine's patient could read only his name. Some patients attempted to read letters, and Holmes (1950) cites several examples of incorrect letter-naming which are difficult to account for on the basis of frequent visual confusions, for example, *N* named as *G, B → Z, K → S*. Holmes commented: "It was obvious that his mistakes were never due to failure to see the whole letter; N was never called V; nor were they due to confusion of letters of somewhat similar shape, as M and W, or B and D. The letter O was usually recognized, probably as it resembled the numeral 0 (nought), and as will be seen later he was able to identify numerals." The patient could rearrange scattered block letters in alphabetic sequence, although he was unable to name them, but he was able to transcribe capital letters into cursive script only when he could identify them. His own comment about his failure to identify more than one-letter words was: "I can see them, but I have forgotten their names and what they mean," or "I feel I can read the letters, but when I try they seem to get mixed up and blurred."

It has been suggested, however, that patients with "pure" (agnosic) alexia tend to be better at letter-naming than word-reading, whereas the converse pattern is associated with aphasic dyslexia (Alajouanine, Lhermitte, & Ribaucourt-Ducarne, 1960). Hinshelwood (1900) described a 53-year-old man who suddenly developed a severe verbal dyslexia (i.e., word-blindness) but could read letters fluently and had no aphasia "on the most careful examination." He occasionally managed to read small function words (e.g., *the, of, to*) and could decipher words if allowed to spell them out letter by letter. Ajax's (1967) patient, with a less severe but nonetheless isolated reading disability, named letters without error.

Thus, there is clinical evidence of remarkably dissociated reading defects in a small group of patients. It is hardly surprising that such cases are rare since focal lesions sited so precisely as to disconnect occipital cortex from the language area without disrupting writing, naming, and speech are exceptional. It may also be that a relatively static and permanent disability (Déjerine, 1892; Ajax, 1967) implies a complete disconnection; and such cases stand in sharp contrast to the patients who recover from word-blindness in a period of up to 6 months after surgical resection of the left occipital lobe (Hécaen, Ajuriaguerra, & David, 1952), although these patients are thereafter disinclined to read and complain of fatigue when reading for more than a short period, a condition formerly ascribed by Berlin (as cited by Hinshelwood, 1900), to partial interruption of transmission fibers, and rapidly exhausted powers of conduction).

At the other extreme from cases of "disconnection" dyslexia are instances where dyslexia presents as one aspect of a more or less severe (central) disorder of language. Thus a case reported by Low (1931) showed dyslexia as the salient symptom although other dysphasic signs were present. The patient "spoke in well-formed sentences, though with some difficulty in finding words." He could carry out simple commands, although he was unable to carry out complicated orders. Object-naming was well preserved, but the patient could not describe the uses of objects. The reading of single words was characterized by both visual and semantic errors:

shirt	→ skirt	*Dad*	→ father
life	→ wife	*child*	→ girl
sword	→ words	*vice*	→ wicked

[Low, 1931]

Short "function" words, such as *at, to, as, in* could not be read, although performance on three-letter nouns, adjectives and verbs, such as *son, pin, red, cow,* was good. Nonsense syllables, as for example, *sim, fik, tek,* could not be read. When an attempt was made to read them, the responses were words possessing considerable visual similarity to the stimulus, either in whole or part.

fal	→ fat
jun	→ jump
sto	→ story
tla	→ atlas
cor	→ corrupt
lom	→ lemon

[Low, 1931]

Quasi-random word strings presented for reading were "regularized" in terms of syntax and meaning:

play waiters food	→ "waiters sell food"
make stop listen	→ "stop, look, and listen"

A related case is described by Albert, Yamadori, Gardner, and Howes (1973): severe dyslexia in the context of a mild but widespread aphasia following removal of a Grade 3 glioma from the left temporo-occipital area. The patient, a 57-year-old right-handed man displayed fluent, albeit circumlocutory, speech with verbal paraphasia and "occasional pauses due to word-finding difficulties." Object-naming was impaired and likewise contaminated by verbal paraphasia. Some comprehension deficit was observed on complex material. Dyslexia and dysgraphia were both pronounced although spelling ability was relatively well preserved; reading errors included both circumlocutions and frank semantic paraphasias, for example, *symphony* → "I think it has something to do with music," *ant* → "it's a small animal," *jacket* → "coat." Of particular interest in this case is the fact that comprehension of written words was relatively well preserved. For instance, when shown a picture of a lion and required to point to the correct word from the alternatives *cat, lion, bear,* the patient succeeded. But he then went on to read *lion* as "Black. No. Horse, I imagine. Yeah, Black." ("Black" was a perseverative utterance from the immediately preceding stimulus.)

Similar patterns are reported in Simmel and Goldschmidt (1953), who describe a case of posteclamptic aphasia in a left-handed woman. The patient's spontaneous speech was good, although "she occasionally searched for names of objects, persons, or activities." Verbal paraphasias were in evidence, although infrequently. Complicated instructions or explanations were not understood, although simple instructions and questions were handled with ease. Object-naming was severely defective and occasioned frequent circumlocutions and verbal paraphasias. Writing was almost abolished—only the alphabet, the number series, and the patient's name could be produced—and reading was severely impaired.

Function words could not be read at all, nor could many short (three-letter) nouns and verbs. Errors were predominantly visual confusions, although many verbal paraphasias were also detected.

Case W. G.

of	→	for
on	→	no
and	→	can
but	→	put
was	→	as, ask, as
chairman	→	airmail
town	→	down
shell	→	tell
one	→	two . . . no, one
cents	→	pennies
blades	→	razor
napkin	→	napkin, towels, no . . . not towels,
		rags, napkin, tablets

[Simmel & Goldschmidt, 1953]

A very similar clinical picture is seen in Goldstein's case 23 (1948). The patient, a 26-year-old left-handed man with occlusion of the left carotid artery and cerebral infarction, spoke very little spontantneously. His speech was telegrammatic and restricted to concrete content. Simple commands were understood, but comprehension was impaired for utterances containing two or more propositions. Object-naming was severely impaired and frequently displayed verbal paraphasias, such as *pipe* → "smoke, cigar." Reading was grossly impaired, and writing, especially to dictation, was very poor. Visual errors, for example, *war* → "was," *ward* → "warm," *nip* → "tip," *smooth* → "smart," *puddle* →

"puppy," were observed, but the predominant error-type in reading was semantic paralexia; examples are provided in the following list. "Mutilated words", like *Hsptl,* or *gradn,* were immediately read as "hospital" and "garden," respectively.

1.	*brunette*	→ red, girl
2.	*draw*	→ paint . . . pencil
3.	*tide*	→ water
4.	*era*	→ time
5.	*wed*	→ marry
6.	*edit*	→ to write
7.	*big*	→ small, little
8.	*black*	→ dark
9.	*down*	→ up
10.	*little*	→ small
11.	*low*	→ small
12.	*oven*	→ hot
13.	*security*	→ loan, money, safe
14.	*Philadelphia*	→ Greek

[Goldstein, 1953]

It would seem, then, that acquired disorders of reading can be placed on a continuum according to the extent and severity of the associated symptoms of dysphasia (de Massary, 1932). One might furthermore expect the *nature* of the dyslexia to vary with the degree and type of concomitant dysphasia and hence with the underlying anatomy. We accordingly present a sequence of eight dyslexic subjects in support of this putative continuum.

CASE 1 (A.G. NO. 514723)

This patient, aged 58, was admitted to the Department of Neurological Surgery at Oxford on July 3, 1971, with the presumptive diagnosis of a space-occupying lesion. The subjective complaints were loss of recent memory, difficulty in finding his way about, and deterioration in vision. The patient's family noted the first sign of illness some 6 months before admission to hospital when he had fainted at work and seemed worried, moody, and tired at the end of each working day. Two months before admission, he complained about his eyesight, saying that he was not focusing well, and shortly afterward he got lost on a familiar walk with the family. Five weeks prior to admission he went on a family holiday to his hometown but failed to identify the old family home and tried to enter a neighbor's house. Twenty-four hours after return from holiday he could not remember that the family had been away. He then had difficulty finding his way around his own home and got lost when buying provisions from a local shop 5 minutes' walk away from his home.

On clinical examination he was found to have a right homonymous hesnianopia, bilateral papilloedema, an extensor left plantar response, increased tendon jerks, as well as bilateral impairment of vibration sense, graphesthesia, and stereognosis. Brain scan showed increased uptake in the posterior parieto-temporal region in the left hemisphere and an even denser uptake on the right side. A left carotid angiogram indicated the presence of a mass in the posterior parieto-temporal region with pathological circulation. A butterfly tumor of the splenium of the corpus callosum was diagnosed, and a bilateral glioblastoma was found at post-mortem on August 19, 1971.

The first psychological examination was on July 4, 1971. The patient was then disoriented in time and place but not in person. Topographical disorientation and topographical memory loss were apparent as well as a generalized impairment of memory functions. He also had a severe degree of visual imperception, including severely impaired recognition of letters, words, faces, and colors. In contrast, tactual recognition of letters and objects was unimpaired. There was little, if any, convincing evidence of aphasia: He certainly could not name visually presented objects, but he had very little difficulty in naming them when they were presented tactually. Moreover, if an object was described verbally by the examiner (e.g., "What is the musical instrument that Teddy Brown played?" or "What apparatus does a scientist use to examine minute specimens?", the patient was able to name it, and he achieved a normal score on an object-naming task presented in this fashion. Also, his vocabulary score was above average and his definition of words good and to the point, (e.g., *Fortitude* → "strength in adversity"). His speech was grammatical and coherent, automatic word series were preserved, and his digit span was 5.

The impairment of this patient's reading was marked and disproportionately severe compared with writing and oral spelling. For example, with two lists of 40 three-letter words, he made no mistakes in oral spelling and wrote approximately 75% of the words correctly, but he could read less than 25% of them. He was relatively better at reading short words than the individual letters of which these words were composed. He read only 6 of 26 uppercase letters of the alphabet and 4 lowercase letters, whereas he was able to write 21 uppercase letters and 20 lowercase letters. He was not able to name colors on demand, nor could he point to named colors when an array of 5 were used (red, blue, black, green, yellow). However, he could sometimes name the color of items named by the examiner. He did not sort colors spontaneously on request, and when groups of primary colors were shown to him, he described them as all grey, "some lighter than the others." Visual acuity, uncorrected, was adequate for reading; he could detect horizontal and vertical grids (A50 4/4 A.100 3/4) and the larger Snellen rings. He could also match upper- and lowercase letters (with one error: $f \rightarrow t$), and abstract patterns.

It is consistent with this clinical picture that all the reading errors made by A. G. can be described as visual misidentifications and omissions. Examples are provided in Table 6.1.

The errors, however, are constrained by the patient's intact knowledge of his language, and thus no neologisms were produced. This constraint ceased to operate when the subject named the individual letters (prior to attempting to read the word), for example, *did* → "L,A,L . . . L,I,D . . . lid." It would seem that it was the sequential nature of this strategy that lead to the constraint being broken, for neologisms were much in evidence on writing to dictation, for example, *sun* → "sut," *rib* → "pib," *sob* → "sodu." Furthermore, the subject's control of spelling patterns was impaired; he thus wrote *nag* and *nip* as "knag" and "knip," respectively. His writing errors also included a solitary example of paraphasic involvement; asked to write *cow*, he wrote "calve." In general, however, A.G.'s dyslexic and dysgraphic impairment had a strong visuo-spatial component.

CASE 2 (A.T. NO. 8843/464)

This patient sustained a penetrating missile wound of the left occipital region of the brain at the age of 23 in 1944. He was operated on within 48 hours of wounding, when three small bone chips were removed from 2 cm of brain track that crossed two definite aulci. The tangle of vessels gave a lot of trouble from bleeding. At a depth of about 3 cm, a large bone fragment about 1.5 cm in diameter and 1 cm thick was found and removed. On examination, 3 weeks after operation, he was found to have a slightly spastic right arm and a spastic right leg. A visual field defect was noted, but the visual field charts are missing from the early records. The patient could recognize and name common objects

TABLE 6.1 Reading Errors Made by A.G. (Case 1)

1. *cat*	→	car
2. *pod*	→	dug
3. *balloon*	→	bloom
4. *greet*	→	street
5. *valley*	→	alley
6. *tomato*	→	domino
7. *rid*	→	H, I . . . hid
8. *ran*	→	can
9. *snail*	→	oil
10. *narrow*	→	saw
11. *sparrow*	→	narrow
12. *easel*	→	Hansel

and obey simple commands. According to early notes, he could read letters but left some out (e.g., *official* → "offcal"). The patient's own recollections are that he had been virtually blind for a short period during the acute phase and that, as vision gradually returned, he saw colors before shapes and probably the color red more clearly than others. One of his first visual memories was of seeing a mass of green which he realized was grass in the hospital grounds. He was then able to identify a cigarette package held up by the examining doctor, by paying attention to its color and shape (there is a note in the records stating that he was able to identify a yellow package of Goldflake cigarettes some 3 weeks after injury).

The most recent neurological examination of this patient, in 1969, showed a spastic right hemiplegia, minimal wasting of the right leg and arm, and decreased sensation to light touch and pin prick on the right side. He had a complete bilateral, altitudinal, visual field defect and also a defect in the upper fields which was not congruous, almost certainly as a result of his inability to maintain fixation. Visual acuity, corrected, was J6 in both eyes. Psychological examinations have consistently shown a pattern of selective language deficit against a background of average nonverbal ability. The difficulty with spelling and writing has persisted despite an average vocabulary. He has no difficulty in naming objects to confrontation, and his speech is grammatical and coherent, although slightly hesitant and slurred.

The patient recalls that he began to read again 3 or 4 months after leaving hospital, although at that time the print seemed blurred. His reading gradually improved, reaching its present level about 18 months after discharge. He still finds it tiring to read, particularly at night, after a busy day. He worked full time as a pay-office clerk in a government department until his recent retirement. The scope of his work was always strictly limited by the severe visual field defect, which led to his missing or colliding with objects in the peripheral visual field.

The nature of A.T.'s reading errors is very similar to the pattern observed in A. G. An overwhelming majority of errors are visual confusions, omissions and transpositions. These are illustrated in Table 6.2.

The effects of syntactic class, word frequency, and word length upon A.T.'s reading performance are minimal or nonexistent. Semantic and derivational errors were never observed. Neologisms did occur, albeit very rarely, for example, *build* → "bliber . . . blib," and they were recognized as such.

Although the visuo-spatial component clearly predominants in A.T.'s errors, it may not be the only source of impairment; errors of the type *fad* → "fade," *met* → "meet," *rid* → "ride," *rob* → "robe," *rut* → "root" are frequently in evidence. It is possible that the vowel-lengthening which characterizes these errors is the result of the subject's having adopted the (covert) strategy of naming the medial vowel.

TABLE 6.2 Reading Errors Made by A.T. (Case 2)

1. *car*	⟶	oar
2. *lit*	⟶	hit
3. *nap*	⟶	map
4. *paw*	⟶	pew
5. *rid*	⟶	rig
6. *street*	⟶	treat
7. *angel*	⟶	angle
8. *song*	⟶	snug
9. *broad*	⟶	board
10. *saucer*	⟶	secure
11. *persuasion*	⟶	precision
12. *arrangement*	⟶	argument

CASE 3 (R.B. NO. 22042)

This patient, aged 20, was admitted to the Department of Neurological Surgery at Oxford on October 15, 1972. He was unconscious at the time, responding only to painful stimuli, and had a right hemiparesis. A left carotid angiogram showed a large left-temporal, avascular lesion. At operation, approximately 50 mg of blood was aspirated from what was possibly an astrocytomatous cyst, situated in the mid-part of the superior temporal gyrus in the left hemisphere. The brain smear examined at operation indicated that he had a Grade I glioma, but subsequent studies of other specimens of tissue taken from the middle and inferior temporal gyri did not show any frank tumor although there was an increase in astrocytes.

The patient regained consciousness and, during the first post-operative week, showed a moderate degree of expressive dysphasia. Dyslexia was reported as the salient feature and was disproportionately severe compared with spontaneous speech and object-naming. The patient's reading difficulties were observed on October 25, 10 days after the operation. At that time, he could understand simple instructions. His speech was slow and somewhat slurred, but he spoke grammatically and fairly fluently; automatic word series, with the exception of the alphabet, were intact. Naming difficulties, barely discernible in conversation, could be detected on formal testing, although they were not marked. The patient made numerous errors in reading individual words; and writing (although legible) and spelling were also impaired.

The patient then had a course of radiotherapy and when reexamined by the consultant radiotherapist, on February 9, 1973, was judged to have made a good general improvement. No residual aphasia was detected in clinical examination. Psychological testing also reflected this improvement: His vocabulary and verbal IQ scores were in the bright–average range; his digit span had increased and was

TABLE 6.3 Reading Errors Made by R.B. (Case 3)

1. *greet*	$\longrightarrow$	green
2. *elope*	$\longrightarrow$	envelope
3. *factory*	$\longrightarrow$	facts
4. *lend*	$\longrightarrow$	leg
5. *abolish*	$\longrightarrow$	boil
6. *had*	$\longrightarrow$	hat
7. *led*	$\longrightarrow$	leg
8. *hat*	$\longrightarrow$	/pag/
9. *mow*	$\longrightarrow$	/mau/
10. *moist*	$\longrightarrow$	/mŏst/
11. *oust*	$\longrightarrow$	/ost/
12. *applaud*	$\longrightarrow$	/àpplau/

within normal limits; no impairment was detected in verbal memory and learning tasks; and he no longer made errors in individual word reading, though his speed of reading for comprehension was slower than normal.

The majority of R.B.'s reading errors bear a clear visual similarity to the stimulus items. Errors involve predominantly, although not solely, the terminal letters of the stimuli; the words appear to have been read globally. It is as if minimal cues have triggered a response which is not controlled by the fine detail of the visual configuration (see Table 6.3, 1–8).

In addition, however, R.B. does not produce a number of errors (e.g., 9–12 in Table 6.3) which seem to indicate a lack of control over the relationship between orthography and the sound pattern of English. These "grapheme–phoneme" errors are much in evidence when he is attempting to read words containing vowel-digraphs, although it is, of course, difficult to rule out a visual interpretation of such cases. R.B. does not make semantic substitutions or circumlocutions when reading individual words; such word-finding difficulties are, however, in evidence on his object-naming performance, for example, *horseshoe* → "horse . . . of its feet," *anvil* → "thing a blacksmith uses." The effect of syntactic class is detectable in R.B.'s reading: Concrete nouns are considerably easier for him than either adjectives or verbs; very occasionally a putative derivational error occurs, for example, *silent* → "silence." Word frequency plays only a small role in determining his performance.

CASE 4 (J.C. NO. 17959/922)

This patient was wounded in 1945 at the age of 20, when he was hit by a grenade fragment in the posterior region of the left cerebral hemisphere, sustaining a depressed fracture. He was taken prisoner at the time, and the wound was debrided in a field hospital. About 3 months later, rejoining the Allied forces, he was found to have a large left temporo-parietal lesion, with brain fungus. He was severely aphasic, had a right hemiparesis and was deaf in his left ear. He started to speak again when he was repatriated and his speech recovered substantially in about a year. He did not spontaneously recall any marked difficulty in understanding speech during the acute phase, but there are no clinical notes to describe his condition at that time.

On examination in 1947, the patient was found to have a right hemianopia and a right hemiparesis with cortical sensory loss. He had marked difficulty in reading and writing but his spontaneous speech was considered to be good; however, he himself reported occasional word-finding difficulties. There has been no change in his neurological condition since that time, nor has he noticed any significant improvement in reading and writing.

When he was examined in 1969, the patient was found to have a right hemianopia and a right hemiparesis. There was good power in all the limbs, but the left arm and leg were stronger than the right. Reflexes were normal and symmetrical, and the plantars were flexor. Light touch, pin prick, joint position sense, and vibration sense were intact in the extremeties; and stereognosis and two-point discrimination were normal in both hands. There was a loss of position sense in the right hand. The patient still has occasional nocturnal major epileptic fits.

The salient feature of the patient's psychological examination in 1969 was his gross difficulty in reading and writing. He could print his address but little else. Oral spelling was also severely impaired, and digit span was reduced. His immediate and delayed recall of story material was virtually normal, but he was impaired in tests of paired-associate learning, right–left orientation, and calculation. He obtained average scores in most of the nonverbal, performance tasks, including block design and maze learning. Nominal difficulties were barely detectable in formal testing and his speech was remarkably fluent and grammatical: He had been elected a shop steward in his union—presumably in view of his effective speech and ready wit—but reading difficulties made it impossible for him to accept the office. Visual acuity, corrected, was J4 in the right eye and J6 in the left. He works full time as a skilled electrician and has no difficulty in deciphering wiring diagrams.

The most notable feature of J.C.'s performance is that he frequently appears to read as if he does not know the language but rather is acting as a simple orthography-to-sound "translator." Some words J.C. reads quickly and accurrately; in such cases J.C. claims that he did not "read" the words, but rather "recognized" them. Other words he reads slowly and laboriously, sometimes "sounding out" the constituent elements; these items, which J.C. says he is "reading," are frequently, although not invariably misread. It is a well-known fact of English orthography that the correct phonetic values for graphemes often cannot be assigned in a single left-to-right pass over the individual letters of a

TABLE 6.4 Reading Errors Made by J.C. (Case 4)

1. *route*	⟶	rote . . . rut-th . . . rout
2. *monarch*	⟶	monarutch
3. *disease*	⟶	decease
4. *of*	⟶	off
5. *guest*	⟶	just
6. *barge*	⟶	bargain
7. *listen*	⟶	Liston
8. *island*	⟶	izland
9. *bike*	⟶	bik
10. *omit*	⟶	ommit
11. *different*	⟶	difference
12. *govern*	⟶	guv . . . guver . . . governer

word; the "unit" of visual-to-acoustic coding is usually longer than a latter. J.C., however, frequently attempts to assign sound values on the basis of "one letter, one syllable." If one adopts such a strategy, English letters become ambiguous— compare the values of *a* in *fan, fade,* and *father,* or the values of *g* in *girl* and *gin*. It is consistent with this "one letter at a time" procedure that J.C. is particularly liable to error when attempting to read words that contain vowel diagraphs, consonant clusters, highly ambiguous consonants such as *s, f, c, g, f,* and *r,* and silent consonants. Examples of some of J.C.'s errors are given in Table 6.4.

CASE 5 (H.A. NO. 325591)

This patient, aged 36, was admitted to hospital on January 30, 1970, with a diagnosis of myocardial infarction. Two days before admission he had had palpitations, and the day before admission, he had experienced a severe, crushing pain in the chest lasting 2 to 3 hours. His previous medical history was negative with the exception of migraine. An EKG showed an inferior infarct, and he was admitted to the coronary care unit. The day after admission, he had nodal tachycardia with hypotension for which he received treatment, and 24 hours later, he produced purulent sputum, with pyrexia of over 100°F. Despite anti-coagulant treatment, on February 13, he suddenly developed a right-sided stroke with facial weakness, right hemiplegia, and severe dysphasia. The weakness gradually resolved, and on March 2, he was discharged to a rehabilitation center where he remained for several months. There was no visual field defect and visual acuity was unimpaired. He was judged to have made a good recovery and started to work in an assembly plant in June.

The first psychological examination of this patient took place in October 1971, when a mild expressive dysphasia was apparent. His spontaneous speech was extremely fluent but occasionally paraphasic. There were slight word-finding

TABLE 6.5 Reading Errors Made by H.A. (Case 5

1. *regular*	$\longrightarrow$	regardless
2. *intrude*	$\longrightarrow$	interlude
3. *prefer*	$\longrightarrow$	preface . . . or prefix
4. *frail*	$\longrightarrow$	fragile
5. *Jane*	$\longrightarrow$	Janet
6. *Helen*	$\longrightarrow$	Henry
7. *siege*	$\longrightarrow$	scene, or Wild West days
8. *high*	$\longrightarrow$	height
9. *persuade*	$\longrightarrow$	persuasion
10. *calmness*	$\longrightarrow$	calm
11. *arrival*	$\longrightarrow$	arrive
12. *furniture*	$\longrightarrow$	furnish

difficulties, but he had no problem with a formal object-naming task. Rote speech was intact, and he had a digit span of 5. There was a moderate verbal memory deficit: His recall of narrative was meagre, and he had difficulty in a paired-associate, word-learning task. The salient residual symptoms were dyslexia and dysgraphia. (Army efficiency certificates established that he had previously been fully literate.) He could name all the letters of the alphabet, and he could write the words that he could spell orally, and vice versa, but he made errors at the 5- to 6-year-old level in spelling three-letter words.

The vast majority of H.A.'s reading errors show a strong visuo-spatial component; the first letters (the first syllable of multisyllabic words) are almost invariably read correctly. (This can be seen in examples 1–3 of Table 6.5.) Overall word-shape is often preserved. Although only one outright semantic circumlocution was noted (example 7 in Table 6.5), it is possible that a certain mild lexical instability is represented by the combined visual and semantic errors shown in examples 4, 5, and 6. Semantic paraphasias do occur, albeit very occasionally, in H.A.'s spontaneous speech; for example, "reading" for *writing* and "Ireland" for *Wales*.

Derivational errors appear quite frequently in H.A.'s misreadings (Table 6.5, examples 8 to 12); these take the form of both predicate to nominal (e.g., *defend* → "defendant," *heroic* → "hero") and nominal to predicate misreadings (e.g., *classification* → "classified," *truth* → "true"). The latter error-type is, however, much more frequent than the former (in the approximate ratio of 3 to 1). No word-frequency bias is to be found in this subject's misreadings, although concrete nouns are read with greater accuracy than either adjectives or verbs.

CASE 6 (K.U. NO. SM/900)

This man was wounded in 1944 at the age of 23, when he sustained a penetrating left parieto-occipital gunshot wound; at least one metal foreign body penetrated forward to reach the region of the thalamus, on the left side. The wound was debrided, but convalescence was complicated by the development of hernia cerebri and cerebral abscess. The patient had been wounded in India and was in hospital in the Far East. During that time, his speech was described as slow and slurred; and he showed word-finding difficulties but no obvious difficulty in understanding what was said to him. He had a right homonymous hemianopia and a right hemiparesis.

During hospital admissions in the U.K. in 1947 and 1948, the patient was reported to have a right hemianopia, right facial palsy of the upper motor neurone type, and a right hemianaesthesia. His aphasia was assessed by a speech therapist in 1948, who described a marked degree of expressive aphasia with slowness in recalling words rather than a failure to retrieve them. The speech was slow but not dysarthric. The dyslexia was described as a severe disability: "Reading of nouns is now roughly 90% accurate but the reading of the small connecting words is about 5% only." He had gross difficulties in writing and could write only his name, address, and a few words; however, he could copy. Follow-up reports from a speech therapist in 1962 described speech as adequate for conversation but sometimes telegrammatic, especially when hurried or excited.

This patient emigrated and was seen briefly in 1970 when he returned to the hospital for a brief visit. Neurological examination showed a right hemianopia, a right supranuclear facial palsy, and a very mild nerve deafness on the right. There was a severe spastic right hemiparesis, especially involving the right hand. There was no movement of dorsiflexion of the right foot, and a caliper was worn for this. There was blunting of sensation to all superficial modalities on the right side, more marked in the right upper limb, and especially in the right hand. Tactile localization was grossly impaired in the right arm, especially in the right hand. Postural loss could be demonstrated in the finger and wrist on the right. Vibration sense was impaired on the right, but there were no cerebellar signs.

A short psychological examination, during the above-mentioned brief visit to the U.K., was focused almost entirely on the problem of dyslexia. There was, however, evidence of word-finding difficulty in spontaneous speech. The patient was usually able to get across the gist of his message but used phrases rather than sentences, interspersed with stereotyped and repetitive expressions. He occasionally had difficulty in grasping the meaning of a question. Rote speech was slow but intact. Oral and written spelling were severely impaired. He was, however, able to name 19 out of 20 photographs of objects including "microscope" and "stethoscope." For the past 4 years, he has worked as a part-time electronics technician in a university laboratory abroad, and there is therefore at least circumstantial evidence that the impairment of language is selective and does not stem from a more generalized intellectual impairment.

K.U.'s reading performance is very similar to that reported for the previous case (H.A.). The majority of K.U.'s errors possess a considerable degree of visual similarity to the stimulus item. (This can be seen in examples 1–3 of Table 6.6).

TABLE 6.6 Reading Errors Made by K.U. (Case 6)

1. *expect*	$\longrightarrow$	explain
2. *remote*	$\longrightarrow$	renovate
3. *insect*	$\longrightarrow$	secure
4. *Susan*	$\longrightarrow$	Susie
5. *frail*	$\longrightarrow$	fragile
6. *diamond*	$\longrightarrow$	necklace
7. *news*	$\longrightarrow$	paper
8. *luxury*	$\longrightarrow$	luxurious
9. *truth*	$\longrightarrow$	true
10. *wise*	$\longrightarrow$	wisdom
11. *prefer*	$\longrightarrow$	preference
12. *inquire*	$\longrightarrow$	inquiry

Very occasionally the possibility arises that semantic factors may be interacting with the apperceptive failures (examples 4 and 5). Two outright semantic paralexic errors were observed: *diamond* → "necklace," and *news* → "paper." It is interesting in the light of Case 8 that these errors are more plausibly regarded as syntagmatic than as paradigmatic paralexias.

Substantial numbers of derivational errors are also to be found in the corpus collected from K.U. (examples 8 to 12). In the case of verbs and their nominals, errors are always in the direction of misreading a base verb as its related nominal, never vice versa; in the case of adjectives and their related nominals, errors are usually in the direction of misreading a nominal as its underlying adjective. Errors in the reverse direction occur very rarely. Nouns (concrete but not abstract) are read with slightly greater accuracy than predicates, and a noticeable effect of word frequency can be detected.

CASE 7 (B.R. NO. 531434)

This woman, aged 44, was admitted to hospital in February 1972 with the diagnosis of right hemiplegia and dysphasia following a stroke. She had been very well until the morning of her admission, when she was found lying on the floor, aphasic, with a right-sided weakness. There was no previous history of hypertension. On examination, the CVS pulse was 80 regular and the blood pressure was 170/105. Examination of the nervous system showed a conjugate deviation of the eyes to the left, a right homonymous hemianopia, right facial weakness, flaccid paralysis in the right arm and leg, and increased tendon reflexes on the right with an extensor right plantar. No papilloedema or hypertensive changes in the fundi were observed. The CSF was bloodstained, with a pressure of 175 mm of water; EKG sinus showed rhythm with no evidence of hypertension. Biochemical screening was normal. A left carotid angiogram showed that the middle cerebral artery and its branches were depressed outward and a little downward, and there was some midline shift. An intracerebral haematoma was aspirated through a burrhole on March 6. The patient was transferred on March 21 for rehabilitation and was discharged home in June 1972 to be seen at regular intervals at follow-up clinics.

A year after the stroke, the patient's condition was judged to be static. She showed a residual right hemiparesis with a spastic right arm: Elbow flexion and finger flexion were present and the fingers could be extended passively; hip flexion and ankle dorsiflexion were weak on the right, although tone was normal and knee extension good. There was impairment of joint position sense in the right fingers and toes and of vibration sense in the right wrist. Pinprick was reported to have an unpleasant quality on the right side of the body, and there was sensory inattention to pinprick on the right side. The patient showed a severe, predominantly expressive dysphasia but could usually make herself understood with a combination of speech, paraphrase, and gesture. Vocabulary and story recall scores were very low, but her score on a nonverbal, intelligence test (Ravens Progressive Matrices) was at the 82nd percentile for her age group.

Reports of her attempts to read during the early phase of rehabilitation note that she was often confused by "common words such as 'the' and 'of'." A later report in June 1973 stated that she could recognize and name common objects and produce appropriate yes—no answers to simple questions. She had difficulty, however, in repeating digits and sentences and in reading aloud from a news-paper. A tendency to produce substitutions was noted (e.g., *trapped* → "prison-er," *sea* → "river"). The present reading data were obtained in May 1973.

Case 7 presents a range of error-types similar to, albeit slightly wider than, those of cases 5 and 6. Substantial numbers of B.R.'s errors are visually similar to the stimulus items (see examples 1—4, Table 6.7). In contradistinction to cases 5 and 6, however, the locus of the visual misapprehension frequently involves the initial segments of the word (see example 1; also, e.g., *defend* → "fend," *imply* → "reply," *elope* → "lope"). While such errors do appear in the corpora collected from H.A. (Case 5) and K.U. (Case 6), they are extremely rare (e.g. from H.A., *gentleness* → "forgetfulness"; and from K.U., *insect* → "secure"). The presence of uncorrected neologisms (examples 5 and 6) is perhaps indicative of a wider aphasic involvement in B.R.'s reading. Similarly, the presence of putative (example 7) and outright (examples 8—10) semantic errors or circumlocutions is consistent with the type of word-finding difficulties that are apparent in B.R.'s spontaneous speech.

When putative derivational errors occur (examples 11 and 12), they are always in the direction of misreading a nominal form as a predicate. However, given B.R.'s tendency to drop entire syllables in her misreadings (e.g., *defend* → "fend," *domicile* → "mobile," *destruction* → "struction"), it is by no means clear that a derivational analysis of such erorrs is appropriate. Nonetheless, the presence of

TABLE 6.7 Reading Errors Made by B.R. (Case 7)

1. *impact*	⟶	pact
2. *stale*	⟶	snail
3. *hierarchy*	⟶	hereditary
4. *porous*	⟶	porcupine
5. *evade*	⟶	vading, is it?
6. *expect*	⟶	expeek
7. *frail*	⟶	fragile
8. *January*	⟶	February, no March . . . no this one here . . . January
9. *parent*	⟶	No . . . oh, my Father and Mother
10. *infection*	⟶	No . . . when you've got a cut
11. *subtraction*	⟶	subtract
12. *inducement*	⟶	induce . . . no, introduce

semantic misreadings, particularly noticeable when B.R. is reading sentences (e.g. *She had a new frock* → "This had a new dress"), points to a lexical instability over and above failures of visual apprehension. Finally, concrete nouns are read more accurately than either adjectives or verbs, although there is no detectable effect of word frequency in B.R.'s corpus.

CASE 8 (G.R. NO. 8713/6)

This man was wounded accidentally in 1944 at the age of 20, when a bullet from his own sten-gun penetrated his brain in the region of the left Sylvian fissure and emerged in the superior parietal lobe of the left hemisphere. This severe through-and-through injury resulted in global aphasia and a right hemiplegia. Five weeks after the injury, the patient was using grunts to express "yes" and "no" but was unable to repeat any words; he could not read or write. Subsequently, there was a gradual improvement in understanding language and spontaneous speech, but severe difficulties in reading and writing persisted.

Neurological examination more than 20 years after injury showed right anosmia, a right homonymous hemianopia more marked in the upper quadrant, mild right facial weakness of upper motor neurone type, and a profound right spastic hemiplegia with relative sparing of the leg; all sensory modalities were moderately impaired in the right limbs. The patient has continued to have occasional epileptic fits.

Preliminary accounts of follow-up investigations (1963, 1964, 1965) have been published elsewhere (Marshall & Newcombe, 1973; Newcombe & Marshall, 1975). Psychological examination showed well-preserved nonverbal intelligence (WAIS Performance Scale and Ravens Progressive Matrices) and nonverbal visual and spatial skills (visual recognition memory and maze-learning tasks). Comprehension of language was relatively good for ordinary conversational purposes, but impairment could be demonstrated on formal testing (Token Test and other experimental language tasks).

The patient's spontaneous speech was telegrammatic and halting, with marked word-finding difficulties. Reading, writing, and oral spelling were severely impaired. His span for digits or unrelated nouns was 3; and his immediate and delayed recall of narrative was limited to approximately three items.

The accuracy with which G.R. can read single words is critically dependent upon the variables of word frequency and syntactic class. The patient reads correctly between 60% and 90% of the concrete nouns with which he has been presented, but only about 10% of the adjectives, verbs, and abstract nouns. With other parts of speech (function words), his accuracy is no better than 1%. A sample of G.R.'s erroneous responses is given in Table 6.8. Although G.R. makes substantial numbers of visual errors (example 9), his predominant error-type is semantic. Over 50% of G.R.'s misreadings bear a close semantic similarity to the stimulus item which was presented (examples 1–6); the ratio of semantic to visual errors is greater for nouns than for either adjectives or verbs (Marshall & Newcombe, 1966). The majority of G.R.'s paralexic errors are outright semantic substitutions which are easily distinguishable from circumlocutory responses of the type illustrated in examples 7 and 8. Having made a semantic error, G.R. usually considered that his response was correct, although occasionally such a response would be preceded by the remark "I'm not sure" or succeeded by "Not quite right." He was not invariably confident about correct responses. Approximately 5% of G.R.'s errors would appear to involve a visual misapprehension followed by a semantic substitution (examples 10–12): thus *gratitude* → "alone" is presumably mediated internally by "solitude," *allegory* → "lizard" by "alligator," and *perfect* → "scent" by "perfume." Syntactic response biases are also to be observed in G.R.'s misreadings. Thus nominalized adjectives, such as *truth*, are frequently misread as their underlying form (*true*); the reverse bias, however,

TABLE 6.8 Response Errors Made by G.R. (Case 8)

1. *soccer*	⟶	football
2. *arsenic*	⟶	poison
3. *beggar*	⟶	tramp
4. *bivouac*	⟶	camping
5. *ill*	⟶	sick
6. *close*	⟶	shut
7. *amusement*	⟶	something to do with fun fair
8. *learn*	⟶	something to do with books
9. *perform*	⟶	perfume
10. *gratitude*	⟶	alone
11. *allegory*	⟶	lizard
12. *perfect*	⟶	scent

obtains with verbs. Nominals, such as *arrival,* are read more accurately than their base forms (*arrive*), and errors of the type *arrive* → "arrival" are common (Marshall, Newcombe & Marshall, 1970). Semantic errors are also observed when G.R. reads sentences, for example, *Put five shillings on a good horse* → "Five bob . . . best horse," and when he is asked to construct a sentence which contains a particular (written) word, as for example, *watch* → "My clock fast," *common* → "House where Lords speak."

COMPARISONS AMONG THE EIGHT CASES

One would expect on an a priori basis that a skill as complex as reading should be susceptible to breakdown on a number of levels, and it is clearly the case in the foregoing sequence of dyslexic subjects that the range of impairments (and the range of functions preserved) is considerable. Thus subject 1 (A.G.) presents with a deficit in linguistic skills restricted to the modality of written language. His intact command of the language (and, in particular, the absence of any detectable word-finding difficulties) serves to constrain his output when reading aloud; easy access to lexical representations—which can be addressed by way of a visual stimulus—restricts A.G.'s reading errors to English words. The absence of syntactic or frequency biases (at least in conditions when no time pressure is imposed) seems to indicate that the full range of the lexicon is available to A.G., a suggestion consistent with the clinical inference of a disconnection syndrome. Errors are interpretable in terms of visual misapprehensions—a form of impairment which, in A.G.'s case, extends considerably beyond his disabilities in perceiving visual language. Subject 2 (A.T.) demonstrates that a similar, albeit less severe, impairment may be found as a salient, residual sign of occipital injury. The relative degree of dyslexic impairment in the two patients is reflected not only in the number of errors made by A.G. and A.T. but also in the fact that A.T.'s erroneous responses are visually much more similar to the stimulus item than are A.G.'s responses.

The pattern of dyslexic impairment begins to change, however, once features of word-finding difficulty begin to enter the clinical picture. Subject 3 (R. B.) manifested such difficulties, albeit infrequently, at the time that the reading errors shown in Table 6.3 were collected; thus circumlocutions were observed on formal tests of object-naming (e.g., *anvil* → ". . . thing a blacksmith uses"). Associated with this picture, we see that R.B.'s reading performance does show slight effects due to word frequency (Hf > Lf) and substantial effects of syntactic class (N > $\frac{A}{V}$). In this situation where the correct word is unavailable, two further possibilities for erroneous responses (other than visual errors) are open to the subject: (1) Given that the visual stimulus has elicited an internal semantic representation, the subject may produce a circumlocutory response or an outright semantic substitution. (2) If an internal semantic representation is not available, the subject may attempt to read by converting the visual representation into sound through grapheme–phoneme correspondence rules. As is well known, English orthography is somewhat complex and irregular when seen from such a viewpoint. One would expect, then, that neologisms will be much in evidence when a patient adopts this strategy. Such errors are indeed to be found in R.B.'s performance—for example, *mow* → "mau." Unless one "recognizes" the word *mow*, there is no way in which one can tell that it rhymes with *low* and *tow* rather than with *how* and *now.*

Difficulties in recognizing visual words qua words (i.e., as semantically interpretable stimuli) can, however, be found in the absence of word-finding difficulty in spontaneous speech or in formal naming tests (Case 4). In such cases, the dyslexia may be interpreted as a (partial) disconnection syndrome, and in subject 4 (J.C.), it is perhaps significant that a deficit in (directly) addressing semantic representations from orthography should be seen in the context of paired-associate learning difficulties. J.C. does "recognize" some words—with a fairly substantial bias towards concrete nouns and a slight frequency bias—but his errors indicate that, when recognition fails, the subject adopts a "sounding-out" (grapheme-to-phoneme) strategy which is peculiarly liable to error. Neologisms abound, and when "by accident," an error is a real English word (or even a rough approximation to one), J.C. assigns the meaning appropriate to his response, not a meaning appropriate to the stimulus item.

When reading is not controlled by grapheme–phoneme correspondence rules, visual errors may again predominate, and generalized word-finding difficulty will be reflected in circumlocutions and frank semantic substitutions. Subject 5 (H. A.) presents with a relatively mild condition of this type. Semantic paraphasias occur, albeit very rarely, both in spontaneous speech and in reading. Similarly, systematic derivational errors point to a mild instability of lexical representations. Subject 6 (K.U.) demonstrates that a very similar pattern of reading disability may persist as a residual condition some 25 years after injury. "Central" deficits of lexical access—which are made manifest by word-finding difficulties and various syntactic biases in erroneous responses—may be highly resistant to "spontaneous recovery," formal retraining, and the adoption of strategies whereby the patient can circumvent his disability.

A similarly wide range of error-types—visual, semantic, and, perhaps, derivational—is to be found in subject 7's performance. Here the severity of the aphasic condition at the time of testing is such that—as contrasted with cases 6 and 8—lexical knowledge does not invariably constrain the patient's responses to the set of English words. Her word-finding difficulty will sometimes show itself in a circumlocution (examples 9 and 10), and on other occasions frank neologisms are found (e.g., "vading," "expeek"). This does imply, however, that the subject can—albeit imperfectly—utilize grapheme–phoneme correspondences in her attempts at reading. But this strategy is not sufficiently well preserved to allow the subject to retrieve the pronounciation of "infection" subsequent to her circumlocutory demonstration that she has comprehended the word ("No . . . when you've got a cut").

In case 8, it would appear that the use of grapheme–phoneme correspondences is totally unavailable to the subject. The nature of his errors (visual and/or semantic) combined with his inability to read nonsense syllables (the latter customarily provoke the response "Don't know") imply that some fairly direct route from visual analysis to semantic representation is being utilized. The nature of the "semantic representation" has been the subject of some discussion recently, and it has been suggested that "images" (particularly visual images) may be the initial form of coding for meaning which such patients adopt (Shallice & Warrington, 1975; Richardson, 1975a). Although there is evidence for this view in the fact of substantial correlations between the rated imageability of words and the success rate for reading them in cases of "deep" dyslexia, it remains to be shown that the nature of the errors can be explicated by postulating that "internal images" are being named when such patients read aloud. Examples from G.R., which appear embarrassing to such an account, include *history* → "geography," *comradeship* → "friendship," *bravery* → "hero," *answer* → "question," *cost* → "price," *finished* → "the end."

In outlining this taxonomy of error, we are not proposing that linguistic patterns of error can invariably be linked with either locus or etiology of lesion. There is, however, a link between these patterns and the relative preponderance of literal or verbal errors. Studies of well-defined cases of dyslexia have shown an association between literal dyslexia and anterior lesions and between verbal dyslexia and posterior lesions (Hécaen, 1967; Wechsler, Weinstein, & Antin, 1972). Benson et al. (1971) state that these two varieties of alexia "do exist clinically and indicate significant variations in the site of pathology." These authors also distinguish between two groups of patients with literal dyslexia: those with anterior lesions in Broca's area who can nevertheless point to named letters, and those with lesions of the angular gyrus who cannot either name letters or point to letters on command (cf. Benson & Geschwind, 1969). It is not uncommon for patients with global aphasia to show a specific difficulty in letter naming (see Alajouanine et al., 1960; Mohr, Sidman, Stoddard, Leichester, & Rosenberger, 1973), and our patient, G.R., fits into this schema: He cannot name half the letters of the alphabet, although he can read words composed of these letters, and he cannot point to letters on command. The lesion has caused extensive damage to the language areas, undoubtedly involving both Broca's area and the region of the angular gyrus. X-rays of the entry and exit site of the bullet, and the neurosurgical report of the operation, however, suggest that the occipital lobe was spared. In contrast, patient A.T., whose injury was clearly posterior, shows no difficulty with individual letter recognition but makes visual errors, especially when reading short words for which there are several alternative responses based on a single error (e.g., *bid* → "lid," "bid," "mid," "did," "hip," "hit").

The pattern of error in an individual patient may change considerably in the course of a few months or even a year. Time of testing, therefore, may be an important factor in assessing the linguistic and anatomical correlates of dyslexia. Accordingly, we have undertaken a few longitudinal studies of individual patients with acquired reading difficulties. These were also designed to provide data concerning the natural history of recovery, its time scale, and prognostic implications. Previous studies have shown the recovery of reading skills after left temporal lobectomy (Hécaen *et al.*, 1952) or substantial improvement after carefully designed training (Luria, 1970). Conversely, negligible improvement after two years of "intensive efforts at retraining in reading" was reported (Ajax, 1967) for a young, highly motivated student who developed a relatively pure dyslexia after the surgical removal of a left occipital arteriovenous malformation. The contrast would appear to be that between a pure and permanent disconnection syndrome (comparable to that shown by Déjerine's patient during the last 4 years of his life, prior to his second and fatal stroke) and partial damage to areas critically involved in the reading process. The four patients whom we have tested repeatedly fall into the latter category, and brief case histories are presented below.

Patient M.B., aged 41, whose history has been described in detail in previous publications (Newcombe & Marshall, 1973; Newcombe *et al.*, 1975; Marshall, Newcombe, & Hiorns, 1975), developed a large left occipital abscess secondary to a pulmonary infection. She had a transient hemiparesis and a right homonymous hemianopia which persisted. Initially, she had a global aphasia which slowly receded, leaving a permanent residual dyslexia and moderate nominal difficulties. Comprehension and spontaneous speech were fairly well restored.

Patient W.M., aged 67, was surgically treated for the removal of a meningioma arising from a pedicle of the choroid plexus, discovered in the course of routine investigations after a road traffic accident. There was a rapidly improving dysphasia, mainly of the expressive type, following the operation. Slight nominal defects persisted, detectable in a naming task with a wide range of items but barely noticeable in spontaneous conversation. The ability to read individual words was virtually restored, with the exception of a very occasional visual error.

Patients T.R. and G.P. were young men of 17, who incurred closed head injuries in separate road traffic accidents. There were no permanent neurological sequelae. Dysphasic features, present in the acute phase, resolved rapidly. Dyslexia was the salient symptom and cleared more slowly. T.R.'s capacity to read was restored; G.P., who had never been a competent reader, probably regained his former level.

The performance of these four patients in successive tests of object naming and word reading is plotted in Figure 6.1. The time course varies greatly: M.B. improved over a period of at least 60 weeks; W.M. and T.R. recovered their ability to read single words in 12 weeks. The shapes of the recovery curves, however, had features in common, and we have already suggested (Newcombe *et al.,* 1975) that they can be described mathematically in a simple formula, incorporating the asymptote ($y = \alpha + \beta e^{\chi}$, when α represents the asymptote, β the constant, that is, the number of errors, e the rate of learning, and χ represents time). In cases where the recovery of function is complete (for example, all four patients recovered the ability to name letters and to point to named letters before they reached their asymptote in the word-reading tests), the data can be described in terms of a simple linear regression model. These recovery curves, we suggest, carry information about the duration and limits of spontaneous recovery by indicating when and at what level of performance an asymptote value is reached. They do not speak to the linguistic changes that may be occurring as the patient improves. If we consider one variable—syntactic class—we see that it may be significant for some patients (e.g., M.B. and W.M.)

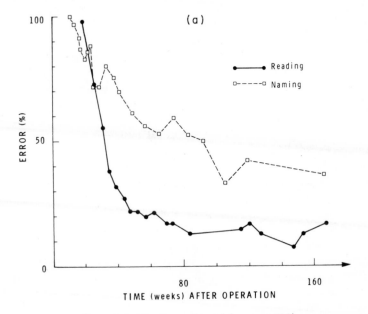

Figure 6.1   (Caption and part (c) on page 282)

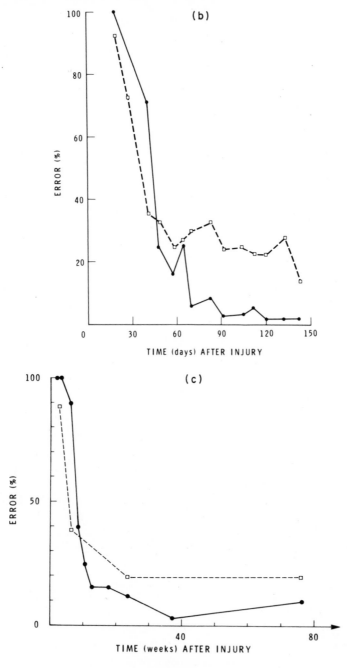

Figure 6.1

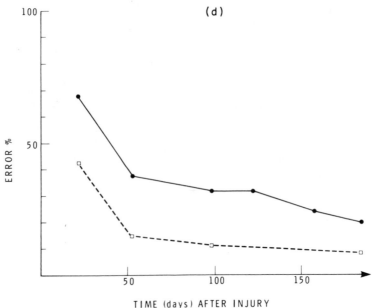

Figure 6.1 (a) Patient M.B.: Successive recordings of error percentage on reading (List 1) and object-naming tasks. (b) Patient W.M.: Successive recordings of error percentage on reading (List 1) and object-naming tasks. (c) Patient T.R.: Successive recordings of error percentage on reading (List 1) and object-naming tasks. (d) Patient G.P.: Successive recordings of error percentage on reading (List 1) and object-naming tasks.

during the initial sessions of testing when they were only able to read a few words, mainly nouns. Errors were often mixed, including both visual and grapheme–phoneme mistranslations. This syntactic bias was not apparent during the final sessions when their reading had improved. Their residual errors had a clear-cut phonological or visual basis, independent of syntactic class.

The noun bias, which we reported earlier (Marshall & Newcombe, 1966) as a striking feature of one of the patients (G.R.) and which is probably characteristic of patients with reading difficulties in the setting of frank dysphasia, raises interesting questions about the development and nature of the lexicon. Normal children between the age of 6 and 11 have shown the same bias on our reading material, List I (Newcombe, Marshall & Richardson, in preparation). It may be that the names of objects are acquired earlier than verbs and are more resistant to interference with the reading process than verbs or adjectives, and age of acquisition may be an important variable to be considered in addition to, or in conjunction with, word frequency (cf. Carroll & White, 1973).

Within the noun class, however, concrete nouns are reputedly easier for the aphasic patient to read than abstract substantives (see Goldstein, 1948), and there has been some experimental support for this view (see Halpern, 1965). Faust (1955), referring to a patient who made semantic errors in reading, noted that "it is not the length of the word which is crucial for the recognition of it, but rather its relation to concrete objects and to what is visually picturable," and he interprets the difficulty in reading function words, shown by such patients, in this light. Subsequent studies have invoked the role of imagery as an alternative (nonverbal) coding system in facilitating the performance of dyslexic patients (Shallice & Warrington, 1975; Richardson, 1975a,b). It is certainly interesting to consider semantic errors as the result of using the coding system of imagery just as a patient with a disorder of object recognition may be using a picture lexicon to get at a certain class of objects without being able to recognize all its distinguishing features and hence its specific identity.

There are some indications that the use of imagery cannot always explain the performance of patients showing a strong syntactic bias and a tendency to make semantic errors in reading. Saffran and Marin (1975) have reported that their patients found it significantly easier to read words like *brown* and *holly* when they were presented as proper names than as color adjectives or plants although the latter two categories are eminently picturable. There may also be wide individual differences in the use of imagery. In fact, we speculate that Beringer and Stein's case of "pure" dyslexia, who made numerous semantic errors, might have had a strongly developed imagery system before the illness. Otherwise, this patient is the only clear example that we have been able to find of a subject, apparently without dysphasia, who produced semantic errors in reading. We have not, however, been able to track down the reply to Minkowski's (1930, p. 475) unequivocal question about the possibility of dysphasic symptoms in this case.

In summary, a number of variables have to be taken into account when describing the restitution or improvement of language skills. These include the etiology and natural history of the disease, the underlying anatomophysiological basis, and the changing pattern of linguistic error. Remedial programs and prognosis are clearly dependent on these and other critical factors. Ajax (1967), commenting on the persistence of the deficit in a case of pure dyslexia, has emphasized that "disrupted language circuitry tends to produce resistant defects. Imaginative new approaches in aphasia therapy are overdue."

Our studies have so far been restricted to the reading of single words, individually presented. We are also concerned with the wide discrepancies that undoubtedly exist between scores on standard language tests or our own reading tasks and the patient's functional efficiency. Patient M.B. has improved her capacity to read individual words, but she can make very little use of linguistic context when attempting to read narrative. Patient W.M. can read individual words but cannot read a few lines of print without losing her place in the row. Other patients that we examined with focal left posterior lesions (due to missile injury) have regained reading skills but dislike reading for more than a few minutes for reasons that they cannot formulate precisely, including fatigue and a subjective feeling of unpleasant strain (see also Hécaen *et al.*, 1952, for a similar report).

We have not yet speculated on the process underlying spontaneous improvement or recovery in our cases. We have shown, however, that for two of the cases (M.B. and W.M.), improvement was not confined to performance on one list but was comparably reflected on matched tests which were only administered at the end of the recording period (Newcombe *et al.*, 1975). We assume that a process of physiological reorganization has continued to take place, after the patient has recovered from the secondary consequences of the lesion. We are inclined to think that there is some advantage in systematically repeating a task during the period after illness or accident when the patient continues to improve. This could have a basis in perceptual learning and generalization. It could have a nonspecific but nevertheless important effect on the patient's confidence and morale. To continue is to expose further areas of ignorance. We therefore wish to relate our preliminary concern with taxonomy to future studies of the acquisition of language skills and their restitution after cerebral disease.

REFERENCES

Ajax, E. T. 1967. Dyslexia without agraphia. *Archives of Neurology, 17,* 645–652.

Alajouanine, Th., Lhermitte, F., & Ribaucourt-Ducarne, Bl. de. 1960. Les alexies agnosiques et aphasiques. In Th. Alajouanine (Ed.), *Les Grandes Activités du Lobe Occipital.* Paris: Masson.

Albert, M. L., Yamadori, A., Gardner, H., & Howes, D. 1973. Comprehension in alexia. *Brain, 96,* 317–328.

Baron, J. 1973. Phonemic stage not necessary for reading. *Quarterly Journal of Experimental Psychology, 25,* 241–246.

Benson, D. F., Brown, J., & Tomlinson, E. B. 1971. Varieties of alexia: Word and letter blindness. *Neurology, 21,* 951–957.

Benson, D. F., & Geschwind, N. 1969. The alexias. In P. J. Vinken and G. W. Bruyn (Eds.), *Handbook of clinical neurology.* Vol. 4. Amsterdam: North-Holland.

Broadbent, W. H. 1872. Cerebral mechanism of speech and thought. *Medical and Chirurgical Transactions, 55,* 145–194.

Brown, J. W. 1972. *Aphasia, apraxia and agnosia.* Springfield, Ill.: Charles C Thomas.

Carroll, J. B., & White, M. N. 1973. Word frequency and age of acquisition as determiners of picture-naming latency. *Quarterly Journal of Experimental Psychology, 25,* 85–95.

Casey, T., & Ettlinger, G. 1960. The occasional "independence" of dyslexia and dysgraphia from dysphasia. *Journal of Neurology, Neurosurgery and Psychiatry, 23,* 228–236.

Charcot, J. M. 1889. On a case of word-blindness. In *Clinical lectures of diseases of the nervous system.* Vol. 3. The New Sydenham Soc. London. Pp. 130–140.

Déjerine, J. 1892. Contribution a l'étude anatomopathologique et clinique des differents varietes de scecité verbale. *Comptes Rendues des Sceances de la Societé de Biologie, 4,* 61.

Faust, C. 1955. *Die zerebralen Herdstörungen bei Hinterhauptsverletzungen und ihr Beurteilung.* Stuttgart: Thieme.

Geschwind, N., & Fusillo, M. 1966. Color-naming defects in association with alexia. *Archives of Neurology* (Chicago), *15*, 137–146.

Gloning, I., Gloning, K., & Hoff, H. 1968. *Neuropsychological symptoms and syndromes in lesions of the occipital lobe and the adjacent areas.* Paris: Gautheir-Villars.

Goldstein, K. 1948. *Language and language disturbances.* New York: Grune and Stratton.

Greenblatt, S. H. 1973. Alexia without agraphia or hemianopia: Anatomical analysis of an autopsied case. *Brain, 96,* 307–316.

Halpern, H. 1965. Effect of stimulus variables on dysphasic verbal errors. *Perceptual and Motor Skills, 21,* 291–298.

Hécaen, H. 1967. Aspects des troubles de la lecture (alexies) au cours des lésions cérébrales en foyer. *Word, 23,* 265–287.

Hécaen, H., Ajuriaguerra, J. de, & David, M. 1952. Les déficits fonctionnels après lobectomie occipitale. *Monatsschrift für Neurol. u. Psychiat., 123,* 239–291.

Hinshelwood, J. 1900. *Letter-, word-, and mind-blindness.* London: H. K. Lewis.

Holmes, G. 1950. Pure word blindness. *Folia Psychiat. Neurol. Neerl.* (Amsterdam), *43,* 279–288.

Low, A. A. 1931. A case of agrammatism in the English language. *Archives of Neurology and Psychiatry, 25,* 556–597.

Luria, A. R. 1970. *Traumatic phasia.* The Hague: Mouton.

Lyman, R. S., Kwan, S. T., & Chao, W. H. 1938. Left occipito-parietal brain tumour with observations on alexia and agraphia in Chinese and in English. *Chinese Medical Journal, 54,* 491–516.

Marshall, J. C., & Newcombe, F. 1966. Syntactic and semantic errors in paralexia. *Neuropsychologia, 4,* 169–176.

Marshall, J. C., & Newcombe, F. 1973. Patterns of paralexia: A psycholinguistic approach. *Journal of Psycholinguistic Research, 2,* 175–199.

Marshall, J. C., Newcombe, F., & Hiorns, R. W. 1975. Dyslexia: Patterns of disability and recovery. *Scandanavian Journal of Rehabilitation Medicine, 7,* 37–43.

Marshall, M., Newcombe, F., & Marshall, J. C. 1970. The microstructure of word-finding difficulties in a dysphasic subject. In G. B. Flores D'Arcais and W. J. M. Levelt (Eds.), *Advances in psycholinguistics* Amsterdam: North-Holland.

Massary, J. de 1932. L'Alexie. *Encephale, 1, 2,* 53–78, 134–164.

Meyer, D. E., Schvaneveldt, R. W., & Ruddy, M. G. 1974. Functions of graphemic and phonetic codes in visual word-recognition. *Memory and Cognition, 2,* 309–321.

Minkowski, M. 1930. Cited in Beringer, K., & Stein, J. 1930. Analyse eines falles reiner alexie. *Zeitschrift für Neurologie, 123,* 475.

Mohr, J. P., Sidman, M., Stoddard, L. T., Leicester, J., & Rosenberger, P. B. 1973. Evolution of the deficit in total aphasia. *Neurology, 23,* 1302–1312.

Newcombe, F., Hiorns, R. W., Marshall, J. C., & Adams, C. B. T. 1975. Acquired dyslexia: Patterns of deficit and recovery. In R. Porter and D. W. Fitzsimons (Eds.), *Outcome of severe damage to the central nervous system.* Ciba foundation symposium 34, Amsterdam: Associated Scientific. Pp. 227–244.

Newcombe, F., & Marshall, J. C. 1973. Stages in recovery from dyslexia following a left cerebral abscess. *Cortex, 9,* 329–332.

Newcombe, F., & Marshall, J. C. 1975. Traumatic dyslexia: Localization and linguistics. In K. J. Zülch, O. Creutzfeldt, and G. C. Galbraith (Eds.), *Cerebral localization.* New York: Springer-Verlag. Pp. 272–290.

Newcombe, F., Marshall, J. C., Carrivick, P. J., & Hiorns, R. W. 1975. Recovery curves in acquired dyslexia. *Journal of the Neurological Sciences, 24,* 127–133.

Newcombe, F., Marshall, J. C., & Richardson, J. 1976. Developmental and syntactic aspects of word-reading. In preparation.

Poppelreuter, W. 1917. *Die psychischen Schadigungen durch Kopfsschuss im Kriege 1914– 1916: die Storungen der neideren un hoheren Sehleistungen durch Verletzungen des Okzipitalhirns.* Leipzig: Voss.

Richardson, J. T. E. 1975a. The effect of word imageability in acquired dyslexia. *Neuropsychologia, 13,* 281–288.

Richardson, J. T. E. 1975b. Further evidence of the effect of word imageability in dyslexia. *Quarterly Journal of Experimental Psychology, 27,* 445–449.

Saffran, E., & Marin, O. 1975. Semantic errors in paralexia. Presented at the Third Annual Meeting of the International Neuropsychology Society, Florida, February 5–7.

Shallice, T., & Warrington, E. K. 1975. Word recognition in a phonemic dyslexic patient. *Quarterly Journal of Experimental Psychology, 27,* 187–200.

Simmel, M. L., & Goldschmidt, K. H. 1953. Prolonged posteclamptic aphasia. *American Medical Association Archives of Neurology and Psychiatry, 69,* 80–83.

Wechsler, A. F., Weinstein, E. A., & Antin, S. P. 1972. Alexia without agraphia. *Bulletin of the Los Angeles Neurological Society, 37,* 1–11.

7

The Question of Electro-physiological Asymmetries Preceding Speech

Ronald S. Levy

HENNEPIN COUNTY MEDICAL CENTER,
MINNEAPOLIS

INTRODUCTION

The literature on slow potentials preceding speech contains considerable controversy. The issue of artifact has commanded much attention; the issue of task parameters, comparatively little. Since the latter issue may bear heavily on the nature and reliability of the findings—and because attention to it may help clarify some apparent discrepancies in the literature—it, along with other variables, merits attention. This study investigates pertinence of some task parameters, recording sites, time-course of analysis, and possible artifact sources to prearticulatory slow potentials. It uses the *readiness potential* (RP) methodology (Kornhuber & Deeke, 1965; Gilden, Vaughan, & Costa, 1966; Vaughan, Costa, & Ritter, 1968), a technique which has revealed reliable potentials of cerebral origin that precede and are time-locked to voluntary movement.[1]

---

[1] In this technique, the activity is recorded with amplifiers sensitive to low frequencies (e.g., DC amplification), and averaged backward in time from a "trigger" point indicating the onset of movement (i.e., back-averaging). This electrocortical event starts approximately 1 sec prior to the movement and slowly slopes negatively until just before the movement. It has been called the *readiness potential* (RP), the *Bereitschafts potential* (BP), or the *motor potential* (MP); consistent nomenclature has not been universally adopted. (If many trials are averaged, a small, positive inflection can be seen immediately following the RP; this latter phenomenon, *pre-motor positivity* (PMP), is probably not relevant to the present study since not enough trials have been averaged). The above investigators have typically mapped the parameter of RP with respect to limb movements. Collectively, these investigations have indicated that the potentials are bilaterally distributed with focal activity

A number of early studies claiming that certain cerebral events (slow potentials) characteristically precede articulation (Ertl & Schafer, 1967; Schafer, 1967; Ellis, 1971) studied only relatively simple articulations (e.g., *tea*) and did not deal with bilateral comparisons of homotopic loci. Collectively, these data seem to represent complex potentials arising from complex, but essentially undetermined, factors. Schafer (1967) describes utterance- and area-specific potentials from one subject (himself) recorded over right sensorimotor cortex (C_4-A_2, international standards) and left temporal "speech-association" area (T_5-A_1) for the utterances T, O, and P. Ellis (1971), studying potentials over left hemisphere sites only, preceding the articulation of [kæ] and other tasks loosely classified as "verbal" (e.g., counting) or "nonverbal" (e.g., jaw opening, toe tapping), noted some distinctions. A number of methodological considerations (see below), particularly the lack of controls for vocal tract configuration, make most of these findings difficult to interpret. Ertl and Schafer (1969) published an "erratum" which pointed to a close correspondence between integrated lip EMG preceding articulation and the scalp-recorded potentials they originally reported. The relevance of these findings for studies emphasizing asymmetrical activity between bilateral, homotopic areas is not entirely clear; however, key methodological problems were identified which are only now being settled.

McAdam and Whitaker (1971a) published the first evidence of an asymmetry preceding the articulation of certain complex utterances. Their findings are from simultaneous comparison of left and right inferior frontal and precentral loci preceding utterance of polysyllabic words beginning with p or k or nonspeech gestures, the latter basically single segmental syllables [pʰʌ] and [kʰʌ].[2] The left–right differences of visually integrated amplitudes of the computer averaged

---

over areas of the Rolandic cortex associated with the responding musculature but attain maximal negativity over Rolandic areas contralateral to the responding limb (for review, see McAdam, 1974). (For contractions of the lower face and tongue, maximal potentials were found over the low Rolandic area; Vaughan *et al.*, 1968.) Studies on slow potential antecedents of speech which are mentioned in this report—unless otherwise noted—used variations of this methodology (back-averaging).

[2] The term *segmental syllable* is provisional. The word *syllable* is used because of the airburst associated with the articulation, and the modifier *segmental* is used to indicate a restricted level of complexity in comparison with voiced syllables typical in English phonology. The nomenclature does not imply that its referent is "language." Although the sound of some of the utterances may be described as "speech sounds," this type of utterance, in both McAdam and Whitaker (1971a) and the present experiment, was taught as "nonspeech" oromotor movements. The term *segmental syllable* is basically synonymous with the terms *nonspeech gesture* (McAdam & Whitaker, 1971a) *nonspeech oromotor response* (Anderson & Jaffe, 1973), and *phoneme* (Szirtes & Vaughan, 1973). The latter term is technically incorrect, since phonemes can not be articulated. It remains to be decided which is the clearest and most useful term.

slow potentials during the last 150 msec prior to overt articulation (marked by "air-burst" trigger) showed significantly greater negativity in slow potentials over the left hemisphere sites preceding the polysyllabic word tasks. Furthermore, the left–right difference over the inferior frontal sites (presumably Broca's area and its right homologue) were significantly greater (for a .05, one-tail test) than the difference between precentral motor areas. Differences in potentials preceding the single segmental syllabic gestures [$p^h_ʌ$] and [$k^h_ʌ$] were not significant.

Because of its possible relevance to neurolinguistics and to clinical neurology, the study by McAdam and Whitaker (1971a) became a focus for a variety of follow-up studies. Among these, several looked at the possibility that McAdam and Whitaker's results were artifactual. Various extracerebral sources were considered, including artifact primarily from lip muscles (orbicularis oris) (Morrell & Huntington, 1971); "glosso-kinetic" (tongue) movement (Grabow & Elliott, 1974); palatal movement (Zimmerman, Knott, Mendel, & Keuhn, 1975); and eye movement (Anderson & Jaffe, 1973).

While it is impossible to prove that extracerebral generators are not responsible for scalp-recorded asymmetry in EEG, the probability that such extracerebral generators are artifactual sources of the scalp-recorded findings is highly questionable. McAdam and Whitaker (1971b) noted that the use of control utterances and bilateral sites in their study lessens the possibility that bilateral articulatory muscles were responsible for asymmetrical activity on the scalp. Morrell and Huntington (1972), on the basis of a careful study simultaneously comparing scalp-recorded activity over various sites with the EMG of various articulators (as well as EOG on occasion), conclude that the potentials are probably *cerebral* in origin.[3] The most thorough study of artifact to date (Grözinger, Kornhuber, & Kriebel, 1975) examines the above sources of artifact and others (e.g., respiration, GSR, EMG of temporal, neck, and shoulder muscles) and concludes that reports of scalp-recorded asymmetry represent a bioelectric correlate of hemispheric dominance. (They also confirm McAdam & Whitaker's, 1971b, contention that the use of *voice onset time* [VOT] is a

---

[3] They monitored, by separate EMG leads, larynx, lip, tongue, jaw, and eye movements preceding a range of utterances and presented several lines of evidence

consistent with a cerebral origin of speech-locked potentials. Recordings from an array of electrodes over both hemispheres indicate that (a) there are amplitude gradients for such potentials along both para-sagittal and coronal planes which are not readily referable to scalp musculature effects, (b) hemispheric differences for symmetrically placed electrodes are not expected from articulatory muscle artifact, (c) reiterative averages for the same spontaneous speech token may show no consistent change of amplitude of the scalp-recorded potentials, while simultaneous recordings of articulatory muscle activity may show marked reduction with repetition, (d) distinct differences in the time course of scalp-recorded and electromyographic activity preceding phonation can be demonstrated. [Morrell & Huntington, 1972, p. 921–922] particularly poor way to trigger back-averaging, and they note, in addition, that potentials for 100 msec prior to their own EMG [orbicularis oris] trigger should be interpreted cautiously.)

Another source of variance in the literature concerns the reliability of bioelectric asymmetries. It is difficult to dichotomize the above studies into camps supporting or contesting the reliability of bioelectric asymmetries preceding speech because of differences in the tasks, general methodology, and ways of assessing reliability which they used, but there have been assertions (Grabow & Elliot, 1974) of insignificance (when relying on "visually apparent" differences, tasks, and procedures different from McAdam & Whitaker, 1971a). Typically, the studies which produced more or less unreliable results have employed procedures which maximized the occurrence of extracerebral artifact (generally whichever source was being touted). The observation of extracerebral artifact coupled with the failure to successfully replicate McAdam and Whitaker (1971a) does not provide logical grounds for intimating that extracerebral artifact was the source[4] of asymmetries shown by McAdam and Whitaker.

On the other hand, some studies have partially supported and extended McAdam and Whitaker (1971a). These include: (a) work using slow potential techniques based on the CNV[5] paradigm (Low, Wada, & Fox, 1974a,b, in press; Zimmerman & Knott, 1973, 1974, in press); (b) a study which, like McAdam and Whitaker (1971a), utilized a back-averaging technique (Szirtes & Vaughan, 1973); (c) work using back-averaging and other analysis which revealed hemi-

---

[4] A more straightforward interpretation is that extracerebral artifact contributes mainly to the noise (thus obscuring the "signal") in the S/N ratio that characterizes any paradigm involving signal-averaging. Another possible interpretation is that differences in the articulatory tasks among the experiments were a source of discrepancies between their results and McAdam and Whitaker's—most other studies used mainly or only short or single-syllable utterances. Thus their tasks and findings might be viewed as consistent with the control conditions of McAdam and Whitaker (1971a). An additional complication in comparing these studies is their manifold differences in basic procedure (i.e., with respect to baseline, synchronization event [trigger] for averaging, measurement, number of trials averaged, time periods examined, etc.). Grabow and Elliot (1974), for example, essentially took their baseline during a period in which the present study and others find well-developed asymmetries. Regardless of these latter interpretations, these studies still raise questions as to the reliability of the phenomena observed by McAdam and Whitaker (1971a), or more cogently suggest that artifact control and other methodological factors may be important for the demonstration of asymmetries.

[5] In the CNV technique, averaging of slow potentials takes place between and with respect to fixed S_1-S_2 intervals. This is essentially a reaction time paradigm, with the S_1 being the "warning stimulus" and the S_2 being the "imperative stimulus"; the subject must respond as quickly as possible following S_2. Typically, a negative shift occurs between S_1 and S_2; this has been related to "expectancy" (Walter, Cooper, Aldridge, McCallum, & Winter, 1964), "conation" (intention to respond) (Low, Borda, Frost, & Kellaway, 1966) "motivation" (Irwin, Knott, McAdam & Rebert, 1966) and "attention" (Tecce & Scheff, 1969). For a general review of CNV phenomenon as well as its relationship to the RP, see Cohn (1969) and Tecce (1972).

spheric asymmetries in α waves, θ waves, and a wave called the R-wave, correlated with respiration (Grözinger, Kornhuber, Kriebel & Murata, 1974; Grözinger, Kornhuber, & Kriebel, 1973, 1975, in press); (*d*) an independent pilot study for this experiment, which, like the present study, was performed in McAdam's laboratory; (*e*) an additional observation by McAdam and Whitaker (mentioned in McAdam & Whitaker, 1971b, & Whitaker, 1971a) that polysyllabic nonsense words seem to occasion similar phenomena to the real polysyllabic words employed in their original study; and (*f*) this study. Except for the last, these studies did not explicitly include or report the averaging and statistical analysis of both the EMG and EOG contemporary with the EEG preceding speech. Anderson and Jaffe (1973) express a valid possibility that the "averaging" technique might accrue subtle extracerebral artifact at scalp sites that is not visually apparent in the single-trial monitoring of those extracerebral channels.

An additional aim of the present study was to develop and test hypotheses based upon some linguistic, psycholinguistic, and clinical models concerning articulatory demands (tasks). Although other studies, beginning with Shafer (1967), reported observations which might indicate that articulatory task variables could have importance, comparisons between tasks having grossly different vocal tract configuration are problematic (see "Discussion"). The clearest indication, until now, that task demands may influence asymmetries is composed of McAdam and Whitaker's (1971a) findings which suggest that the brain may process demands for polysyllabic English words beginning with "p" or "k" differently from the way it processes such single segmental syllables as $[p^h\Lambda]$ or $[k^h\Lambda]$ which were used to control for initial vocal tract configuration. There are many differences between the McAdam and Whitaker polysyllabic word condition and the condition of single segmental "nonspeech gestures." The former required variability of response, verbal memory, semantic value, syntactic value, and lexical value, and it was recognized as language (verbal). The various words were also phonologically complex: They were polysyllabic, composed of English morphemes and syllables consisting of consonant–vowel sequences involving "voicing," took longer to produce—regardless of the number of syllables—and involved "coarticulation." This list of differences, hierarchical for the most part, is not encyclopedic, nor are its differences mutually exclusive, but it should serve to place possible hypotheses in perspective.

At one basic level, articulation of polysyllabic words requires rapid sequential shifting (which can be called *switching*) from one articulatory position to different ones. Sequential shifting may also require the ability to repeat, in a staccato fashion, any articulatory position; this multiple linking of the ostensibly same articulatory position will be called *chaining*.

Pilot observations have shown that utterances which apparently lack semantic, lexical, or syntactic proporties but which consist of the rapid and precise repetition (in clusters of four) of a particular articulatory position can also result in findings similar to those reported by McAdam and Whitaker (1971a). These observations, in the light of the voluminous body of clinical literature (for reviews, see Brown, 1972; Schuell, Jenkins, & Kiminez-Pabon, 1964), suggest that more explicit hypotheses bearing on "phonological complexity" might be fruitful.

Experimental hypotheses may be founded on a more general theoretical proposition that states that an additional set of demands are imposed on brain mechanisms by the programming of rapid multiple output which "tracks" a precisely defined "target" (e.g., in terms of number of units, stress, and duration), that is, additional demands in comparison with the tracking required for "all-or-none" output of a singular target. This notion is related to arguments such as those of Lashley (1951), Martin (1972), MacNeilage (1970), and Anderson (in press) which, taken collectively, imply that motoric behavior, particularly speech, which is sequential, rhythmic, and ballistic, requires special mechanisms for its production. In speech, at least—if not in other types of behavior requiring rapid, sequential, precisely timed bilateral movement—it would be efficient for the mechanism which synchronizes, organizes, or otherwise "tracks" the target to be represented, at some level, asymmetrically. Asymmetries in the slow potentials preceding speech might reflect, among other things, the activity of such a mechanism. Clinical evidence, particularly Luria (1966, 1970), who includes anatomical evidence, and Johns and Darley (1970), Shankweiler and Harris (1966), who present precise analysis of the articulatory errors of (essentially) motor aphasics, suggests that Broca's area might have particular significance for the serial organization of speech. Thus, one might expect to see maximal asymmetries in EEG leads overlying Broca's area (when compared to its contralateral homologue) associated with tasks requiring such organization.

Tasks in the present experiment which might require such organization are termed *multiple* (syllable or component) utterances. Other tasks, which control for the vocal tract configuration of the multiple utterances are termed *single* utterances in that they can consist of a single, unvoiced (segmental) syllable or a single consonant—vowel syllable as in English phonology; the single utterances begin with the same segment as the multiple utterances to which they correspond but are less complex in terms of the amount or, perhaps, type of sequential coordination they require for execution.

The single utterances in this experiment are the single English syllable *pa* [pʰæ], the "single puff" [pʰʌ̥] (i.e., the "spit" condition of McAdam and Whitaker), and the "single huff" [hʌ̥]. Articulation of *pa* as in *pat* is included for many reasons: being an English syllable, it is lexical, it involves "voicing" and "coarticulation," and in general it has more types of phonological complexity than the single puff but less than a multiple-syllable word. It is also included to clarify the meaning of studies which have tried and failed to replicate the polysyllabic word condition of McAdam and Whitaker (1971a) by using mainly or only short words. There are three corresponding multiple utterances used here. One, the polysyllabic nonsense word *patapute* [pʰ ˈætʌpʰjuwt ˈh] exemplifies switched sequential complexity. The other two multiple utterances, *multiple puff* and *multiple huff,* exemplify "chained" sequential complexity. The experimental hypotheses predict that the rapid and rhythmic articulation of the multiple utterances is *sufficient* to provide bioelectric reflections of cerebral dominance preceding those utterances (even though they—particularly the chained multiple utterances—have no ostensible semantic, syntactic, or lexical value). These reflections of cerebral dominance for right-handed subjects, on the basis of previous literature, are periods of analysis indicating *relative* negativity (viz., left-more-negative: LMN) derived from left–right comparisons of waveforms; this predicted asymmetry should be strongest between left and right inferior frontal sites. No such predictions are made for the single utterances since previous literature suggests that at least for these methods the asymmetries preceding short utterances might be comparatively unreliable.

Confirmation of such hypotheses could provide evidence for the neurophysiological reality of mechanisms relating to assembly function, and may suggest that to dichotomize cerebral dominance for vocal tract control into "verbal versus nonverbal" categories, without consideration of the level of complexity that the task (verbal or nonverbal) involves, may overlook common neuroanatomical substrates (see De Renzi, Pieczuro, & Vignolo, 1966).

METHOD

Subjects

Subjects were eight right-handed females, aged 18–23, students in an introductory psychology course. They were unaware of the specific purposes of the experiment.

Tasks

There were six tasks (i.e., utterances): single huff (*h*), multiple huff (*hhhh*), single puff (*p*), multiple puff (*pppp*), single syllable (*pa*), and multi-syllable nonsense word (*patapute*). All these utterances were pronounced "explosively" beginning from the *same* "neutral position," which was a relaxed but completely immobile position of the mouth with the tongue on the floor of the mouth, the jaw muscles relaxed, the teeth and lips slightly parted, and the eyes fixated on a spot. The single huff, essentially a glottal fricative, was a short, vigorous expulsion of air through the already parted lips (i.e., the neutral position) produced by rapidly expelling breath using the diaphragm. It was not a "blow-ing" gesture, nor was it "voiced." The multiple huff was a rapidly executed sequence of four single huffs, produced as rapidly as the subject could form them while still retaining some distinctness of the individual huffs. The single puff, essentially a bilabial voiceless plosive, was a spit-like gesture consisting of a rapid "stop" formed by lip closure coupled with a short, explosive puff of air to form a plosive sound. This gesture is identical to the "spit gesture" of McAdam and Whitaker (1971a). The multiple puff was a rapidly executed sequence of four single puffs. (At no time during the experiment were the single or multiple puffs and huffs described as "speech sounds"; they were introduced and treated as "praxic" movements; see footnote 6). The single syllable was *pa* (the *a* rhymes with the vowel in *hat*), and the multiple syllable nonsense word was *patapute* (the *a* in *pa* rhymes with the vowel in *hat*, the *a* in *ta* rhymes with *the*, and *pute* is said similarly to the *pute* in *compute*, but the *pute* received secondary stress and the *t* was aspirated so it added a component to the sequential complexity); in both these tasks, the initial *p* was produced explosively, in a similar manner to both "puff" conditions (within the limitations of coarticulation effects). In practice, the first segment of each of the multiple utterances (*hhhh*, *pppp*, and *patapute*) was stressed; thus these multiple utterances might be considered "rhythmic" as opposed to merely "concatenated" according to the analysis of Martin (1972).

Electrical Recording

Ag/AgCl recording electrodes (Beckman miniature biopotential electrodes) were placed bilaterally over inferior frontal areas (11 cm down from vertex and 4 cm anterior to the interaural line) and precentral gyri (9 cm down from vertex and 2 cm anterior to the interaural line). These are the same placements as McAdam and Whitaker (1971a) used. Grabow and Elliott (1974) and Zimmerman and Knott (1974) have reported data from autopsies indicating that the inferior frontal placements lie over Broca's area and its right homologue, while precentral placements lie over the portion of the primary Rolandic motor cortex controlling articulatory musculature. Left and right inferior frontal placements will be referred to as LB and RB, respectively, and the left and right precentral placements will be referred to as LR and RR. Linked electrodes over left and right mastoids served as the reference for recordings from these four sites; a forehead electrode served as ground. Prior to application of electrodes, the underlying skin was abraded and, after application, at least 20 minutes passed before recording began. A tissue impedance meter was used to assure that resistances between electrodes were approximately equal and in no case exceeded 3000 ohms.

Eye and mouth movements were also recorded. The eye placements, referred to each other, were approximately 1 cm above the left outer canthus and 1 cm below the right outer canthus; this array is particularly sensitive to lateral movement of the eyes while it also reflects vertical movement and blinks. The mouth electrodes, referred to each other, were approximately 1 cm above the outer canthus of the left side of the mouth and 1 cm below the outer canthus of the right side of the mouth. This array was empirically chosen to reflect both lateral and vertical movements of the lips (orbicularis oris) and tongue, as well as other movements involving jaws, cheeks, and so on.

Apparatus

A Grass polygraph (Model 78) traced the electrophysiological events and synchronized pulses in addition to supplying them to a Precision Instrument 6280 eight-channel tape recorder with FM capabilities. Grass (chopper stabilized) preamplifiers (Model 7DAC) and their attendant driver amplifiers (Model 7PIA) provided DC amplification for the brain signals. Other Grass amplifiers (Model 7P511) (with 1/2 amplitude frequency attenuations of .1–1000 Hz) were used for eye (EOG) and mouth (EMG) activity.

The airburst associated with each utterance defined the onset of the utterance (i.e., served as the "trigger" for analysis of the utterance). This airburst was detected by the microphone of a sound pressure meter (General Radio, Model 1561-A) placed approximately 2.5 cm directly in front of the subject's mouth. Set at 80 db, with "flat" weighting and "fast" response time, this sound pressure meter provided an amplified signal which triggered a Grass S88 stimulator to put a square wave on the airburst trigger channel of the tape recorder.

The trials selected for analysis, off-line, were averaged by a Nuclear–Chicago DRC signal averager, and the results were written out by a Leeds and Northrup Speedomax X–Y plotter running at its fastest speed.

Procedure

Following the subjects' arrival, they were questioned as to their degree of right-handedness, family history of handedness, and lack of ambidexterity. Only subjects who considered themselves "strongly right-handed" were used. After the electrodes were applied, subjects were given instructions.[6]

---

[6] Subjects were first instructed and rehearsed in the neutral position for each of the six utterances. Instructions for the puff conditions included telling the subject to imagine a small piece of paper stuck to her bottom lip and to "spit it away" using a small, but explosive, puff of air through briefly closed lips. Instructions for the huff conditions were much the same, except that the subjects were told not to actively move their lips. Similar degrees of "abruptness of onset" and intensity were shaped by practice for all six utterances. For the multiple utterances (including the nonsense word), subjects were told to produce them as rapidly as possible while still maintaining some degree of distinctness for the components. In no case was it suggested to the subjects that multiple utterances are more linguistic than single utterances.

After the subjects had learned each utterance competently, they were instructed as to the importance of remaining completely motionless for approximately three seconds prior to the utterance (they were also warned not to count). Movements which might normally precede an utterance, such as tongue movements, jaw movements, licking or pursing the lips, taking a breath, or tightening of the mouth and facial muscles, were defined as "prearticulatory" movement. The subjects received extensive rehearsal to minimize such prearticulatory movement. Verbal feedback from the experimenter and training with a mirror were employed.

Each subject, then, was led into a sound-proof chamber and seated in a comfortable high-backed chair where she viewed a fixation spot. The subject was told that the experimenter, via intercom, would randomly request performance of each of the utterances. It was emphasized that the subject should not respond "immediately" or "automatically" to each of the requests, but rather should wait until she herself was ready and had eliminated prearticulatory movement. Great emphasis was placed on the elimination of movement artifact.[7] After the subject received the instructions, she was given approximately 10 minutes of further practice during which the experimenter, observing the EMG and EOG, provided her with feedback on how well she was minimizing prearticulatory movement.

The collection of data began. The experimenter requested each of the six utterances 40 times in a randomized sequence. (A constraint on the randomness was that the same utterance could not be requested more than two times in succession.) Each of the requests was spaced so that the subject was responding approximately once every 10–15 seconds. Following the subject's completion of the 240 trials, she was asked to rank the utterances along subjective dimensions of "phonological difficulty" (i.e., how hard they were to say) and "linguistic-

---

[7] A sequence of movement-eliminating procedures was suggested in a manner similar to the following: "Suppose you have just made an utterance. Now is a good time to blink, move your eyes, or slightly shift position. When I have determined that the grosser aspects of your movement have disappeared and you have presumably resumed the *neutral position*, I will specify the next utterance. You will not make this utterance immediately; you will wait until you have eliminated the finer aspects of movement and are absolutely ready to explosively produce the utterance. You should eliminate your movement in several progressive stages: when I give you the utterance you should check your neutral position to be sure it is perfect to the finest degree; when you are thus certain, I want you to give me a *clear* period. A clear period is a period of time (approximately three seconds—but do not count) during which you are not only generally relaxed in the neutral position with your eyes fixated, but also during which you have halted your respiration at the highest point of an inspiration." (Note: Although Caspers, 1963, has shown that changes in pO_2 and pCO_2 can influence cortical steady potentials as measured in rats by chronically implanted electrodes, it is unlikely that behavior such as stopping respiration at the height of inspiration for a few seconds would be reflected in grosser scalp EEG. At least, no obvious effects were seen during the collection of pilot data. In any case, it would be desirable to regularize across the

ness" (i.e., how much they seemed like words of her language). Also, the subject was asked to rate the "meaningfulness" of the nonsense word *patapute*, and she was asked if any of the other utterances had or attained a semantic connotation during the experiment.

Analysis

Subjects were eliminated whose records showed excessive DC "drift" (i.e., more or less long-term changes in DC levels which are probably electrode artifact), excessive movement or muscular artifact of a general nature (e.g., tenseness, fidgeting), or excessive prearticulatory movement in more than 25 trials of any utterance. (Note: Although prearticulatory movement cannot be completely eliminated, pilot work has shown that with practice a subject can usually confine the greatest amount of prearticulatory movement—at least with the utterances and electrode placements used in this experiment—to approximately 100 msec prior to onset of utterance (as measured by the airburst trigger). "Excessive" prearticulatory movement was defined as "prearticulatory movement, as measured by EMG and EOG, which increases rapidly prior to approximately 100 msec before onset of the utterance.")

Using the subjects who passed the initial screening described above, the trials most free of prearticulatory movement were selected for computer averaging. In order to avoid favoring the signal-to-noise characteristics attending one utterance as opposed to another, for each subject each type of utterance had the same number of trials selected for computer averaging. Different subjects might have different numbers of utterances eligible for computer averaging, but in no case did any subject have fewer than 18 utterances or more than 37 of each type averaged (the mean, across subjects, was 29 trials averaged).

---

various utterances any subtle effects respiration might have by requesting the subject to explicitly exercise the same sort of breathing pattern before each type of utterance. It should also be noted that this approach distinguishes the present study from other studies on speech-linked potentials, as far as known; this distinction might be particularly important in comparing the present study with those by Grözinger and co-workers who find an asymmetrical wave correlated with respiration prior to speech.) "You should make no attempt to take an extra large breath, but rather handle it as a normal catching of the breath preceding speech. Once you have caught your breath, you should begin to get ready to explosively release your utterance after approximately three seconds. You should abort the utterance attempt if, during the clear period, you notice any blinking, eye movement, or other prearticulatory movement such as tightening of the mouth. You should also abort the attempt if you notice any discomfort whatsoever from catching your breath; if you feel any need to breathe whatsoever, you should take the breath and give me another clear period."

After paraphrasing these instructions in detail, the experimenter observed the subject performing the sequence of movement-elimination-and-articulation a number of times. Special emphasis was placed on making sure the subject did not take an abnormally large breath immediately prior to the clear period and the utterance.

To average the potentials which preceded each type of utterance, a magnetic tape containing the brain potentials, EMG, EOG, and airburst triggers was played backward into a Nuclear–Chicago DRC signal averager. The appropriate airburst triggers activated a 2.5 sec sweep of the signal averager. This, performed off-line, is the traditional back-averaging technique. The relevant segment of the averaged activity written out by the Speedomax plotter was traced on graph paper.

The integrated value of the 125 msec period commencing approximately 1.25 sec prior to utterance onset served as baseline for the analysis of the six successive 125 msec (approximately) periods immediately preceding the defined onset of articulation (i.e., the airburst trigger); that is, activity preceding the onset of articulation up to approximately 750 msec was analyzed by separately integrating the values of six successive 125 msec periods. This was done for all brain channels, EMG, and EOG.[8] These values were tabulated and converted to μV's by computation based on calibration signals fed to all six recording channels for each subject.

This "uncorrected" data was used to develop three sets of "corrected" data by employing a specially developed model similar to analysis of covariance (see Appendix to the chapter). This model embodies some of the assumptions of standard analysis of covariance (ie., additivity and linearity) but does not assume that volume conductance from sources of artifact (EMG and EOG) are necessarily the same for all subjects. A program written in OMNITAB calculated these corrections for each of the four scalp loci: the data were corrected for (a) "mouth EMG," (b) EOG, and (c) EOG and mouth EMG simultaneously. An OMNITAB program also made the appropriate comparisons among these scalp loci for both the uncorrected and corrected sets of the data. The comparisons consisted of LB − RB, LR − RR, LB − LR, RB − RR, and [(LB − LR) − (RB − RR)]; this latter expression is mathematically equivalent to [(LB − RB) − (LR − RR)]. Expressions such as LB − RB mean "activity recorded over the LB site (left inferior frontal) minus activity recorded over the RB site (right interior frontal)"; this sort of abbreviation is used subsequently in this report.

RESULTS

The ONEWAY program of OMNITAB was used to compute means and 95% confidence intervals for each time period of analysis. These values are computer

---

[8] The integration was visually accomplished (in a manner similar to that used by McAdam & Whitaker, 1971a) by drawing, for each time period, a line intersecting the waveform such that the area enclosed above the line is equivalent to the area enclosed below the line. (The outer boundaries in each case, of course, are the raw tracings of the potentials, the vertical lines on the graph paper making the start and end of the 125 msec epoch.) The height and sign of each of the six analysis period lines was measured with respect to the baseline of each averaged potential.

plotted for the EOG and "mouth EMG" values and for the uncorrected and the corrected EEG comparisons (see Figures 7.1, 7.2, 7.3, 7.4, 7.5).

The data of three of the subjects were eliminated prior to any averaging and analysis because their records were not sufficiently free of artifact to yield enough "clean" trials for averaging. The EOG channel from one of the remaining five subjects was missing because of apparatus failure. Thus, in Figure 7.1, the EOG analyses are based on the data of four subjects and the EMG analyses are based on the data of five subjects. The analyses in Figure 7.2 (uncorrected data set) and Figure 7.3 (EMG corrected data set) are based on the data of five subjects, while the analyses in Figure 7.4 (EOG corrected data set) and Figure

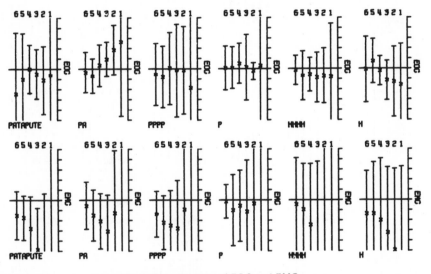

Figure 7.1   Analysis of EOG and EMG

Figures 7.1–7.5 Negative is up. The y-axis is marked in 1 μV intervals. The middle of the y-axis represents 0 with respect to the baseline. The x-axis represents the six successive time periods, each nominally 125 msec; period 1 is closest to articulation. Vertical lines limited by crossbars represent 95% confidence intervals for the integrated activity for each time period; "x" marks the mean. If either the cross-bar or the "x" is not marked on a particular vertical line, that value is off-scale. The six columns on each figure correspond to the six tasks.

Figure 7.1 pictures the analysis of the averaged EOG and EMG, respectively. Figures 7.2, 7.3, 7.4, and 7.5 picture the following comparisons of scalp-recorded activity: Row 1, LB – RB; Row 2 LR – RR; Row 3, LB – LR; Row 4, RB – RR; Row 5 [(LB – RB) – (LR – RR)] or [(LB – LR) – (RB – RR)], i.e., the "difference of differences" comparison. (For further explanation of the comparisons, see the text section "Methods"). The "/U" after each comparison indicates that the comparison is based on "uncorrected data"; "/M" indicates data "corrected" for activity recorded by the "mouth EMG" channel; "/E" indicates data corrected for EOG; and "/S" indicates data corrected for the "simultaneous" abstraction of the waveforms for both eye and "mouth" artifact.

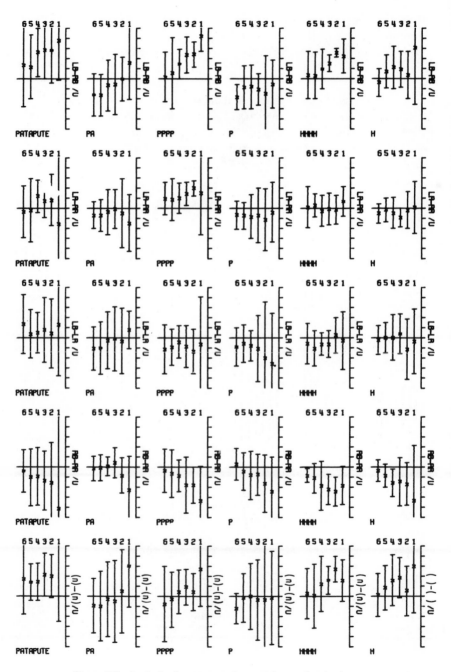

Figure 7.2 Analysis of uncorrected comparisons of scalp-sites.

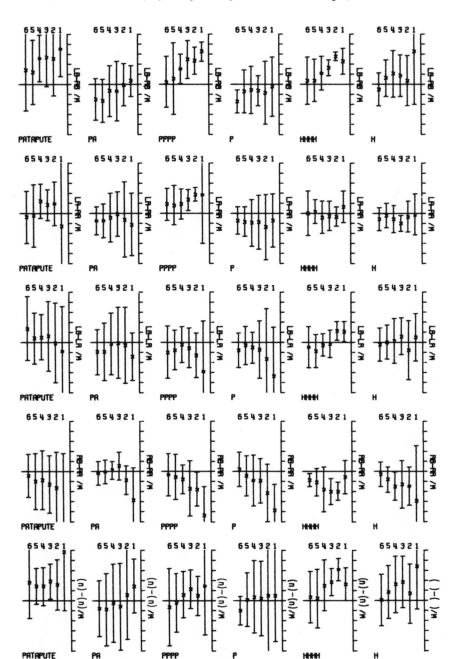

Figure 7.3 Analysis of EMG-corrected comparisons of scalp-sites.

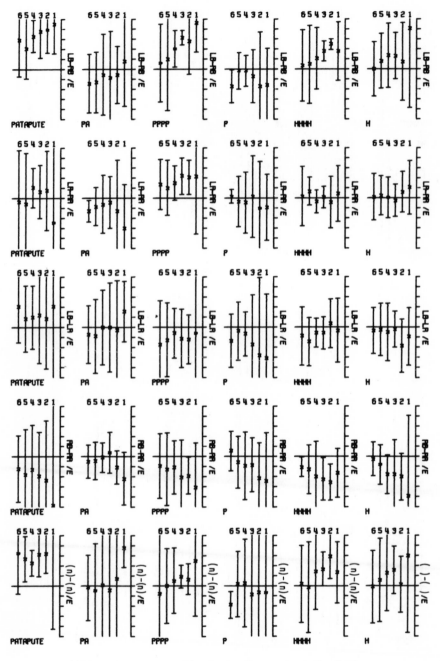

Figure 7.4 Analysis of EOG-corrected comparisons of scalp-sites.

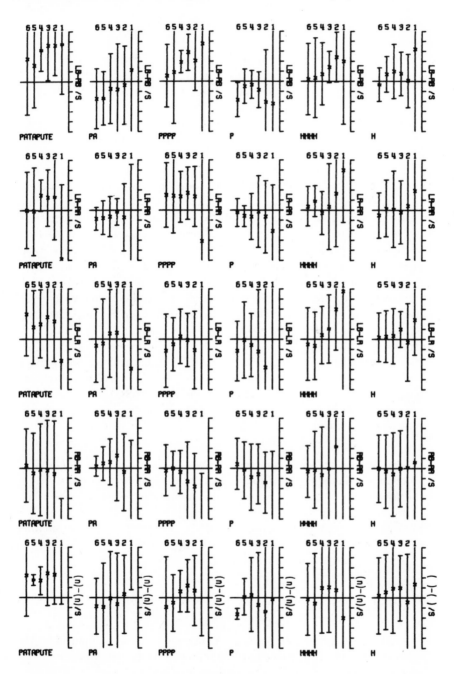

Figure 7.5 Analysis of simultaneous EMG/EOG-corrected comparisons of scalp-sites.

7.5 (simultaneous correction for EMG and EOG) are based on the data of four subjects.

Periods during which the more positive (lower) cross-bar of the 95% confidence interval is on or above the O μV baseline are called significantly negative here with respect to the first member of the comparison (e.g., LB in the comparison LB − RB), or significantly positive with respect to the second member. An analogous procedure is followed where the more negative (upper) cross-bar of the confidence interval is on or below the baseline.

The EMG and EOG data, recorded and analyzed simultaneously with the EEG data, provide only one statistically significant observation (out of 72 possibilities): the third time period of mouth EMG for *patapute* (see Figure 7.1, column 1, row 2). Note, however, that the amount of EMG activity in the first time period of all the utterances—though highly variable and thus statistically insignificant—is quite large. These observations along with those of corrected and uncorrected comparisons might be considered in advancing a conservative evaluation of the scalp-recorded findings deleting mention of (*a*) findings for the first time period (but note that this period is sometimes significant as predicted); (*b*) findings which are not statistically significant in the uncorrected version (Figure 7.2); and (*c*) findings which, while significant for the uncorrected version, do not continue to maintain significance for either the simultaneous correction of EMG and EOG or for both the separate corrections for EMG and EOG. (Observations which narrowly miss this latter criterion are noted in parentheses. Findings for the third analysis period of *patapute* which pass the preceding criteria but which might be considered "less conservative"—see above—are also mentioned in parentheses). Findings which meet the conservative criteria along with the noted exceptions follow:

For LB − RB
1. Negativity in the second and third periods of the multiple huff (*hhhh*).
2. Negativity in the third and fourth periods of the multiple puff (*pppp*).
3. Negativity in the fourth period of the multisyllabic word *patapute*; (note that the third period is similar to the fourth).
4. A difference in the confidence intervals for the third period of the multiple puff compared to the third period of the single puff.
5. Positivity in the sixth period of the single puff (*p*).

For LR − RR
6. Negativity in the second and third period of the multiple puff.

For RB − RR
7. Positivity in the second, third, and sixth periods of the multiple huff. (The fourth period of the single huff (*h*) follows a similar pattern but narrowly misses significance for the EOG correction).
8. Positivity in the second period of the multiple puff.

For the "difference of differences" scores—which are labeled in the figures as
() − () because they can be interpreted either as differences in degree of
asymmetry [(LB − RB) − (LR − RR)] or as interhemispheric differences of
intrahemispheric gradients [(LB − LR) − (RB − RR)] :

9. Negativity in the second and third periods of the multiple huff. (Also note
   the third period of the multisyllabic word *patapute* which shows a similar
   pattern to the multiple huff for this comparison).

For each of these findings the reader should see the appropriate rows and
columns of Figures 7.2, 7.3, 7.4, and 7.5.

Analysis of variance for ranked data (Winer, 1962, p. 136) was performed on
the subjects' ratings of the utterances. The means of the ranks for their ratings of
subjective judgments of how much "like a word of their normal language
(English)" each utterance seemed ran, from most "like language" to least "like
language" in their experience, as follows: *patapute, pa, p, h, pppp, hhhh.*
"Lexicality" might be the appropriate linguistic label for the dimension along
which this data falls. For this data, there was significance beyond the .05 level
(χ^2 rank = 21.80). The rankings for "subjective difficulty" ran, from most
difficult through least difficult, as follows (based on mean of rank): *hhhh, pppp,
patapute, h, pa,* and *p.* This order, however, narrowly missed significance at the
.05 level (χ^2 rank = 10.83, where 11.17 is required for $p \leqslant .05$). A closer look at
the data, in any case, has yet to reveal a simple correspondence between
subjective difficulty and asymmetry over scalp loci: The subject who showed the
largest left-more-negative asymmetry (LB − RB) for *patapute* ranked it as the
easiest utterance. Ratings for the meaningfulness of *patapute* confirmed that it
was more or less semantically void.

DISCUSSION

The major and most general findings were reliable hemispheric differences in
slow-potential activity in which left sites were more negative than homologous
sites on the right prior to articulation of the sequentially complex (multiple)
utterances. This predicted observation of left-more-negative (LMN) was most
evident in,[9] but not completely limited to, the inferior frontal comparison (see
LB − RB, Figures 7.2, 7.3, 7.4, 7.5).

---

[9] It is tempting to make strong claims of "lateralization and localization" of function from
the data in this experiment, but the following caveats should temper any such inferences:
(*1*) Limited arrays of recording sites have limited value in localizing activity. (*2*) Bilaterally
symmetrical scalp placements might not overlie bilaterally symmetrical areas of cortex. This
is the implication of such studies as Geschwind and Levitsky (1968) and Whitaker and
Selnes (in press). Although this caveat can apply to any electrode locus, it seems particularly
potent for posterior temporoparietal sites (Rubens, Mahowald, & Hutton, 1976). (*3*) Cautious interpretation should be attached to the meaning of direction and degree of polarity

These findings, in the main, concur with those of McAdam and Whitaker (1971a). While it is difficult to compare the results of the present study with those of other studies which used more disparate procedures either in the context of back-averaging (Morrell & Huntington, 1971, 1972; Schafer, 1967; Anderson & Jaffe, 1973; Grözinger *et al.*, 1973, 1974, 1975, in press; Szirtes & Vaughan, 1973; Grabow & Elliott, 1974) or CNV (Low *et al.*, 1974a,b; Zimmerman & Knott, 1974), *it can be agreed that* (*1*) potentials recorded over individual scalp sites are complex waveforms which may be positive or negative, are generally variable in form, and are sometimes more negative over precentral than inferior frontal sites—these observations do not mean that the site of greater intrahemispheric negativity is necessarily the site of greater interhemispheric negativity, nor does variability at single scalp-sites preclude *relative* negativity (i.e., LMN) when measurements from these sites are compared; (*2*) interhemispheric asymmetries may begin to arise quite early prior to articulation, are usually small, and may even show polarity reversals or variability of asymmetry over a range of different articulations.

The results of this experiment support the hypotheses that sequentially complex articulations which demand high fluency, regardless of whether the articulations consist of ostensibly similar (chained) or different (switched) components, and even if the articulations have no apparent semantic, syntactic, or lexical value, are sufficient to yield bioelectric reflections of cerebral dominance. (It is interesting that *pa*, which was judged relatively "language-like" by all subjects, does not foster reliable LMN for any bilateral comparison of scalp loci in this study, whereas the multiple puff and multiple huff, which were usually judged to be the least "like language" both foster reliable LMN between left and right inferior frontal regions). These findings in combination with similar findings for English polysyllabic words (McAdam & Whitaker, 1971a) and the pilot observation that polysyllabic nonsense words (reported in McAdam & Whitaker, 1971b, and Whitaker, 1971a) also yield reliable LMN suggest the following conservative inference: *Broca's area participates in the staging of complex oromotor sequences.* These sequences may be basic to the contextural, "syntagmatic" (Jakobson, 1971) organization of speech.

These findings, however, do not exclude the potential importance of other linguistic or nonlinguistic factors for the establishment, degree, and spatial

---

when comparing recordings overlying different cytoarchitectures and geometries (see Vaughan & Ritter, 1970; Vaughan, 1974). (*4*) It should not be assumed that the waveforms reflect only one underlying mechanism. They may represent—perhaps depending on the time period of analysis and electrode location—spatio-temporal summation from generators (either diffuse or localized) which serve different functions (e.g., the programming of "macro-sequential" events, the activation of cortical areas concerned with the mobilization of particular muscle groups, reafference or feedback from peripheral musculature). Discussion which centers on a particular mechanism should be viewed as heuristic. See Vaughan (1974) for further discussion.

distribution of the LMN effect. (Nor do the findings argue against propositions that Broca's area may participate in linguistic activities beyond the phonological level.) It may be that "sequential complexity" is neither the only, nor the most crucial explanation of the findings. Alternative hypotheses fall into several classes. One class consists of hypotheses which are subsets or refinements of sequential complexity. Perhaps "stress/rhythm" or "rapidity of production" are crucial determinants of the bioelectric phenomena associated with sequentially complex articulations. A second class of hypotheses focuses on aspects of the articulations which are incidently the properties of sequentially complex utterances but which may also be the properties of specially instructed single syllable utterances. These hypotheses might be based upon "force of articulation integrated over time," or "planned inhibition of ongoing movement," or other factors pertaining to "timing independent of sequential timing." Would, for example, a single puff, huff, or voiced syllable, greatly extended in duration, occasion similar results to multiple puffs, huffs, or polysyllabic words? A third class of hypotheses is more general in nature. Perhaps any sort of increased "task demand," especially when it requires considerable conscious attention to precision of output, tends to evoke greater or more reliable LMN asymmetries. Exploration of some of these possibilities is planned. In any case, some of the above hypotheses such as "sequential complexity" or the more general notion of task demand are consistent with the performance of motor aphasics (see below) and may thus have enhanced stature as valid explanations. Since sequential complexity characterizes much of the phonological complexity of normal language and also provides a convenient way to describe and manipulate articulatory demands, it may have greater usefulness as a "working hypothesis" than other plausible hypotheses.

A consideration of the level of sequential complexity is important. The data are consistent with the notion that Broca's area is involved in programming related to "macro-sequential" assembly (i.e., assembly functions which occupy a relatively high position in a hierarchy of activities that can be considered sequentially complex). It should be noted that linguistic analyses[10] describe

---

[10] The findings in this study also have potential, though loose, relevance to questions raised by current linguistic studies. Such questions involve neural mechanisms for the sequential patterning of articulation (Lashley, 1951), the importance of rhythmic and/or ballistic constraints in such articulation (Martin, 1972; Anderson, in press), the existence of buffer zones for containing the articulatory segments to be tracked and the type of units contained in such buffers (Whitaker, 1971b; Ohala, 1970; MacKay, 1970); the role of open-loop (i.e., preprogrammed) and closed-loop (i.e., determined by ongoing afferent feedback) control of such patterning (MacNeilage, 1970), and the identity and neurophysiological reality of "minimal articulatory units." See Kim (1971) for a review of these issues. For example, if the multiple utterances (*pppp, hhhh,* and *patapute*) in this experiment were articulated rapidly enough to require open-loop programming, the scalp-recorded findings for such utterances might reflect the activity of mechanisms involved in such programming. Unfortunately, the lack of precise scaling in the present study of the utterances along

intricate sequential coordination among different groups of articulatory muscles for the articulation of single syllables or even smaller segments (see Lennenberg, 1967, and Kim, 1971, for discussion). While the present data are not conclusive as to these latter levels of sequential assembly, it may be that these micro-assembly factors are not accompanied by robust enough electrophysiological events to be detected by the techniques or sites used here. It is not implied that other applications of the back-averaging technique or other paradigms (e.g., CNV) are unable to detect similar neural concomitants for tasks lower on a hierarchy of sequential complexity (see Low *et al.*, 1974a; Grözinger *et al.*, 1975, in press). It is interesting that the clinical literature shows that motor aphasics, in addition to showing greater impairment as word-length increases, make more errors on fricatives, affricatives, and especially on complex consonant clusters (e.g., *spl* as in *split*) as compared to simple consonants which are lower on a dimension of sequential complexity (Shankweiler & Harris, 1966; Johns & Darley, 1970; Deal & Darley, 1972). Whether the "macro-sequential assembly mechanism" is actually a different type of mechanism or merely reflects greater involvement of the same mechanism which handles the assembly of single syllables or smaller components is moot.

Sequential complexity hypotheses draw support from clinical literature. Luria (1966, 1970, 1973) concludes that Broca's area may be involved in "complex consecutive synthesis." He observes that patients with damage to Broca's area have particular difficulty in shifting smoothly from one articulatory position to the next in a chain of consecutive movement s comprising "kinetic melody" of speech. He proposes that the essence of Broca's aphasia (or "*efferent* motor aphasia" as he calls it) is a

> disturbance in complex consecutive syntheses encompassing an inability to construct complex systems of articulation and difficulty in inhibiting preceding articulations for a smooth transfer from one articulation in a series to the next. [Luria, 1966, p. 207]

Observations by other aphasiologists corroborate Luria's hypotheses; Deal and Darley (1972), for example, characterize some of the symptoms of Broca's aphasia, a subset which they call "apraxia of speech," as a "disorder of the

---

articulatory dimensions (e.g., stress, rapidity), as well as the lack of appropriate control utterances, prevent adequate discrimination as to the precise role of a number of possibilities mentioned above. All that can be said at present is that the findings are consistent with the hypothesis that proposes special involvement of neural mechanisms for articulations which are sequential, rapid, and rhythmic: These three qualities best describe the multiple utterances as performed by the subjects in this experiment. Subsequent experiments which contrast articulations performed fast or slow and articulations varying in rhythmic complexity may allow assessment of the particular role of each of these qualities.

programming of the complex sequencing of neuromuscular events required for speech." Adding to evidence from phonetic analysis (Shankweiler & Harris, 1966), Shankweiler, Harris and Taylor (1968) present EMG data which shows that aphasics of this type have difficulty in the timing of sequential movements. Their overall findings indicated a disruption of coordinated sequencing of muscle groups concerned with articulation.

It is interesting to consider the predictions that clinically based, traditional approaches to the issue of localization (see Luria, 1966, 1974, for review) might make for the outcome of this experiment. A theory of "narrow" localization might predict that potentials over Broca's area alone are associated with speech; an "anti-localization" approach might predict that all areas would show much the same sort of bioelectric response. Neither viewpoint appears to be particularly consistent with the present findings[11] which, in concert with other findings in the bioelectric literature, point to an extremely complex state of affairs with regard to the central control of articulation. This complexity more aptly fits perspectives which emphasize "dynamic, systematic localization" (Luria, 1966, p. 468). This perspective, proposed by Pavlov, developed by Vygotsky, and vitalized by Luria (1966, 1970, 1973, and other works), regards higher cortical processes as "complex dynamically localized functional systems that are affected differently with lesions of different parts of the cerebral hemispheres" (Luria,

---

[11] The findings described as "left-more-negative" (LMN) may, of course, indicate positive voltages from right hemisphere sites as well as negative (or less positive) voltages from left hemisphere sites. Although the mean waveforms (across subjects) of computer averaged potentials from the single (i.e., uncompared) scalp sites are statistically insignificant (and thus not presented here), it is interesting that positivity from right hemisphere sites (particularly RB) sometimes contributes to the LMN score. If the simplistic assumption is ventured that negativity in these slow potentials indicates excitatory processes and positivity indicates inhibitory processes, then some of these observations may reflect excitatory processes over sites in the dominant hemisphere and/or inhibitory processes selectively affecting homologous sites in the nondominant hemisphere. These speculations are highly tentative, but it is interesting that there were some significant intrahemispheric gradient differences between RB and RR, at least for the multiple puffs and huffs (see RB − RR) which could suggest relative positivity for the right inferior frontal site. (Similar observations have been reported, e.g., for speech-related CNVs; Low *et al.*, 1974b.) One could conjecture that such observations might reflect a balancing or area-specific integration of excitatory and inhibitory processes. Such speculations may be related to Luria's concept of "neurodynamic mechanisms" (Luria, 1972), and then are also congruent with some hypotheses of callosal function and hypotheses of the minor hemisphere's relation to articulation which imply that the minor hemisphere might be inhibited from controlling expressive speech, faced with higher threshold than the major hemisphere, or otherwise subject to the tight grip the major hemisphere holds over articulatory channels (Butler, 1971; Butler & Norrsell, 1968; Kinsbourne, 1971; J. Levy, Nebes, & Sperry, 1971; Moscovitch, 1973; Pribram, 1971—but see Selnes, 1974, for critical review of inhibitory hypotheses, and Joynt & Goldstein, 1975, for general review of minor hemisphere function, including the views of Hughlings Jackson and others on possible capacities of the minor hemisphere for speech).

1966, p. 468); it emphasizes "graded localization of function and pluripotential-ism of the brain structures" (Luria, 1966, p. 27) and asserts, for example, that in articulated speech different brain regions contribute different factors to the whole performance depending on the nature of the articulated speech.

An empirical model to describe the pattern of findings in the present study (which could possibly represent the electrophysiological counterparts of Luria's view of "localization") might be called a "mini-gestalt" model of bioelectric activity. It is called "mini" because it predicts that the cerebral activity can reflect small or subtle differences in functional task requirements. This activity may occur nonrandomly over widespread areas (not merely traditional language areas) in such a way that (*a*) different subsets of localized activity can reflect different subsets of functional requirements; and (*b*) these indicants of func-tional differentiation may be best manifested when subsets of localized activity are viewed in relation to each other, so that they can be part of a gestalt extending over a number of areas. This last point may be purely methodological or may reflect a basic principle of cerebral function. The mini-gestalt conceptual framework suggests that future investigators should look for mosaics of activity (perhaps representing gradients of excitation and inhibition) between and within hemispheres, mosaics which can possibly vary according to the particular func-tional demands imposed by a particular task.

Turning to a more pedestrian issue, can extracerebral artifact account for the major scalp-recorded findings in this study? Some lines of evidence suggest this is unlikely. First, the various statistical "corrections" (see Figures 7.3, 7.4, 7.5) for plausible sources of artifact did not substantially change the basic pattern seen in the uncorrected data (Figure 7.2). Within the limitation of the model of statistical analysis (see "Methods" and Appendix to chapter) it is unlikely that artifact recorded by the eye or mouth placements could have been responsible for the major findings. Second, utterances sharing putatively similar vocal tract configurations (e.g., the single puff and multiple puff) yield different patterns of scalp-recorded asymmetries, whereas utterances possessing different vocal tract configurations (e.g., the multiple huff and multiple puff) shared similar patterns of scalp-recorded asymmetry, particularly for the scalp sites closest to articula-tory and ocular generators. There is no reason to believe at present that a possible source of artifact, that is, raising the palate (Zimmerman *et al.*, 1975), would be systematically different for any of the articulations in the present study. Third, since most of the crucial findings involved bilateral comparisons, it is unlikely that articulatory movements, reputedly bilateral, could have influ-enced them unilaterally. Fourth, even if there could have been lateralized articulatory (or other) movements, they would have to correspond to the distinction between single and multiple utterances to account for the data seen here: If such movements or sources of bioelectrical fields could be found, the most meaningful way of understanding them is with reference to differential cerebral processing.[12] Fifth, tests for statistical significance among the averaged EOG and mouth EMG data fail to reveal a pattern which is adequate to account for significant differences seen in scalp-recorded comparisons. Moreover, reliable periods of scalp-recorded asymmetry were generally prior to the period of greatest EMG and EOG activity. Sixth, the gradients of maximal negativity are not always consistent with more anterior sources of artifact. It is not clear how the same source, extracerebral or otherwise, could explain the distribution of findings seen among the multiple utterances.

These lines of evidence, though any one might be inconclusive alone, together imply, buttressed by the detailed studies of Morrell and Huntington (1972) and Grözinger *et al.* (1975), that the major findings in this study are not artifactual, at least in any obvious way.

The findings reported here suggest that task differences might help to explain some apparent discrepancies in the literature but even so, the problems facing this type of research are still formidable. A number of complications concerning methodology should be emphasized.

1. There are some considerations related to the task variables which may be important. Improvement of the literature in general, as well as some points in the present study, might proceed from more specific answers to the following questions. What exactly is the subject asked to do and what degree of precision is expected? (Mere specification of "words," "nonspeech gestures," "articulatory movements" is not adequate). What is the subject's attitude, familiarity, and extent of practice with the task? What is the "context" of the task (that is, the relationship of the particular task to other tasks in the experiment; also, were the tasks performed in blocks or by randomized requests)? How did the subject actually perform (e.g., in terms of speech, accuracy, or errors) each of the tasks? And what were the subject's strategies for performing each task? This last question, although difficult to answer, merits amplification since it may

---

[12] The eyes are a likely source of bioelectrical fields associated with cerebral dominance (Kinsbourne, 1972; Anderson & Jaffe, 1973); the present experiment shows, however, that subjects can be trained to minimize eye movement: Concurrent averaging of eye movement failed to show that peripheral movement was a source of artifact here. Of course, the possibility of special activity arising from cortical regions controlling eye (or other) movement is not eliminated. But put this way, the issue is not one of artifact, strictly speaking. See Grözinger *et al.* (1974, in press) for a discussion of the "R-wave" (a wave of intracranial origin that reflects cerebral dominance and is correlated with respiration prior to speech).

In view of the number of muscles in or near the head, some of which might become active prior to speech (e.g., the middle ear muscles; C. Berlin, personal communication), and in view of other bioelectrical phenemona which might affect slow potentials (e.g., the cephalic skin potential; Picton & Hillyard, 1972; Corby, Roth, & Kopell, 1974), it is more conservative to refer to the data in the present experiment as scalp-recorded potentials than as brain potentials. But the above argument still holds: They probably reflect directly, or conceivably they reflect indirectly, differential cerebral processes.

relate the present data to the performance of Broca's aphasies. It is possible that utterances or even phrases described as "polysyllabic" or consisting of "multiple components" may make different demands on neural substrates depending on how the subject (or patient) "chunks" the components. This chunking may depend in part whether the utterances are highly practiced or stereotyped, on the rapidity of the performance, and on other factors such as the stress/saliency of the utterances (Goodglass, 1973). (The work of Goodglass is also relevant since it shows how prosodic factors may underlie the agrammatisms shown by motor aphasics.) Though some of the preceding questions may be irrelevant, questions such as these have proved to be valuable in the study of electrophysiological phenomenon (see Sutton, 1969; McAdam, 1974).

2. Differences in subject population may partially explain some of the variances in the literature. There is well-established evidence that even within a right-handed population there are differences in degree, and occasionally even direction, of cerebral dominance (Zangwill, 1960; Shankweiler & Studdert-Kennedy, 1975; Branch, Milner, & Rasmussen, 1964). The present study was limited to subjects who considered themselves to be *strongly* right-handed, not ambidextrous, and not having left-handed parents or siblings. These restrictions were not explicitly stated in all other studies in this area. The work of Zimmerman and Knott (1974) on the speech-linked CNV of stutterers has important ramifications for subject variables as well as performance variables. A further complication which might explain some variability in observations is that there is perhaps greater variation in size, shape, and arrangement of cortical areas (Whitaker & Selnes, in press) than is typically assumed. These factors, taken together, imply that extended studies of single subjects are warranted.

3. The findings as to the particular latencies of the asymmetries in the present experiment suggest that measurement procedure encompassing the onset (trigger point) of back-averaging, duration and latency of periods analyzed, and baseline may be quite critical. Asymmetries, though small, are sometimes reliable in periods which considerably precede the onset of articulation. (Mere reliance on visually apparent differences between potentials may not suffice to reveal the reliability of such small asymmetries.) The trend of this data, as well as other studies by Grözinger and co-workers imply that it is not a good idea to establish a baseline during the last 1000 msec prior to articulation. Additionally, it seems important to limit study to articulations which have sharp, reliable onsets because of problems in determining the trigger event. Problems are posed by comparisons between utterances which have grossly different initial vocal tract configurations because of differences in the sources, time course, and magnitude of extracerebral movement which might precede the trigger event. Studies that compare articulations that do not start with the *same initial sound initiated from the same neutral position* (see "Methods") should be considered very critically.

4. One implication of the present experiment is that the particular electrode sites studied might be a more or less crucial variable according to the particular

articulatory task. Electrode sites which differ greatly from those used in the present study might reflect an entirely different pattern of results with respect to distinctions between single and multiple component utterances. In fact, Luria's hypothesis (1966, 1970, 1973) on the functional–anatomical substrate of *afferent* motor aphasia could predict different findings for post-central sites. (Further research on this latter aspect is planned.)

5. Painstaking care in experimental procedure, particularly artifact control, may be requisite for successful demonstration of these phenomena. This conclusion is fostered not only by the literature, but also by the failure to find reliable cerebral asymmetries in an early pilot study, differing in procedure, in which measures to exclude artifcat were much less stringent. Other procedural considerations might also be important. For example, Low *et al.* (1974a), using a CNV paradigm, reported that first test findings were "often equivocal" and retesting was necessary.

The above complications, particularly the importance of minimizing artifact and the need for greater precision in specifying effective experimental parameters, suggest that further refinement of techniques for speech-linked back-averaging is probably required before it is feasible to use these techniques in clinical settings (for determining hemispheric dominance prior to neurosurgery).

The difficulties of this area of research remain formidable, but close attention to task parameters, in addition to other methodological considerations such as artifact control, can begin to surmount them. The present findings for certain complex utterances—particularly for those which are ostensibly foreign to the subject's language system—are consistent with a basic oromotor sequencing mechanism which could serve the contextural organization of speech. Thus, parameters should not be confined to merely "verbal versus nonverbal" domains traditionally associated with cerebral dominance, for parameters which span these domains may also be important.

ACKNOWLEDGMENTS

I am indebted to Dale McAdam, Harry Whitaker, and Michael Davidson for their invaluable assistance. I appreciate the support of the Department of Psychology at the University of Rochester where this study was done.

APPENDIX

A special adaptation of the analysis of covariance, developed with the help of Michael Davidson, was used to correct the EEG data for possible contamination by the electrical concomitants of eye and/or mouth movements. This model assumes, as does the standard analysis of covariance model, that at each scalp locus at each moment of time, there is a contaminating voltage which is additive to the voltage arising from true cerebral generators and which is either proportional to the EMG or the EOG, measured during the same moment of time, or is a linear combination of both. Given this model, least squares procedures estimated the constants of proportionality ($\hat{\beta}$) between voltages recorded at the mouth (EMG) and/or eye (EOG) sites and the contemporary component voltages recorded at scalp loci (nominally EEG) for each of the four scalp loci. A standard model for the analysis of covariance would do likewise. This adapted model, however, additionally allowed these constants of proportionality to vary across subjects. This is the only major difference between this adapted model and the standard model of analysis of covariance.

The estimated constants of proportionality ($\hat{\beta}$) were multiplied by the EMG and/or EOG for each time period of each task as performed by each individual. This yielded an estimate of the contaminating voltage contained in each corresponding period of EEG. These estimates of contaminating voltage, then, were subtracted from each of the corresponding periods of EEG to yield "corrected" EEG values.

In formal terms, the model assumes that each of the uncorrected EEG scores y_{ijk} (the subject is indexed by the subscript i, experimental conditions by the subscript j, and scalp locus by the subscript k) was the sum of the following terms: an overall mean (μ_k) peculiar to a given scalp locus (across subjects and experimental conditions), a term (π_k) peculiar to each individual subject at a particular scalp locus (across experimental conditions); a term (α_{jk}) peculiar to the experimental conditions effect at a given locus (across subjects); estimates of random statistical and experimental error (e_{ijk}); and "contamination" terms consisting of estimates of voltage attributable to EMG and/or EOG sources. The EMG contamination factor would add the following term to the model as stated up to now: a constant of EMG proportionality ($\beta_{EMG\ ik}$)—peculiar not only to the specified scalp locus, but also to the particular individual who generated the measurements—multiplied by the EMG measurement peculiar to that individual for the experimental condition (i.e., the particular task at a particular time period) in question ($x_{EMG\ ij}$). The EOG factor is handled analogously (i.e., $\beta_{EOG\ ik} \cdot x_{EOG\ ij}$).

In summary, the model of analysis used to correct the data states:

$$y_{ijk} = \mu_k + \pi_{ik} + \alpha_{ij} + e_{ijk} + (\beta_{EMG\ ik} \cdot x_{EMG\ ij} + \beta_{EOG\ ik} \cdot x_{EGO\ ij}).$$

This model is for the simultaneous correction for EMG and EOG. The appropriate terms are of course deleted for correction for EMG alone and EOG alone.

The following points are implicit in the above model:

1. The model is linear and additive; it will provide a valid correction of the EEG for contamination by the EMG and/or EOG to the extent the latter(s) is related to the former in a linear and additive manner. This appears to be a reasonable and parsimonious assumption which has received support from work using a linear, additive model to "correct" CNV for eye movements (Hillyard & Galambos, 1970; Hillyard, 1974).

2. One task does not average away the correction factor for another task. For example, if the eyes systematically moved in equal and opposite directions for 2 different tasks, the model would not allow a "zero" correction for each task; it would correct each separately.

3. Analogously, one time period can not affect the correction factor for another time period.

4. The model does not assume that "volume conductance" was consistent across individuals. Thus, separate sets of $\hat{\beta}$'s were estimated for each subject. This is the major strength of the model—it is wise to avoid the assumption, if possible, of consistency between individuals of muscular configuration, facial structure, precise electrode placement, sweating, and any other factors that can influence the impedance and conductivity between electrode points.

Vaughan (1969), for example, states that there can be individual differences in the isopotential distribution of EOG over the scalp.

REFERENCES

Anderson, S. W. In press. Ballistic control of rhythmic articulatory movements in natural speech. *Annals of the New York Academy of Sciences.*

Anderson, S. W., & Jaffe, J. 1973. Eye movement bias and ear preference as indices of speech lateralization in brain. Scientific report no. 15, Department of Communication Sciences, New York State Psychiatric Institute.

Branch, C., Milner, B., & Rasmussen, T. 1964. Intracarotid sodium amytal for the lateralization of cerebral speech dominance: Observations in 123 patients. *Journal of Neurosurgery, 21*, 399–405.

Brown, J. W. 1972. *Aphasia, apraxia, and agnosia: Clinical and theoretical aspects.* Springfield, Ill.: Charles C Thomas.

Butler, S. R. 1971. Organization of cerebral cortex for perception. *British Medical Journal, 4*, 544–547.

Butler, S. R., & Norsell, V. Vocalization possibly initiated by the minor hemisphere. *Nature, 220*, 793–794.

Caspers, H. 1963. Relations of steady potential shifts in the cortex to the wakefulness–sleep spectrum. In M. A. B. Brazier (Ed.), *Brain function.* Vol. 1. *Cortical excitability and steady potentials: Relations of basic research to space biology.* UCLA Forum in Medical Science, No. 1. Los Angeles: University of California Press. Pp. 177–213.

Cohn, J. 1969. Very slow brain potentials relating to expectancy: The CNV. In E. Donchin and D. B. Lindsley (Eds.), *Average evoked potentials: Methods, results, evaluations.* Washington, D.C.: National Aeronautics and Space Administration, NASA SP-191. Pp. 143–198.

Corby, J. C., Roth, W. J., & Kopell, B. S. 1974. Prevalence and methods of control of the cephalic skin potential EEG artifact. *Psychophysiology, 11*, 350–360.

Deal, J. L., & Darley, F. L. 1972. The influence of linguistic and situational variables on phonemic accuracy in apraxia of speech. *Journal of Speech and Hearing Research, 15*, 632–638.

De Renzi, E., Pieczuro, A., & Vignolo, L. A. 1966. Oral apraxia and aphasia. *Cortex, 2*, 50–73.

Ellis, L. 1971. Slow electroencephalographic changes preceding speech production. Unpublished Ph.D. dissertation, University of Illinois, Urbana.

Ertl, J., & Schafer, E. W. P. 1967. Cortical activity preceding speech. *Life Sciences, 6*, 473–479.

Ertl, J., & Schafer, E. W. P. 1969. Erratum. *Life Sciences, 8*, 559.

Geschwind, W., & Levitsky, W. 1968. Human brain: Left–right asymmetries in temporal speech region. *Science, 161*, 186–187.

Gilden, L., Vaughn, H. G., Jr., & Costa, L. D. 1966. Summated human EEG potentials with voluntary movements. *Electroencephalography and Clinical Neurophysiology, 20*, 433–438.

Goodglass, H. 1973. Studies on the grammar of aphasics. In H. Goodglass and S. Blumstein (Eds.), *Psycholinguistics and aphasia.* Baltimore: John Hopkins University Press. Pp. 183–215.

Grabow, J. D., & Elliott, F. W. 1974. The electrophysiologic assessment of hemispheric asymmetries during speech. *Journal of Speech and Hearing Research, 17*, 64–72.

Grözinger, B., Kornhuber, H. H., & Kriebel, J. 1973. Inter- and intra-hemispheric asymmetries of brain potentials preceding speech and phonation. *Electroencephalography and Clinical Neurophysiology, 34*, 737–738. (Abstract)

Grözinger, B., Kornhuber, H. H., & Kriebel, J. 1975. Methodological problems in the investigation of cerebral potentials preceding speech: Determining the onset and suppressing artifacts caused by speech. *Neuropsychologia, 13*, 263–270.

Grözinger, B., Kornhuber, H. H., & Kriebel, J. In press. EEG investigation of hemispheric asymmetries preceding speech: The R-wave. In W. C. McCallum and J. R. Knott (Eds.), *Proceedings of the Third International Congress on Event Related Slow Potentials of the Brain.* Bristol, Eng.: John Wright and Sons.

Grözinger, B., Kornhuber, H. H., Kriebel, J., & Murata, K. 1974. Cerebral potentials during respiration and preceding vocatlization. *Electroencephalography and Clinical Neurophysiology, 36*, 435. (Abstract).

Hillyard, S. A. 1974. Methodological issues in CNV research. In R. F. Thompson and M. M. Patterson (Eds.), *Bioelectric recording techniques.* Part B. *Electroencephalography and human brain potentials.* New York: Academic Press. Pp. 282–304.

Hillyard, S. A., & Galambos, R. 1970. Eye movement artifact in the CNV. *Electroencephalography and Clinical Neurophysiology, 28*, 173–182.

Hogben, D., Peavy, S., & Varner, R. N. 1971. *Omnitab II.* (National Bureau of Standards Technical Note 552). Washington, D.C.: U.S. Government Printing Office.

Irwin, D. A., Knott, J. R., McAdam, D. W., & Rebert, C. S. 1966. Motivational determinants of the contingent negative variation. *Electroencephalography and Clinical Neurophysiology, 21*, 538–543.

Jakobson, R. 1971. *Studies in child language and aphasia.* The Hague: Mouton.

Johns, D. F., & Darley, F. L. 1970. Phonemic variability in apraxia of speech. *Journal of Speech and Hearing Research, 13*, 556–583.

Joynt, R. J., & Goldstein, M. N. 1975. The minor cerebral hemisphere. In W. Friedlander (Ed.), *Advances in neurology. VII. Current reviews of higher nervous system dysfunction.* New York: Raven Press. Pp. 147–183.

Kim, C. 1971. Experimental phonetics. In W. O. Dingwall (Ed.), *A survey of linguistic science.* College Park: University of Maryland.

Kinsbourne, M. 1971. The minor hemisphere as a source of aphasic speech. *Archives of Neurology, 25*, 302–306.

Kinsbourne, M. 1972. Eye and head turning indicate cerebral lateralization. *Science, 176*, 539–541.

Kornhuber, H. H., & Deecke, L. 1965. Hirnpotentialanderungen bei Willkerbewegungen und passiven Bewegungen des menschen: Bereitschaftspotential und reafferente Potentiale. *Pflugers Archiv, 284*, 1–17.

Lashley, K. S. 1951. The problem of serial order in behavior. In L. A. Jeffress (Ed.), *Cerebral mechanisms in behavior.* New York: Wiley. Pp. 112–136.

Lenneberg, E. H. 1967. *Biological foundations of language.* New York: Wiley.

Levy, J., Nebes, R. D., & Sperry, R. W. 1971. Expressive language in the surgically separated minor hemisphere. *Cortex, 7*, 49–58.

Low, M. D., Borda, R. P., Frost, J. D., & Kellaway, P. 1966. Surface-negative, slow-potential shift associated with conditioning in man. *Neurology, 16*, 771–782.

Low, M. D., Wada, J. A., & Fox, M. 1974a. EEG localization of conative aspects of language production in the human brain. *Electroencephalography and Clinical Neurophysiology, 37*, 418–419. (Abstract)

Low, M. D., Wada, J. A., & Fox, M. 1974b. Electrographic localization of certain aspects of language production in the human brain. *Electroencephalography and Clinical Neurophysiology, 36*, 562–563. (Abstract)

Low, M. D., Wada, J. A., & Fox, M. In press. Electroencephalographic localization of conative aspects of language production in the human brain. In W. C. McCallum and J. R. Knott (Eds.), *Proceedings of the Third International Congress on Event Related Slow Potentials of the Brain.* Bristol, Eng.: John Wright and Sons.

Luria, A. R. 1966. *Higher cortical functions in man.* New York: Basic Books.

Luria, A. R. 1970. *Traumatic aphasia.* The Hague: Mouton.

Luria, A. R. 1972. Aphasia reconsidered. *Cortex, 8*, 34–40.

Luria, A. R. 1973. *The working brain.* New York: Basic Books.

Luria, A. R. 1974. Language and brain: Toward the basic problems of neurolinguistics. *Brain and Language, 1*, 1–14.

MacKay, D. G. 1970. Spoonerisms: The structure of errors in the serial order of speech. *Neuropsychologia, 8*, 323–350.

MacNeilage, P. F. 1970. Motor control of serial ordering of speech. *Psychological Review, 177*, 182–196.

Martin, J. G. 1972. Rhythmic (hierarchical) versus serial structure in speech and other behavior. *Psychological Review, 79*, 487–509.

McAdam, D. W. 1974. The contingent negative variations. In R. F. Thompson and M. M. Patterson (Eds.), *Bioelectric recording techniques.* Part B. *Electroencephalography and human brain potentials.* New York: Academic Press. Pp. 245–257.

McAdam, D. W., & Whitaker, H. A. 1971a. Language production: Electroencephalographic localization in the normal human brain. *Science, 172*, 499–502.

McAdam, D. W., & Whitaker, H. A. 1971b. Electrocortical localization of language production. *Science, 174*, 1360–1361.

Morrell, L. K., & Huntington, D. A. 1971. Electrocortical localization of language production. *Science, 174*, 1359–1360.

Morrell, L. K., & Huntington, D. A. 1972. Cortical potentials time-locked to speech production: Evidence for probable cerebral origin. *Life Sciences, 11*, 921–929.

Moscovitch, M. 1973. Language and the cerebral hemispheres: Reaction-time studies and their implications for models of cerebral dominance. In P. Pliner, L. Krames, and T. M. Alloway (Eds.), *Communication and affect: Language and thought.* New York: Academic Press. Pp. 89–126.

Ohala, J. 1970. *Aspects of the control and production of speech.* UCLA Working Papers in Phonetics, No. 15.

Picton, T. W., & Hillyard, S. A. 1972. Cephalic skin potentials in electroencephalography. *Electroencephalography and Clinical Neurophysiology, 33*, 419–424.

Rubens, A. B., Mahowald, M. W., & Hutton, J. T. 1976. Asymmetry of the lateral (sylvian) fissures in man. *Neurology, 26*, 620–624.

Schafer, E. W. P. 1967. Cortical activity preceding speech: Semantic specificity. *Nature, 216*, 1338–1339.

Schuell, H., Jenkins, J. J., & Jiminez-Pabon, E. 1964. *Aphasia in adults: Diagnosis, prognosis, and treatment.* New York: Harper & Row.

Selnes, O. A. 1974. The corpus callosum: Some anatomical and functional considerations with special reference to language. *Brain and Language, 1*, 111–139.

Shankweiler, D., & Harris, K. S. 1966. An experimental approach to the problem of articulation in aphasia. *Cortex, 2*, 277–292.

Shankweiler, D., Harris, K. S., & Taylor, M. L. 1968. Electromyographic studies of articulation in aphasia. *Archives of Physical Medicine, 49*, 1–8.

Shankweiler, D., & Studdert-Kennedy, M. 1975. A continuum of lateralization for speech perception? *Brain and Language, 2*, 212–225.

Sutton, S. 1969. The specification of psychological variables in an average evoked potential experiment. In E. Donchin and D. B. Lindsley (Eds.), *Average evoked potentials; Methods, results, evaluations.* Washington, D.C.: National Aeronautics and Space Administration, NASA SP-191. Pp. 237–297.

Szirtes, J., & Vaughan, H. G., Jr. 1973. Topographic analysis of speech-related cerebral potentials. *Electroencephalography and Clinical Neurophysiology, 34*, 754. (Abstract)

Tecce, J. J. 1972. Contingent negative variation (CNV) and psychological processes in man. *Psychological Bulletin, 77*, 73–108.

Tecce, J. J., & Scheff, N. M. 1969. Attention reduction and suppressed direct-current potentials in the human brain. *Science, 164*, 331–333.

Vaughan, H. G., Jr. 1969. The relationship of brain activity to scalp recordings of event-related potentials. In E. Donchin and D. B. Lindsley (Eds.), *Average evoked potentials: Methods, results, evaluations.* Washington, D.C.: National Aeronautics and Space Administration, NASA SP-191. Pp. 45–94.

Vaughan, H. G., Jr. 1974. The analysis of scalp-recorded brain potentials. In R. F. Thompson and M. M. Patterson (Eds.), *Bioelectric recording techniques.* Part B. *Electroencephalography and human brain potentials.* New York: Academic Press. Pp. 157–207.

Vaughan, H. G., Jr., Costa, L. D., & Ritter, W. 1968. Topography of the human motor potential. *Electroencephalography and Clinical Neurophysiology, 25*, 1–10.

Vaughan, H. G., Jr., & Ritter, W. 1970. The sources of auditory evoked responses recorded from the human scalp. *Electroencephalography and Clinical Neurophysiology, 28*, 360–267.

Walter, W. G., Cooper, R., Aldridge, V. J., McCallum, W. G., & Winter, A. L. 1964. Contingent negative variation: An electrical sign of sensorimotor association and expectancy in the human brain. *Nature, 203*, 380–384.

Whitaker, H. A. 1971a. Neurolinguistics. In W. O. Dingwall (Eds.), *A survey of linguistic science.* College Park: University of Maryland.

Whitaker, H. A. 1971b. *On the representation of language in the human brain.* Edmonton, Can.: Linguistic Research.

Whitaker, H. A., & Selnes, O. A. In press. Anatomic variations in the cortex: Individual differences and the problem of the localization of language functions. Paper presented at the New York Academy of Sciences' Conference on Origins and Evolution of Language and Speech, New York City, September 22–25, 1975.

Winer, B. J. 1962. *Statistical principles in experimental design.* New York: McGraw-Hill.

Zangwill, O. L. 1960. *Cerebral dominance and its relation to psychological function.* Edinburgh: Oliver and Boyd.

Zimmerman, G. N., & Knott, J. R. 1973. Slow potentials preceding speech in stutterers and normal speakers. *Electroencephalography and Clinical Neurophysiology, 36*, 216. (Abstract)

Zimmerman, G. N., & Knott, J. R. 1974. Slow potentials of the brain related to speech processing in normal speakers and stutterers. *Electroencephalography and Clinical Neurophysiology, 37*, 599–607.

Zimmerman, G. N., & Knott, J. R. In press. CNV and stuttering. In W. C. McCallum and J. R. Knott (Eds.), *Proceedings of the Third International Congress on Event Related Slow Potentials of the Brain.* Bristol, Eng.: John Wright and Sons.

Zimmerman, G., Knott, J. R., Mendel, M., & Keuhn, D. 1975. Timing of averaged movement potentials and articulatory events: An EEG, EMG and cineradiographic study. *Electroencephalography and Clinical Neurophysiology, 38*, 542. (Abstract)

Subject Index

A
B 7
C 8
D 9
E 0
F 1
G 2
H 3
I 4
J 5